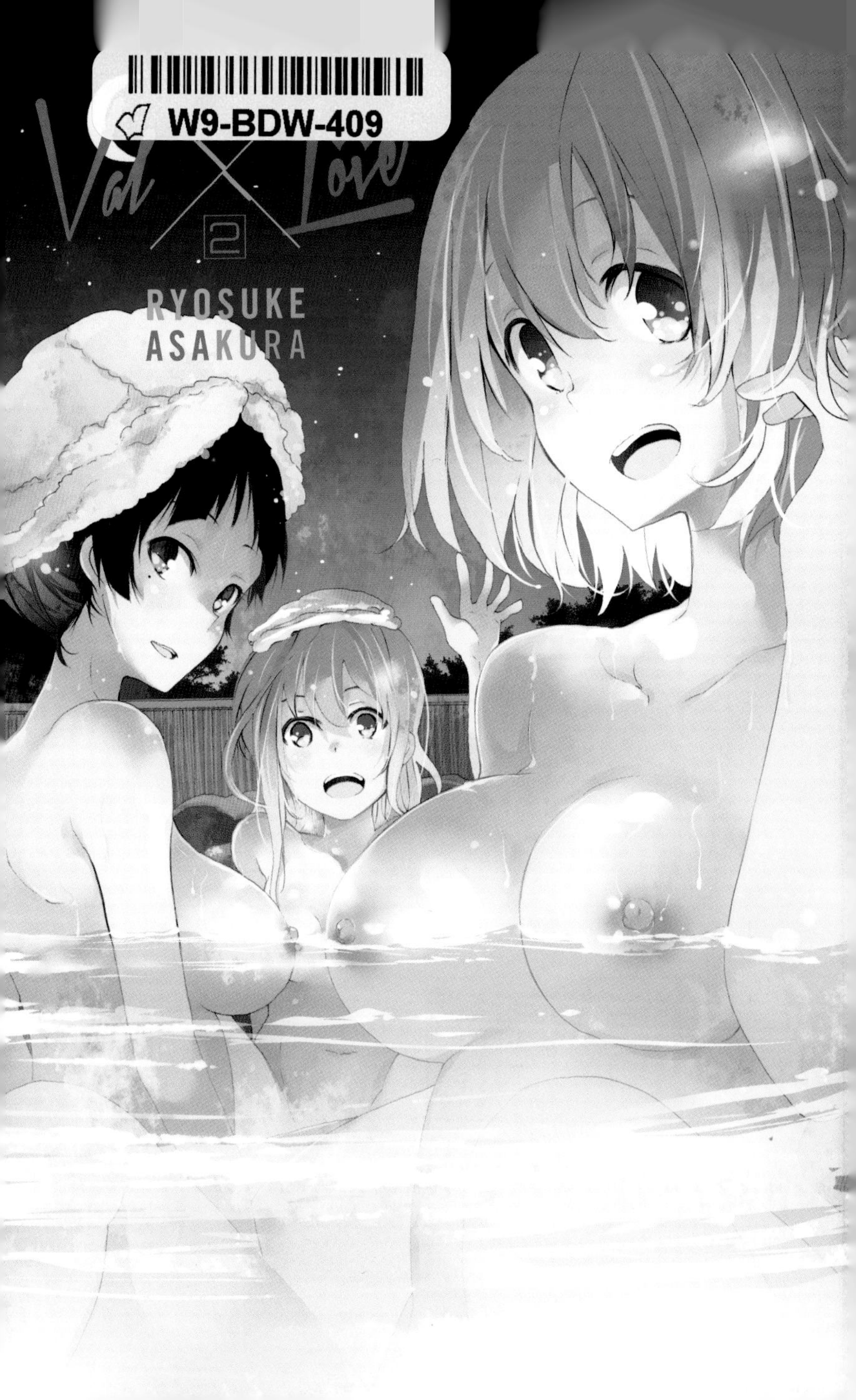
Val × Love
2
RYOSUKE
ASAKURA

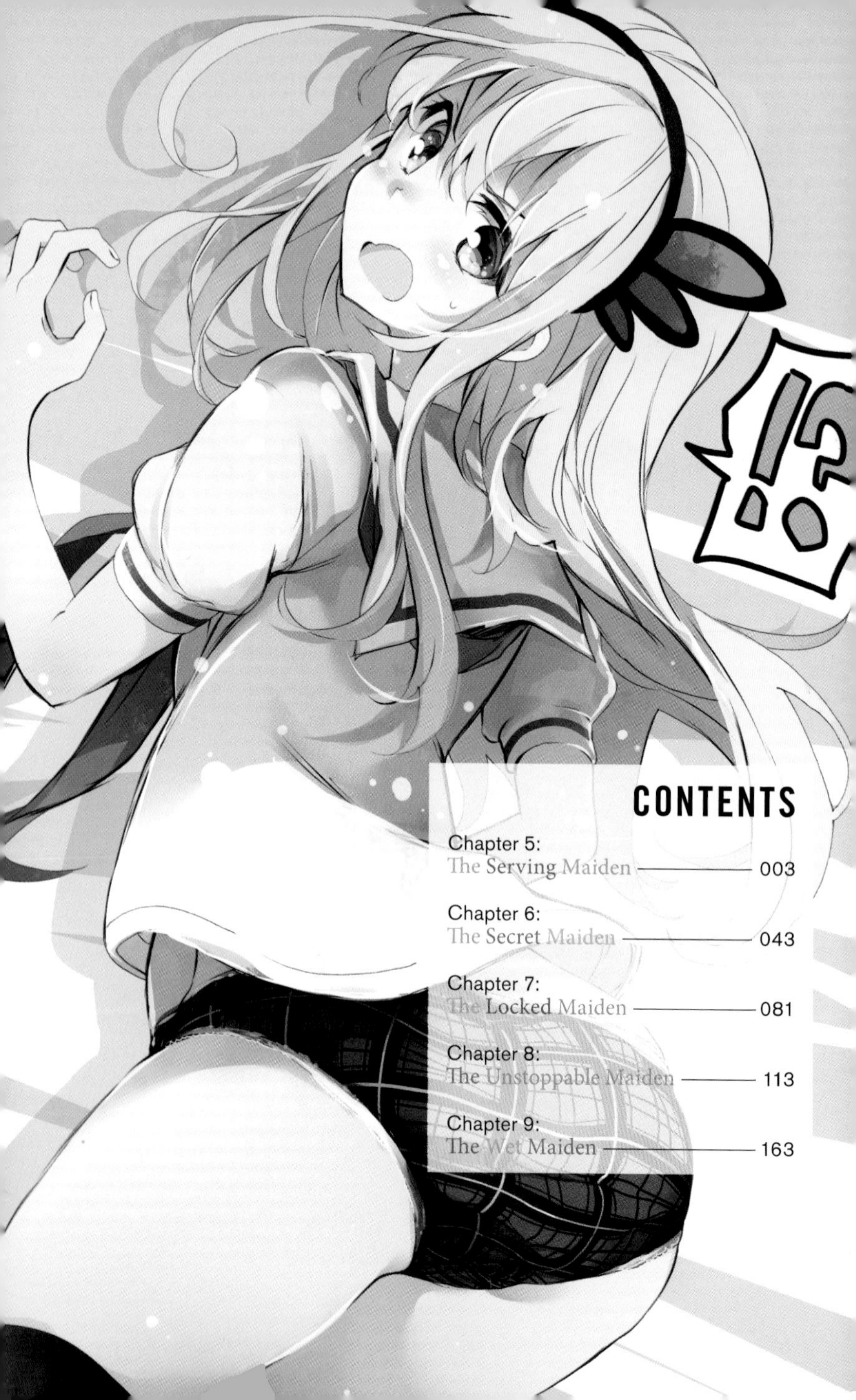
!?

CONTENTS

Chapter 5: The Serving Maiden

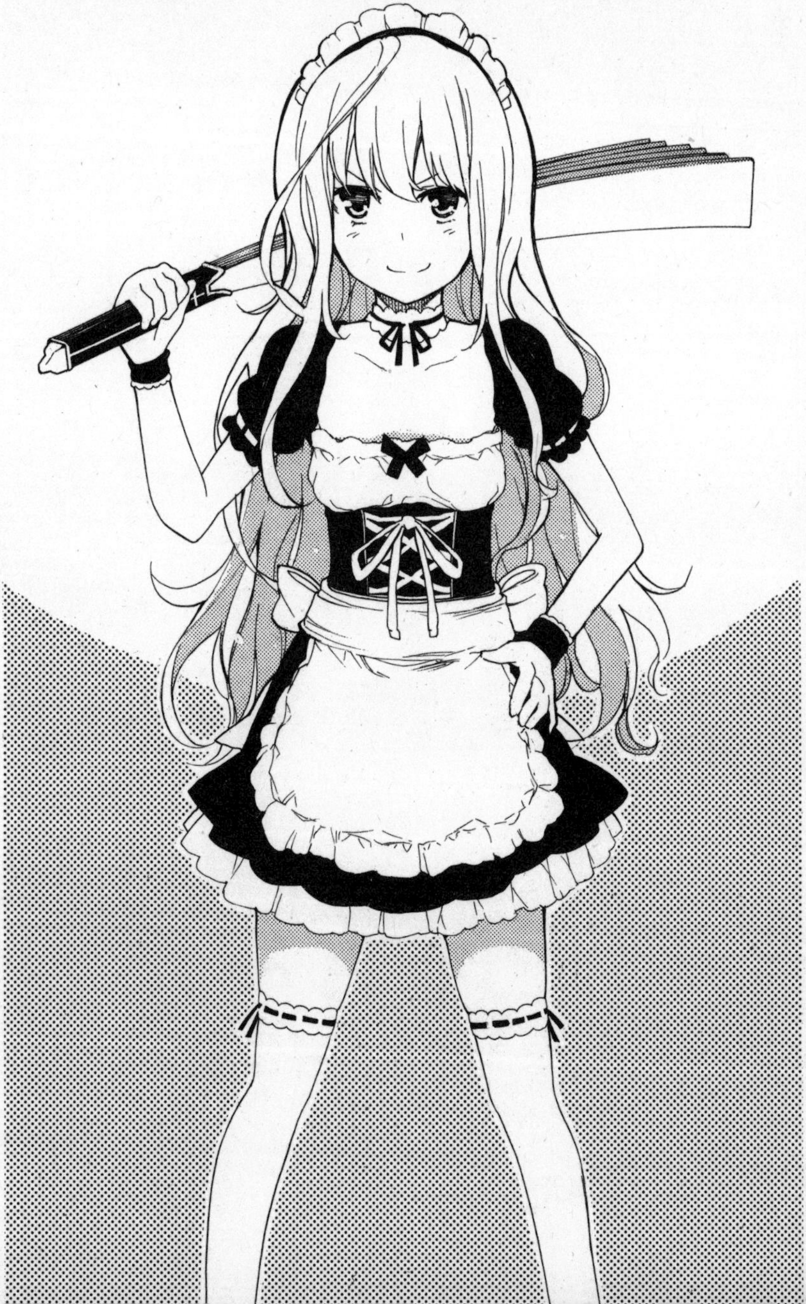

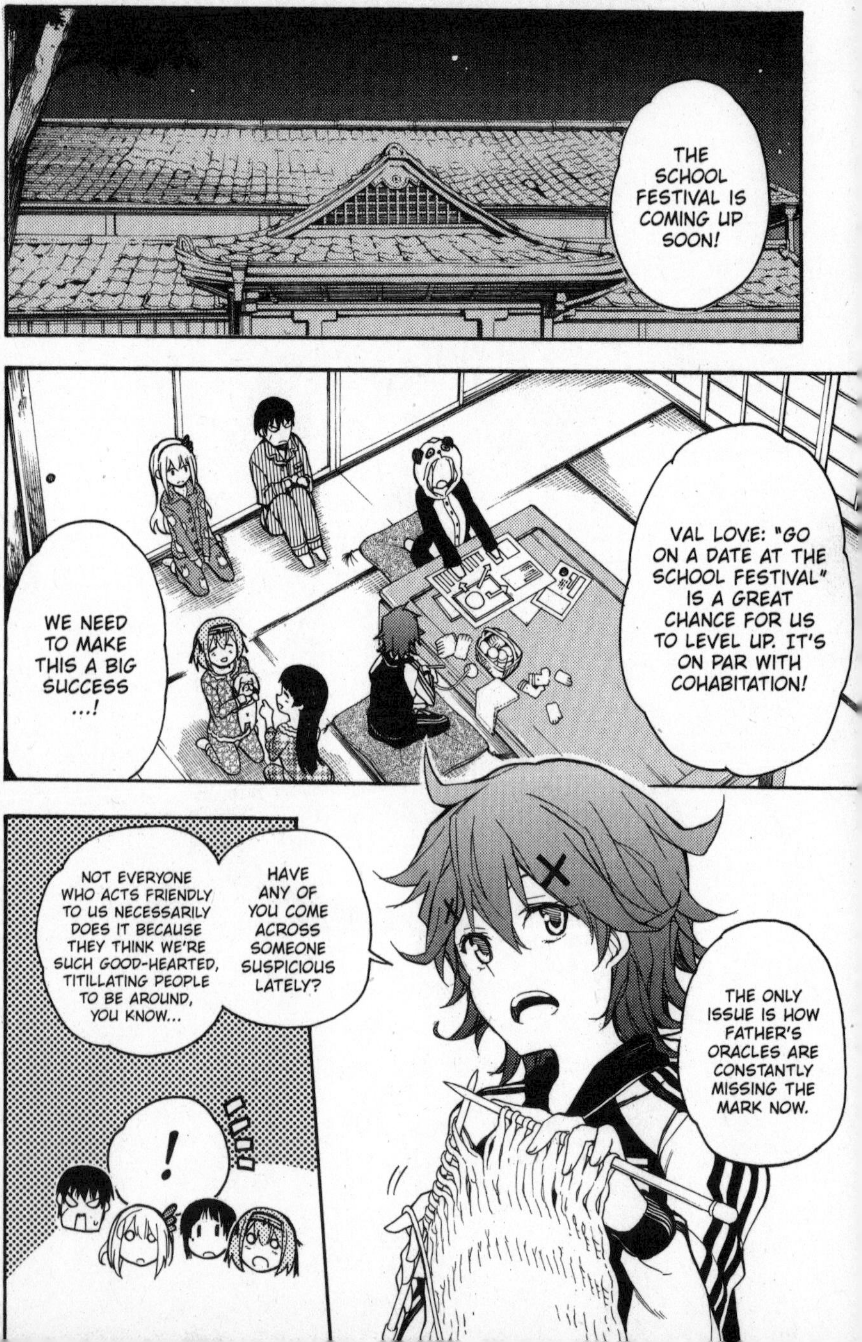
THE SCHOOL FESTIVAL IS COMING UP SOON!
VAL LOVE: "GO ON A DATE AT THE SCHOOL FESTIVAL" IS A GREAT CHANCE FOR US TO LEVEL UP. IT'S ON PAR WITH COHABITATION!
WE NEED TO MAKE THIS A BIG SUCCESS ...!
THE ONLY ISSUE IS HOW FATHER'S ORACLES ARE CONSTANTLY MISSING THE MARK NOW.
HAVE ANY OF YOU COME ACROSS SOMEONE SUSPICIOUS LATELY?
NOT EVERYONE WHO ACTS FRIENDLY TO US NECESSARILY DOES IT BECAUSE THEY THINK WE'RE SUCH GOOD-HEARTED, TITILLATING PEOPLE TO BE AROUND, YOU KNOW...
!

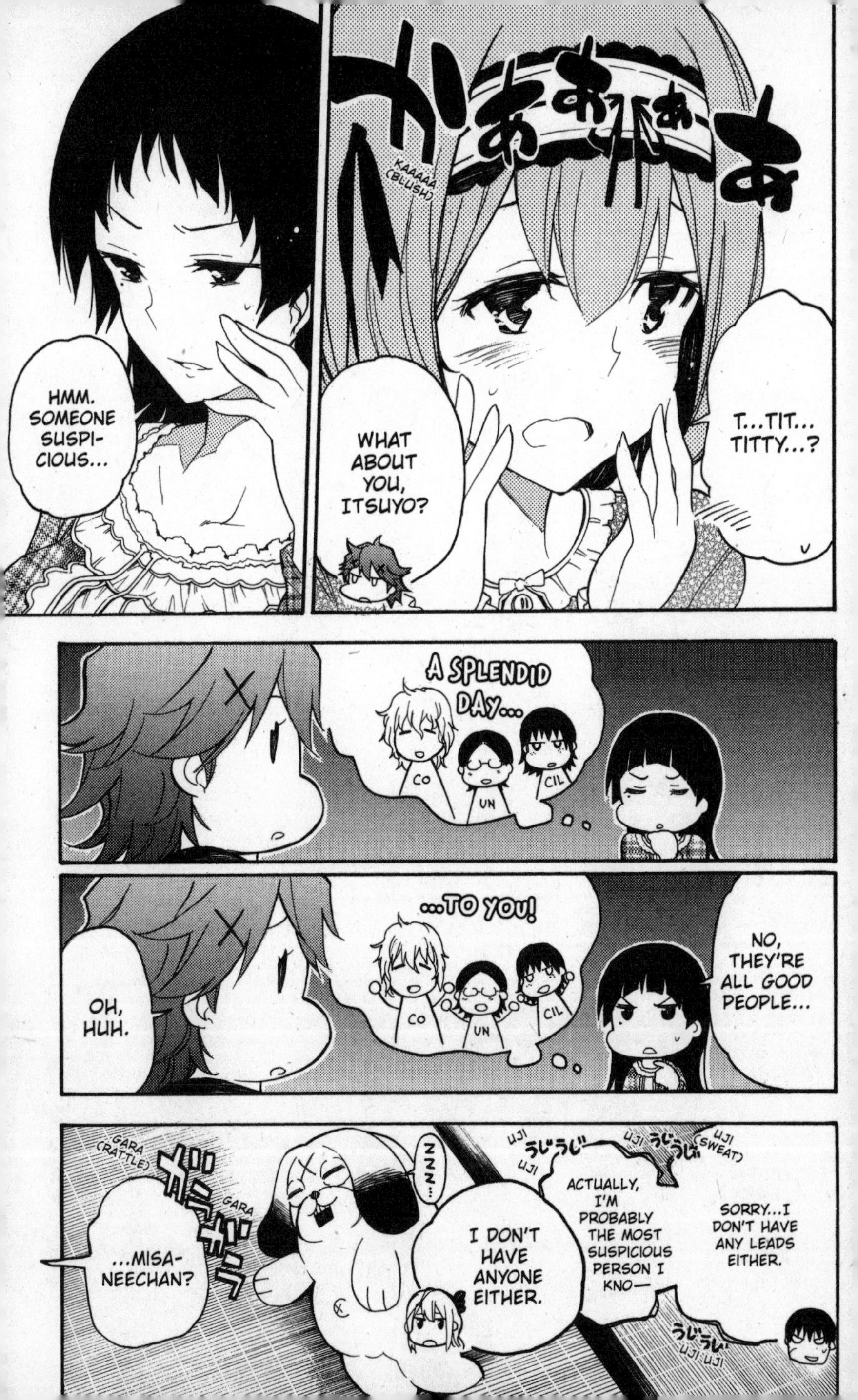
T...TIT... TITTY...?
KAAAAA (BLUSH)
WHAT ABOUT YOU, ITSUYO?
HMM. SOMEONE SUSPICIOUS...
A SPLENDID DAY...
CO
UN
CIL
NO, THEY'RE ALL GOOD PEOPLE...
...TO YOU!
CO
UN
CIL
OH, HUH.
UJI UJI UJI UJI (SWEAT) UJI
SORRY...I DON'T HAVE ANY LEADS EITHER.
ACTUALLY, I'M PROBABLY THE MOST SUSPICIOUS PERSON I KNO—
UJI UJI
I DON'T HAVE ANYONE EITHER.
ZZZ...
GARA (RATTLE) GARA
...MISA-NEECHAN?

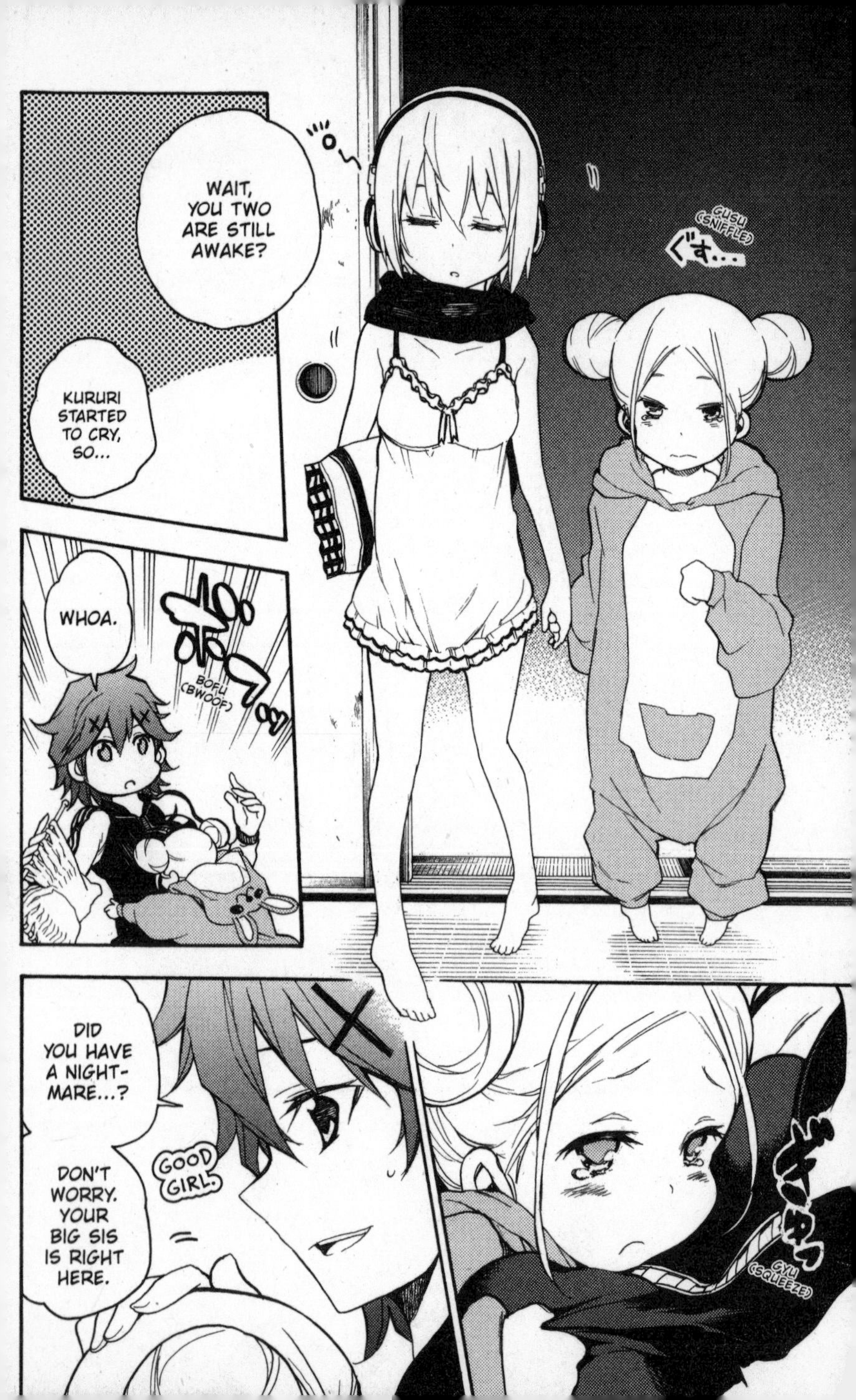
ぐす…
GUSU (SNIFFLE)
WAIT, YOU TWO ARE STILL AWAKE?
KURURI STARTED TO CRY, SO...
WHOA.
BOFU (BWOOF)
GYU (SQUEEZE)
DID YOU HAVE A NIGHT-MARE...?
GOOD GIRL.
DON'T WORRY. YOUR BIG SIS IS RIGHT HERE.

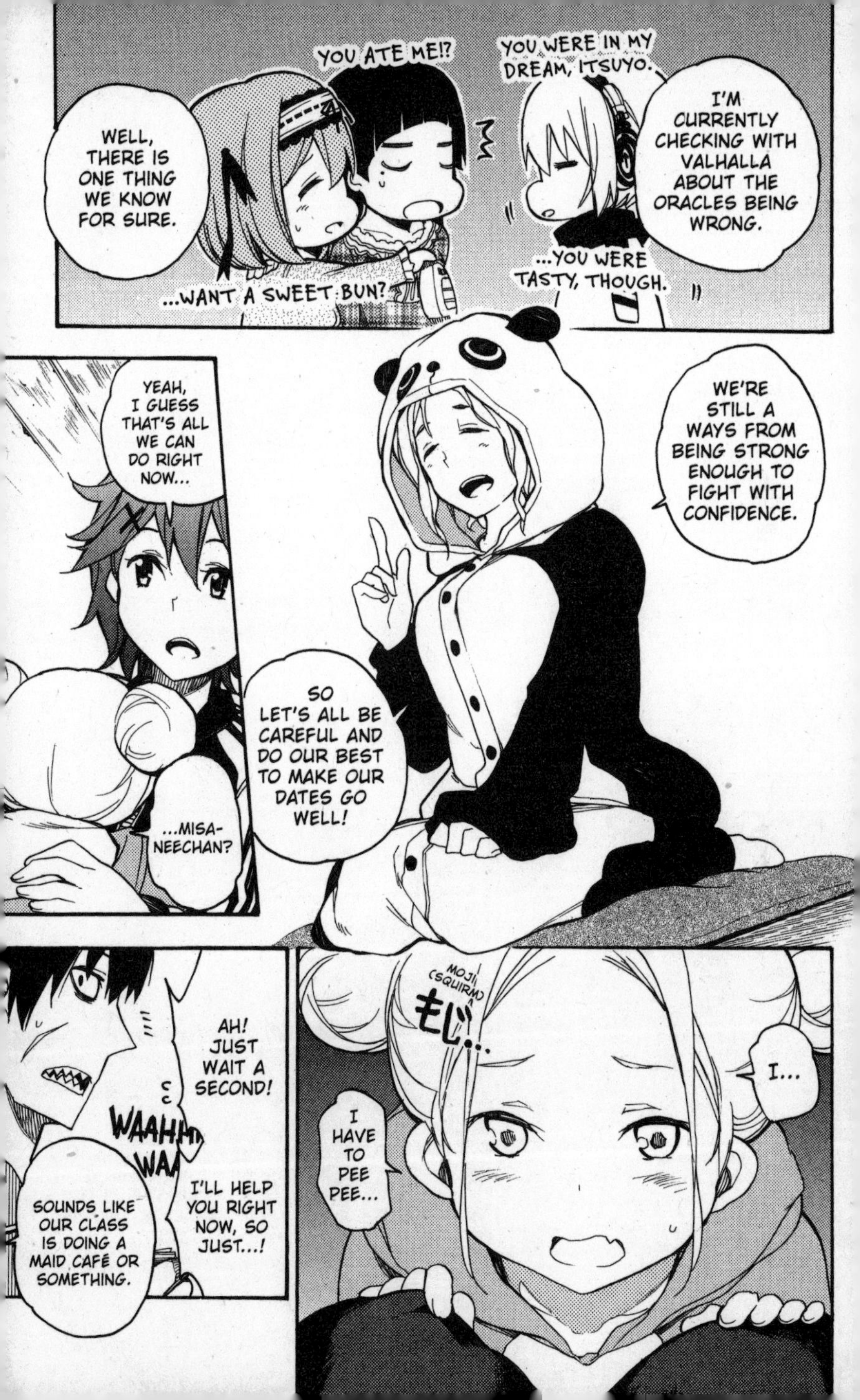
I'M CURRENTLY CHECKING WITH VALHALLA ABOUT THE ORACLES BEING WRONG.
YOU WERE IN MY DREAM, ITSUYO.
YOU ATE ME!?
...YOU WERE TASTY, THOUGH.
WELL, THERE IS ONE THING WE KNOW FOR SURE.
...WANT A SWEET BUN?
WE'RE STILL A WAYS FROM BEING STRONG ENOUGH TO FIGHT WITH CONFIDENCE.
SO LET'S ALL BE CAREFUL AND DO OUR BEST TO MAKE OUR DATES GO WELL!
YEAH, I GUESS THAT'S ALL WE CAN DO RIGHT NOW...
...MISA-NEECHAN?
もじ...
MOJI (SQUIRM)
I...
I HAVE TO PEE PEE...
AH! JUST WAIT A SECOND!
WAAHH
WAA
I'LL HELP YOU RIGHT NOW, SO JUST...!
SOUNDS LIKE OUR CLASS IS DOING A MAID CAFÉ OR SOMETHING.

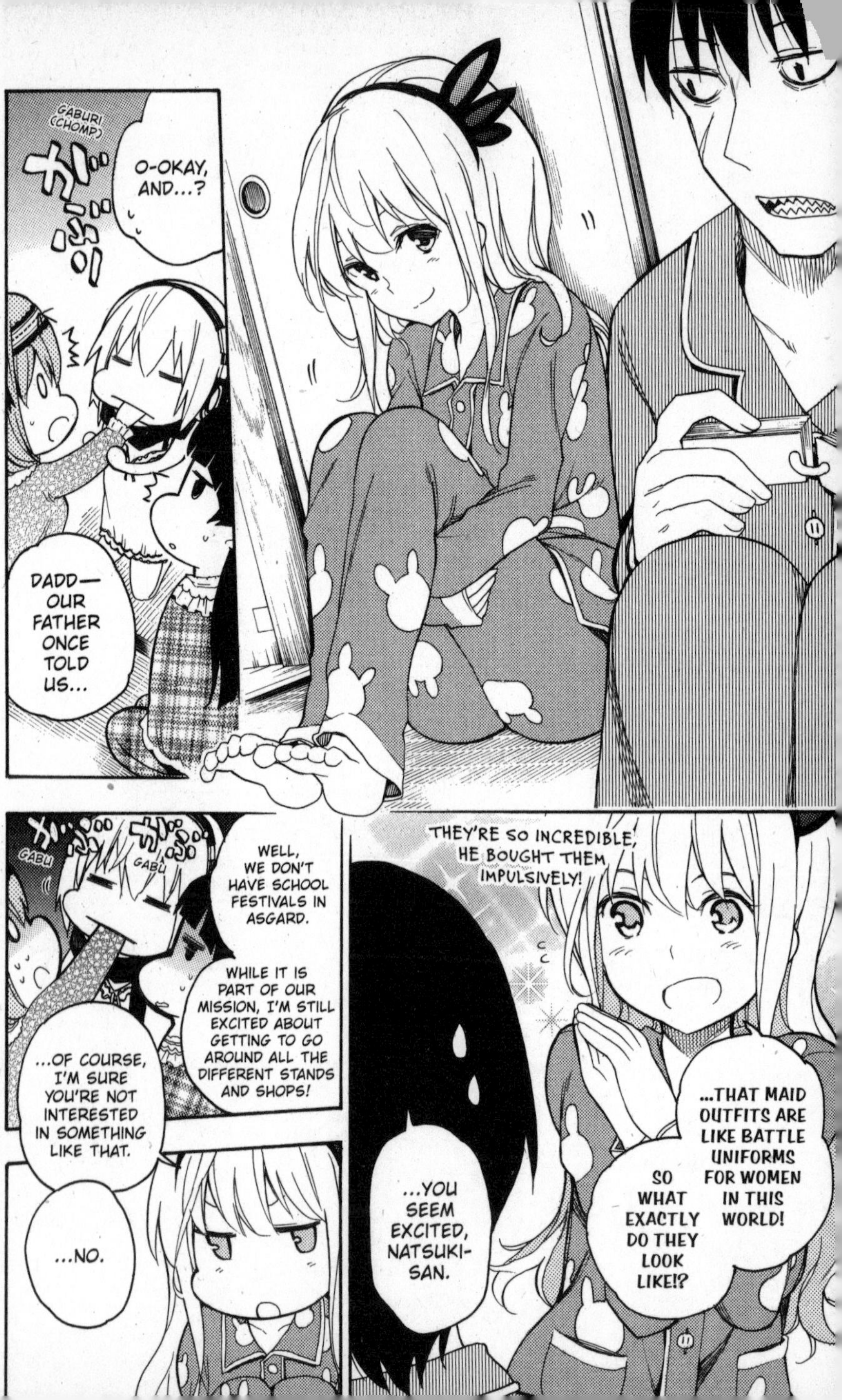
GABURI (CHOMP)
O-OKAY, AND...?
DADD— OUR FATHER ONCE TOLD US...
...THAT MAID OUTFITS ARE LIKE BATTLE UNIFORMS FOR WOMEN IN THIS WORLD!
THEY'RE SO INCREDIBLE, HE BOUGHT THEM IMPULSIVELY!
SO WHAT EXACTLY DO THEY LOOK LIKE!?
...YOU SEEM EXCITED, NATSUKI-SAN.
GABU
GABU
WELL, WE DON'T HAVE SCHOOL FESTIVALS IN ASGARD.
WHILE IT IS PART OF OUR MISSION, I'M STILL EXCITED ABOUT GETTING TO GO AROUND ALL THE DIFFERENT STANDS AND SHOPS!
...OF COURSE, I'M SURE YOU'RE NOT INTERESTED IN SOMETHING LIKE THAT.
...NO.

WHA ...?

DOKI (BADUM)

... FOR THE SCHOOL FESTIVAL TOO.

I'M EXCITED ...

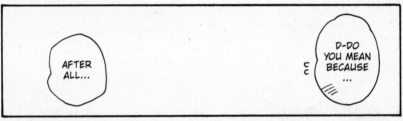

AFTER ALL...

D-DO YOU MEAN BECAUSE ...

PAAAAA (SHINE)

...THERE'S SO MUCH FREE TIME AROUND THE FESTIVAL, I'LL GET TO DO ALL THE STUDYING I WANT!

I CAN REVIEW!

I SEE...

I CAN PREPARE!

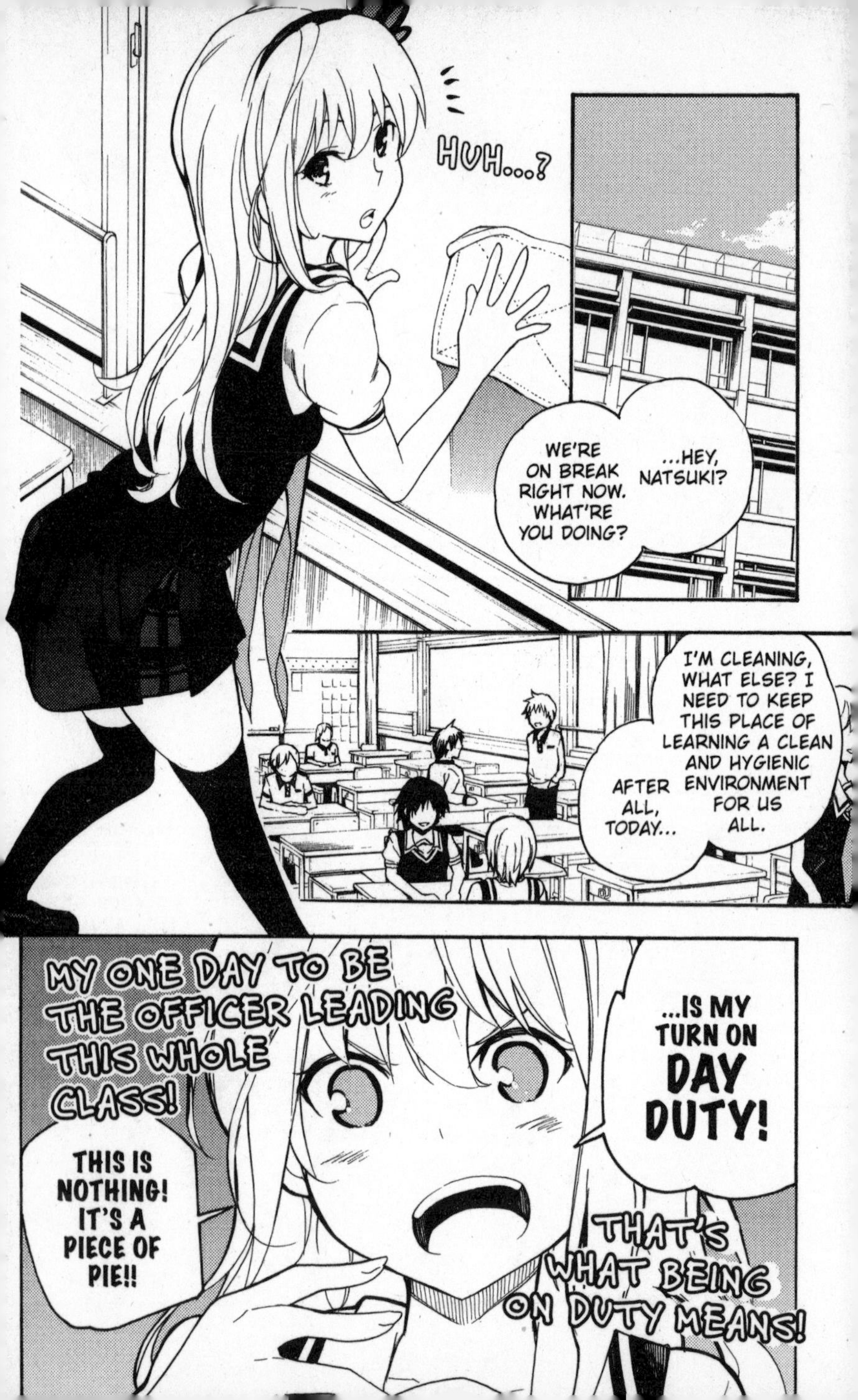
...HEY, NATSUKI?
WE'RE ON BREAK RIGHT NOW. WHAT'RE YOU DOING?
I'M CLEANING, WHAT ELSE? I NEED TO KEEP THIS PLACE OF LEARNING A CLEAN AND HYGIENIC ENVIRONMENT FOR US ALL.
AFTER ALL, TODAY...
HUH...?
...IS MY TURN ON DAY DUTY!
MY ONE DAY TO BE THE OFFICER LEADING THIS WHOLE CLASS!
THIS IS NOTHING! IT'S A PIECE OF PIE!!
THAT'S WHAT BEING ON DUTY MEANS!

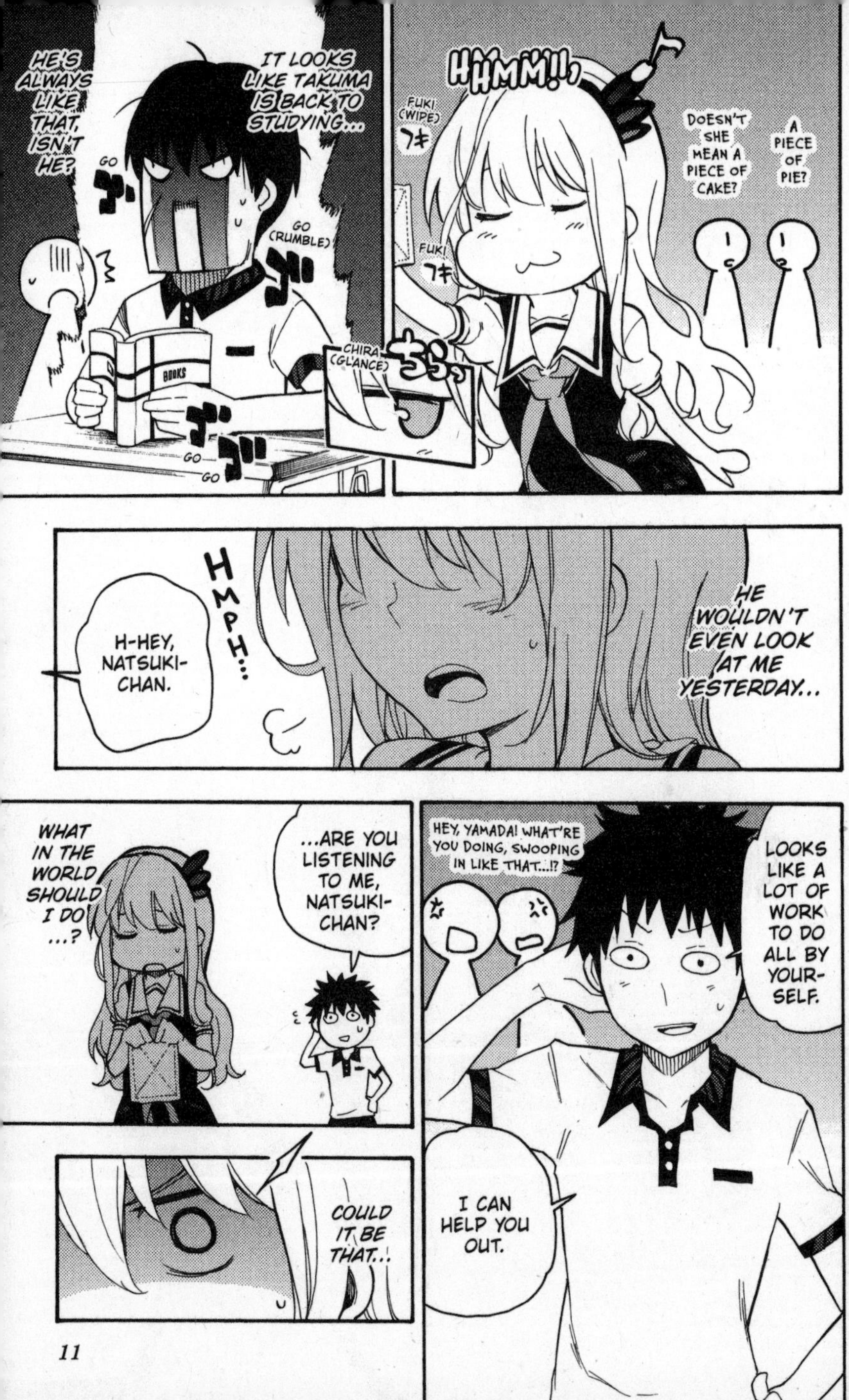

A PIECE OF PIE?
DOESN'T SHE MEAN A PIECE OF CAKE?
HMMM!!,
FUKI (WIPE) フキ
FUKI フキ
CHIRA (GLANCE) ちらっ
IT LOOKS LIKE TAKUMA IS BACK TO STUDYING...
HE'S ALWAYS LIKE THAT, ISN'T HE?
GO ゴ
GO (RUMBLE) ゴ
GO ゴ
GO ゴ
HE WOULDN'T EVEN LOOK AT ME YESTERDAY...
HMPH...
H-HEY, NATSUKI-CHAN.
LOOKS LIKE A LOT OF WORK TO DO ALL BY YOURSELF.
HEY, YAMADA! WHAT'RE YOU DOING, SWOOPING IN LIKE THAT...!?
I CAN HELP YOU OUT.
...ARE YOU LISTENING TO ME, NATSUKI-CHAN?
WHAT IN THE WORLD SHOULD I DO ...?
COULD IT BE THAT...

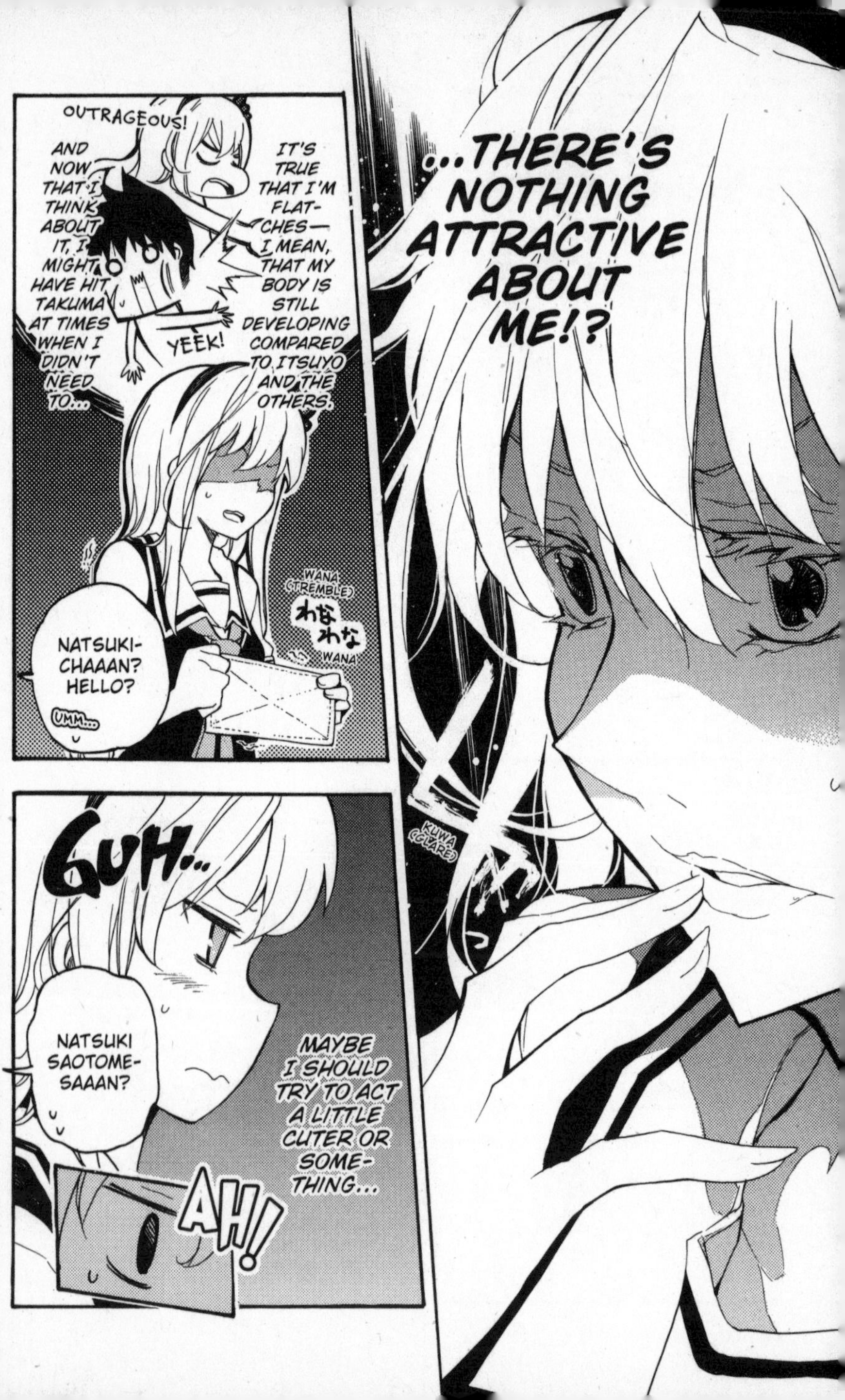
...THERE'S NOTHING ATTRACTIVE ABOUT ME!?
KUWA (GLARE)
IT'S TRUE THAT I'M FLAT-CHES— I MEAN, THAT MY BODY IS STILL DEVELOPING COMPARED TO ITSUYO AND THE OTHERS.
OUTRAGEOUS!
AND NOW THAT I THINK ABOUT IT, I MIGHT HAVE HIT TAKUMA AT TIMES WHEN I DIDN'T NEED TO...
YEEK!
WANA (TREMBLE) わなわな WANA
NATSUKI-CHAAAN? HELLO?
UMM...
MAYBE I SHOULD TRY TO ACT A LITTLE CUTER OR SOMETHING...
GUH...
NATSUKI SAOTOME-SAAAN?
AH!!

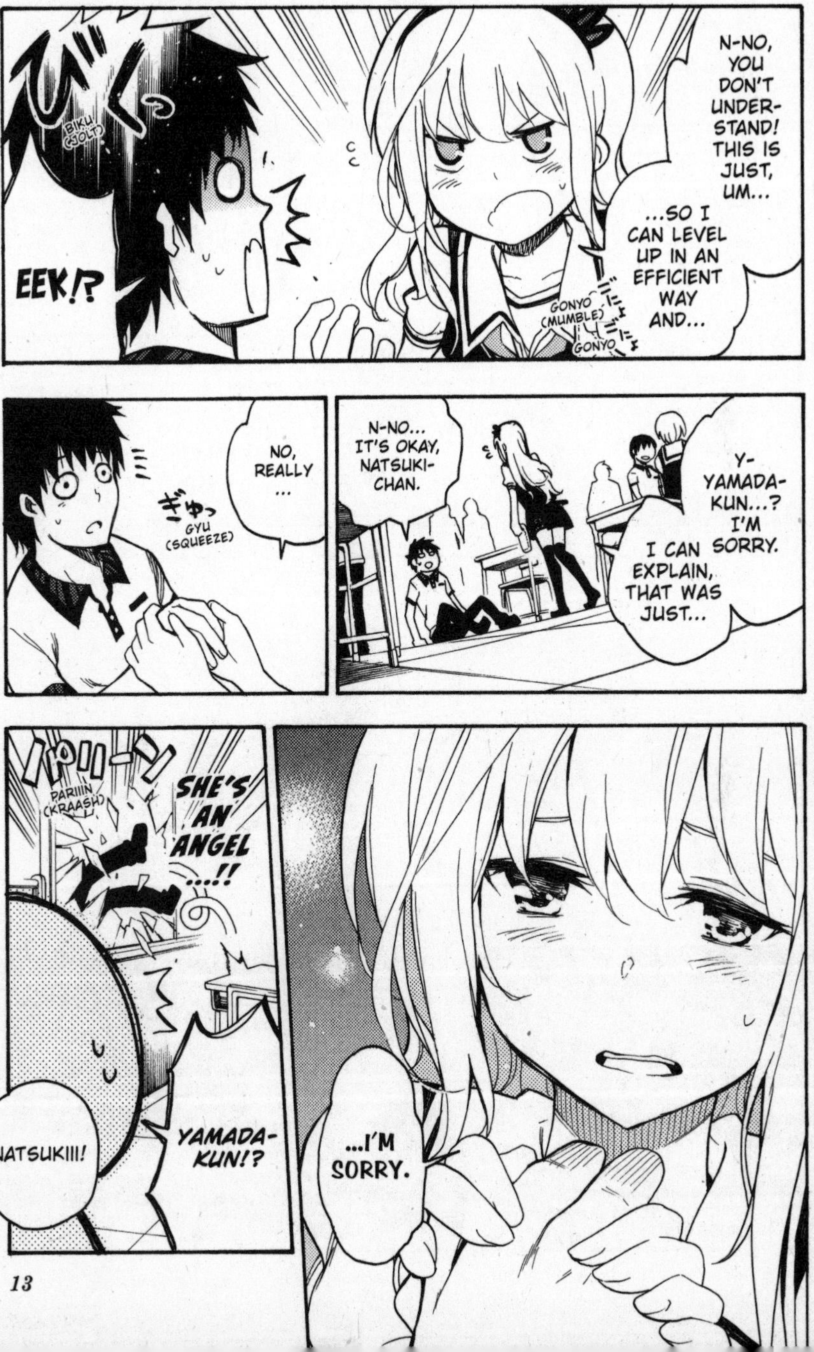
N-NO, YOU DON'T UNDER-STAND! THIS IS JUST, UM...
...SO I CAN LEVEL UP IN AN EFFICIENT WAY AND...
GONYO (MUMBLE)
GONYO
BIKU (JOLT)
EEK!?
Y-YAMADA-KUN...? I'M SORRY.
I CAN EXPLAIN, THAT WAS JUST...
N-NO... IT'S OKAY, NATSUKI-CHAN.
NO, REALLY...
GYU (SQUEEZE)
...I'M SORRY.
PARIIIN (KRAASH)
SHE'S AN ANGEL...!!
YAMADA-KUN!?
NATSUKIII!

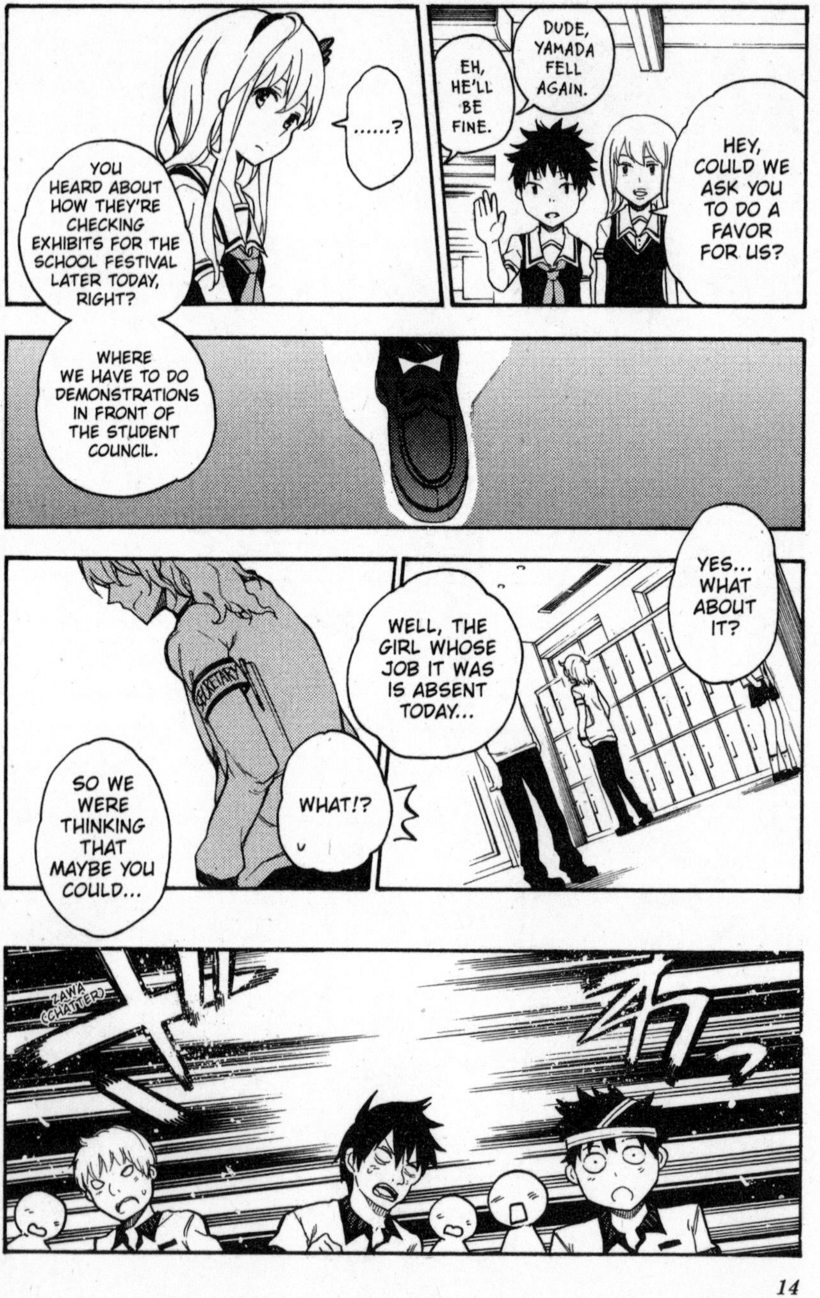
DUDE, YAMADA FELL AGAIN.
EH, HE'LL BE FINE.
HEY, COULD WE ASK YOU TO DO A FAVOR FOR US?
......?
YOU HEARD ABOUT HOW THEY'RE CHECKING EXHIBITS FOR THE SCHOOL FESTIVAL LATER TODAY, RIGHT?
WHERE WE HAVE TO DO DEMONSTRATIONS IN FRONT OF THE STUDENT COUNCIL.
YES... WHAT ABOUT IT?
WELL, THE GIRL WHOSE JOB IT WAS IS ABSENT TODAY...
SO WE WERE THINKING THAT MAYBE YOU COULD...
WHAT!?
SECRETARY
ZAWA (CHATTER)

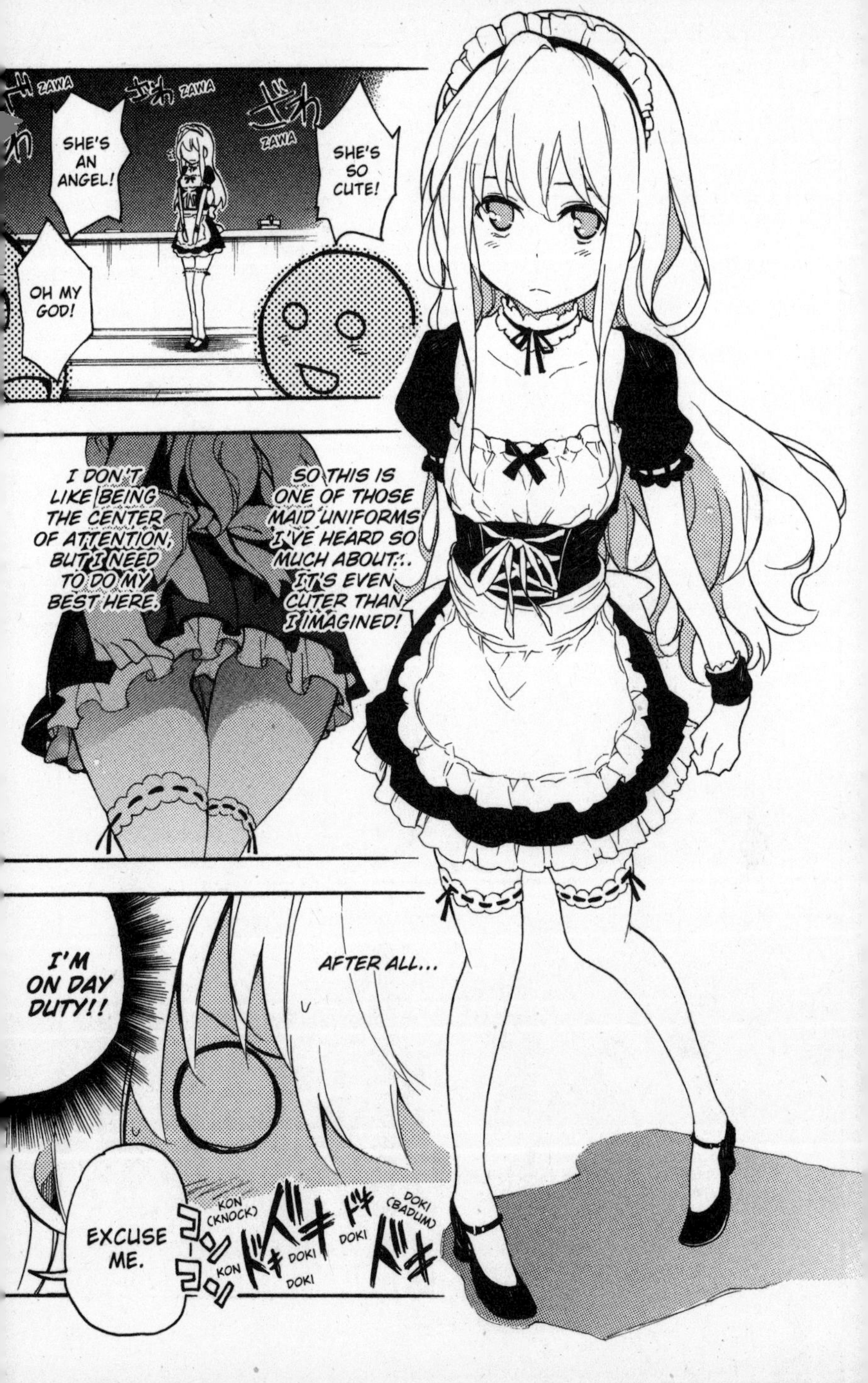

ZAWA
ZAWA
ZAWA
SHE'S SO CUTE!
SHE'S AN ANGEL!
OH MY GOD!
SO THIS IS ONE OF THOSE MAID UNIFORMS I'VE HEARD SO MUCH ABOUT... IT'S EVEN CUTER THAN I IMAGINED!
I DON'T LIKE BEING THE CENTER OF ATTENTION, BUT I NEED TO DO MY BEST HERE.
AFTER ALL...
I'M ON DAY DUTY!!
DOKI (BADUM)
DOKI
DOKI
DOKI
KON (KNOCK)
KON
EXCUSE ME.

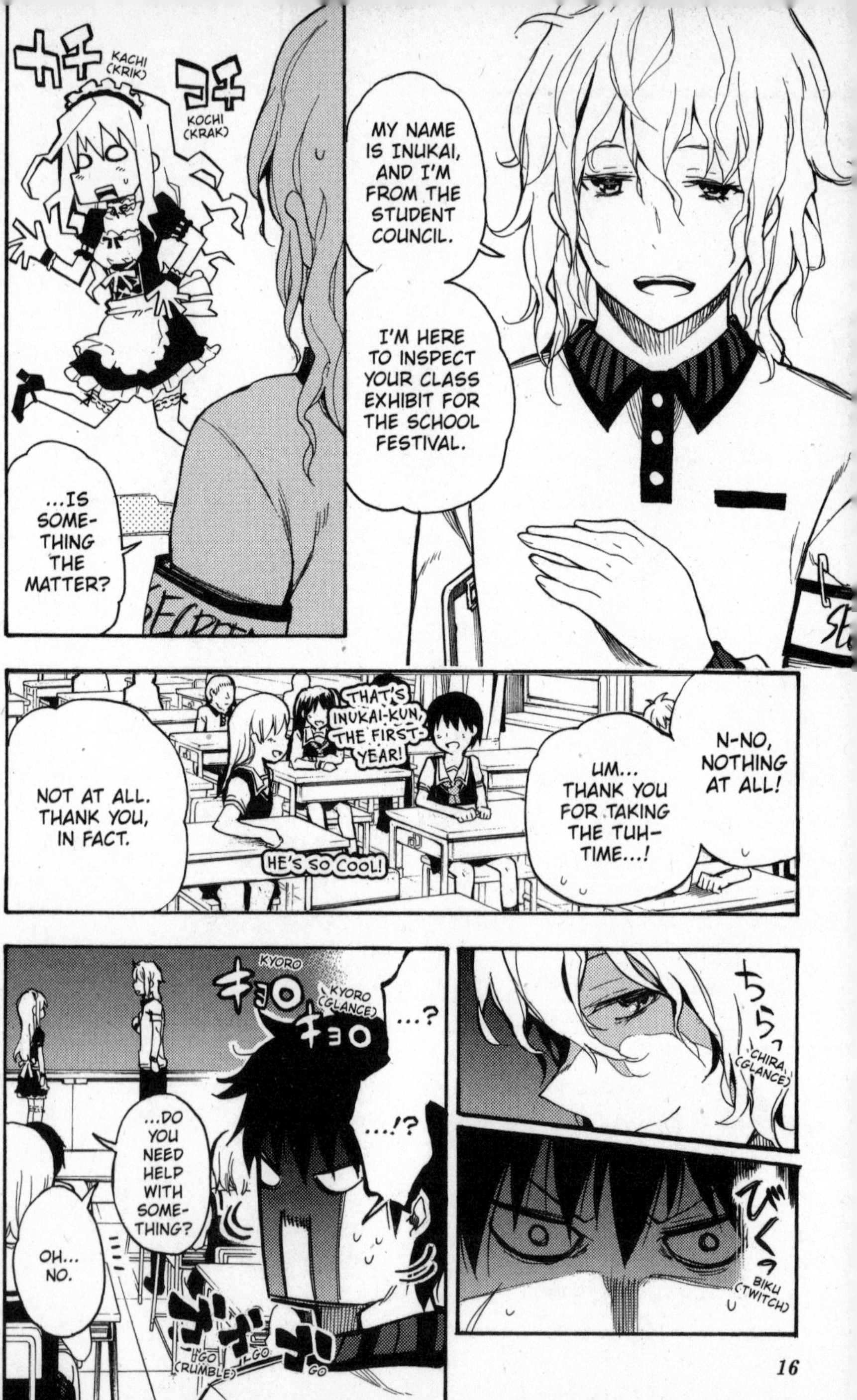
MY NAME IS INUKAI, AND I'M FROM THE STUDENT COUNCIL.
I'M HERE TO INSPECT YOUR CLASS EXHIBIT FOR THE SCHOOL FESTIVAL.
KACHI (KRIK)
KOCHI (KRAK)
...IS SOMETHING THE MATTER?
N-NO, NOTHING AT ALL!
UM... THANK YOU FOR TAKING THE TUH-TIME...!
THAT'S INUKAI-KUN, THE FIRST-YEAR!
HE'S SO COOL!
NOT AT ALL. THANK YOU, IN FACT.
CHIRA (GLANCE)
BIKU (TWITCH)
KYORO
KYORO (GLANCE)
...?
...!?
...DO YOU NEED HELP WITH SOMETHING?
OH... NO.
GO (RUMBLE) GO GO

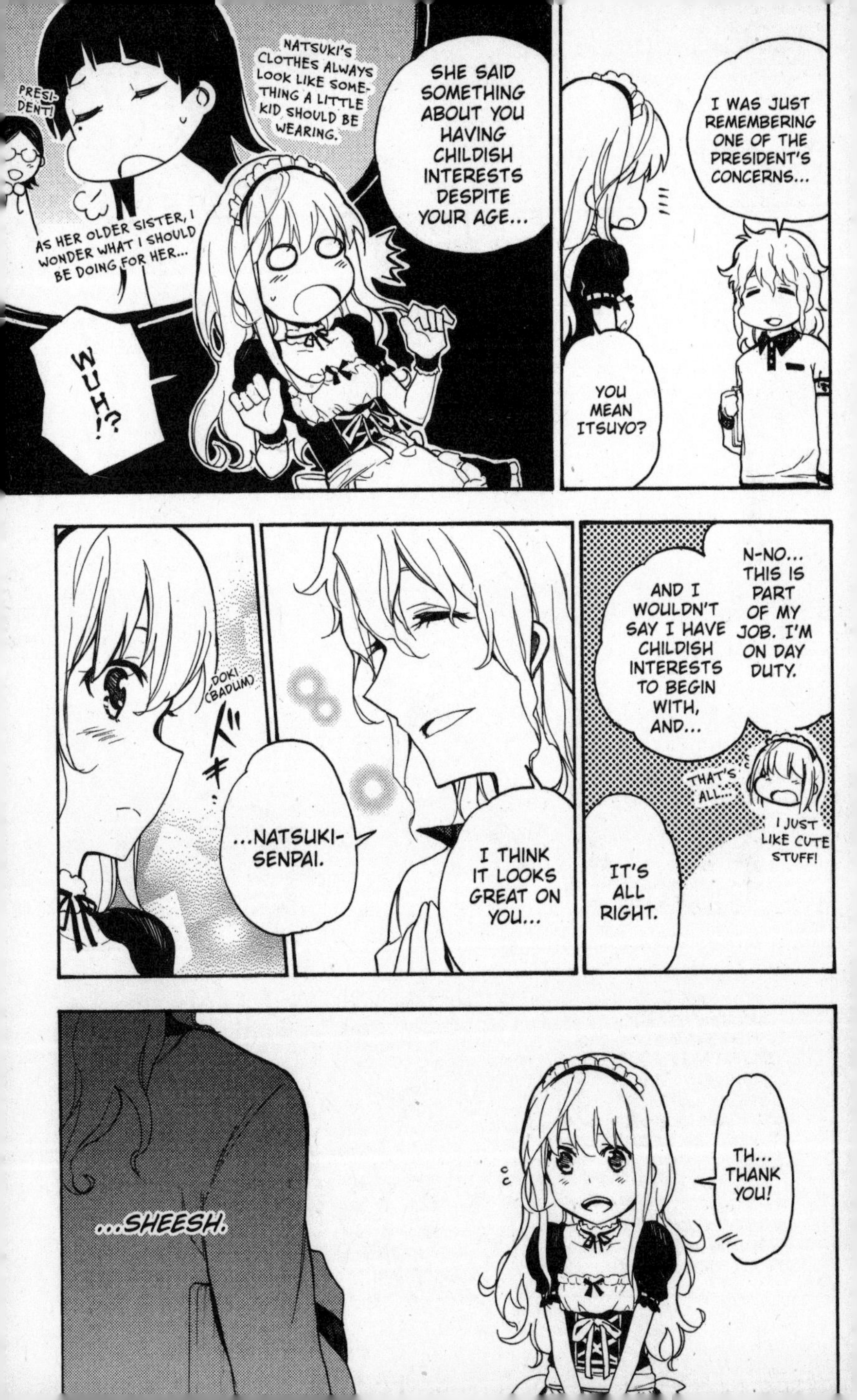
I WAS JUST REMEMBERING ONE OF THE PRESIDENT'S CONCERNS...
YOU MEAN ITSUYO?
SHE SAID SOMETHING ABOUT YOU HAVING CHILDISH INTERESTS DESPITE YOUR AGE...
NATSUKI'S CLOTHES ALWAYS LOOK LIKE SOMETHING A LITTLE KID SHOULD BE WEARING.
PRESIDENT!
AS HER OLDER SISTER, I WONDER WHAT I SHOULD BE DOING FOR HER...
WUH!?
N-NO... THIS IS PART OF MY JOB. I'M ON DAY DUTY.
AND I WOULDN'T SAY I HAVE CHILDISH INTERESTS TO BEGIN WITH, AND...
THAT'S ALL...
I JUST LIKE CUTE STUFF!
IT'S ALL RIGHT.
I THINK IT LOOKS GREAT ON YOU...
DOKI (BADUM)
...NATSUKI-SENPAI.
TH... THANK YOU!
...SHEESH.

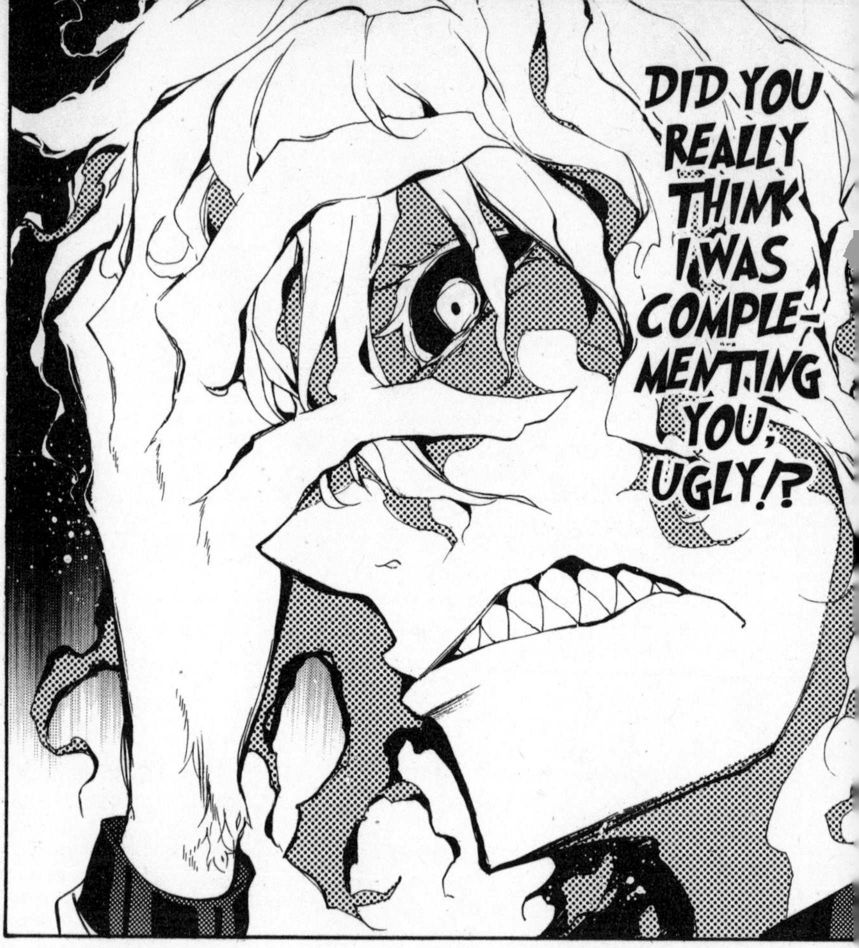
DID YOU REALLY THINK I WAS COMPLE-MENTING YOU, UGLY!?

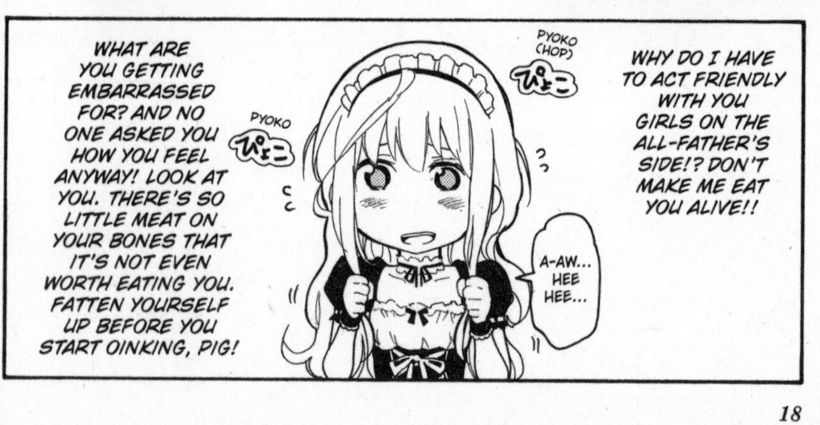
WHY DO I HAVE TO ACT FRIENDLY WITH YOU GIRLS ON THE ALL-FATHER'S SIDE!? DON'T MAKE ME EAT YOU ALIVE!!
PYOKO (HOP)
ぴょこ
PYOKO
ぴょこ
A-AW... HEE HEE...
WHAT ARE YOU GETTING EMBARRASSED FOR? AND NO ONE ASKED YOU HOW YOU FEEL ANYWAY! LOOK AT YOU. THERE'S SO LITTLE MEAT ON YOUR BONES THAT IT'S NOT EVEN WORTH EATING YOU. FATTEN YOURSELF UP BEFORE YOU START OINKING, PIG!

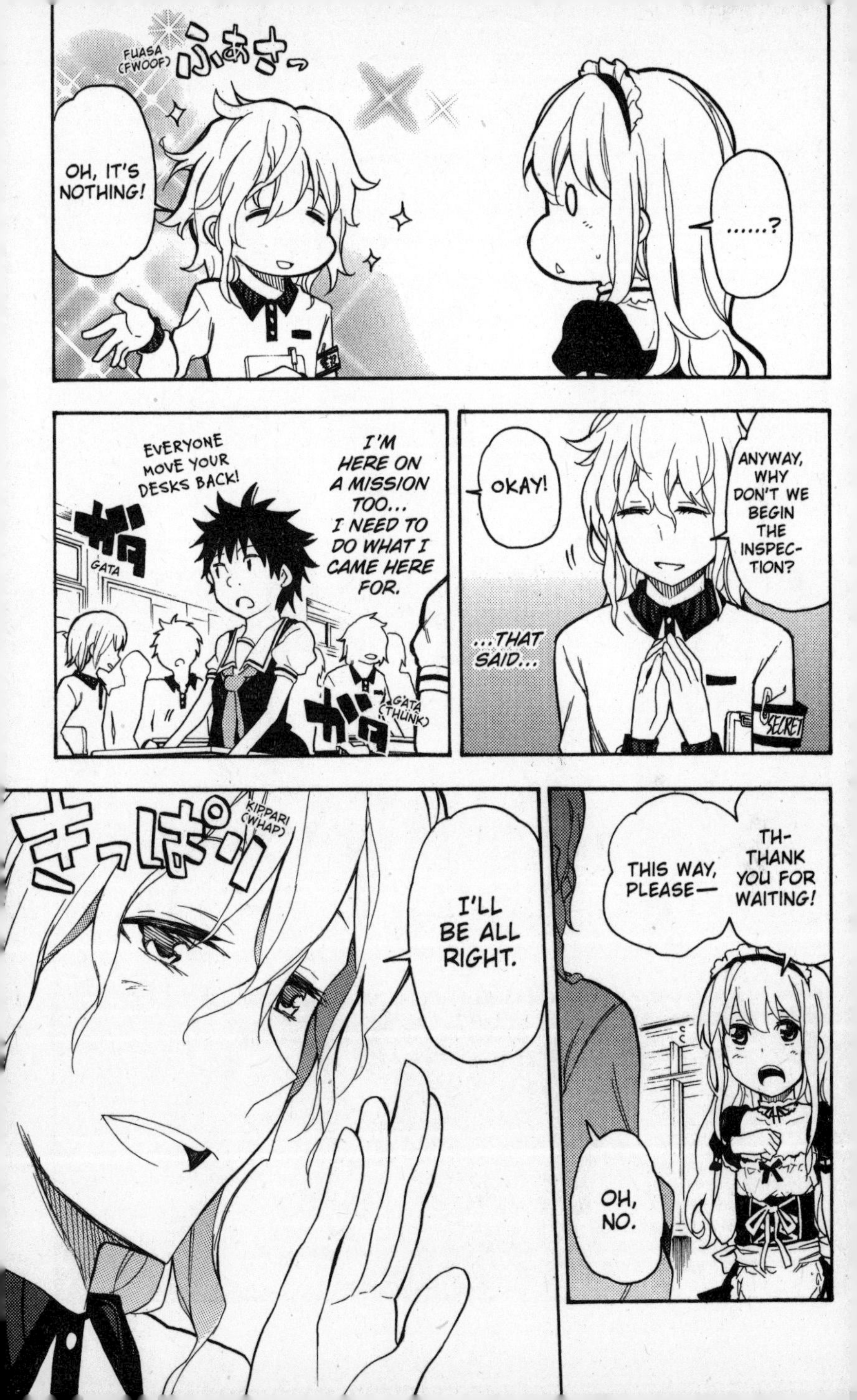
FUASA (FWOOF)
ふぁさっ
OH, IT'S NOTHING!
......?
ANYWAY, WHY DON'T WE BEGIN THE INSPECTION?
OKAY!
...THAT SAID...
SECRET
I'M HERE ON A MISSION TOO... I NEED TO DO WHAT I CAME HERE FOR.
EVERYONE MOVE YOUR DESKS BACK!
ガタ
GATA
GATA (THUNK)
ガタ
TH-THANK YOU FOR WAITING!
THIS WAY, PLEASE—
OH, NO.
きっぱり
KIPPARI (WHAP)
I'LL BE ALL RIGHT.

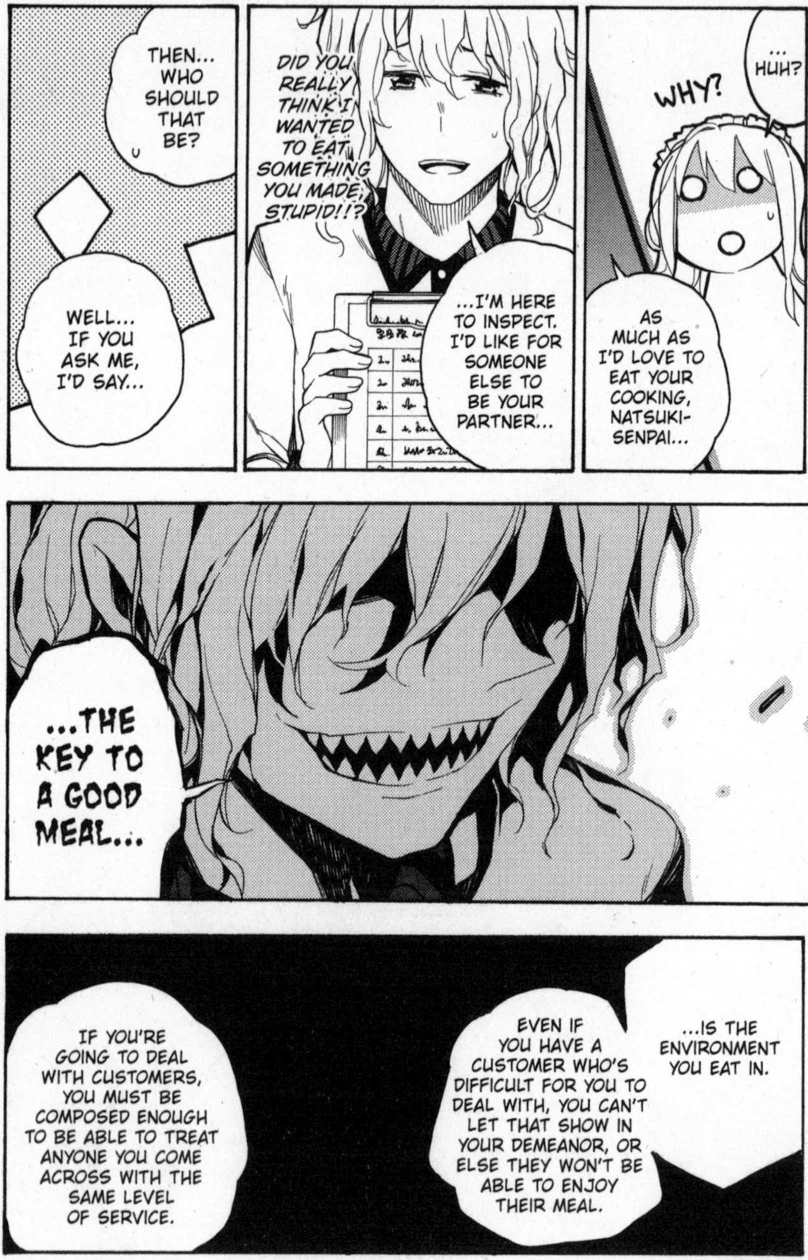
...HUH?
WHY?
AS MUCH AS I'D LOVE TO EAT YOUR COOKING, NATSUKI-SENPAI...
DID YOU REALLY THINK I WANTED TO EAT SOMETHING YOU MADE, STUPID!!?
...I'M HERE TO INSPECT. I'D LIKE FOR SOMEONE ELSE TO BE YOUR PARTNER...
THEN... WHO SHOULD THAT BE?
WELL... IF YOU ASK ME, I'D SAY...
...THE KEY TO A GOOD MEAL...
...IS THE ENVIRONMENT YOU EAT IN.
EVEN IF YOU HAVE A CUSTOMER WHO'S DIFFICULT FOR YOU TO DEAL WITH, YOU CAN'T LET THAT SHOW IN YOUR DEMEANOR, OR ELSE THEY WON'T BE ABLE TO ENJOY THEIR MEAL.
IF YOU'RE GOING TO DEAL WITH CUSTOMERS, YOU MUST BE COMPOSED ENOUGH TO BE ABLE TO TREAT ANYONE YOU COME ACROSS WITH THE SAME LEVEL OF SERVICE.

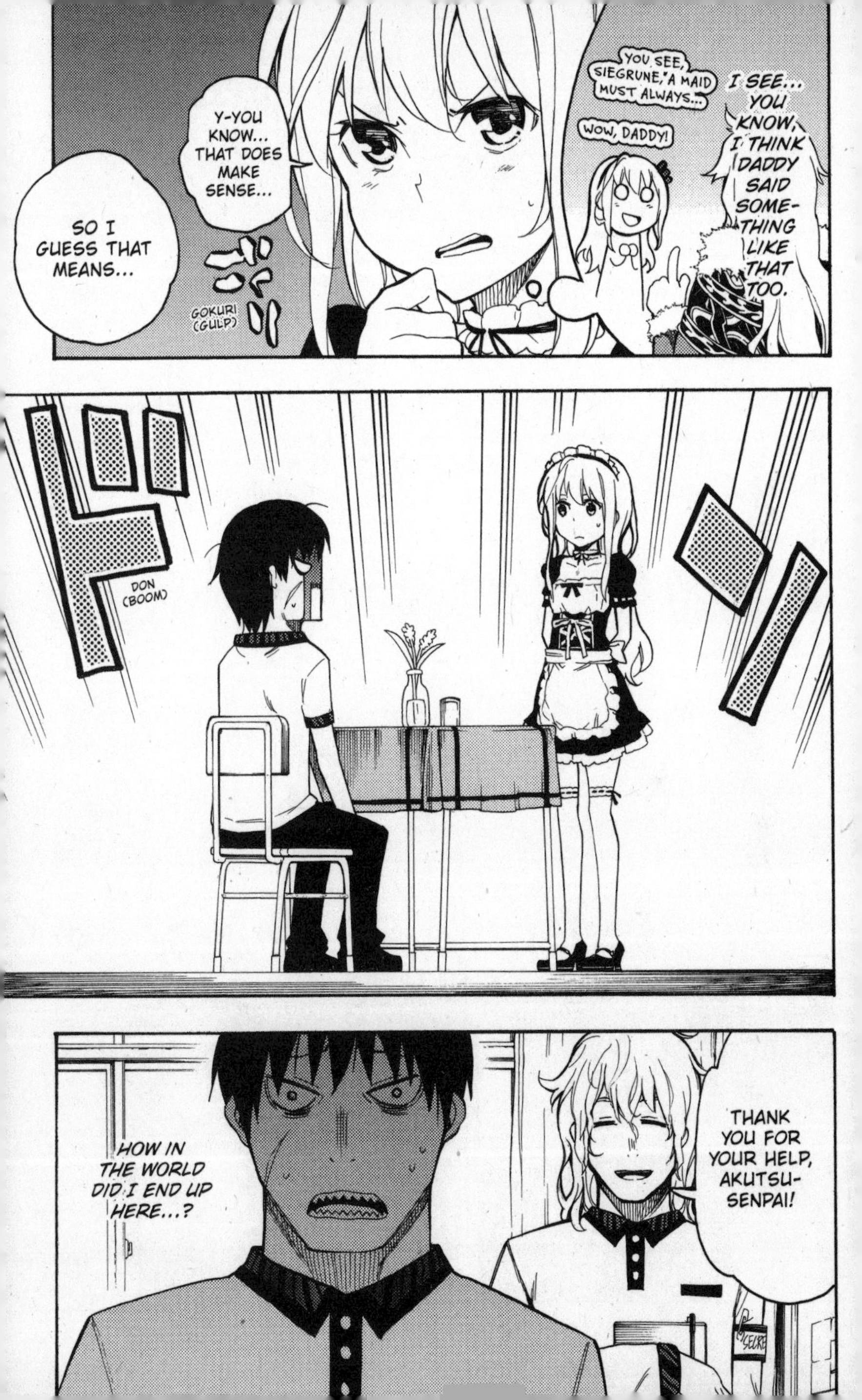
I SEE... YOU KNOW, I THINK DADDY SAID SOMETHING LIKE THAT TOO.
YOU SEE, SIEGRUNE, A MAID MUST ALWAYS...
WOW, DADDY!
Y-YOU KNOW... THAT DOES MAKE SENSE...
GOKURI (GULP)
SO I GUESS THAT MEANS...
DON (BOOM)
THANK YOU FOR YOUR HELP, AKUTSU-SENPAI!
HOW IN THE WORLD DID I END UP HERE...?

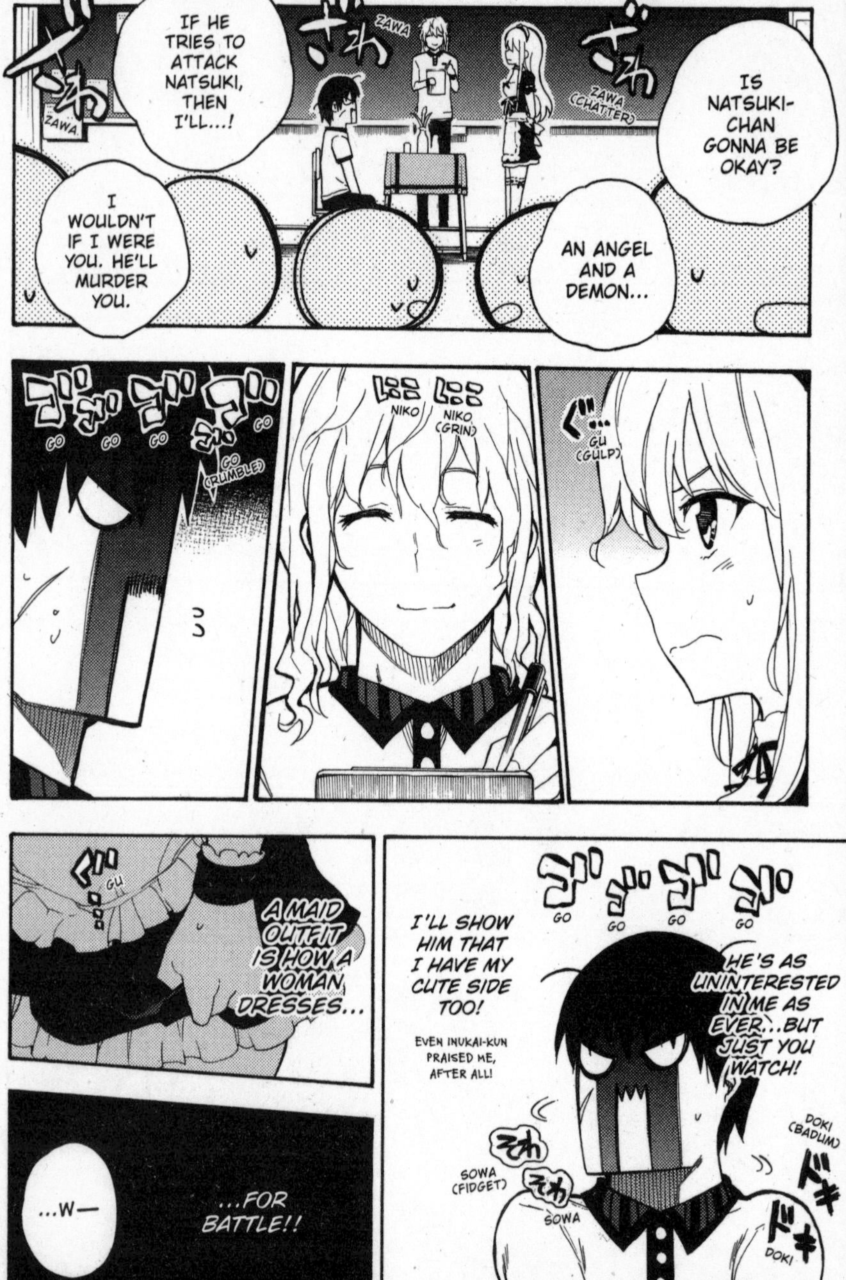
ZAWA
IS NATSUKI-CHAN GONNA BE OKAY?
ZAWA (CHATTER)
AN ANGEL AND A DEMON...
ZAWA
IF HE TRIES TO ATTACK NATSUKI, THEN I'LL...!
I WOULDN'T IF I WERE YOU. HE'LL MURDER YOU.
ZAWA
GU (GULP)
NIKO NIKO (GRIN)
GO GO GO GO GO (RUMBLE)
GO GO GO GO
HE'S AS UNINTERESTED IN ME AS EVER...BUT JUST YOU WATCH!
I'LL SHOW HIM THAT I HAVE MY CUTE SIDE TOO!
EVEN INUKAI-KUN PRAISED ME, AFTER ALL!
DOKI (BADUM)
DOKI
SOWA (FIDGET)
SOWA
GU
A MAID OUTFIT IS HOW A WOMAN DRESSES...
...FOR BATTLE!!
...W—

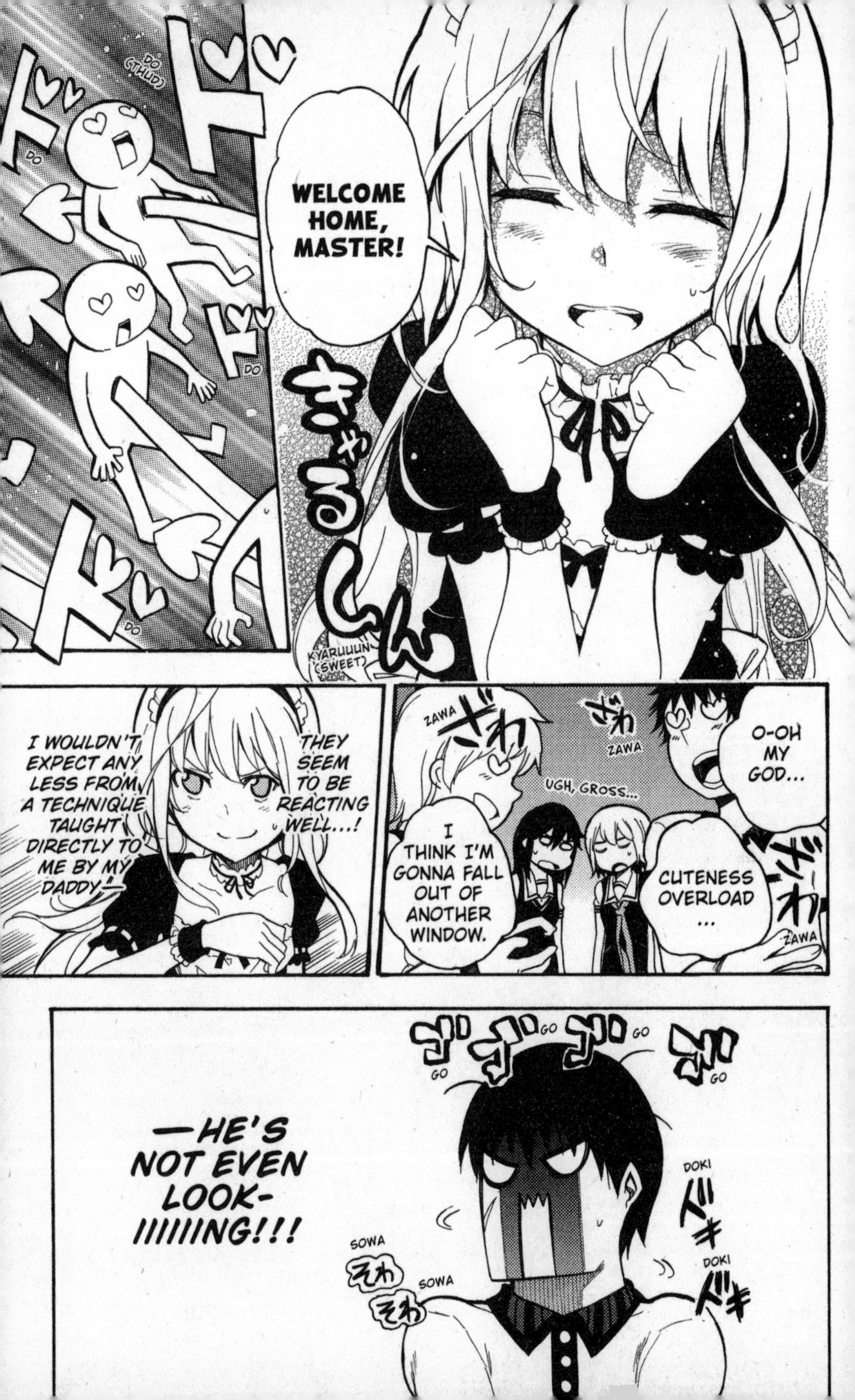
WELCOME HOME, MASTER!
KYARUUUN (SWEET)
DO (THUD)
DO
DO
DO
ZAWA
ZAWA
O-OH MY GOD...
UGH, GROSS...
CUTENESS OVERLOAD ...
I THINK I'M GONNA FALL OUT OF ANOTHER WINDOW.
ZAWA
THEY SEEM TO BE REACTING WELL...!
I WOULDN'T EXPECT ANY LESS FROM A TECHNIQUE TAUGHT DIRECTLY TO ME BY MY DADDY—
GO
GO
GO
GO
DOKI
DOKI
SOWA
SOWA
—HE'S NOT EVEN LOOK-IIIIIIING!!!

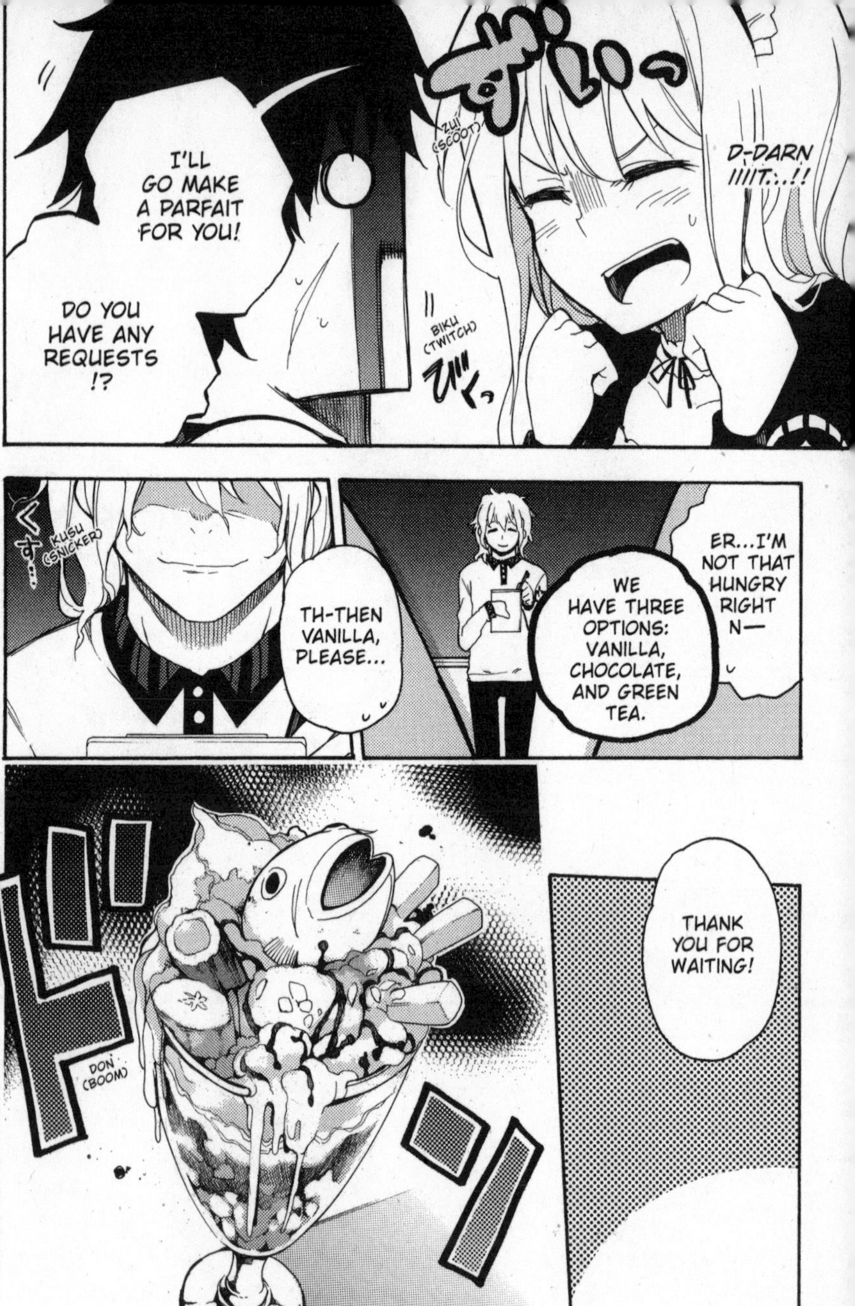

D-DARN !!!!!T...!!
ZUI (SCOOT)
I'LL GO MAKE A PARFAIT FOR YOU!
BIKU (TWITCH)
DO YOU HAVE ANY REQUESTS !?
ER...I'M NOT THAT HUNGRY RIGHT N—
WE HAVE THREE OPTIONS: VANILLA, CHOCOLATE, AND GREEN TEA.
KUSU (SNICKER)
TH-THEN VANILLA, PLEASE...
THANK YOU FOR WAITING!
DON (BOOM)

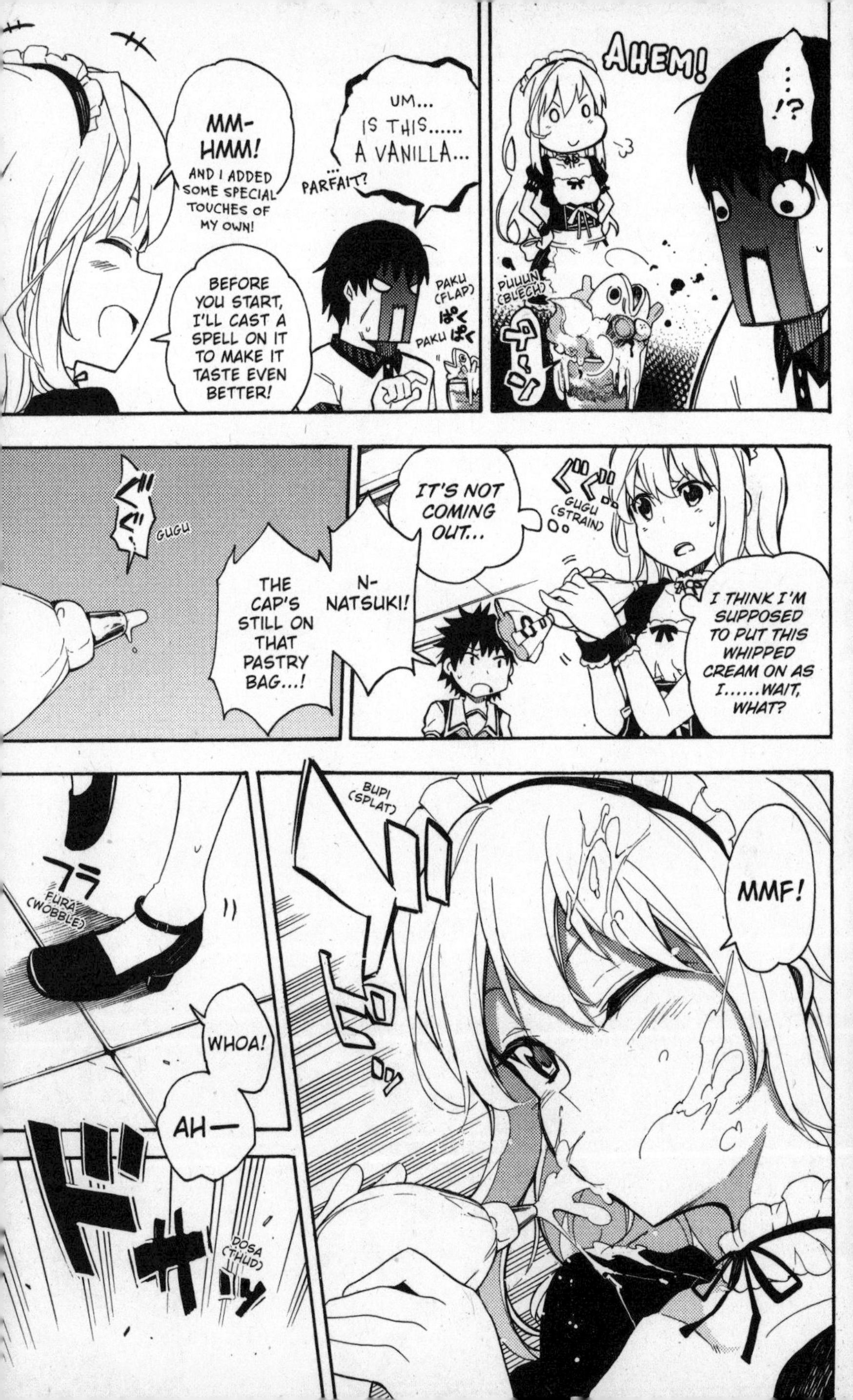
AHEM!
...!?
PUUUN (BLECH)
UM... IS THIS...... A VANILLA... ...PARFAIT?
MM-HMM! AND I ADDED SOME SPECIAL TOUCHES OF MY OWN!
BEFORE YOU START, I'LL CAST A SPELL ON IT TO MAKE IT TASTE EVEN BETTER!
PAKU (FLAP) PAKU
IT'S NOT COMING OUT...
GUGU (STRAIN)
I THINK I'M SUPPOSED TO PUT THIS WHIPPED CREAM ON AS I......WAIT, WHAT?
N-NATSUKI!
THE CAP'S STILL ON THAT PASTRY BAG...!
GUGU
BUPI (SPLAT)
MMF!
FURA (WOBBLE)
WHOA!
AH—
DOSA (THUD)

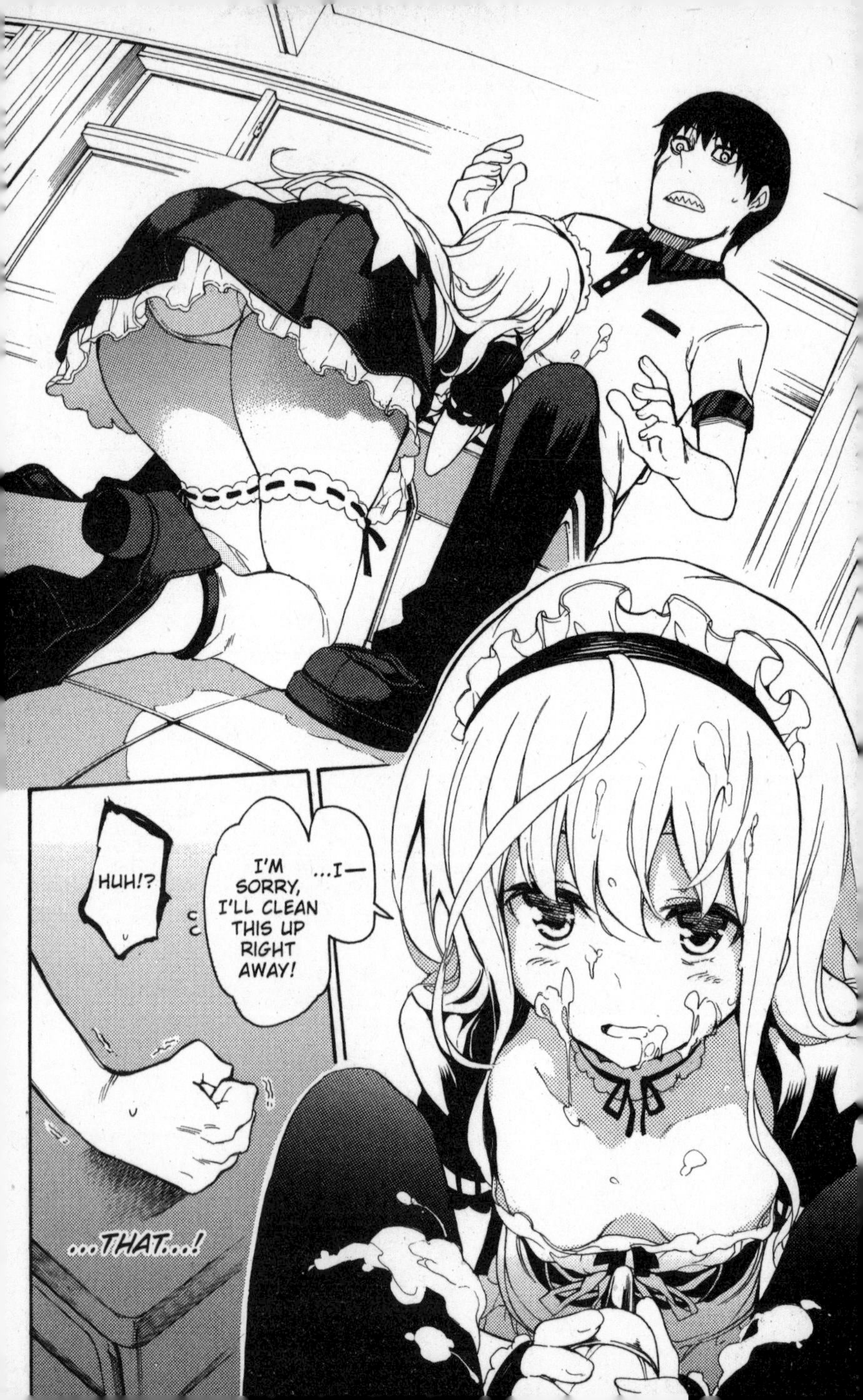
...I—
I'M SORRY, I'LL CLEAN THIS UP RIGHT AWAY!
HUH!?
...THAT...!

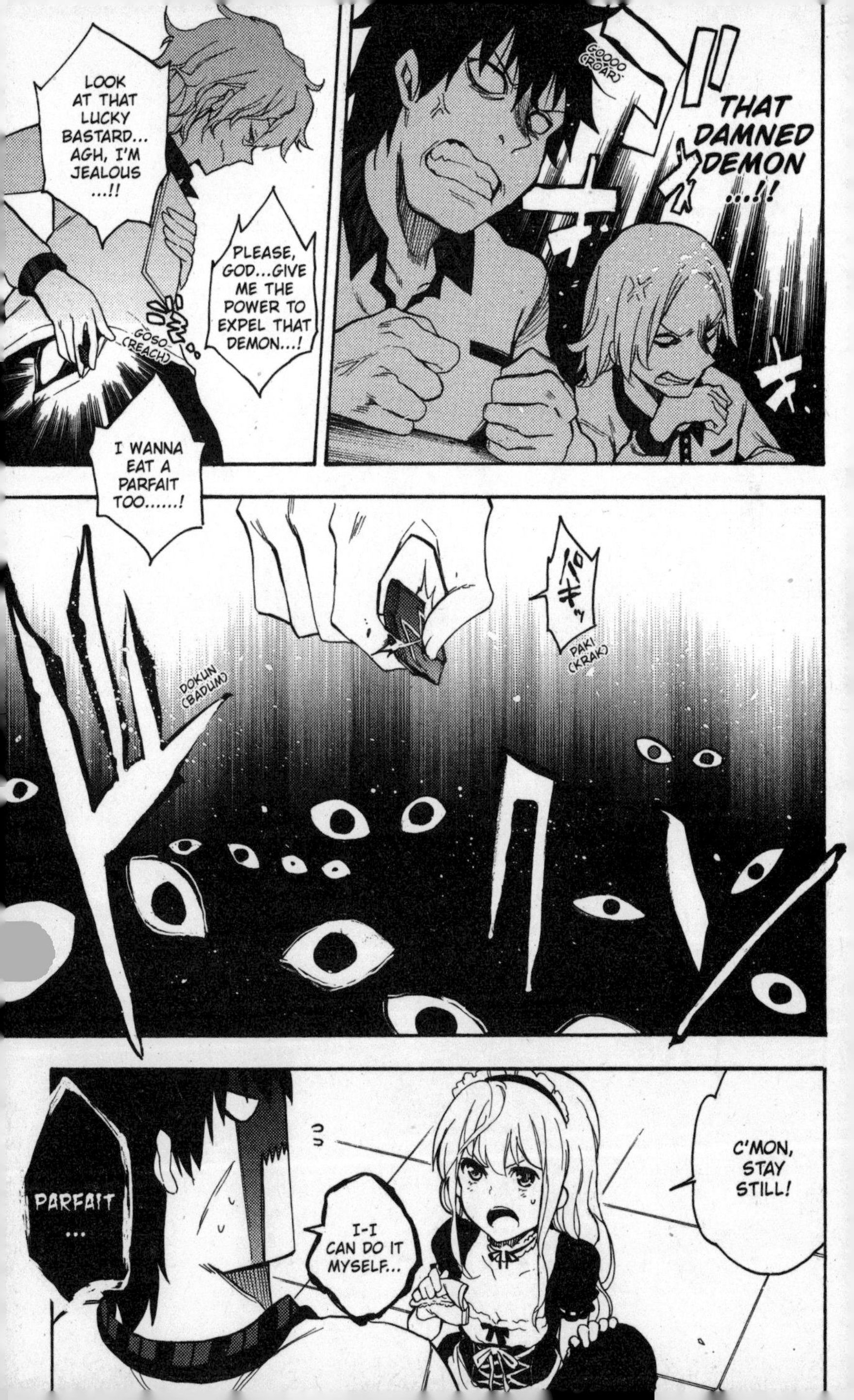
GOOOO (ROAR)
THAT DAMNED DEMON...!!
LOOK AT THAT LUCKY BASTARD... AGH, I'M JEALOUS...!!
PLEASE, GOD...GIVE ME THE POWER TO EXPEL THAT DEMON...!
GOSO (REACH)
I WANNA EAT A PARFAIT TOO......!
パキッ
PAKI (KRAK)
DOKUN (BADUM)
C'MON, STAY STILL!
I-I CAN DO IT MYSELF...
PARFAIT ...

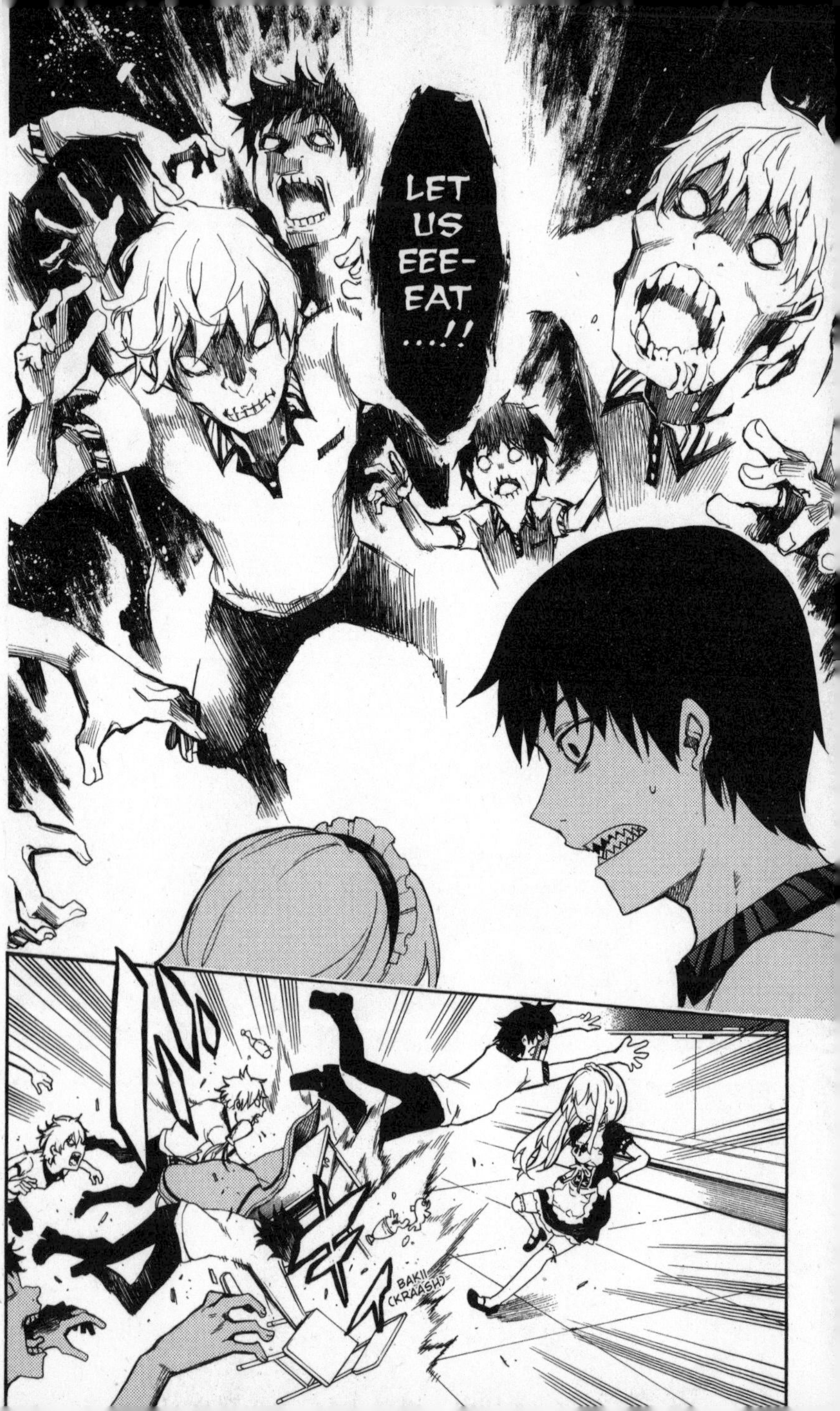
LET US EEE-EAT ....!!
BAKII (KRAASH)

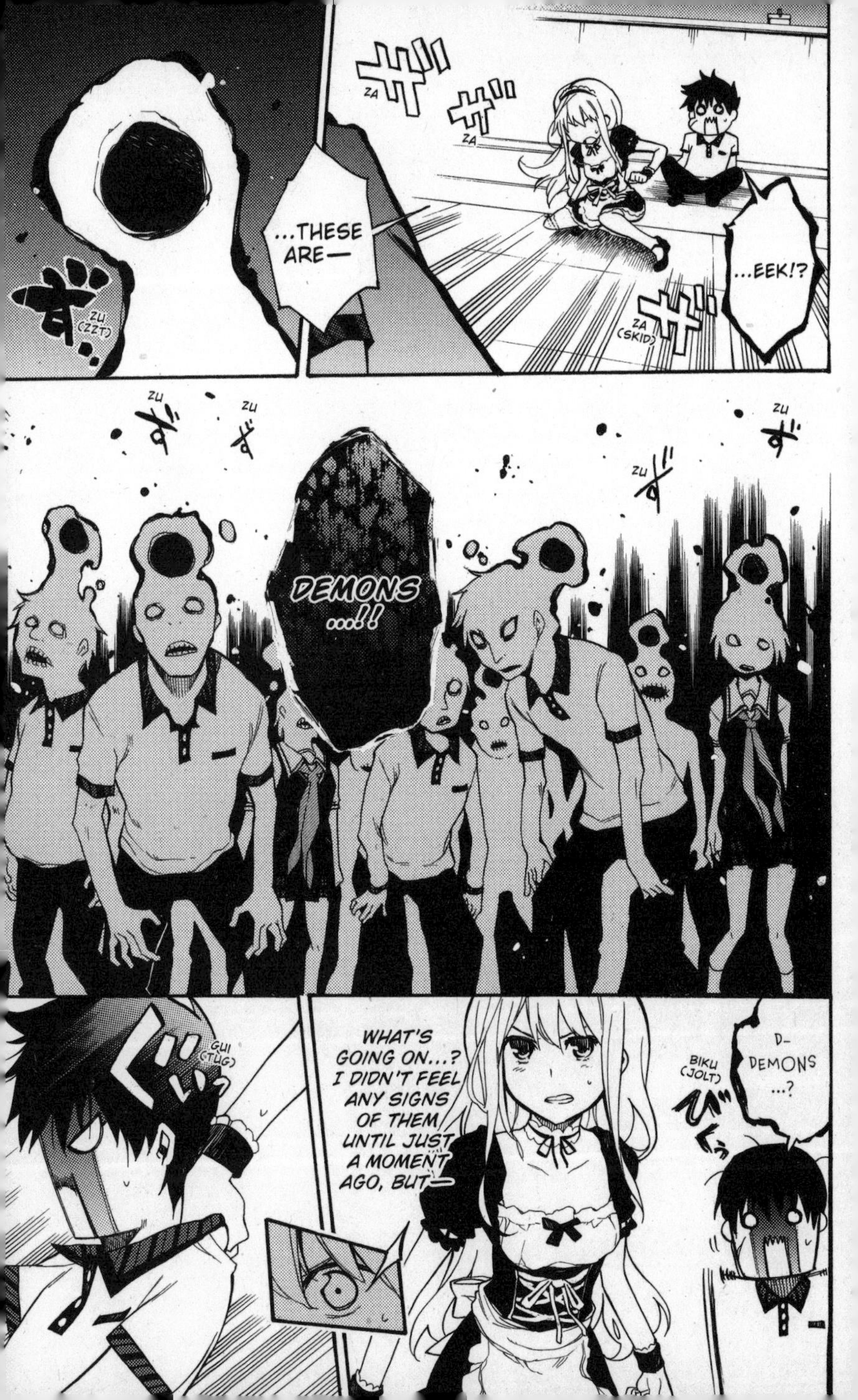
ZA
ZA
...EEK!?
ZA (SKID)
...THESE ARE—
ZU (ZZT)
ZU
ZU
ZU
ZU
DEMONS ...!!
D-DEMONS ...?
BIKU (JOLT)
WHAT'S GOING ON...? I DIDN'T FEEL ANY SIGNS OF THEM UNTIL JUST A MOMENT AGO, BUT—
GUI (TUG)

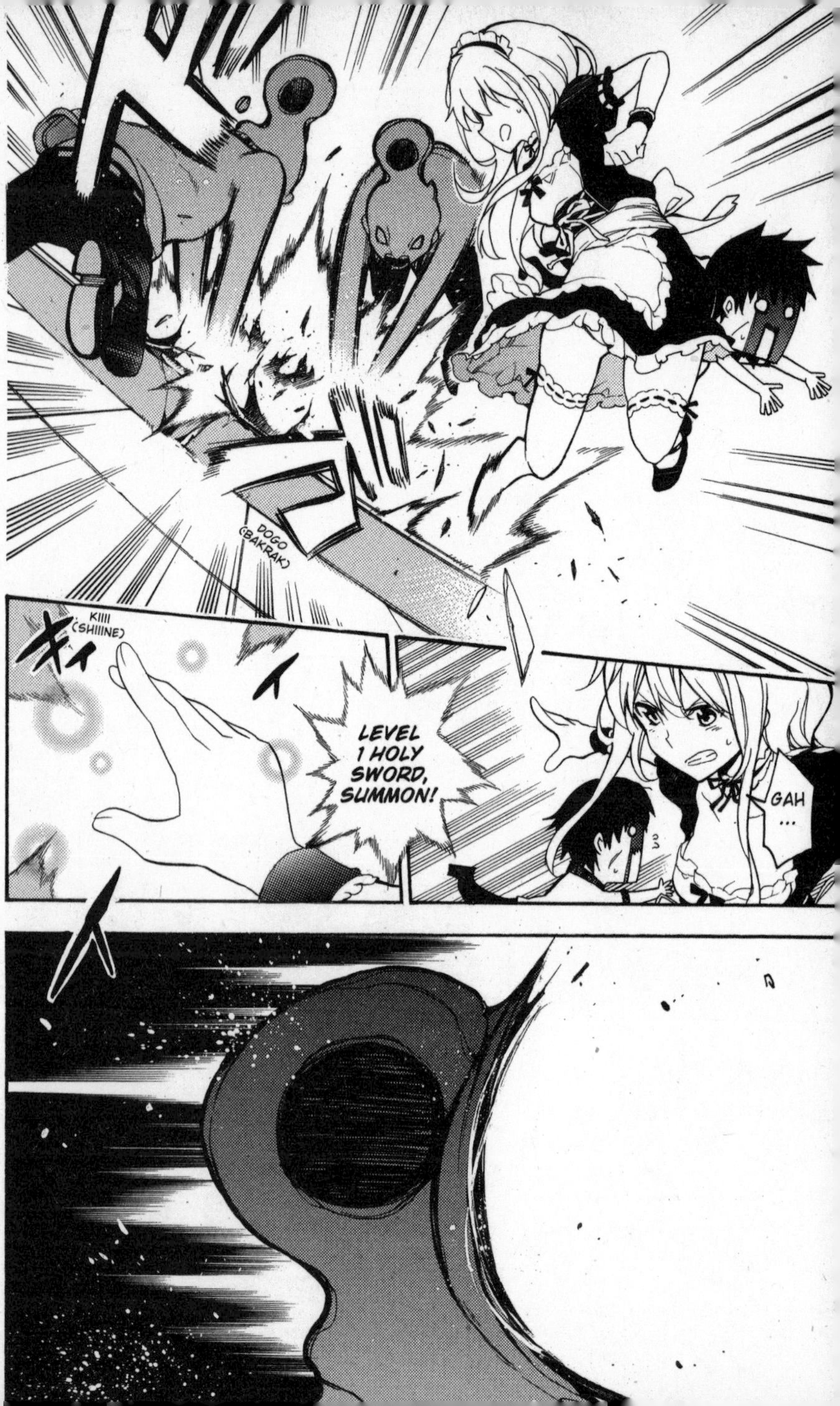
DOGO
(BAKRAK)
KIIII
(SHIIINE)
GAH
...
LEVEL 1 HOLY SWORD, SUMMON!

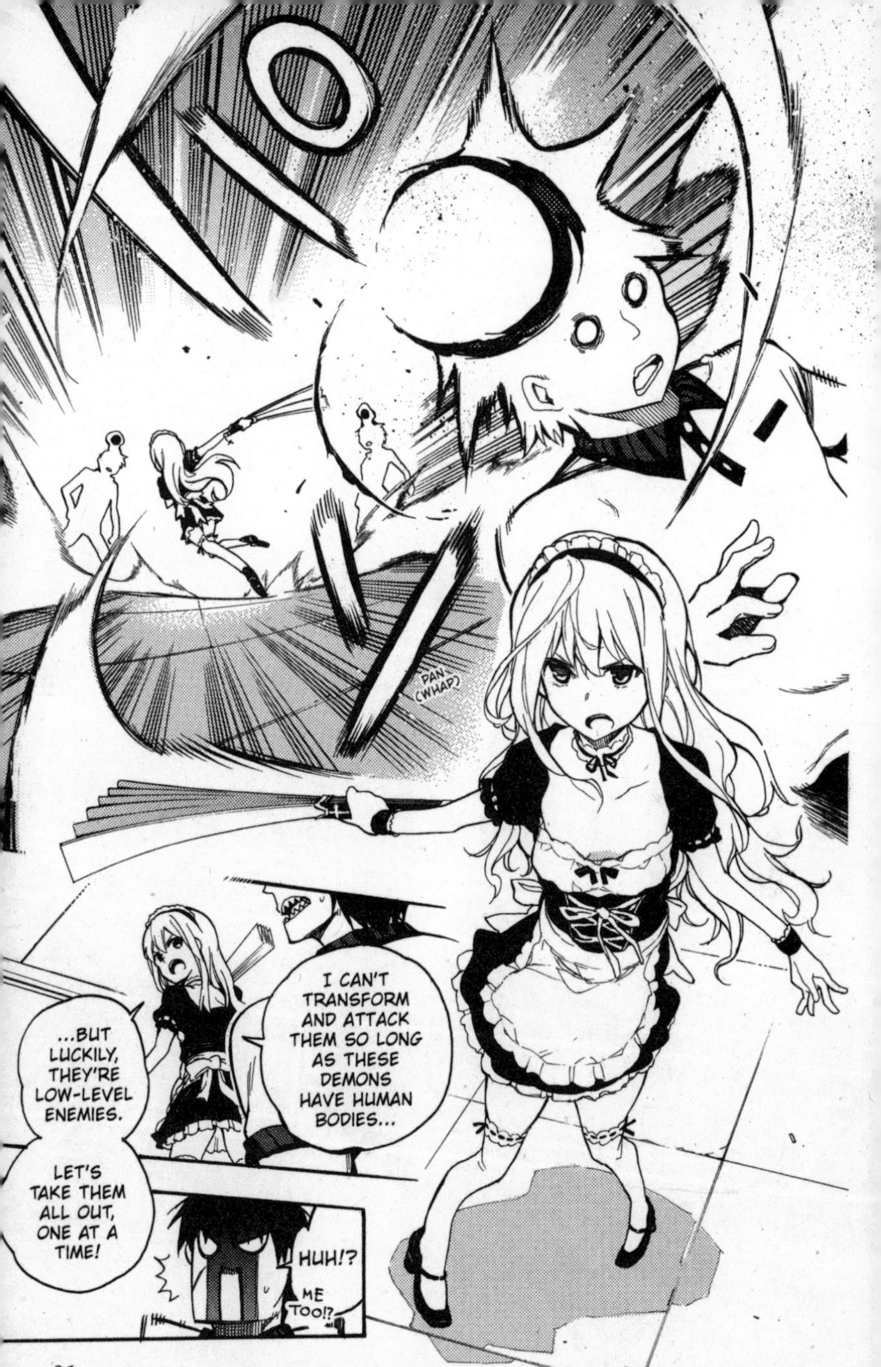
PAN (WHAP)
I CAN'T TRANSFORM AND ATTACK THEM SO LONG AS THESE DEMONS HAVE HUMAN BODIES...
...BUT LUCKILY, THEY'RE LOW-LEVEL ENEMIES.
LET'S TAKE THEM ALL OUT, ONE AT A TIME!
HUH!?
ME TOO!?

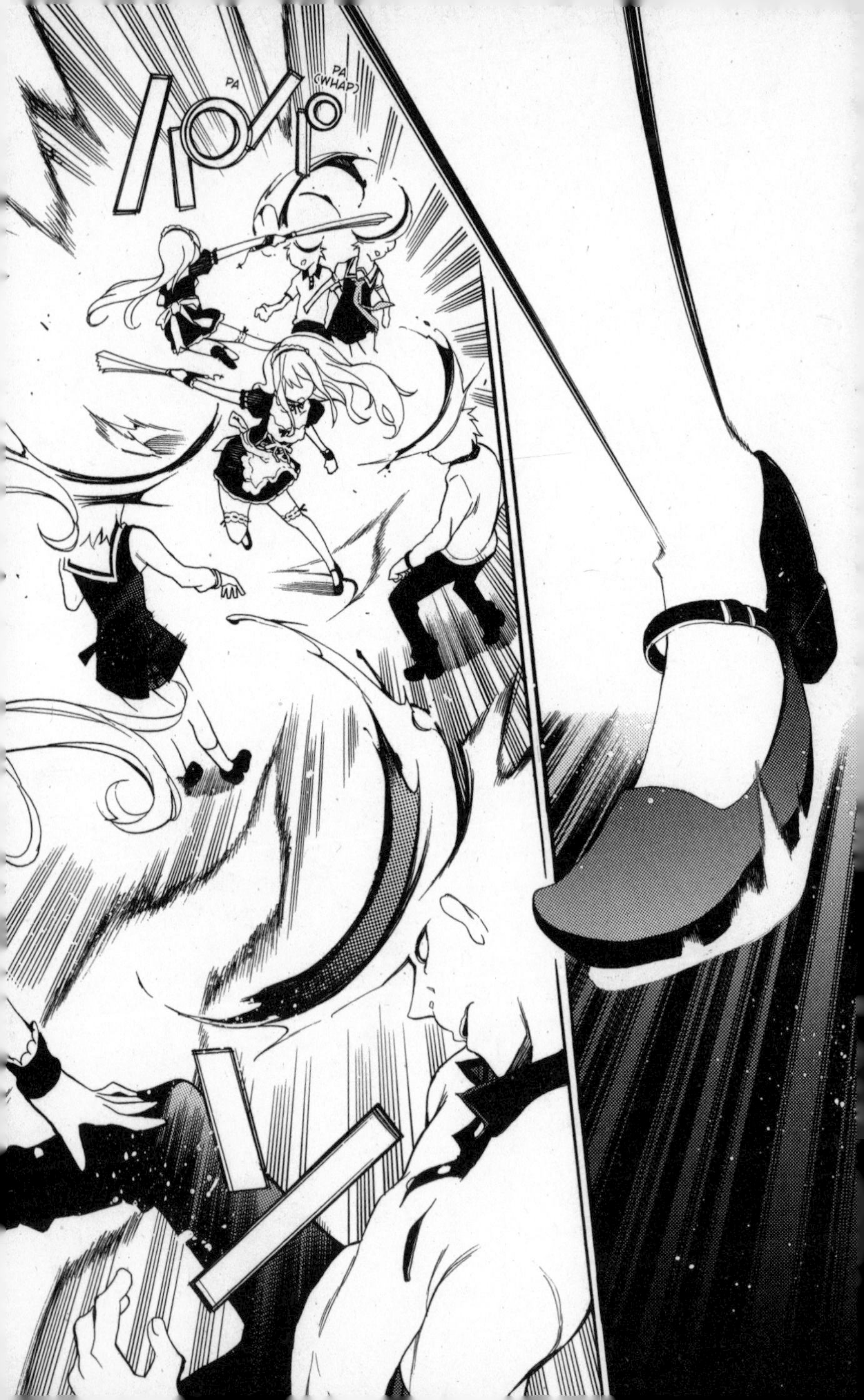
PA
PA
(WHAP)

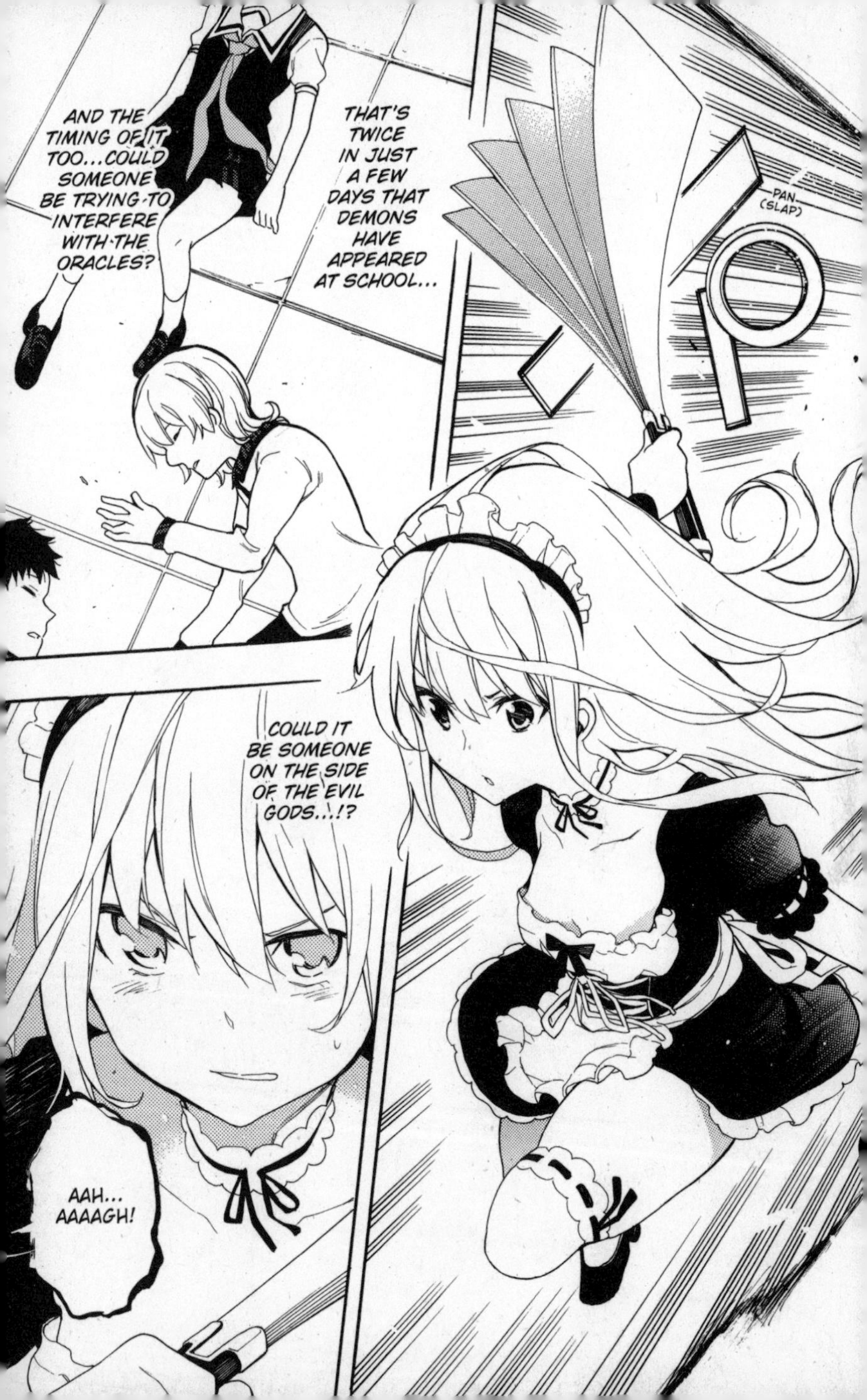

PAN
(SLAP)
THAT'S TWICE IN JUST A FEW DAYS THAT DEMONS HAVE APPEARED AT SCHOOL...
AND THE TIMING OF IT TOO...COULD SOMEONE BE TRYING TO INTERFERE WITH THE ORACLES?
COULD IT BE SOMEONE ON THE SIDE OF THE EVIL GODS...!?
AAH... AAAAGH!

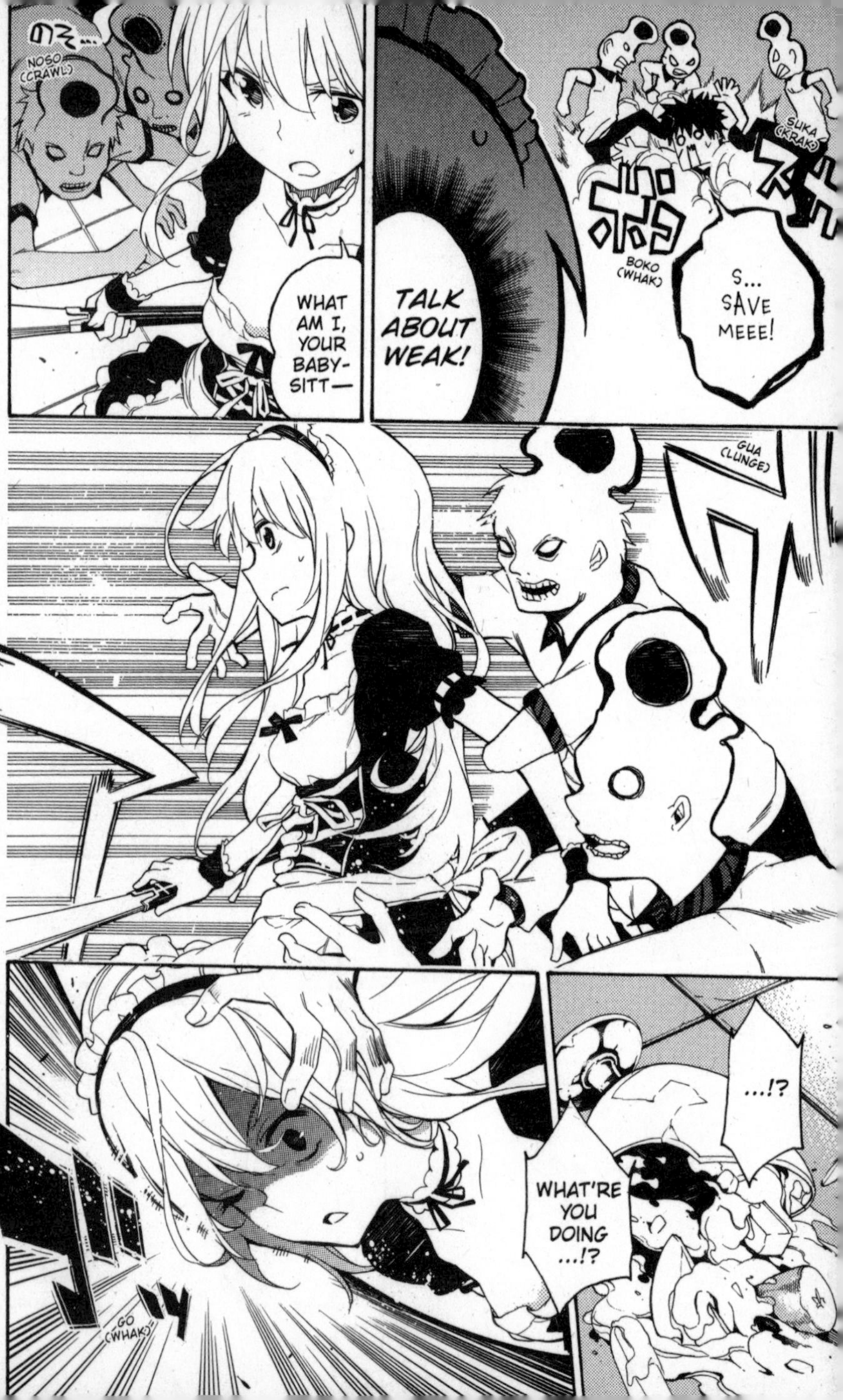
SUKA (KRAK)
BOKO (WHAK)
S... SAVE MEEE!
TALK ABOUT WEAK!
のそ…
NOSO (CRAWL)
WHAT AM I, YOUR BABY-SITT—
GUA (LUNGE)
...!?
WHAT'RE YOU DOING ...!?
GO (WHAK)

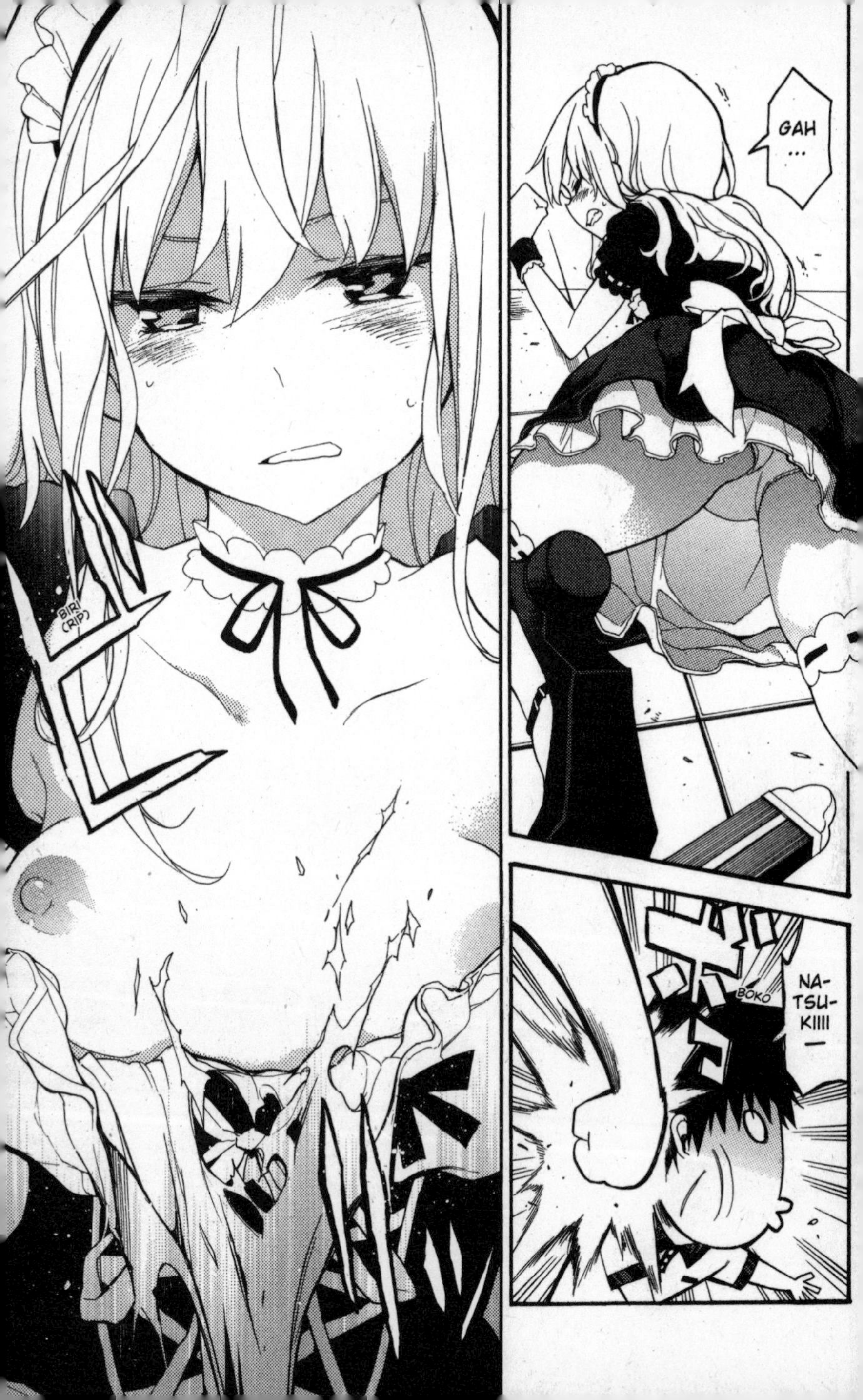
GAH ...
BOKO
NA-TSU-KIIII —
BIRI (RIP)

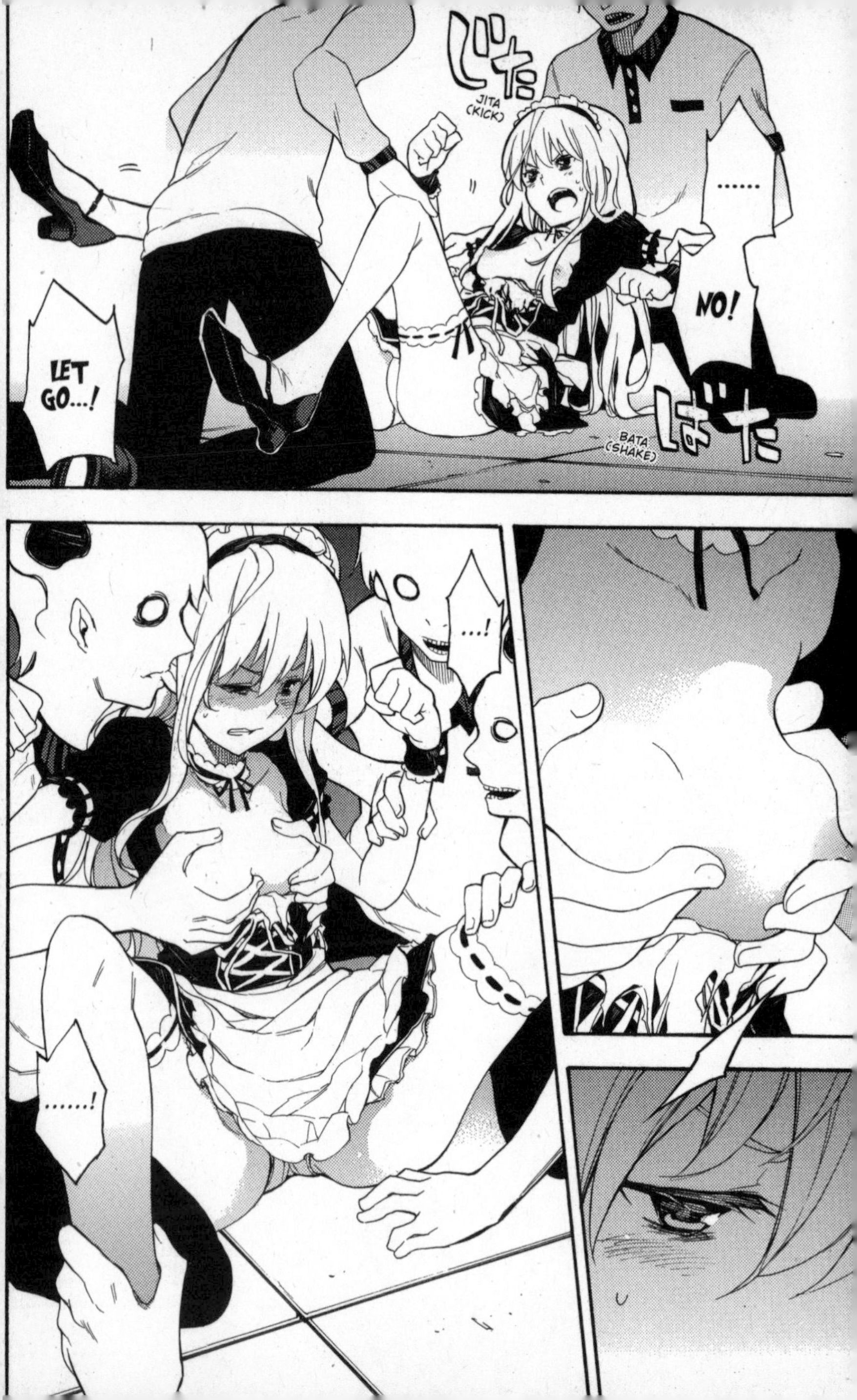
......
NO!
JITA (KICK)
BATA (SHAKE)
LET GO...!
...!
......!

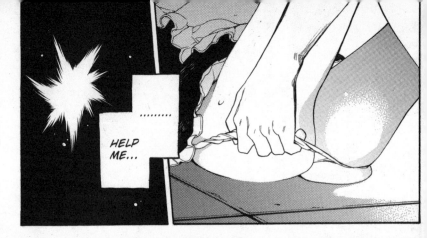

....

HELP ME...

TAKUMA ...!

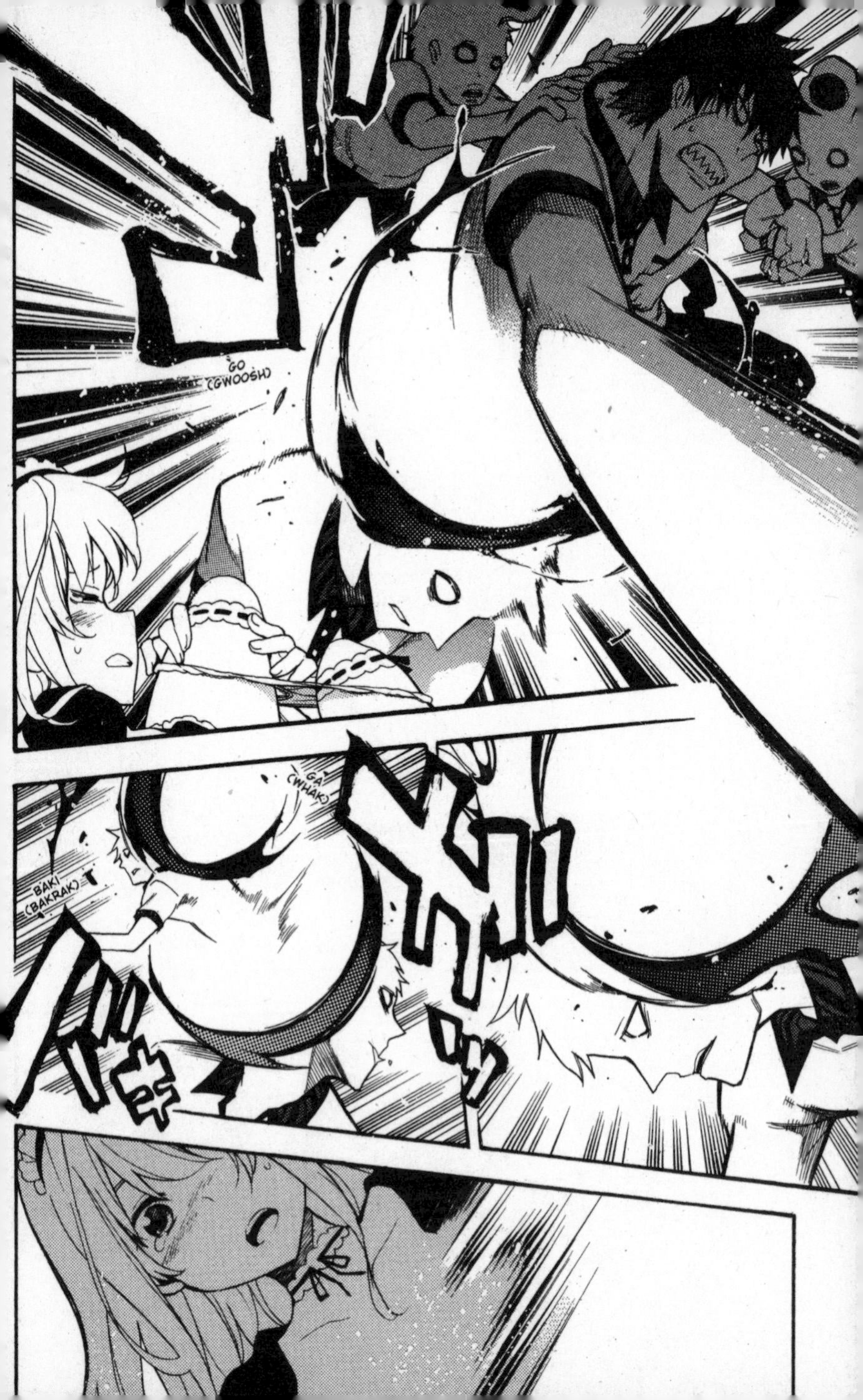
GO
(GWOOSH)
GA
(WHAK)
BAKI
(BAKRAK)

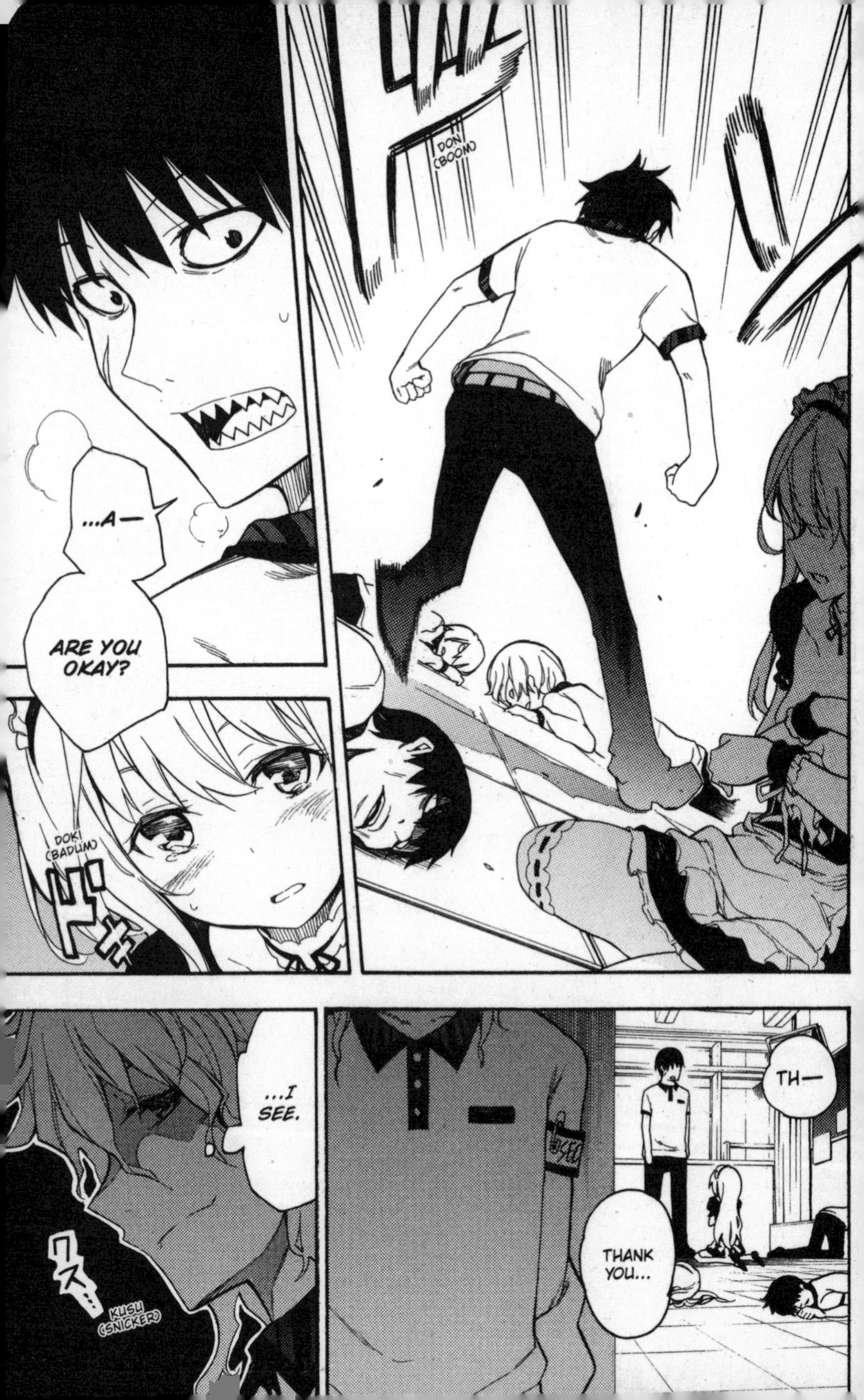
DON (BOOM)
...A—
ARE YOU OKAY?
DOKI (BADUM)
TH—
THANK YOU...
...I SEE.
KUSU (SNICKER)

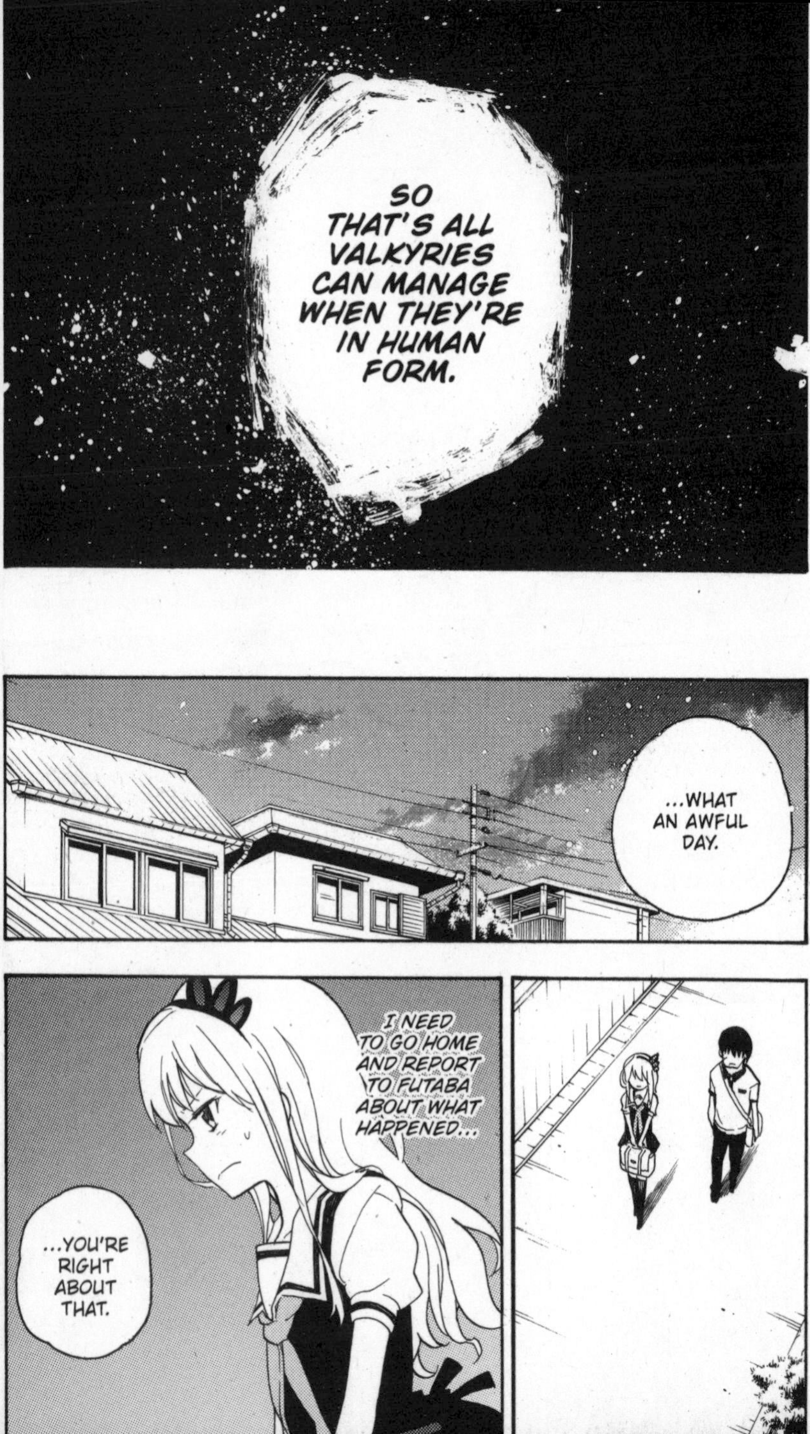
SO THAT'S ALL VALKYRIES CAN MANAGE WHEN THEY'RE IN HUMAN FORM.
...WHAT AN AWFUL DAY.
I NEED TO GO HOME AND REPORT TO FUTABA ABOUT WHAT HAPPENED...
...YOU'RE RIGHT ABOUT THAT.

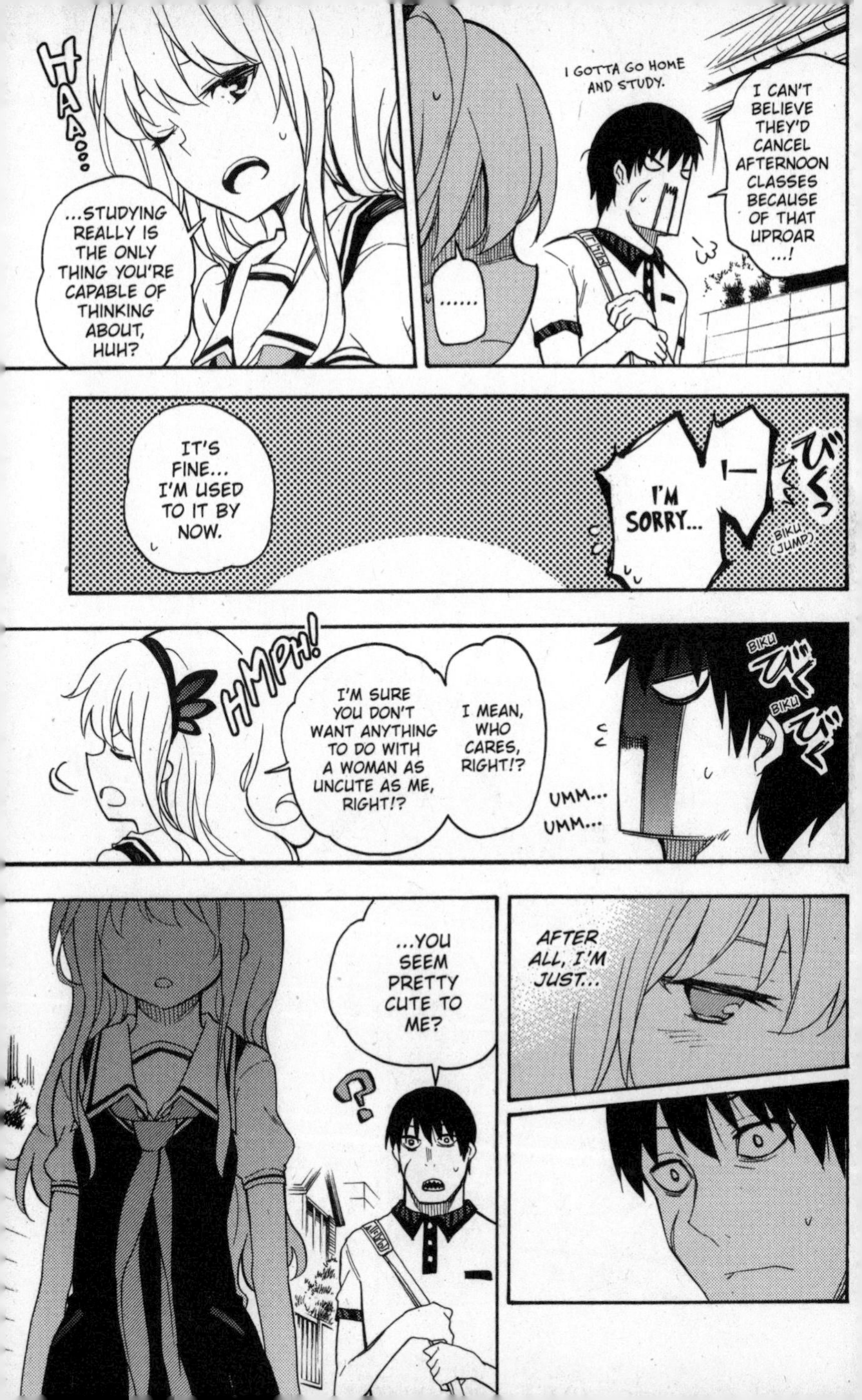
I CAN'T BELIEVE THEY'D CANCEL AFTERNOON CLASSES BECAUSE OF THAT UPROAR...!
I GOTTA GO HOME AND STUDY.
......
HAAA...
...STUDYING REALLY IS THE ONLY THING YOU'RE CAPABLE OF THINKING ABOUT, HUH?
びくっ
BIKU (JUMP)
I— I'M SORRY...
IT'S FINE... I'M USED TO IT BY NOW.
BIKU
びく
BIKU
びく
UMM... UMM...
I MEAN, WHO CARES, RIGHT!?
I'M SURE YOU DON'T WANT ANYTHING TO DO WITH A WOMAN AS UNCUTE AS ME, RIGHT!?
HMPH!
AFTER ALL, I'M JUST...
...YOU SEEM PRETTY CUTE TO ME?
?

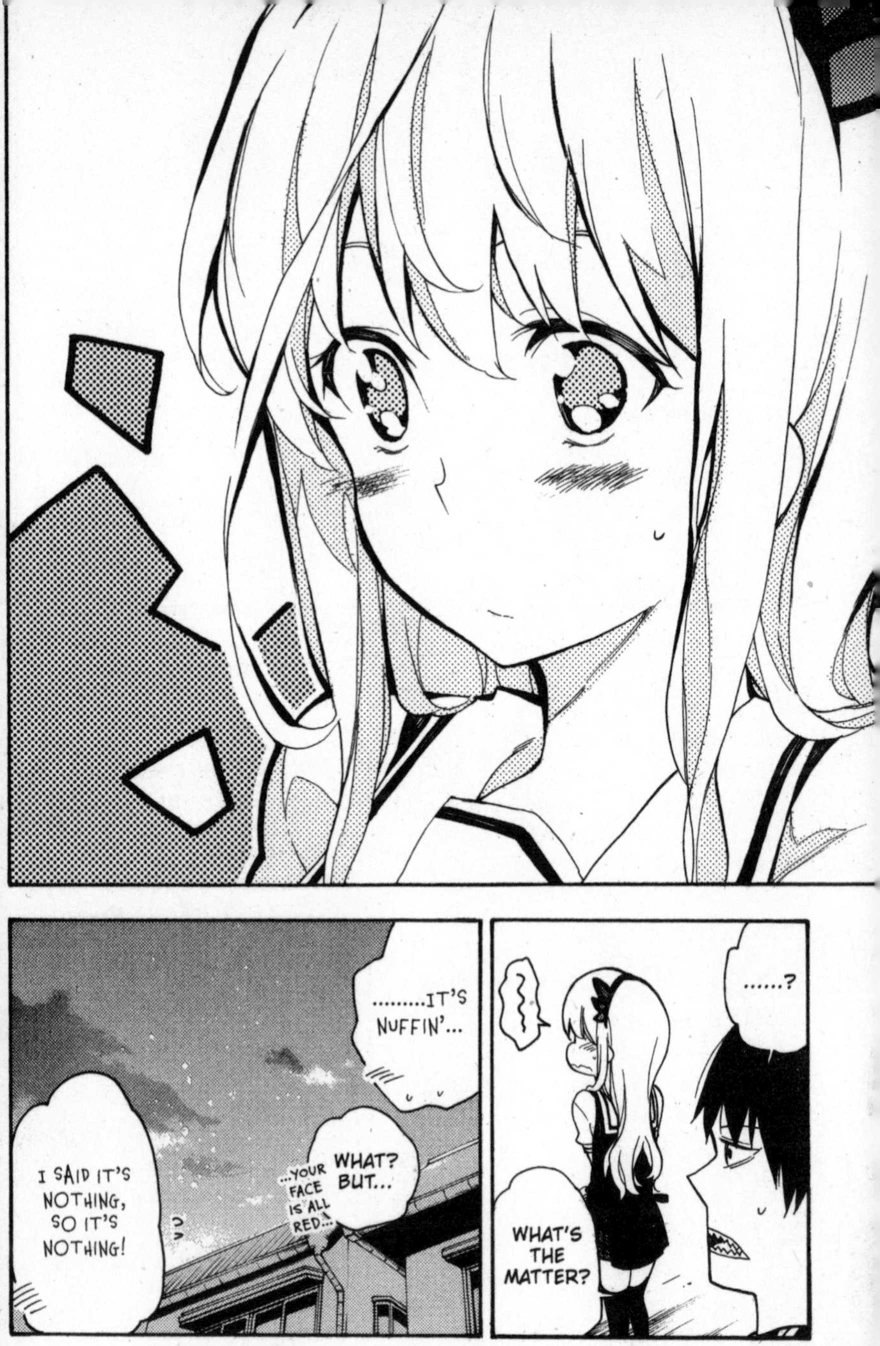
......?
WHAT'S THE MATTER?
.........IT'S NUFFIN'...
WHAT? BUT...
...YOUR FACE IS ALL RED...
I SAID IT'S NOTHING, SO IT'S NOTHING!

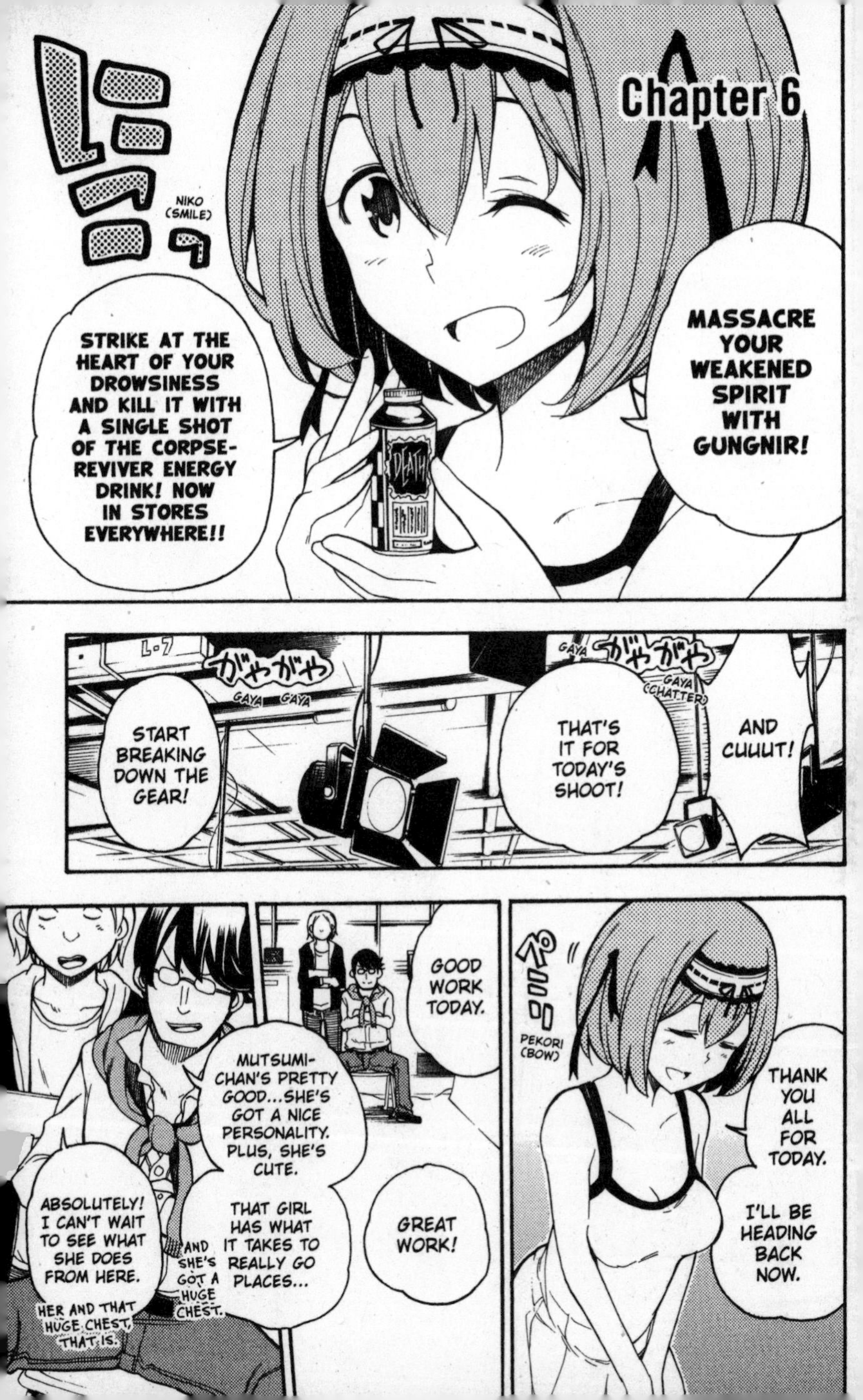
Chapter 6
MASSACRE YOUR WEAKENED SPIRIT WITH GUNGNIR!
NIKO (SMILE)
STRIKE AT THE HEART OF YOUR DROWSINESS AND KILL IT WITH A SINGLE SHOT OF THE CORPSE-REVIVER ENERGY DRINK! NOW IN STORES EVERYWHERE!!
GAYA GAYA (CHATTER)
AND CUUUT!
THAT'S IT FOR TODAY'S SHOOT!
GAYA GAYA
START BREAKING DOWN THE GEAR!
PEKORI (BOW)
THANK YOU ALL FOR TODAY.
I'LL BE HEADING BACK NOW.
GOOD WORK TODAY.
GREAT WORK!
MUTSUMI-CHAN'S PRETTY GOOD...SHE'S GOT A NICE PERSONALITY. PLUS, SHE'S CUTE.
THAT GIRL HAS WHAT IT TAKES TO REALLY GO PLACES...
AND SHE'S GOT A HUGE CHEST.
ABSOLUTELY! I CAN'T WAIT TO SEE WHAT SHE DOES FROM HERE.
HER AND THAT HUGE CHEST, THAT IS.

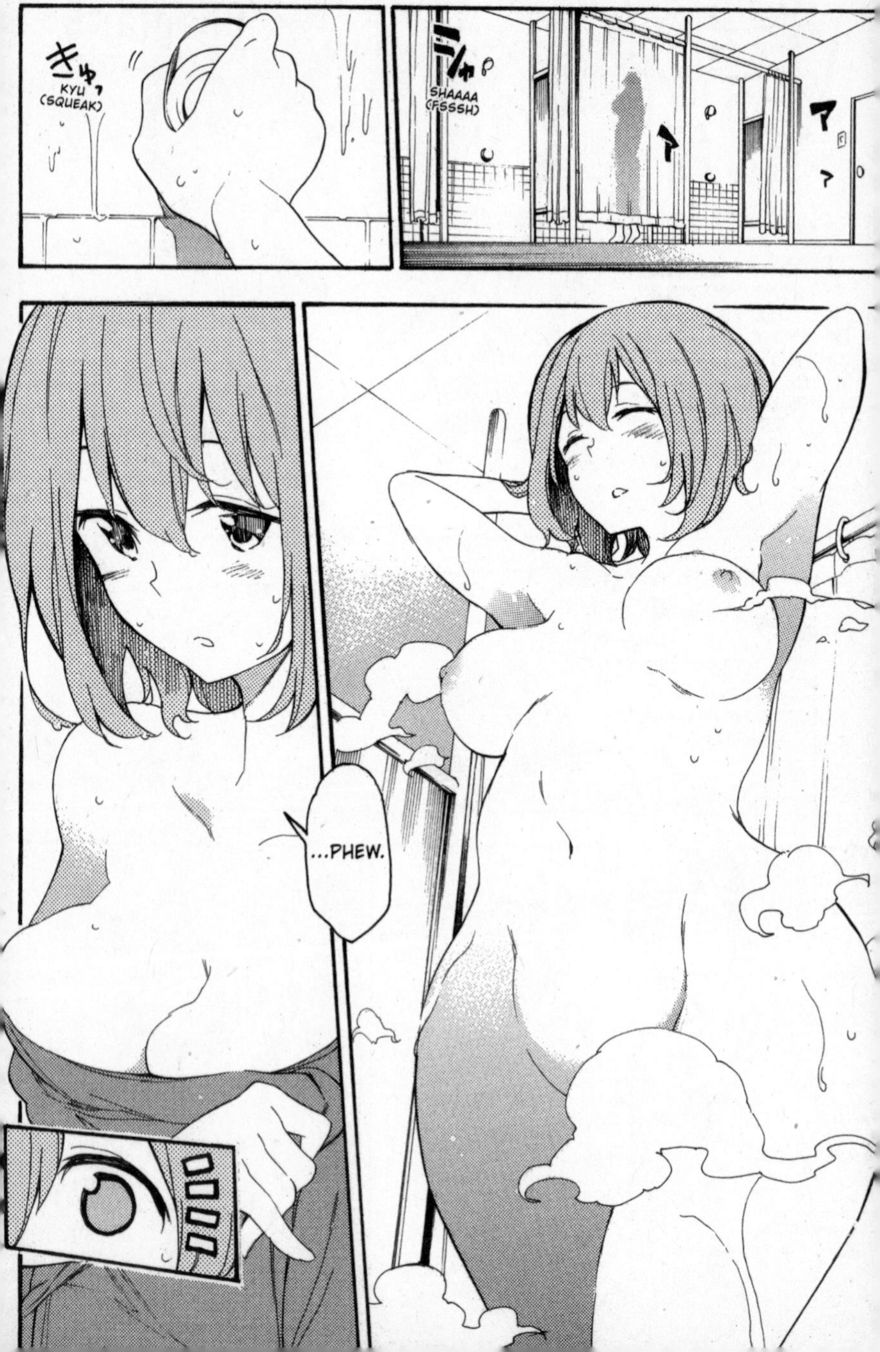
SHAAAA (FSSSH)
KYU (SQUEAK)
...PHEW.

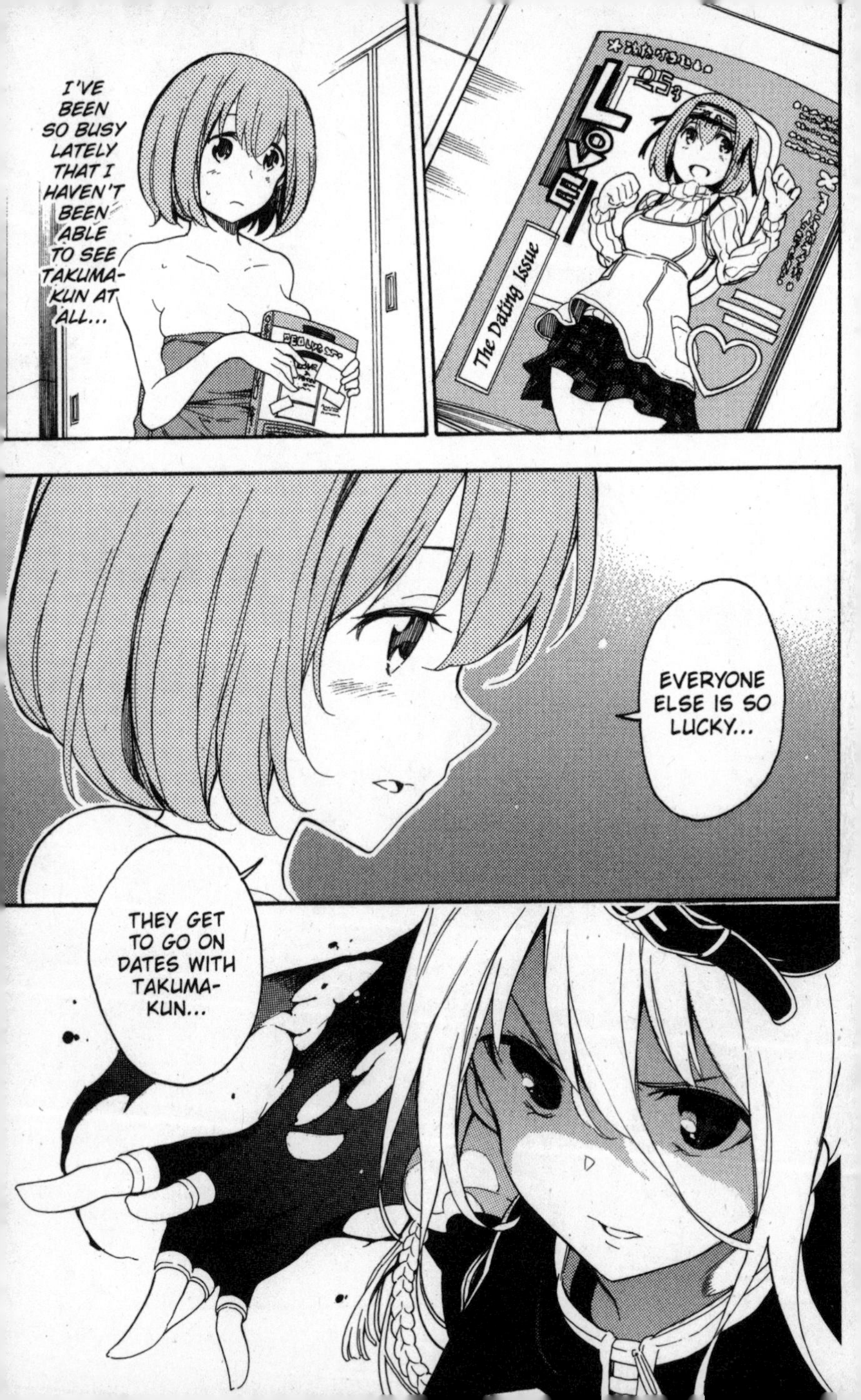
LOVE
The Dating Issue
I'VE BEEN SO BUSY LATELY THAT I HAVEN'T BEEN ABLE TO SEE TAKUMA-KUN AT ALL...
EVERYONE ELSE IS SO LUCKY...
THEY GET TO GO ON DATES WITH TAKUMA-KUN...

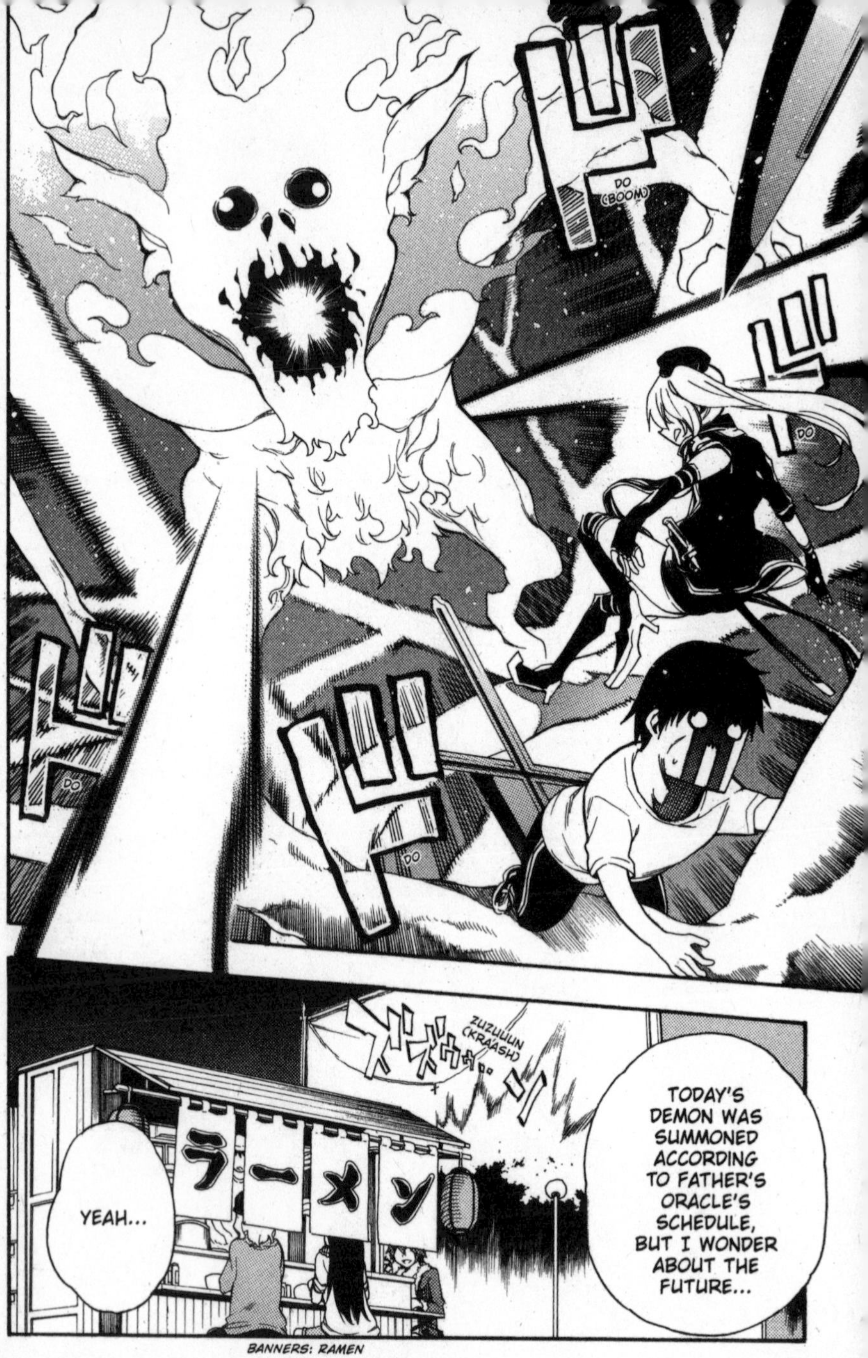
DO
(BOOM)
DO
DO
DO
TODAY'S DEMON WAS SUMMONED ACCORDING TO FATHER'S ORACLE'S SCHEDULE, BUT I WONDER ABOUT THE FUTURE...
ZUZUUUN
(KRAASH)
YEAH...

BANNERS: RAMEN

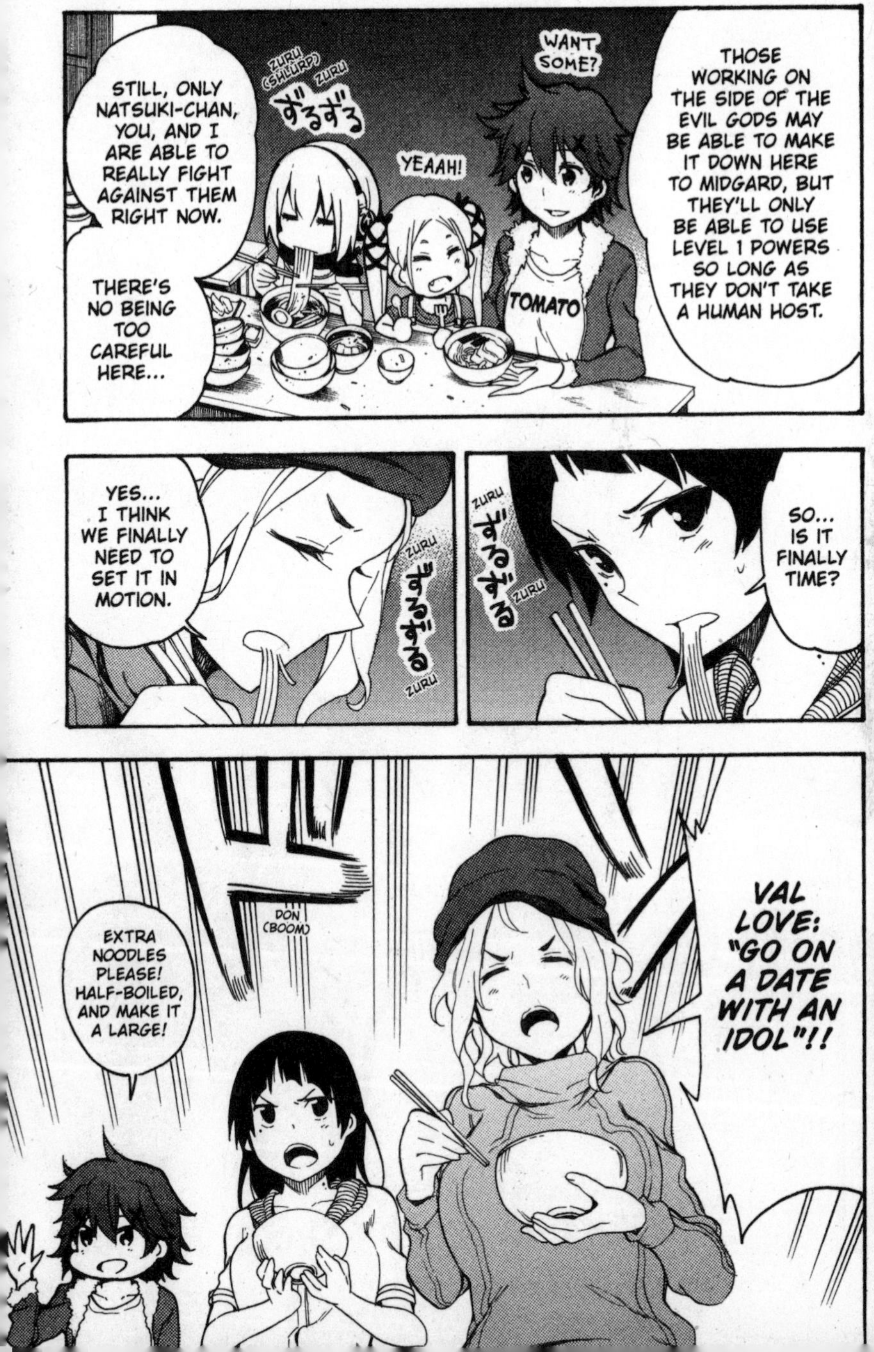
THOSE WORKING ON THE SIDE OF THE EVIL GODS MAY BE ABLE TO MAKE IT DOWN HERE TO MIDGARD, BUT THEY'LL ONLY BE ABLE TO USE LEVEL 1 POWERS SO LONG AS THEY DON'T TAKE A HUMAN HOST.
WANT SOME?
YEAAH!
ZURU (SHLURP) ZURU
ずるずる
STILL, ONLY NATSUKI-CHAN, YOU, AND I ARE ABLE TO REALLY FIGHT AGAINST THEM RIGHT NOW.
THERE'S NO BEING TOO CAREFUL HERE...
SO... IS IT FINALLY TIME?
ZURU ZURU
ずるずる
ZURU ZURU
ずるずる
YES... I THINK WE FINALLY NEED TO SET IT IN MOTION.
VAL LOVE: "GO ON A DATE WITH AN IDOL"!!
DON (BOOM)
EXTRA NOODLES PLEASE! HALF-BOILED, AND MAKE IT A LARGE!

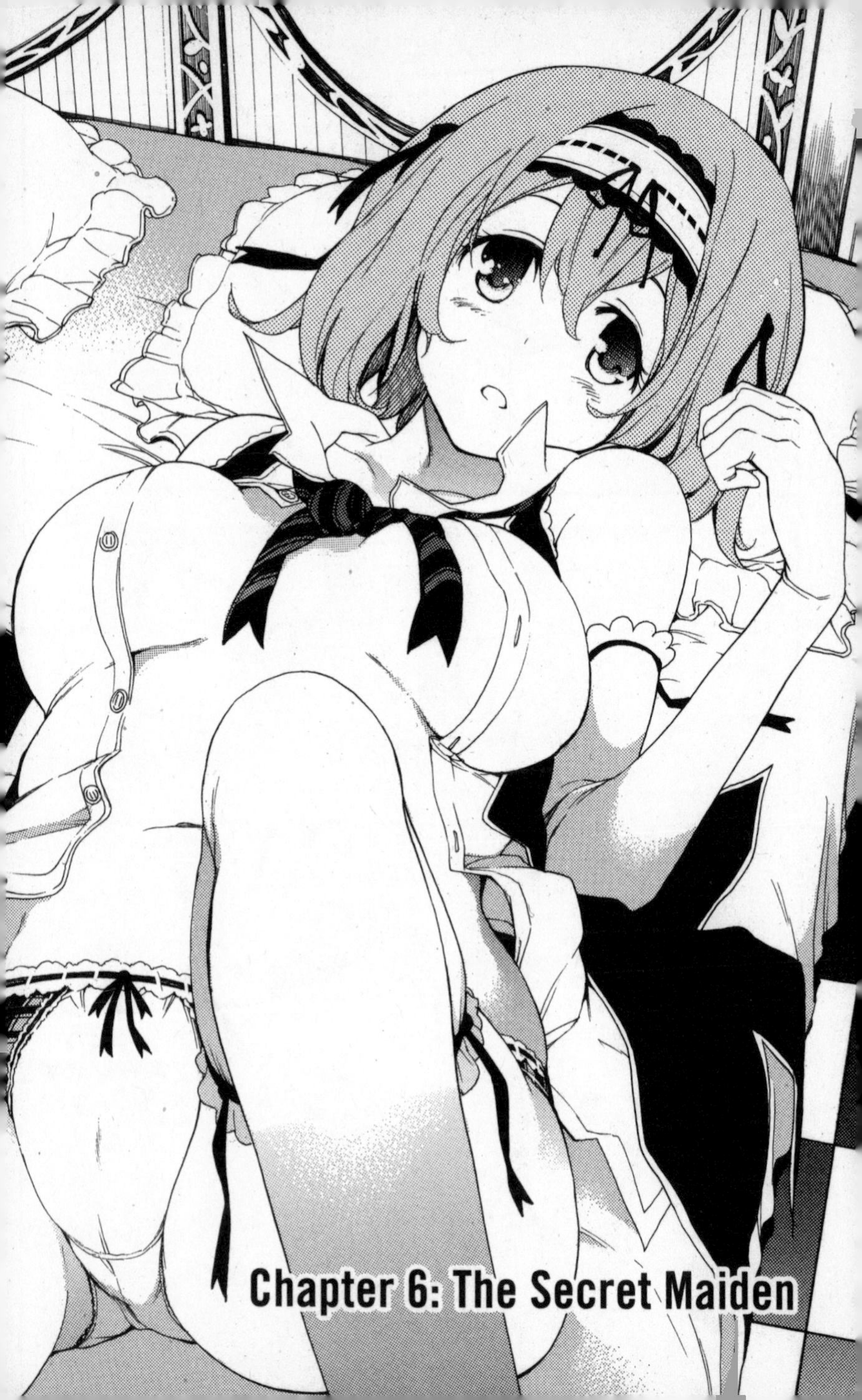
Chapter 6: The Secret Maiden

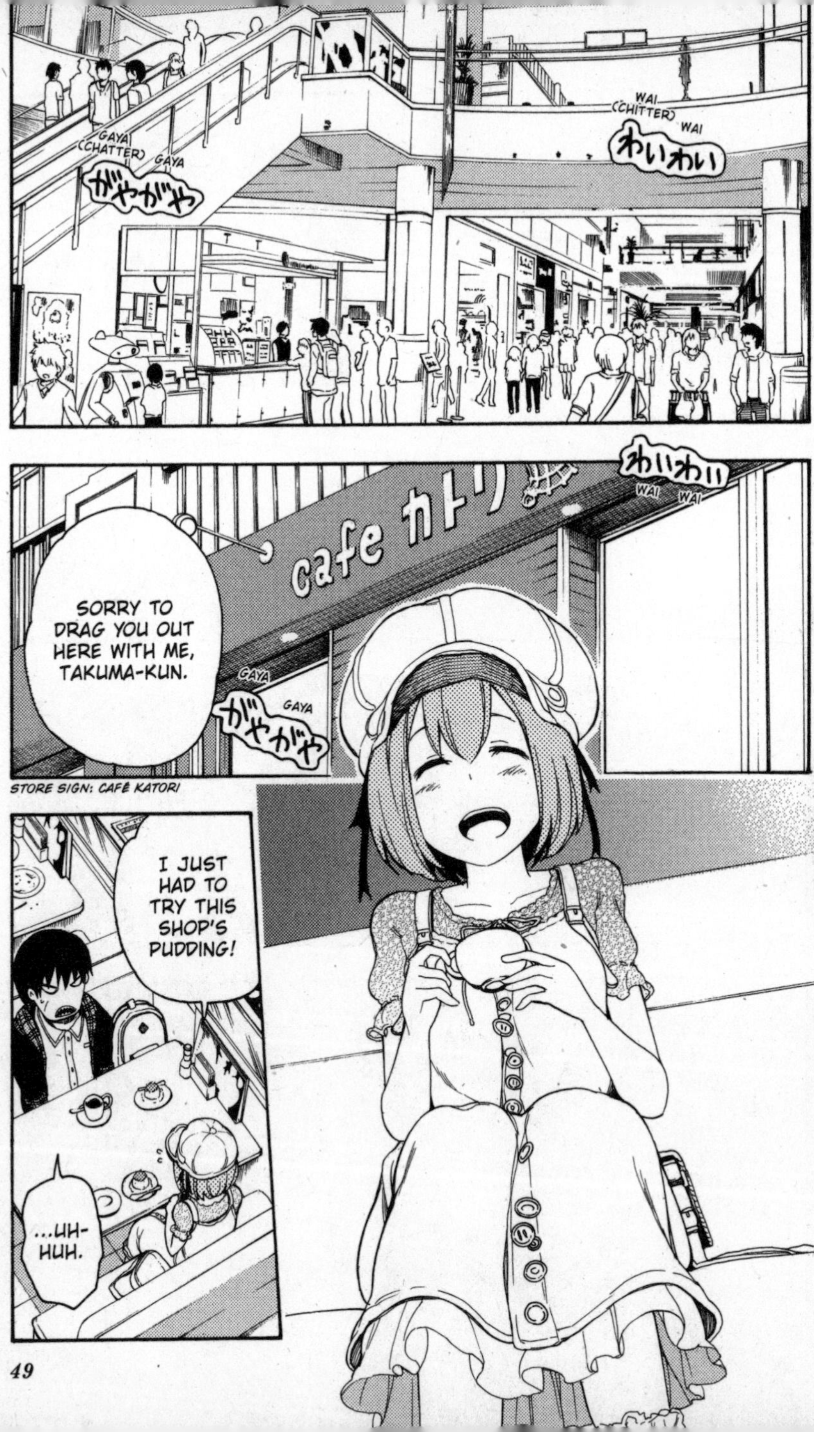
WAI (CHITTER) WAI
わいわい
GAYA (CHATTER) GAYA
がやがや
わいわい
WAI WAI
cafe カトリ
SORRY TO DRAG YOU OUT HERE WITH ME, TAKUMA-KUN.
GAYA GAYA
がやがや
I JUST HAD TO TRY THIS SHOP'S PUDDING!
...UH-HUH.
STORE SIGN: CAFÉ KATORI

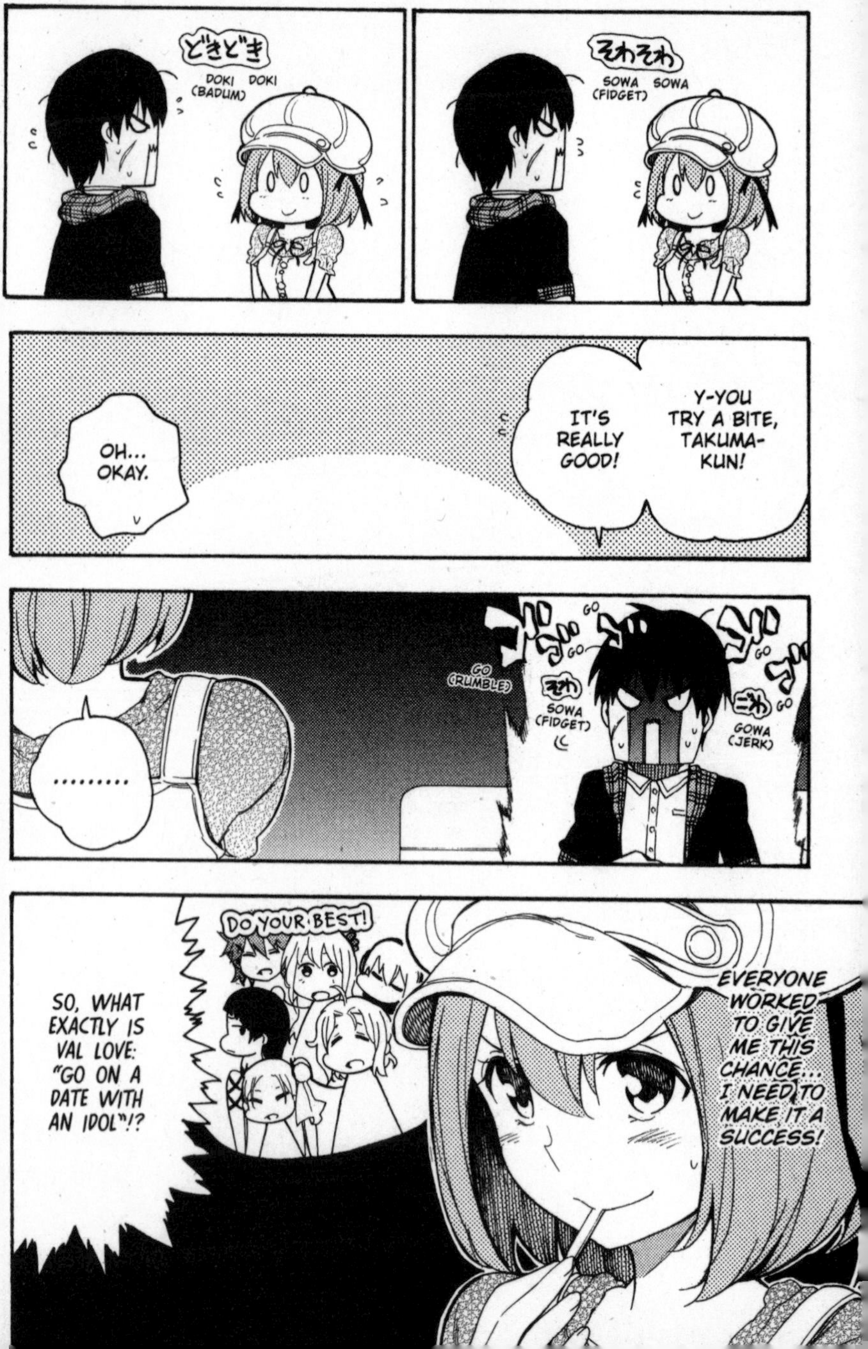
そわそわ
SOWA SOWA (FIDGET)
どきどき
DOKI DOKI (BADUM)
Y-YOU TRY A BITE, TAKUMA-KUN!
IT'S REALLY GOOD!
OH... OKAY.
GO GO GO GO GO
ごわ
GOWA (JERK)
そわ
SOWA (FIDGET)
GO (RUMBLE)
....
EVERYONE WORKED TO GIVE ME THIS CHANCE... I NEED TO MAKE IT A SUCCESS!
DO YOUR BEST!
SO, WHAT EXACTLY IS VAL LOVE: "GO ON A DATE WITH AN IDOL"!?

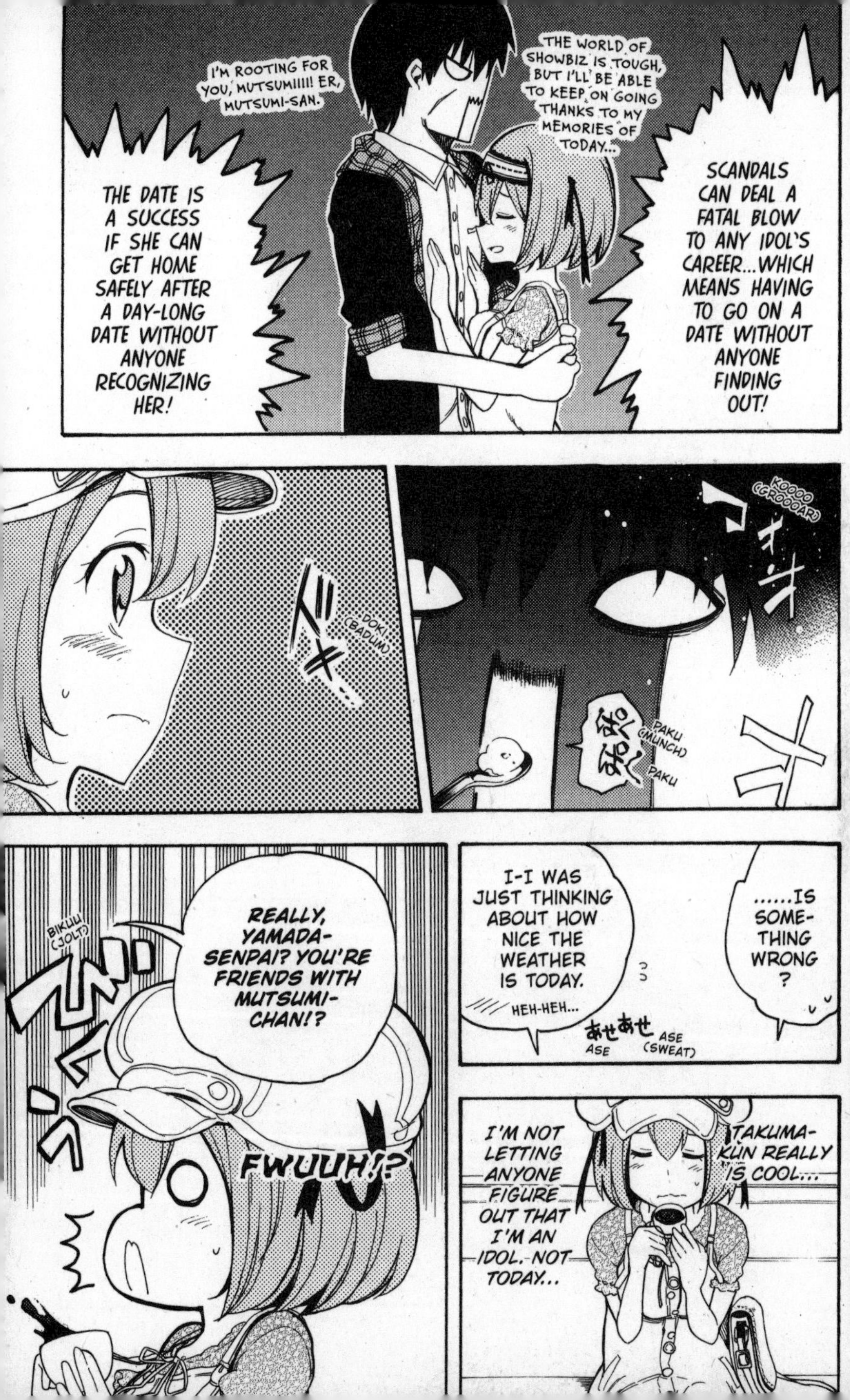
SCANDALS CAN DEAL A FATAL BLOW TO ANY IDOL'S CAREER...WHICH MEANS HAVING TO GO ON A DATE WITHOUT ANYONE FINDING OUT!
THE WORLD OF SHOWBIZ IS TOUGH, BUT I'LL BE ABLE TO KEEP ON GOING THANKS TO MY MEMORIES OF TODAY...
I'M ROOTING FOR YOU, MUTSUMIIIII! ER, MUTSUMI-SAN.
THE DATE IS A SUCCESS IF SHE CAN GET HOME SAFELY AFTER A DAY-LONG DATE WITHOUT ANYONE RECOGNIZING HER!
KOOOO (GROOOAR)
PAKU (MUNCH)
PAKU
DOKI (BADUM)
......IS SOME-THING WRONG?
I-I WAS JUST THINKING ABOUT HOW NICE THE WEATHER IS TODAY.
HEH-HEH...
あせあせ
ASE
ASE (SWEAT)
TAKUMA-KUN REALLY IS COOL...
I'M NOT LETTING ANYONE FIGURE OUT THAT I'M AN IDOL.-NOT TODAY...
REALLY, YAMADA-SENPAI? YOU'RE FRIENDS WITH MUTSUMI-CHAN!?
BIKUU (JOLT)
FWUUH!?

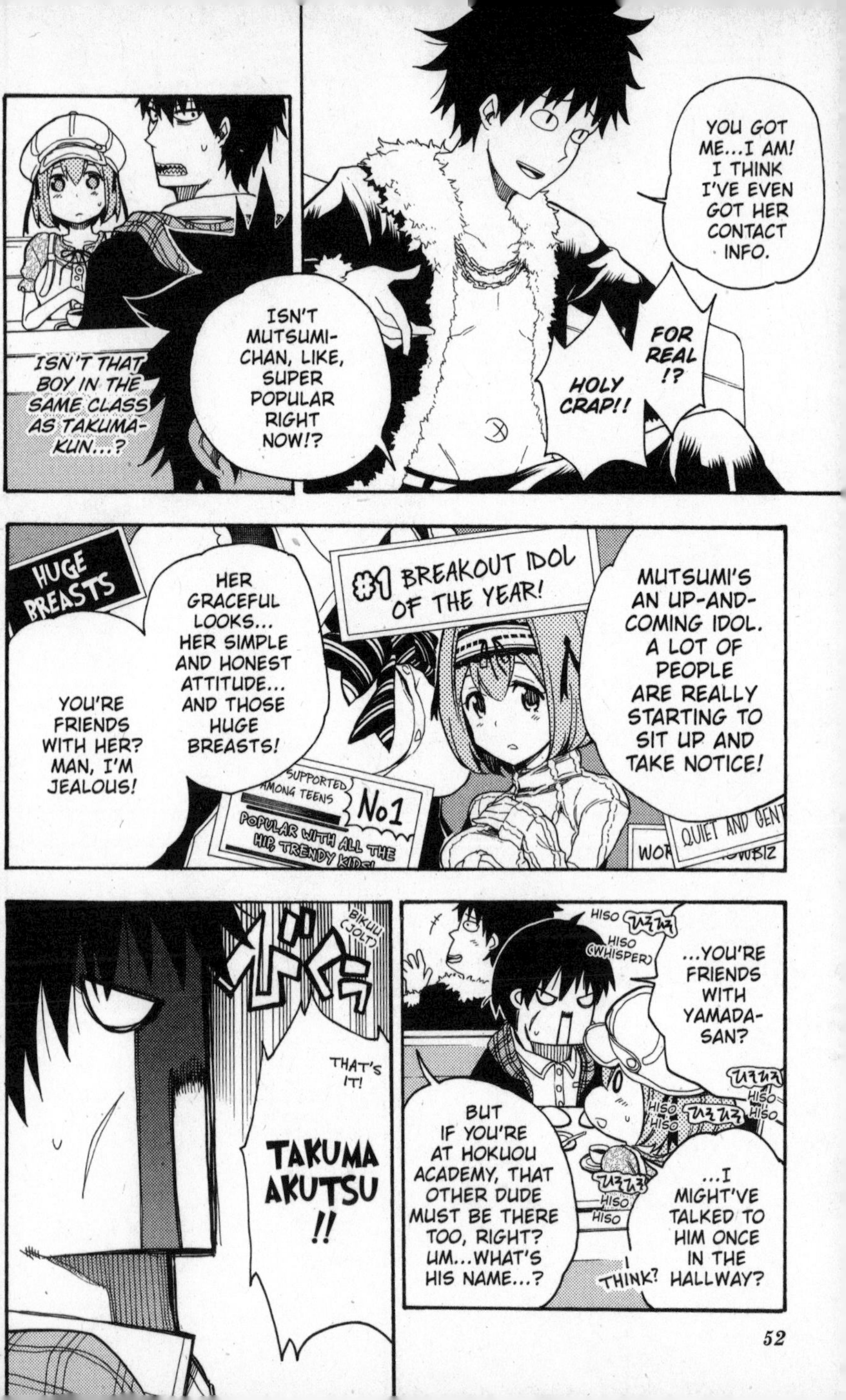
YOU GOT ME...I AM! I THINK I'VE EVEN GOT HER CONTACT INFO.
FOR REAL!?
HOLY CRAP!!
ISN'T MUTSUMI-CHAN, LIKE, SUPER POPULAR RIGHT NOW!?
ISN'T THAT BOY IN THE SAME CLASS AS TAKUMA-KUN...?
MUTSUMI'S AN UP-AND-COMING IDOL. A LOT OF PEOPLE ARE REALLY STARTING TO SIT UP AND TAKE NOTICE!
#1 BREAKOUT IDOL OF THE YEAR!
HER GRACEFUL LOOKS... HER SIMPLE AND HONEST ATTITUDE... AND THOSE HUGE BREASTS!
HUGE BREASTS
YOU'RE FRIENDS WITH HER? MAN, I'M JEALOUS!
SUPPORTED AMONG TEENS No1
POPULAR WITH ALL THE HIP, TRENDY KIDS
HISO HISO (WHISPER)
...YOU'RE FRIENDS WITH YAMADA-SAN?
HISO HISO
BUT IF YOU'RE AT HOKUOU ACADEMY, THAT OTHER DUDE MUST BE THERE TOO, RIGHT? UM...WHAT'S HIS NAME...?
...I MIGHT'VE TALKED TO HIM ONCE IN THE HALLWAY?
I THINK?
BIKUU (JOLT)
THAT'S IT!
TAKUMA AKUTSU!!

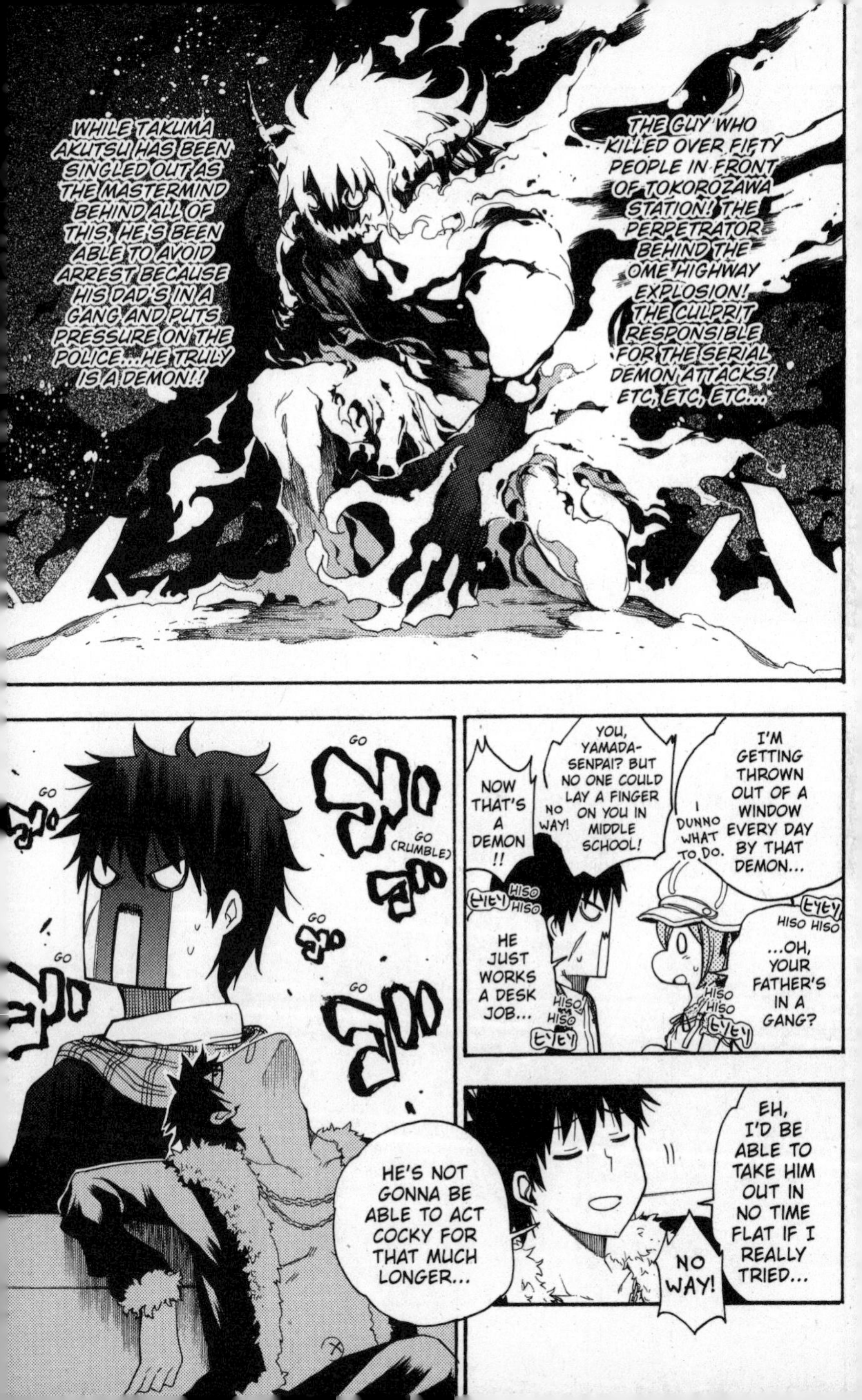
THE GUY WHO KILLED OVER FIFTY PEOPLE IN FRONT OF TOKOROZAWA STATION! THE PERPETRATOR BEHIND THE OME HIGHWAY EXPLOSION! THE CULPRIT RESPONSIBLE FOR THE SERIAL DEMON ATTACKS! ETC, ETC, ETC...
WHILE TAKUMA AKUTSU HAS BEEN SINGLED OUT AS THE MASTERMIND BEHIND ALL OF THIS, HE'S BEEN ABLE TO AVOID ARREST BECAUSE HIS DAD'S IN A GANG AND PUTS PRESSURE ON THE POLICE...HE TRULY IS A DEMON!!
I'M GETTING THROWN OUT OF A WINDOW EVERY DAY BY THAT DEMON...
I DUNNO WHAT TO DO.
YOU, YAMADA-SENPAI? BUT NO ONE COULD LAY A FINGER ON YOU IN MIDDLE SCHOOL!
NO WAY!
NOW THAT'S A DEMON!!
HISO HISO
HISO HISO
...OH, YOUR FATHER'S IN A GANG?
HISO HISO
HE JUST WORKS A DESK JOB...
HISO HISO
EH, I'D BE ABLE TO TAKE HIM OUT IN NO TIME FLAT IF I REALLY TRIED...
NO WAY!
GO
GO (RUMBLE)
GO
GO
GO
GO
HE'S NOT GONNA BE ABLE TO ACT COCKY FOR THAT MUCH LONGER...

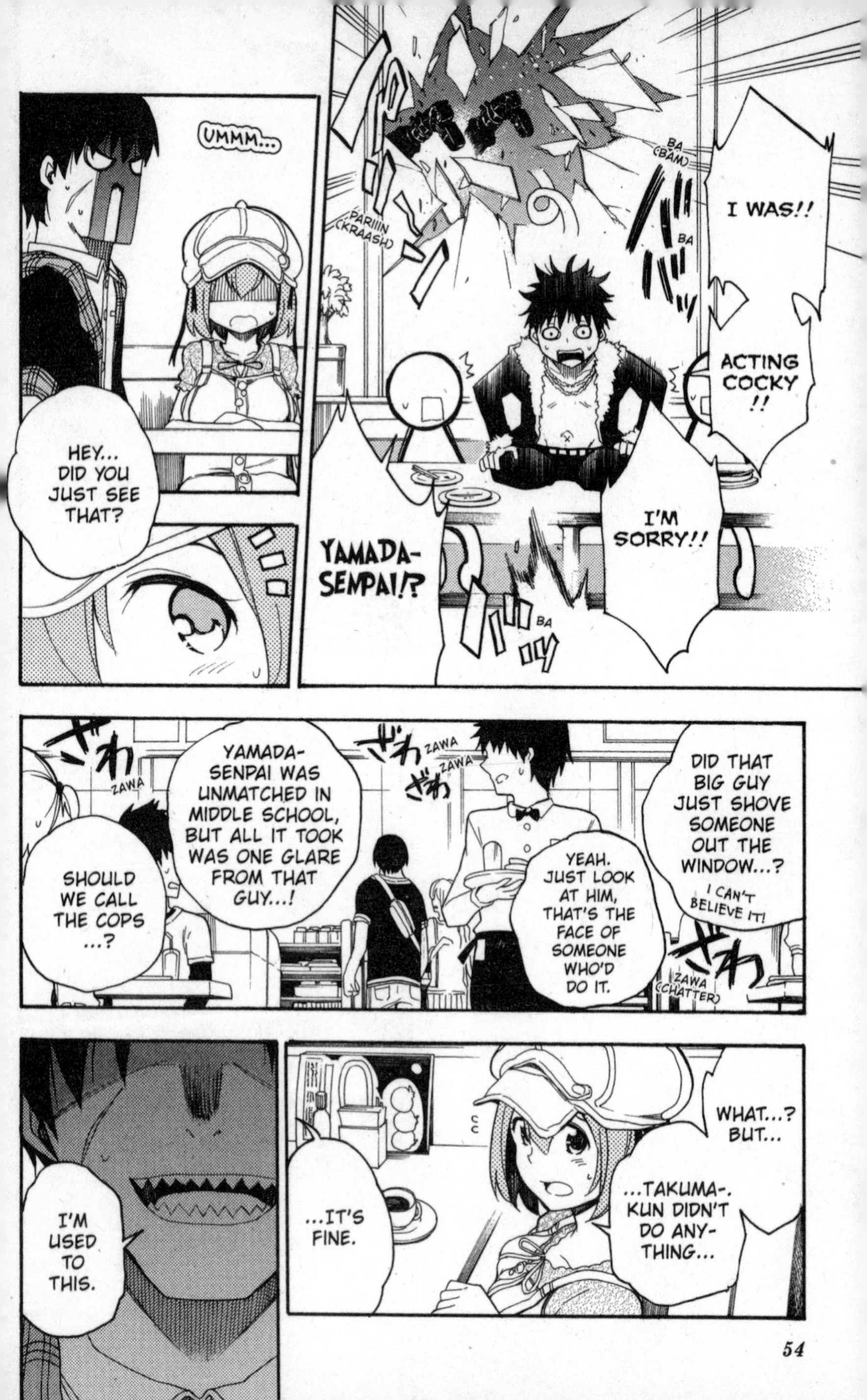
BA (BAM)
I WAS!!
PARIIIN (KRAASH)
BA
ACTING COCKY!!
I'M SORRY!!
YAMADA-SENPAI!?
BA
UMMM...
HEY... DID YOU JUST SEE THAT?
DID THAT BIG GUY JUST SHOVE SOMEONE OUT THE WINDOW...?
I CAN'T BELIEVE IT!
ZAWA (CHATTER)
YEAH. JUST LOOK AT HIM, THAT'S THE FACE OF SOMEONE WHO'D DO IT.
ZAWA
ZAWA
YAMADA-SENPAI WAS UNMATCHED IN MIDDLE SCHOOL, BUT ALL IT TOOK WAS ONE GLARE FROM THAT GUY...!
ZAWA
SHOULD WE CALL THE COPS ...?
WHAT...? BUT...
...TAKUMA-KUN DIDN'T DO ANYTHING...
...IT'S FINE.
I'M USED TO THIS.

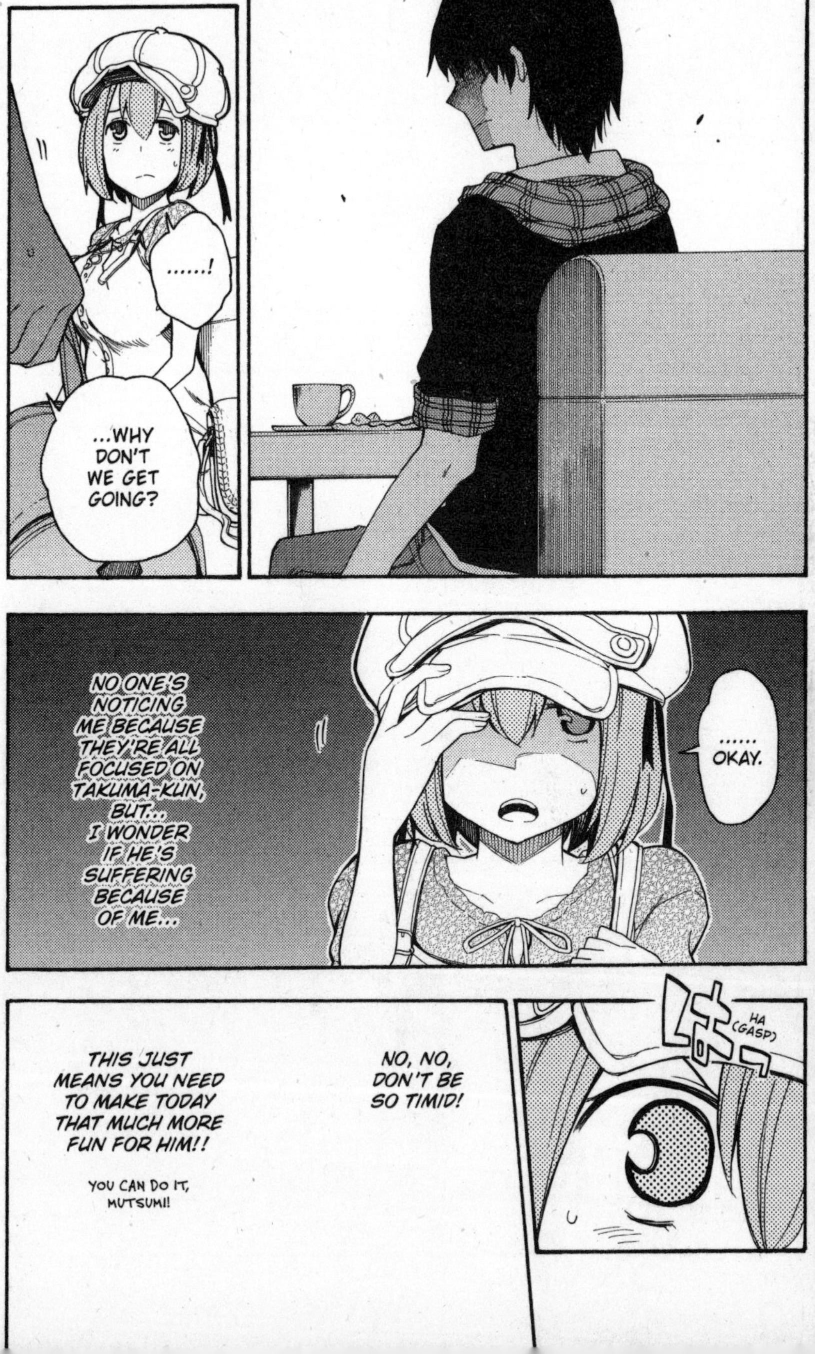
......!
...WHY DON'T WE GET GOING?
......OKAY.
NO ONE'S NOTICING ME BECAUSE THEY'RE ALL FOCUSED ON TAKUMA-KUN, BUT... I WONDER IF HE'S SUFFERING BECAUSE OF ME...
はっ
HA (GASP)
NO, NO, DON'T BE SO TIMID!
THIS JUST MEANS YOU NEED TO MAKE TODAY THAT MUCH MORE FUN FOR HIM!!
YOU CAN DO IT, MUTSUMI!

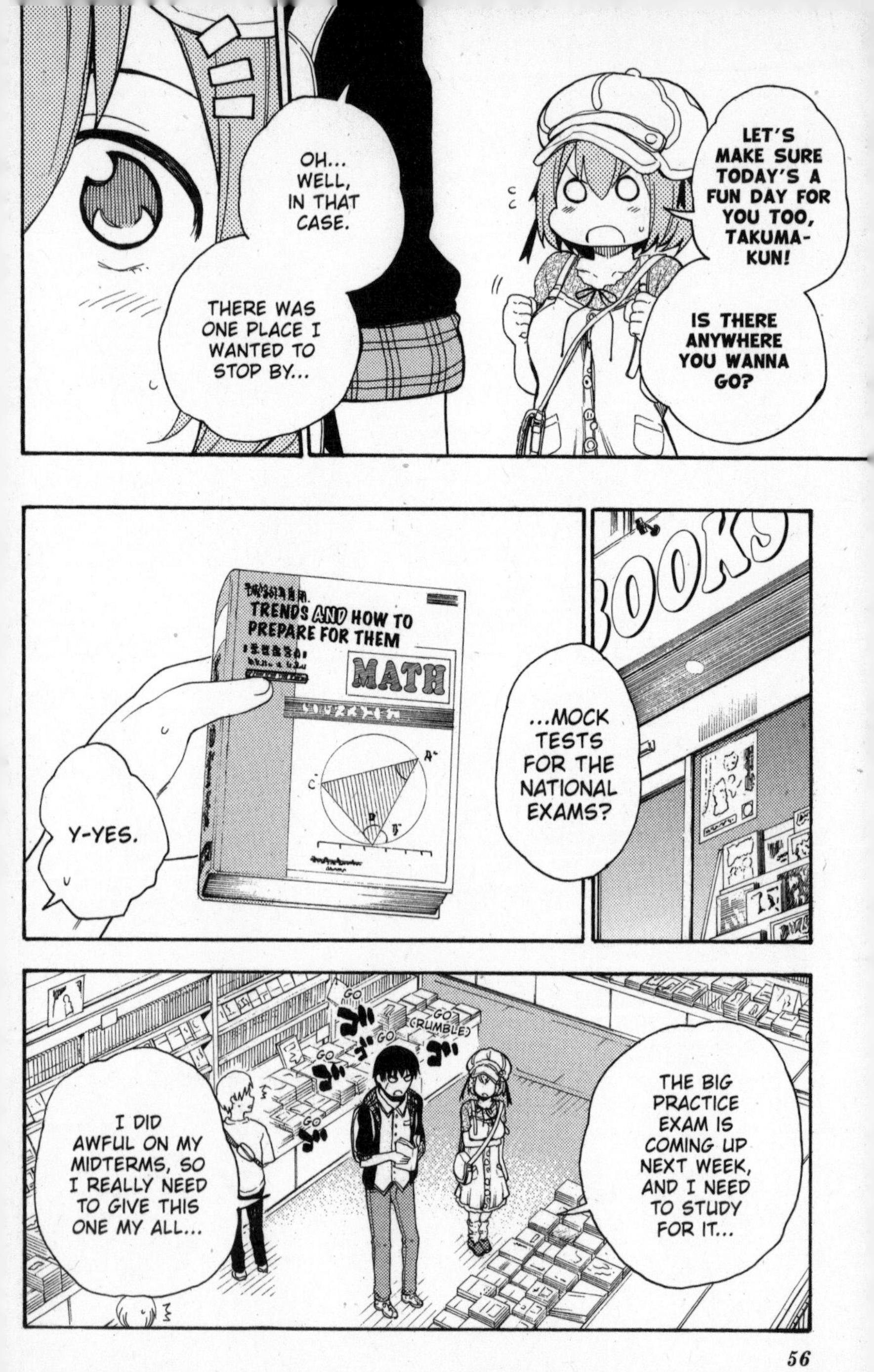
LET'S MAKE SURE TODAY'S A FUN DAY FOR YOU TOO, TAKUMA-KUN!
IS THERE ANYWHERE YOU WANNA GO?
OH... WELL, IN THAT CASE.
THERE WAS ONE PLACE I WANTED TO STOP BY...
BOOKS
...MOCK TESTS FOR THE NATIONAL EXAMS?
TRENDS AND HOW TO PREPARE FOR THEM
MATH
Y-YES.
GO
GO (CRUMBLE)
GO
GO
GO
THE BIG PRACTICE EXAM IS COMING UP NEXT WEEK, AND I NEED TO STUDY FOR IT...
I DID AWFUL ON MY MIDTERMS, SO I REALLY NEED TO GIVE THIS ONE MY ALL...

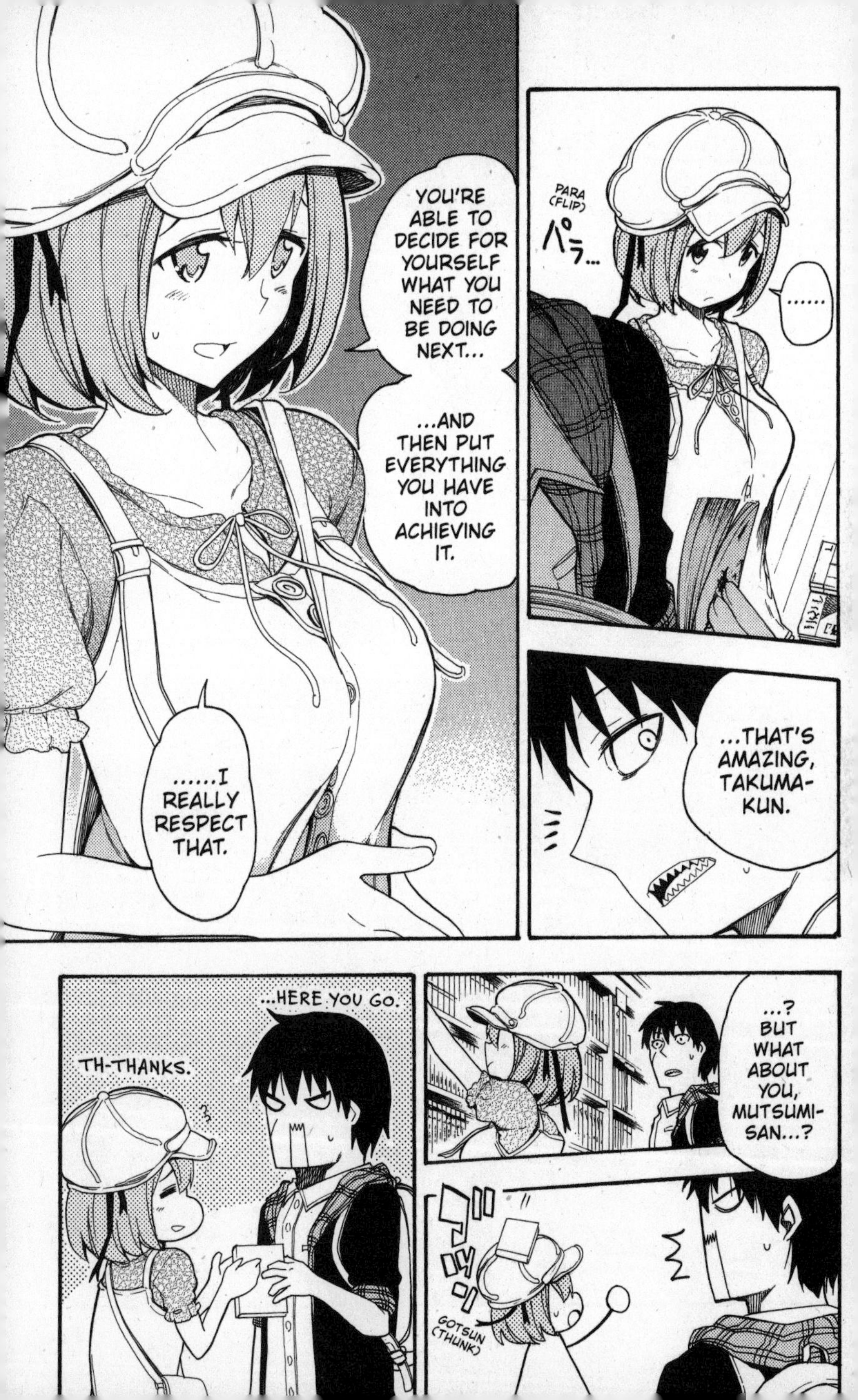
PARA (FLIP)
パラ…
......
...THAT'S AMAZING, TAKUMA-KUN.
YOU'RE ABLE TO DECIDE FOR YOURSELF WHAT YOU NEED TO BE DOING NEXT...
...AND THEN PUT EVERYTHING YOU HAVE INTO ACHIEVING IT.
......I REALLY RESPECT THAT.
...? BUT WHAT ABOUT YOU, MUTSUMI-SAN...?
GOTSUN (THUNK)
...HERE YOU GO.
TH-THANKS.

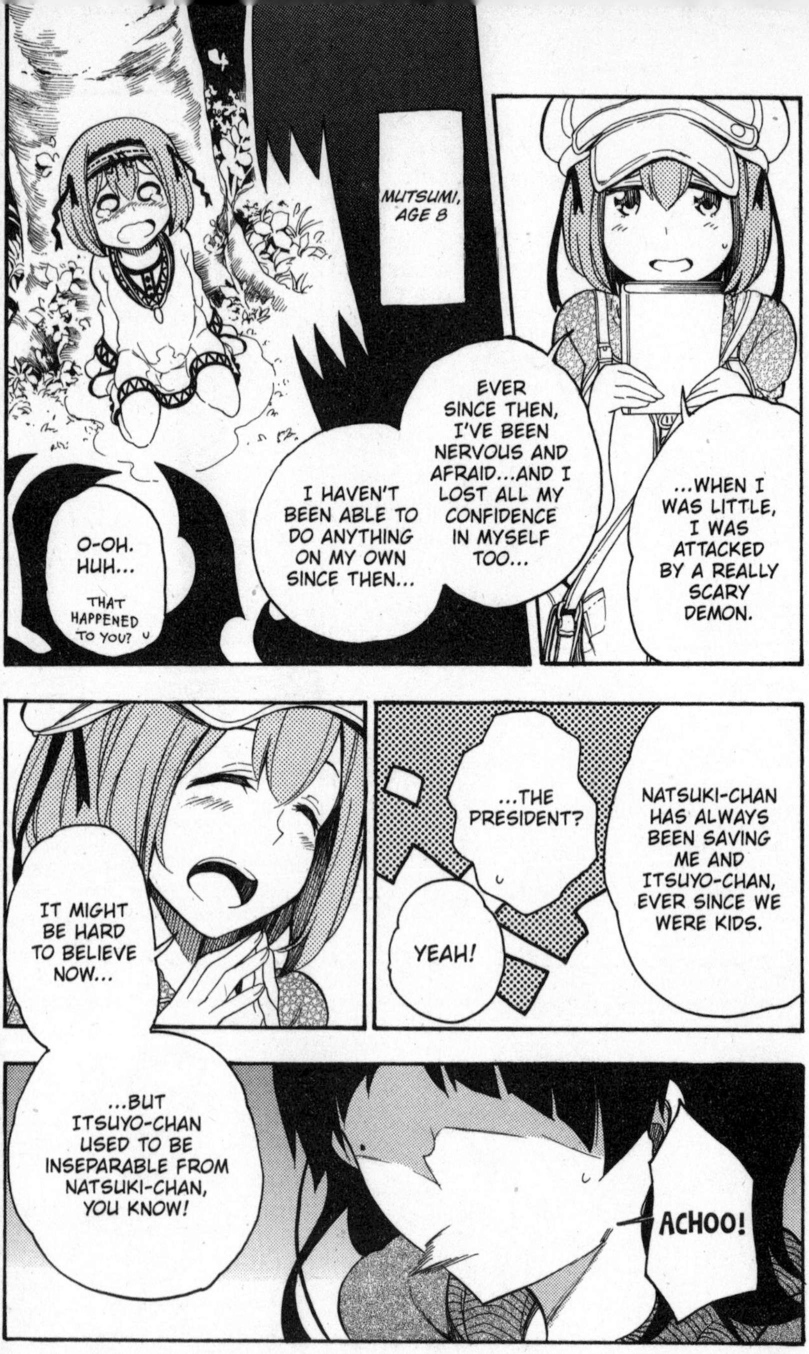
...WHEN I WAS LITTLE, I WAS ATTACKED BY A REALLY SCARY DEMON.
MUTSUMI, AGE 8
EVER SINCE THEN, I'VE BEEN NERVOUS AND AFRAID...AND I LOST ALL MY CONFIDENCE IN MYSELF TOO...
I HAVEN'T BEEN ABLE TO DO ANYTHING ON MY OWN SINCE THEN...
O-OH. HUH...
THAT HAPPENED TO YOU?
NATSUKI-CHAN HAS ALWAYS BEEN SAVING ME AND ITSUYO-CHAN, EVER SINCE WE WERE KIDS.
...THE PRESIDENT?
YEAH!
IT MIGHT BE HARD TO BELIEVE NOW...
...BUT ITSUYO-CHAN USED TO BE INSEPARABLE FROM NATSUKI-CHAN, YOU KNOW!
ACHOO!

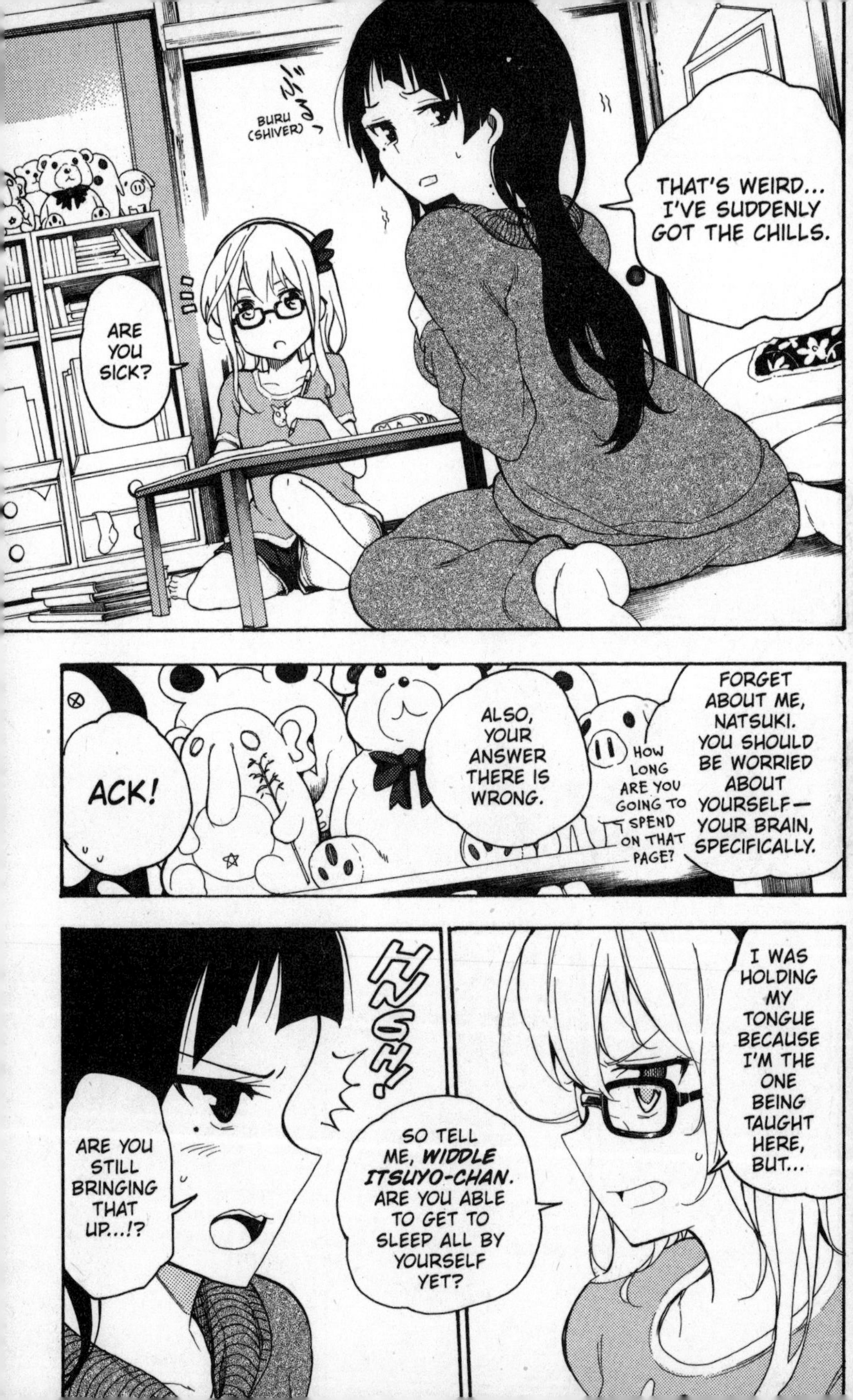

THAT'S WEIRD... I'VE SUDDENLY GOT THE CHILLS.
BURU (SHIVER)
ARE YOU SICK?
FORGET ABOUT ME, NATSUKI. YOU SHOULD BE WORRIED ABOUT YOURSELF—YOUR BRAIN, SPECIFICALLY.
HOW LONG ARE YOU GOING TO SPEND ON THAT PAGE?
ALSO, YOUR ANSWER THERE IS WRONG.
ACK!
I WAS HOLDING MY TONGUE BECAUSE I'M THE ONE BEING TAUGHT HERE, BUT...
SO TELL ME, *WIDDLE ITSUYO-CHAN*. ARE YOU ABLE TO GET TO SLEEP ALL BY YOURSELF YET?
HNGH!
ARE YOU STILL BRINGING THAT UP...!?

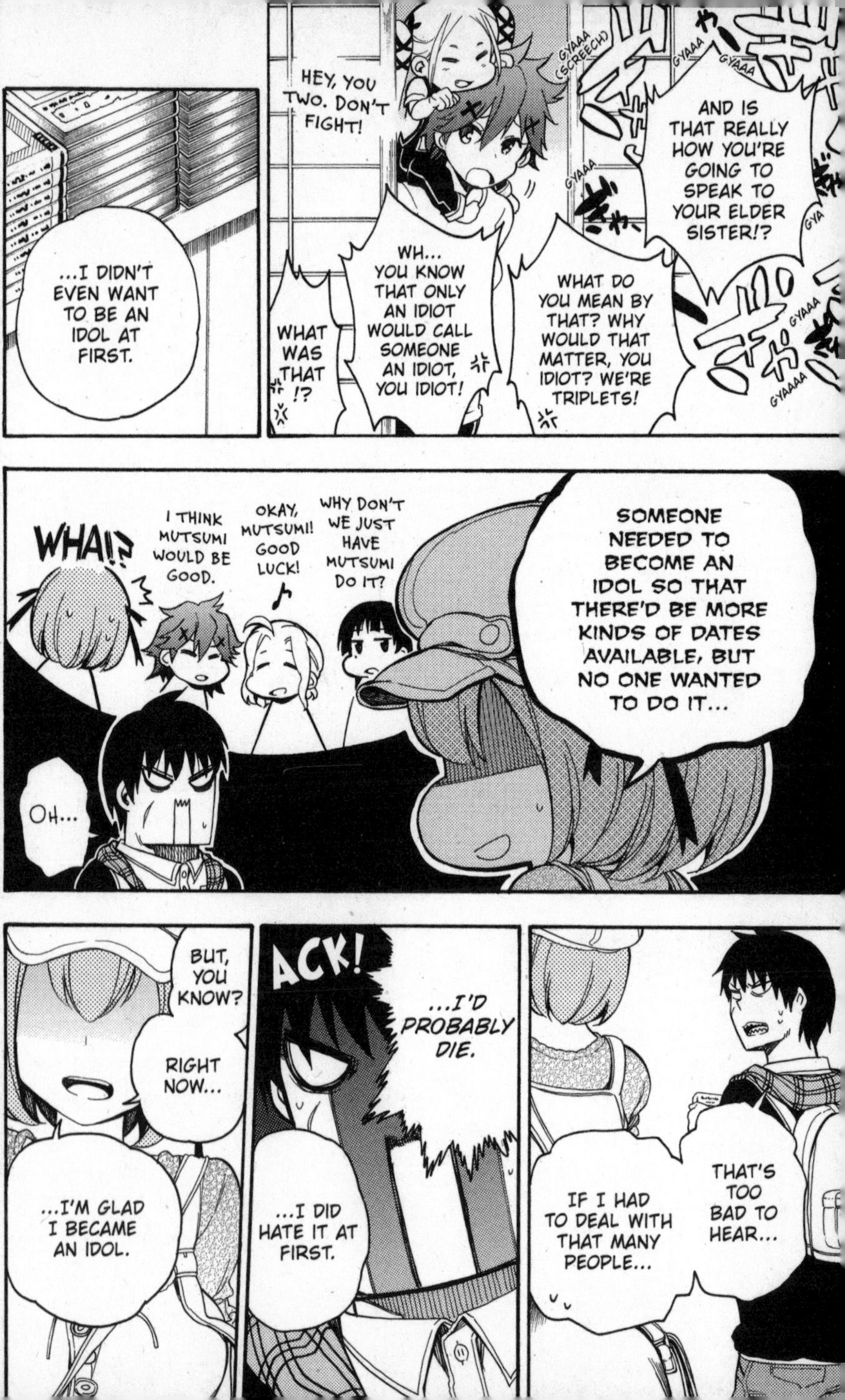
GYAAA (SCREECH)
GYAAA
GYAAA
AND IS THAT REALLY HOW YOU'RE GOING TO SPEAK TO YOUR ELDER SISTER!?
GYA
GYAAA
GYAAA
GYAAAA
HEY, YOU TWO. DON'T FIGHT!
WHAT DO YOU MEAN BY THAT? WHY WOULD THAT MATTER, YOU IDIOT? WE'RE TRIPLETS!
WH... YOU KNOW THAT ONLY AN IDIOT WOULD CALL SOMEONE AN IDIOT, YOU IDIOT!
WHAT WAS THAT!?
...I DIDN'T EVEN WANT TO BE AN IDOL AT FIRST.
SOMEONE NEEDED TO BECOME AN IDOL SO THAT THERE'D BE MORE KINDS OF DATES AVAILABLE, BUT NO ONE WANTED TO DO IT...
WHY DON'T WE JUST HAVE MUTSUMI DO IT?
OKAY, MUTSUMI! GOOD LUCK!
I THINK MUTSUMI WOULD BE GOOD.
WHA!?
OH...
THAT'S TOO BAD TO HEAR...
IF I HAD TO DEAL WITH THAT MANY PEOPLE...
...I'D PROBABLY DIE.
ACK!
...I DID HATE IT AT FIRST.
BUT, YOU KNOW?
RIGHT NOW...
...I'M GLAD I BECAME AN IDOL.

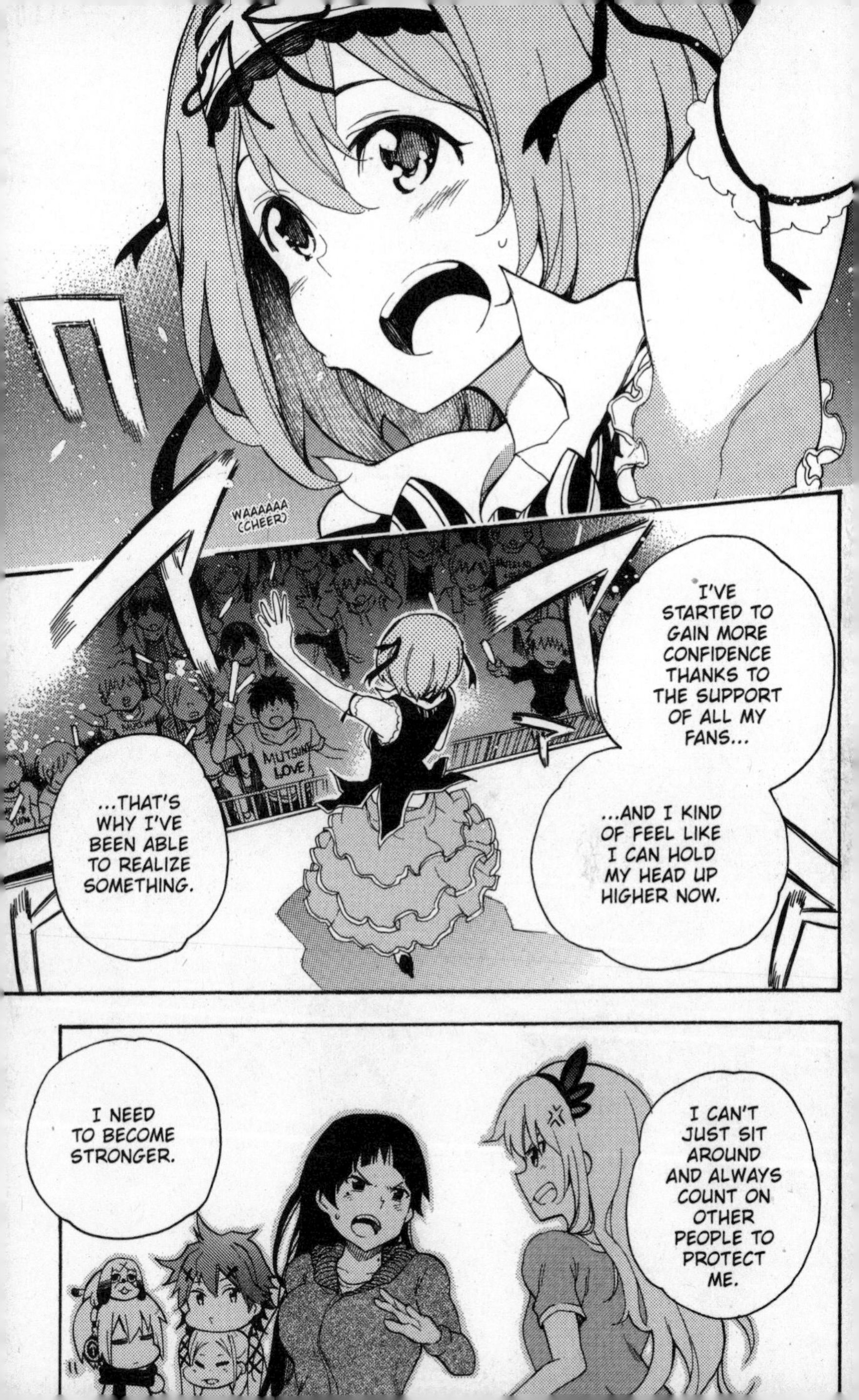
WAAAAAA (CHEER)
I'VE STARTED TO GAIN MORE CONFIDENCE THANKS TO THE SUPPORT OF ALL MY FANS...
...AND I KIND OF FEEL LIKE I CAN HOLD MY HEAD UP HIGHER NOW.
...THAT'S WHY I'VE BEEN ABLE TO REALIZE SOMETHING.
MUTSUKI LOVE
I CAN'T JUST SIT AROUND AND ALWAYS COUNT ON OTHER PEOPLE TO PROTECT ME.
I NEED TO BECOME STRONGER.

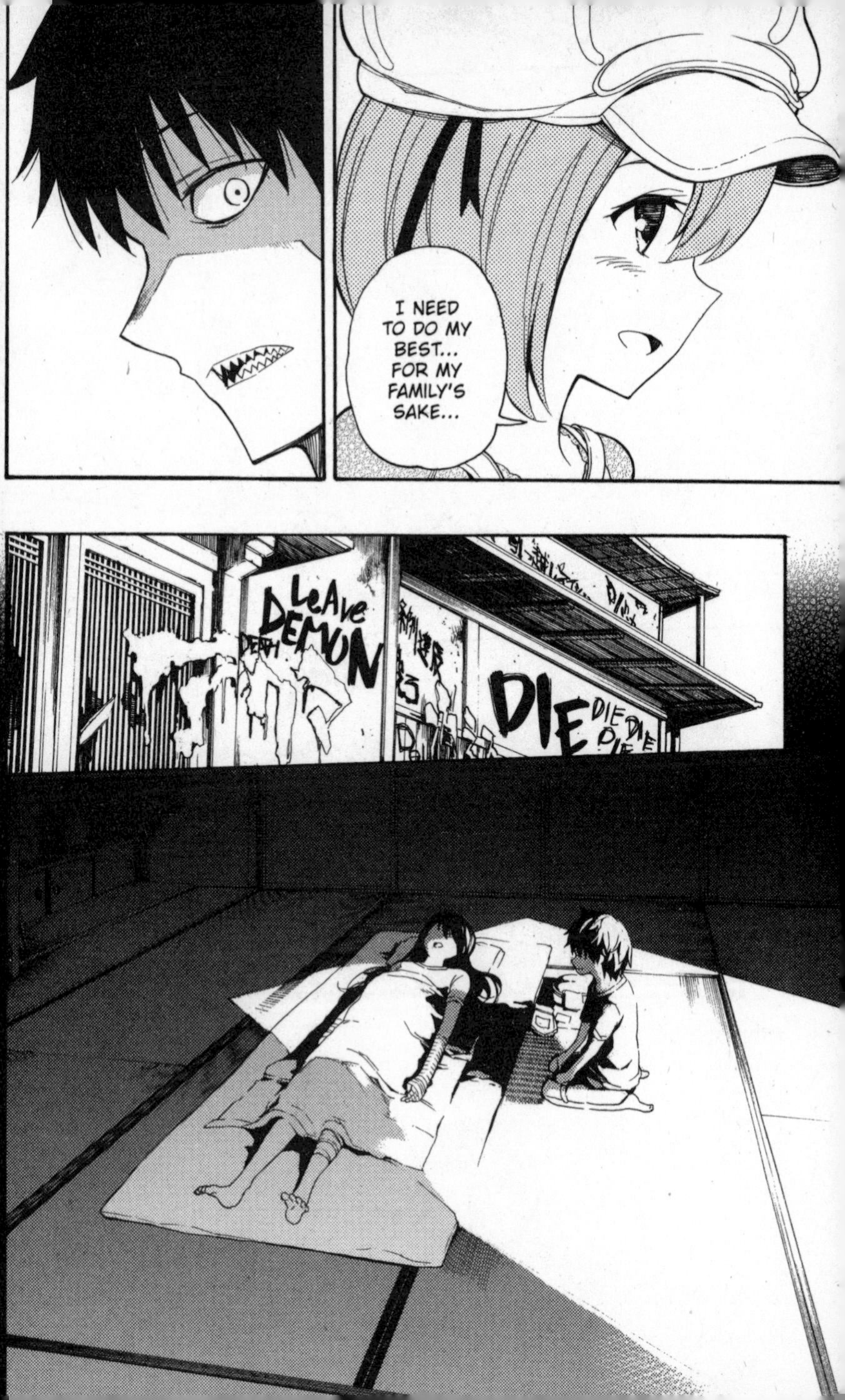
I NEED TO DO MY BEST... FOR MY FAMILY'S SAKE...
LeAve
DEMON
DEATH
DIE
DIE DIE
DIE

IT'S ALL MY FAULT......!

I'M SORRY, MOM.

....

TAKUMA-KUN...?

YOU KNOW... TAKUMA-KUN REALLY DOES REMIND ME...

....

I'M GONNA GO PAY FOR THIS.

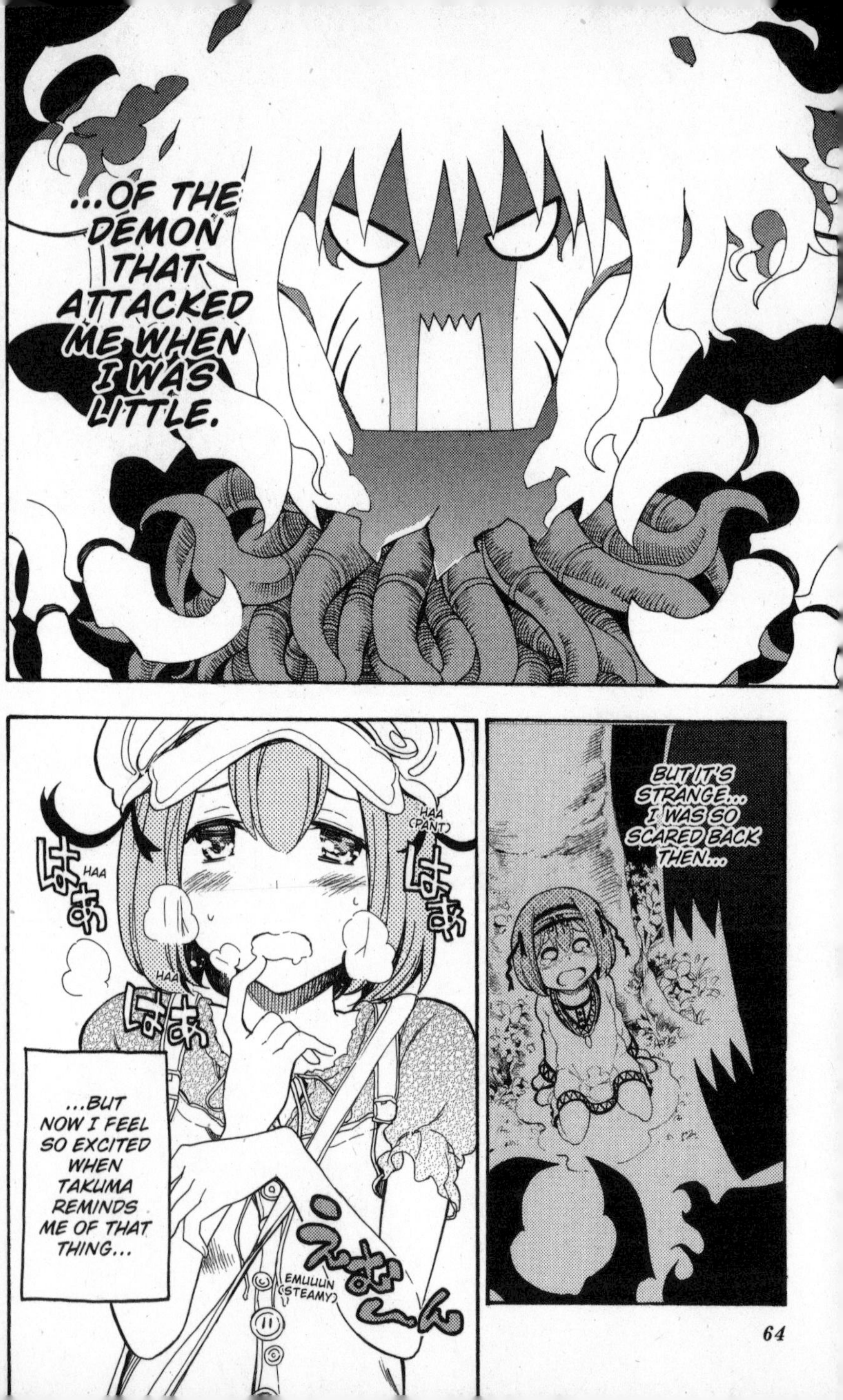
...OF THE DEMON THAT ATTACKED ME WHEN I WAS LITTLE.
BUT IT'S STRANGE... I WAS SO SCARED BACK THEN...
HAA (PANT)
HAA
HAA
...BUT NOW I FEEL SO EXCITED WHEN TAKUMA REMINDS ME OF THAT THING...
EMUUUN (STEAMY)

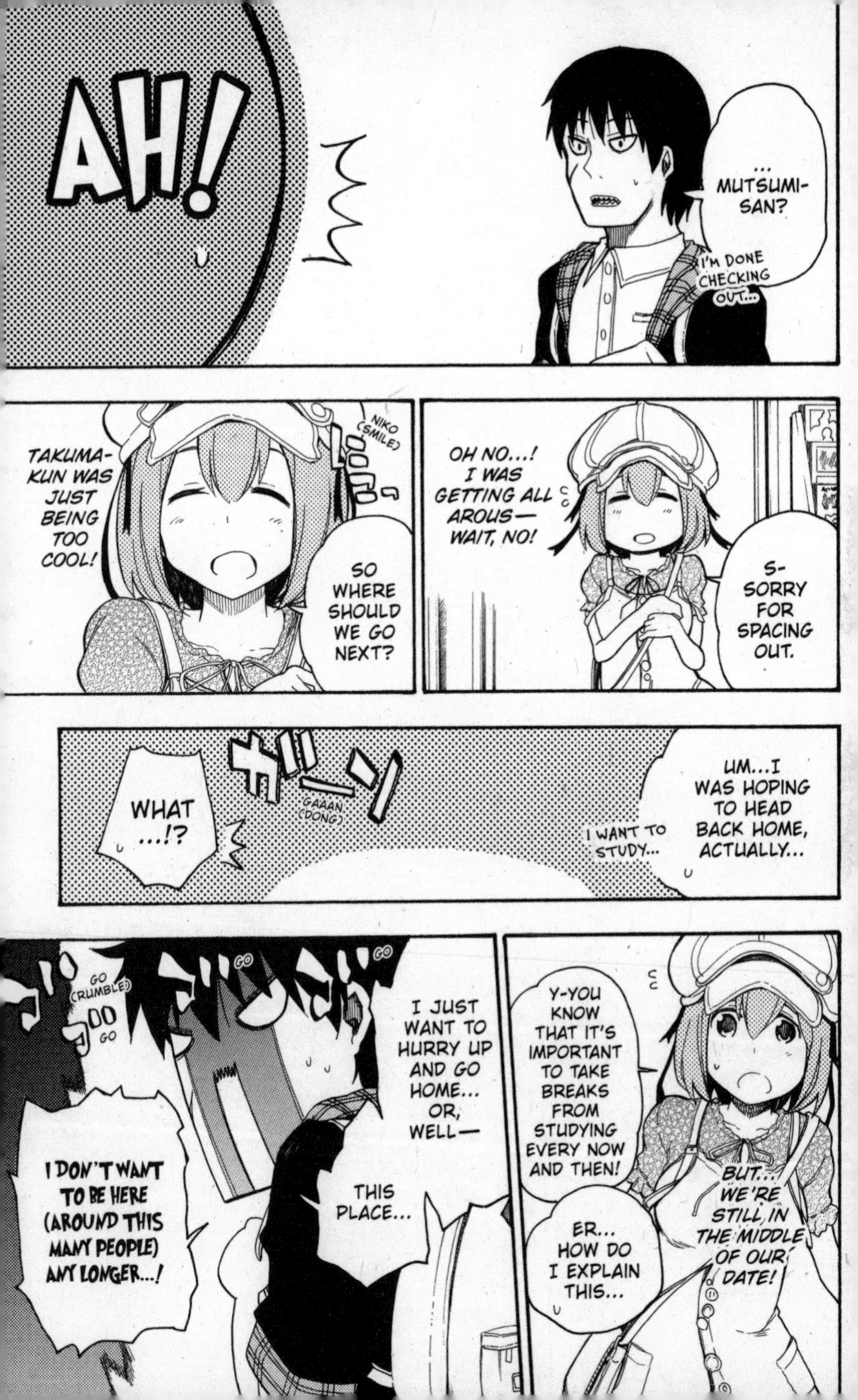

... MUTSUMI-SAN?
I'M DONE CHECKING OUT...
AH!
S-SORRY FOR SPACING OUT.
OH NO...! I WAS GETTING ALL AROUS— WAIT, NO!
NIKO (SMILE)
TAKUMA-KUN WAS JUST BEING TOO COOL!
SO WHERE SHOULD WE GO NEXT?
UM...I WAS HOPING TO HEAD BACK HOME, ACTUALLY...
I WANT TO STUDY...
GAAAN (DONG)
WHAT ...!?
Y-YOU KNOW THAT IT'S IMPORTANT TO TAKE BREAKS FROM STUDYING EVERY NOW AND THEN!
BUT... WE'RE STILL IN THE MIDDLE OF OUR DATE!
ER... HOW DO I EXPLAIN THIS...
GO
GO
I JUST WANT TO HURRY UP AND GO HOME... OR, WELL—
THIS PLACE...
GO (RUMBLE)
GO
I DON'T WANT TO BE HERE (AROUND THIS MANY PEOPLE) ANY LONGER...!

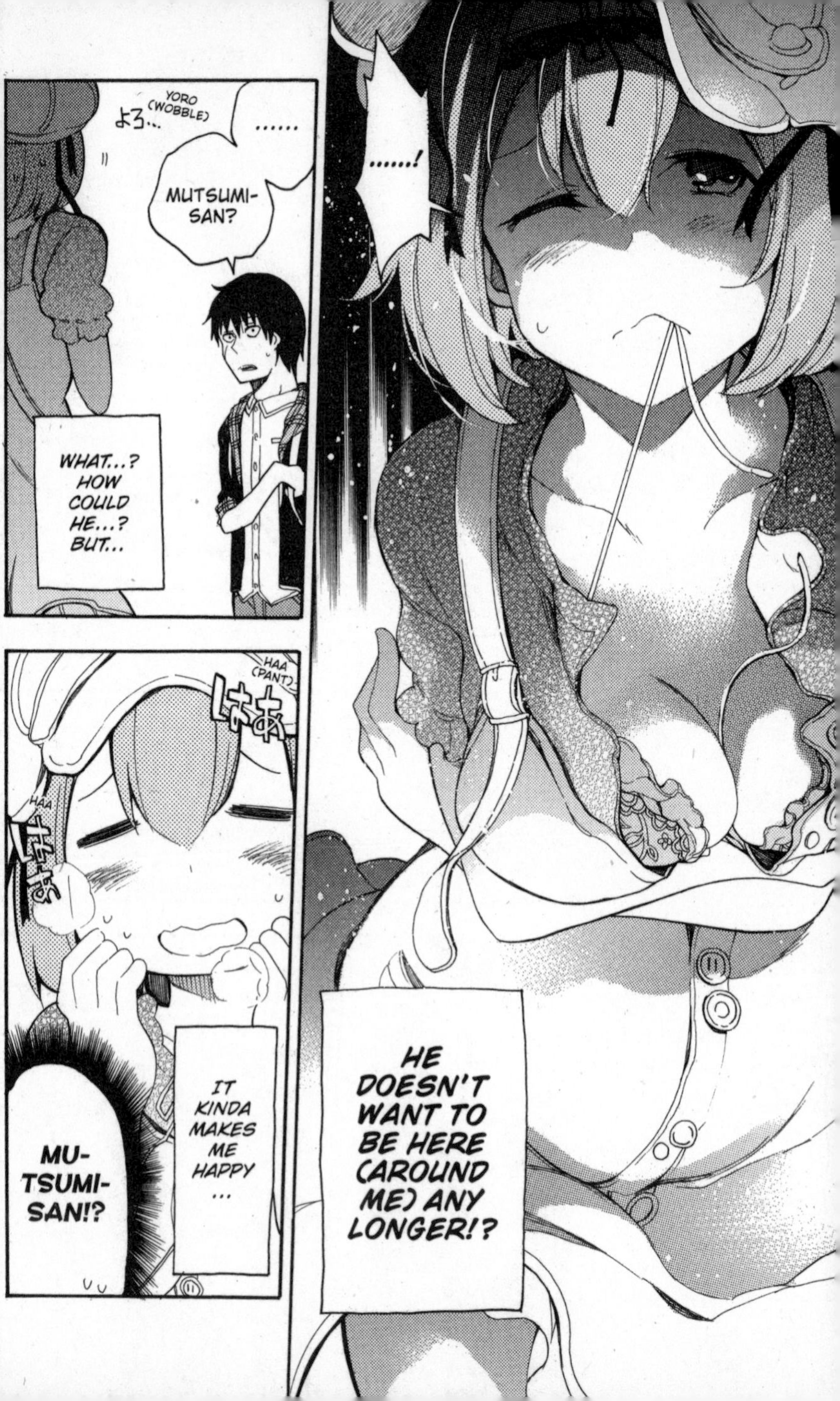
......!
HE DOESN'T WANT TO BE HERE (AROUND ME) ANY LONGER!?
......
MUTSUMI-SAN?
よろ... YORO (WOBBLE)
WHAT...? HOW COULD HE...? BUT...
はあ HAA (PANT)
はあ HAA
IT KINDA MAKES ME HAPPY...
MU-TSUMI-SAN!?

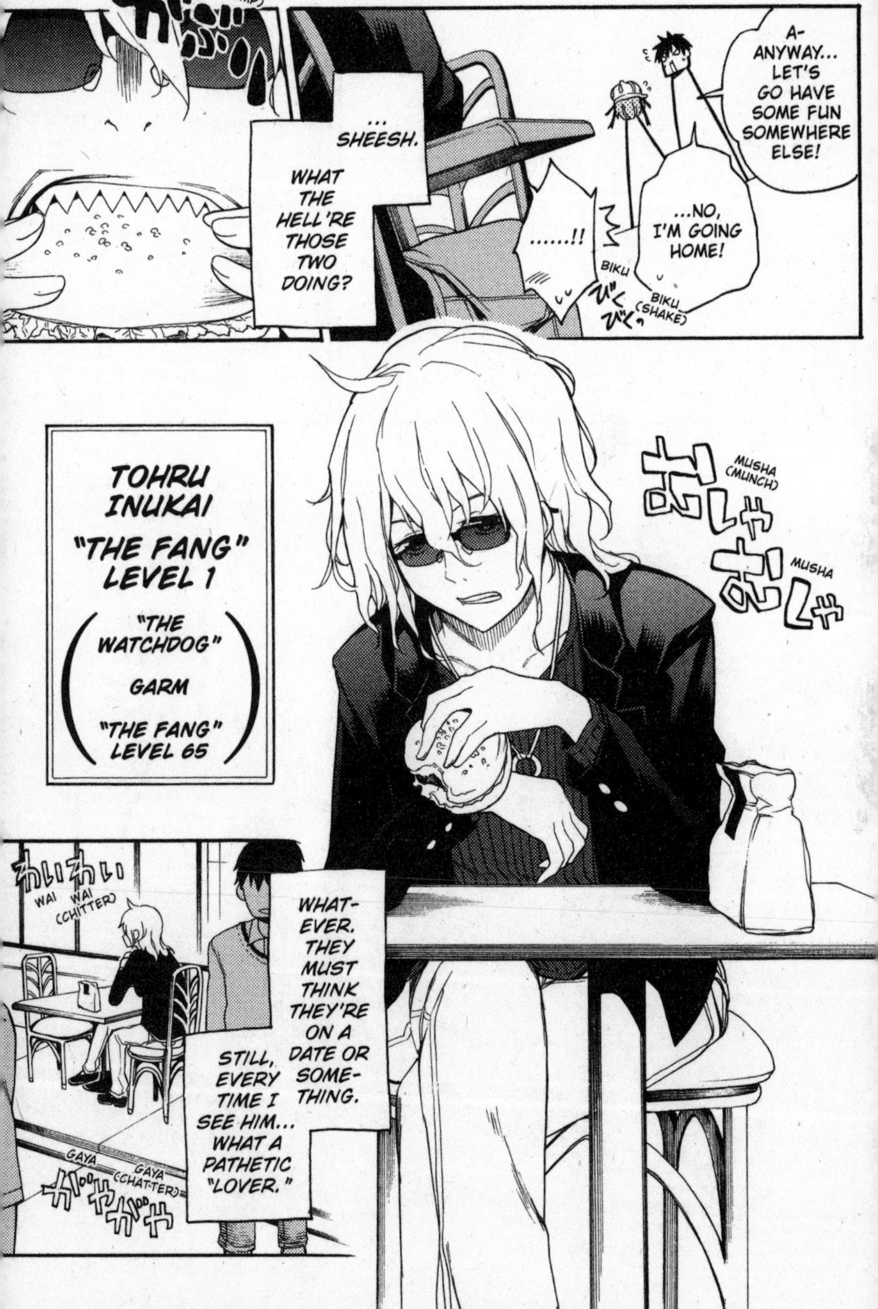
A-ANYWAY... LET'S GO HAVE SOME FUN SOMEWHERE ELSE!
...NO, I'M GOING HOME!
......!!
BIKU BIKU (SHAKE)
...SHEESH.
WHAT THE HELL'RE THOSE TWO DOING?
GABURI (CHOMP)
MUSHA (MUNCH) MUSHA
TOHRU INUKAI "THE FANG" LEVEL 1
("THE WATCHDOG" GARM "THE FANG" LEVEL 65)
WHATEVER. THEY MUST THINK THEY'RE ON A DATE OR SOMETHING.
STILL, EVERY TIME I SEE HIM... WHAT A PATHETIC "LOVER."
WAI WAI (CHITTER)
GAYA GAYA (CHATTER)

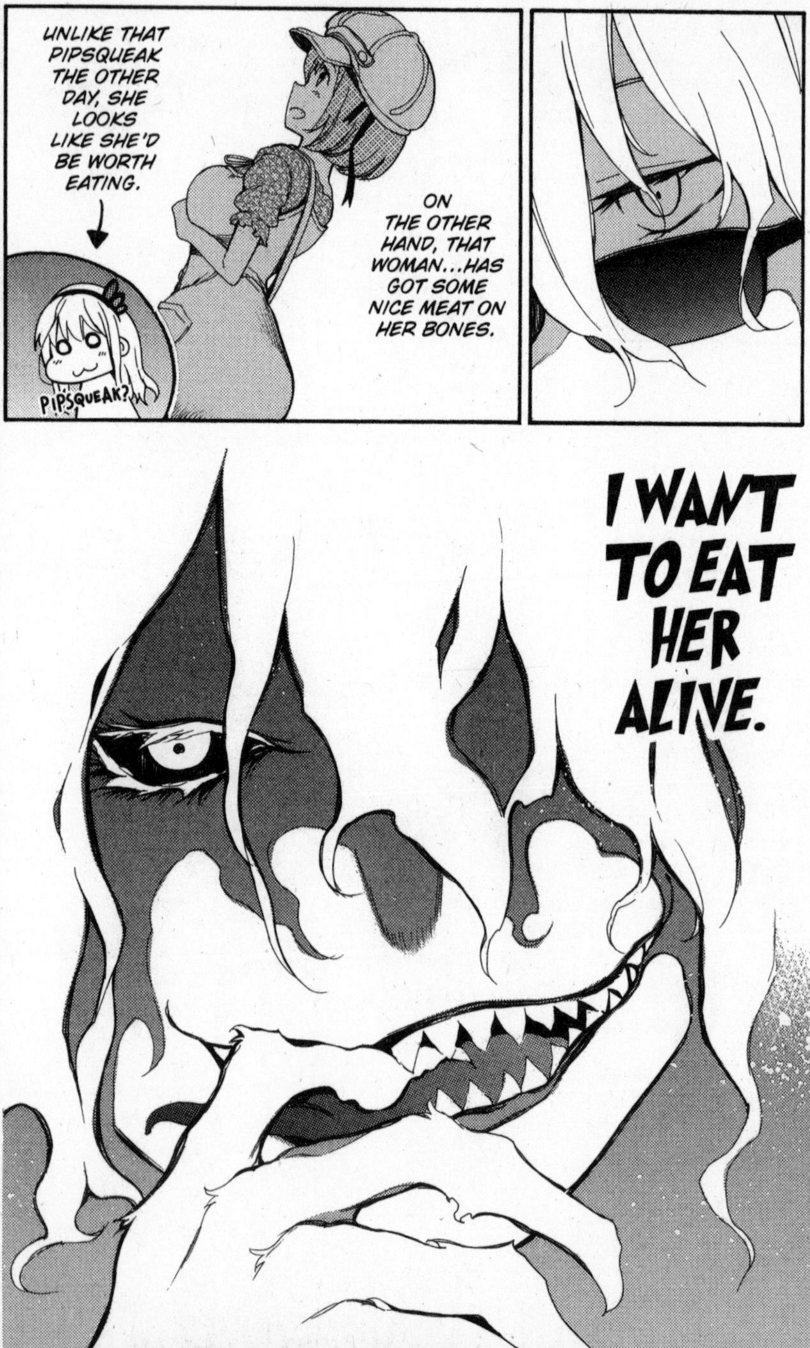
UNLIKE THAT PIPSQUEAK THE OTHER DAY, SHE LOOKS LIKE SHE'D BE WORTH EATING.
ON THE OTHER HAND, THAT WOMAN...HAS GOT SOME NICE MEAT ON HER BONES.
PIPSQUEAK?
I WANT TO EAT HER ALIVE.

GATA ("THUNK")

BIKU (SHIVER)

BIKU

HISO (WHISPER) HISO

IT'S SCARY...

WHY IS HE SMILING LIKE THAT?

HISO HISO

WELL, THIS ONE JUST OPENED UP!

I'M SORRY, WERE YOU TWO YOUNG LADIES LOOKING FOR A SEAT?

IT'LL BE A PAIN IF THEY MANAGE TO LEVEL UP ANY MORE...

PIKU (BLINK)

KYUUUN (THROB)

GUESS I'LL TALK TO THEM AND INTERRUPT THEIR DATE.

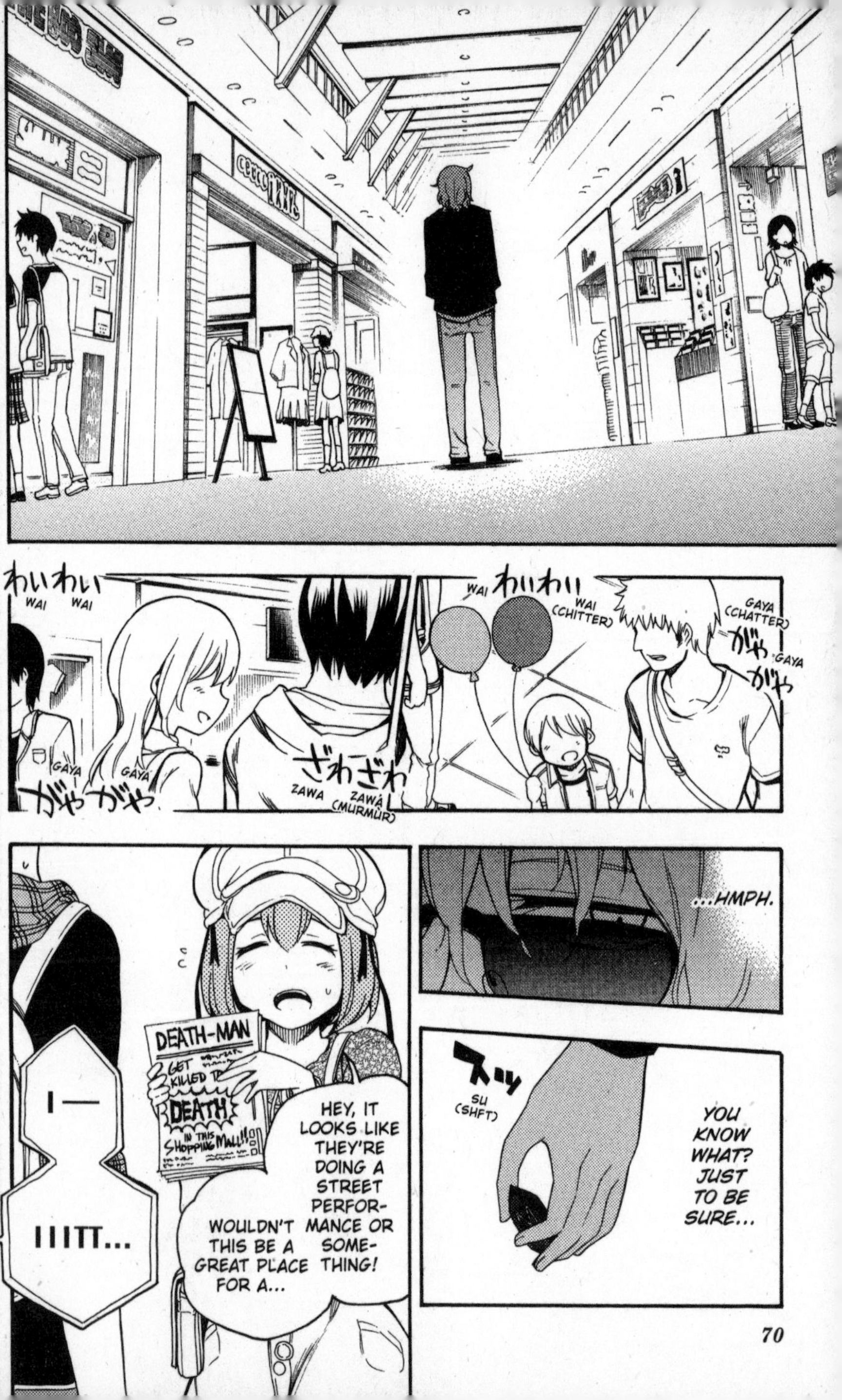

わいわい
WAI WAI (CHITTER)
がやがや
GAYA (CHATTER) GAYA
わいわい
WAI WAI
ざわざわ
ZAWA ZAWA (MURMUR)
がやがや
GAYA GAYA
...HMPH.
スッ
SU (SHFT)
YOU KNOW WHAT? JUST TO BE SURE...
DEATH-MAN
GET KILLED T
DEATH
IN THIS SHOPPING MALL!!
HEY, IT LOOKS LIKE THEY'RE DOING A STREET PERFORMANCE OR SOMETHING! WOULDN'T THIS BE A GREAT PLACE FOR A...
I—
IIITT...

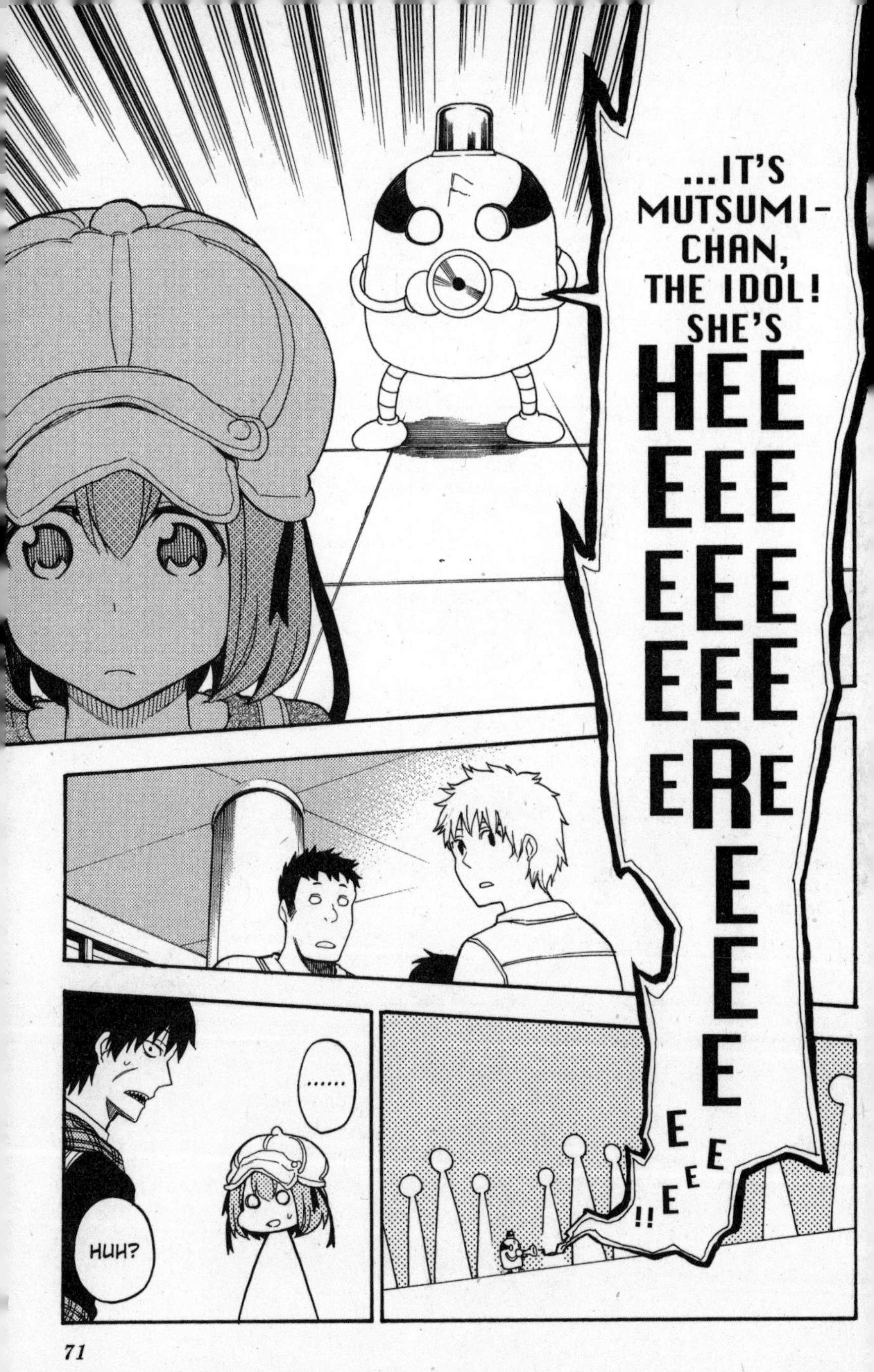
...IT'S MUTSUMI-CHAN, THE IDOL! SHE'S HEEEEEEEEEEEEREEEEEEEEE!!
....
HUH?

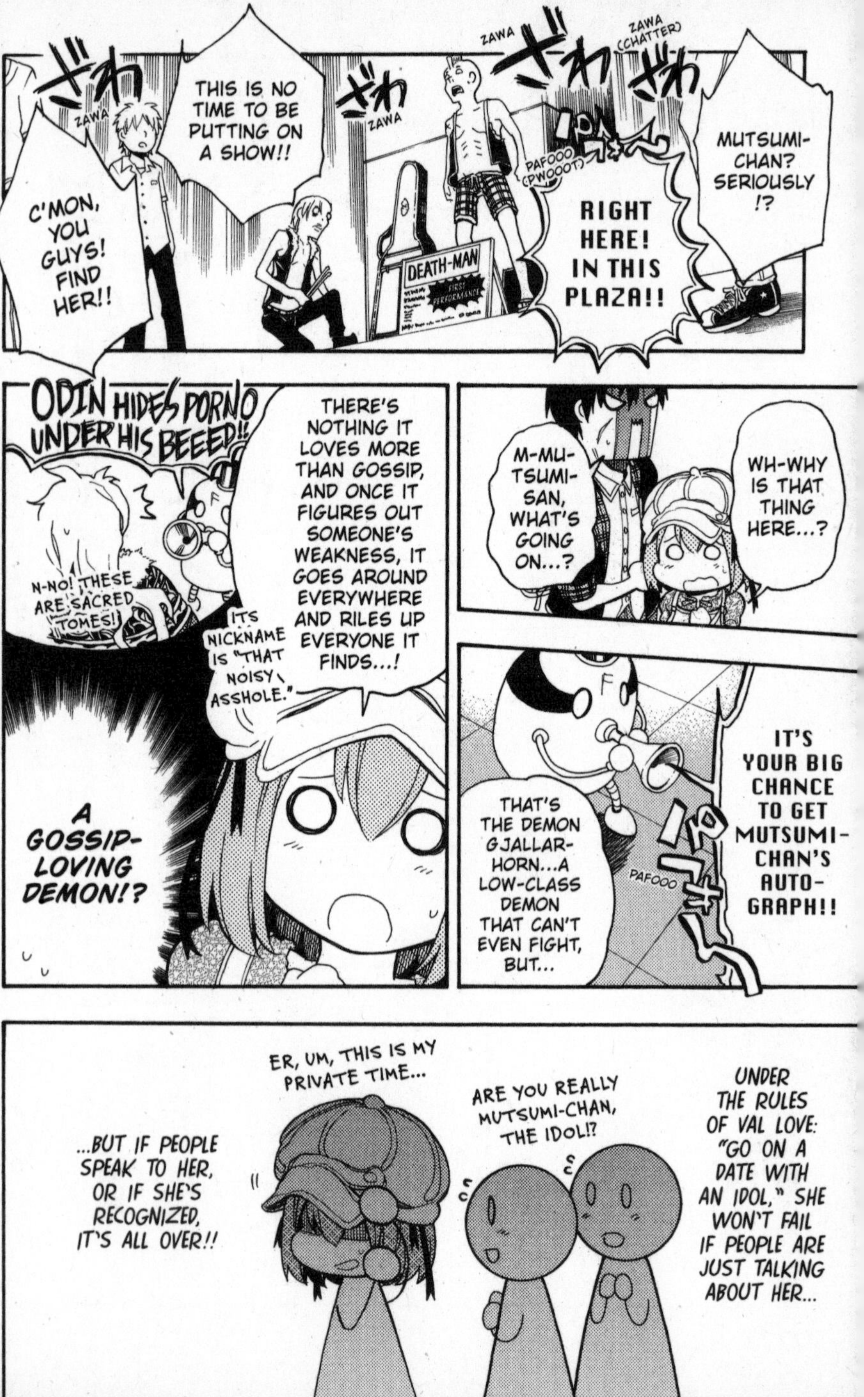
ZAWA ZAWA (CHATTER)
MUTSUMI-CHAN? SERIOUSLY!?
PAFOOO (PWOOOT)
RIGHT HERE! IN THIS PLAZA!!
ZAWA
DEATH-MAN
FIRST PERFORMANCE
THIS IS NO TIME TO BE PUTTING ON A SHOW!!
ZAWA
C'MON, YOU GUYS! FIND HER!!
WH-WHY IS THAT THING HERE...?
M-MUTSUMI-SAN, WHAT'S GOING ON...?
IT'S YOUR BIG CHANCE TO GET MUTSUMI-CHAN'S AUTOGRAPH!!
PAFOOO
THAT'S THE DEMON GJALLARHORN...A LOW-CLASS DEMON THAT CAN'T EVEN FIGHT, BUT...
THERE'S NOTHING IT LOVES MORE THAN GOSSIP, AND ONCE IT FIGURES OUT SOMEONE'S WEAKNESS, IT GOES AROUND EVERYWHERE AND RILES UP EVERYONE IT FINDS...!
ODIN HIDES PORNO UNDER HIS BEEED!!
N-NO! THESE ARE SACRED TOMES!!
ITS NICKNAME IS "THAT NOISY ASSHOLE."
A GOSSIP-LOVING DEMON!?
UNDER THE RULES OF VAL LOVE: "GO ON A DATE WITH AN IDOL," SHE WON'T FAIL IF PEOPLE ARE JUST TALKING ABOUT HER...
ARE YOU REALLY MUTSUMI-CHAN, THE IDOL!?
ER, UM, THIS IS MY PRIVATE TIME...
...BUT IF PEOPLE SPEAK TO HER, OR IF SHE'S RECOGNIZED, IT'S ALL OVER!!

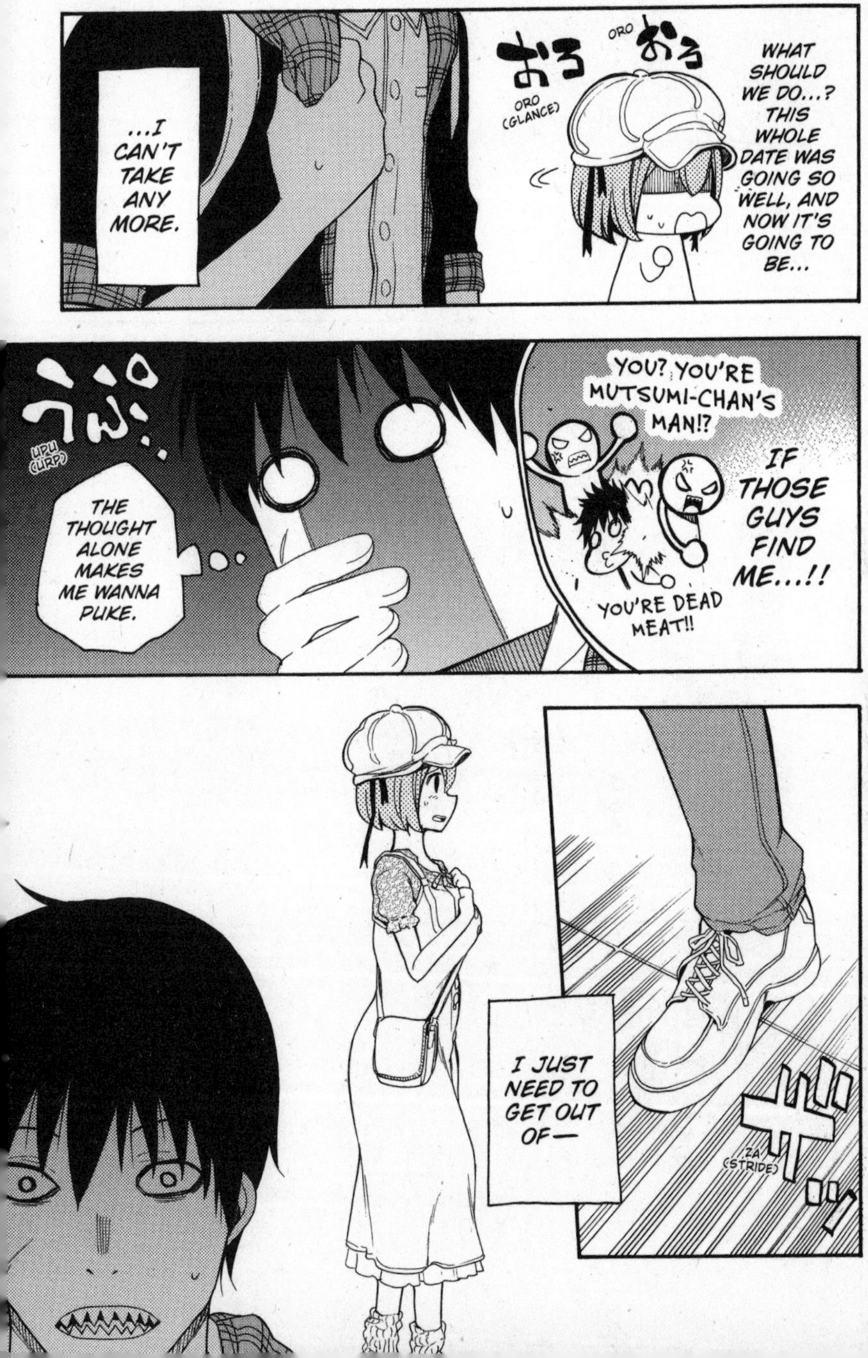

おろ
ORO
おろ
ORO (GLANCE)
WHAT SHOULD WE DO...? THIS WHOLE DATE WAS GOING SO WELL, AND NOW IT'S GOING TO BE...
...I CAN'T TAKE ANY MORE.
IF THOSE GUYS FIND ME...!!
YOU? YOU'RE MUTSUMI-CHAN'S MAN!?
YOU'RE DEAD MEAT!!
うぷ..
UPU (URP)
THE THOUGHT ALONE MAKES ME WANNA PUKE.
ザッ
ZA (STRIDE)
I JUST NEED TO GET OUT OF—

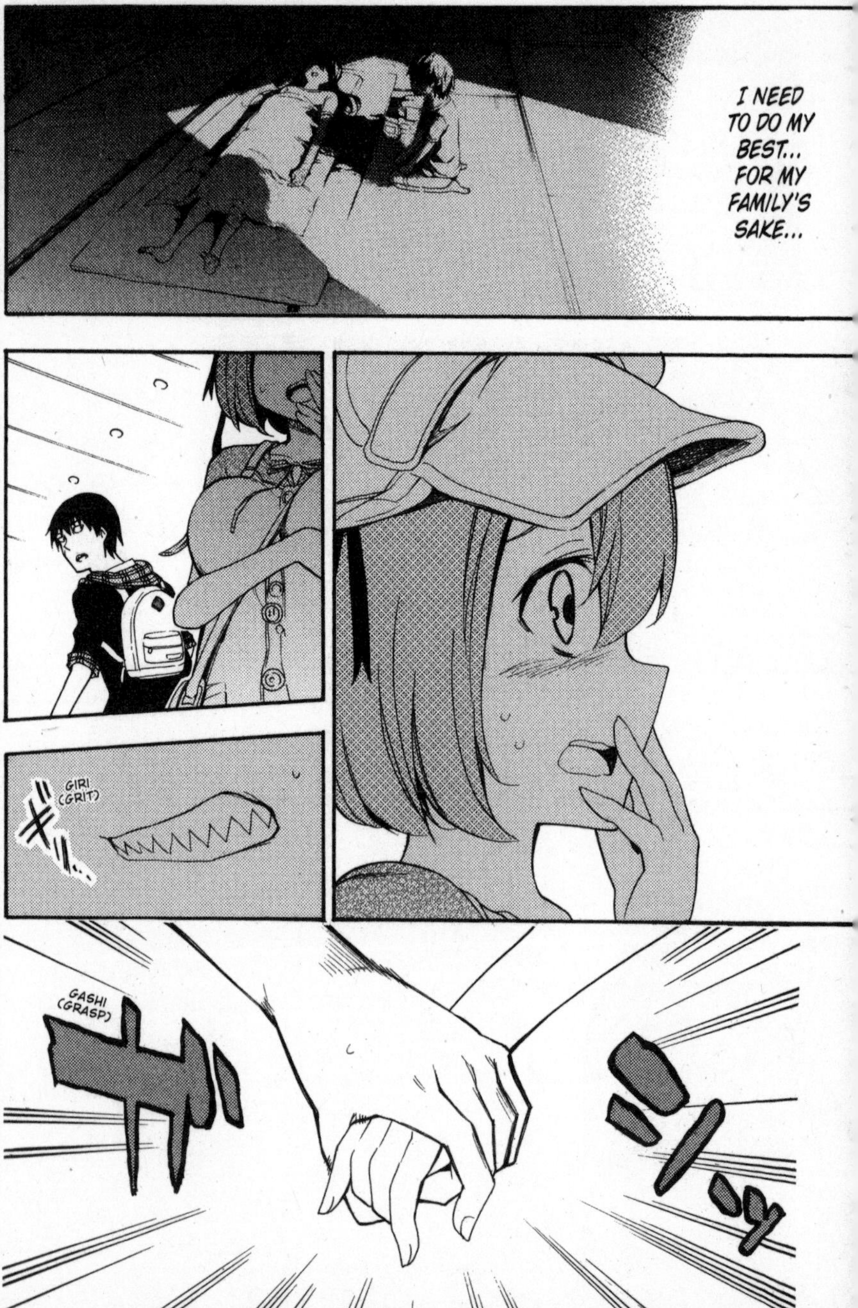
I NEED TO DO MY BEST... FOR MY FAMILY'S SAKE...
GIRI (GRIT)
GASHI (GRASP)

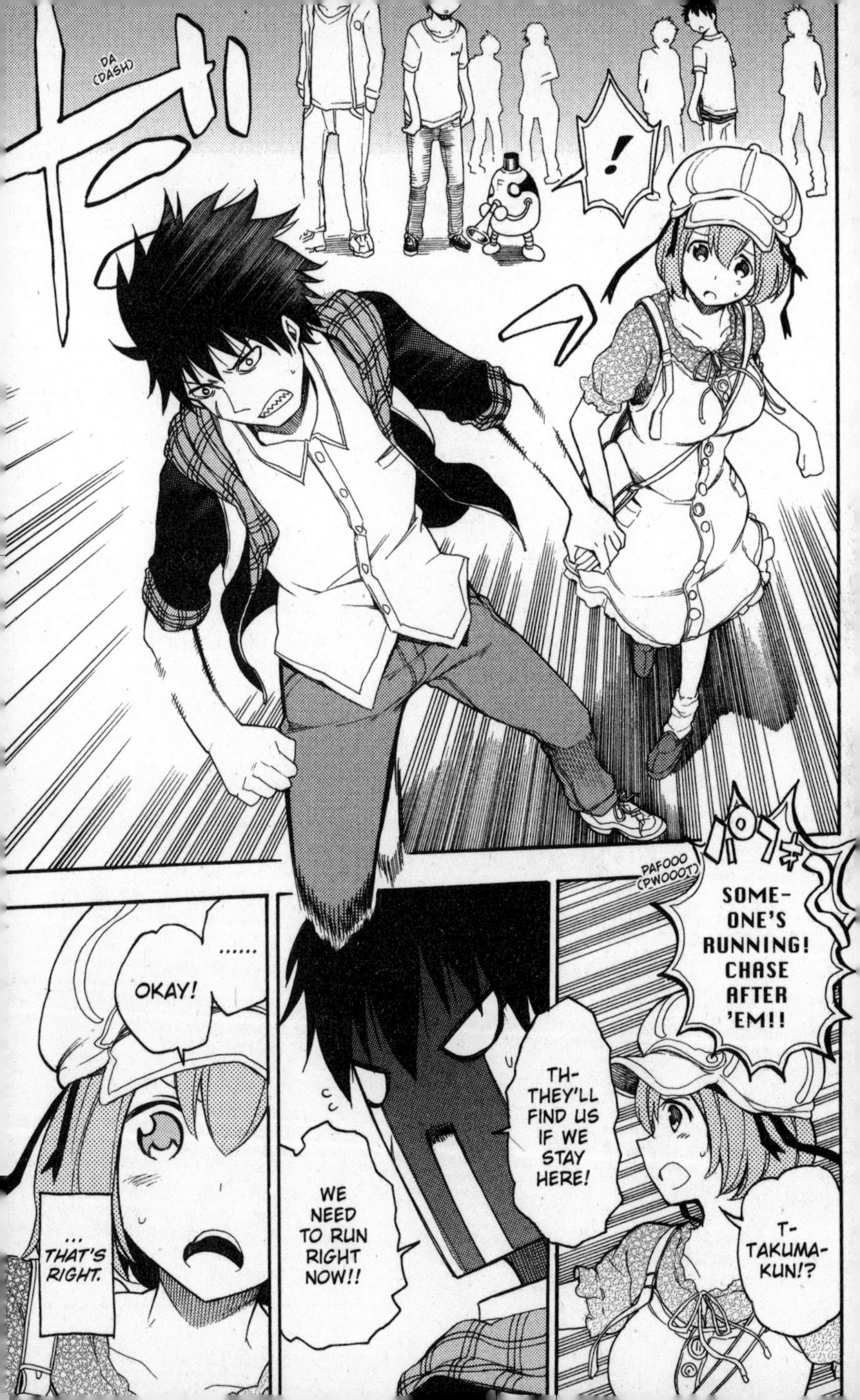
DA (DASH)
!
PAFOOO (PWOOOT)
SOME-ONE'S RUNNING! CHASE AFTER 'EM!!
T-TAKUMA-KUN!?
TH-THEY'LL FIND US IF WE STAY HERE!
WE NEED TO RUN RIGHT NOW!!
......
OKAY!
... THAT'S RIGHT.

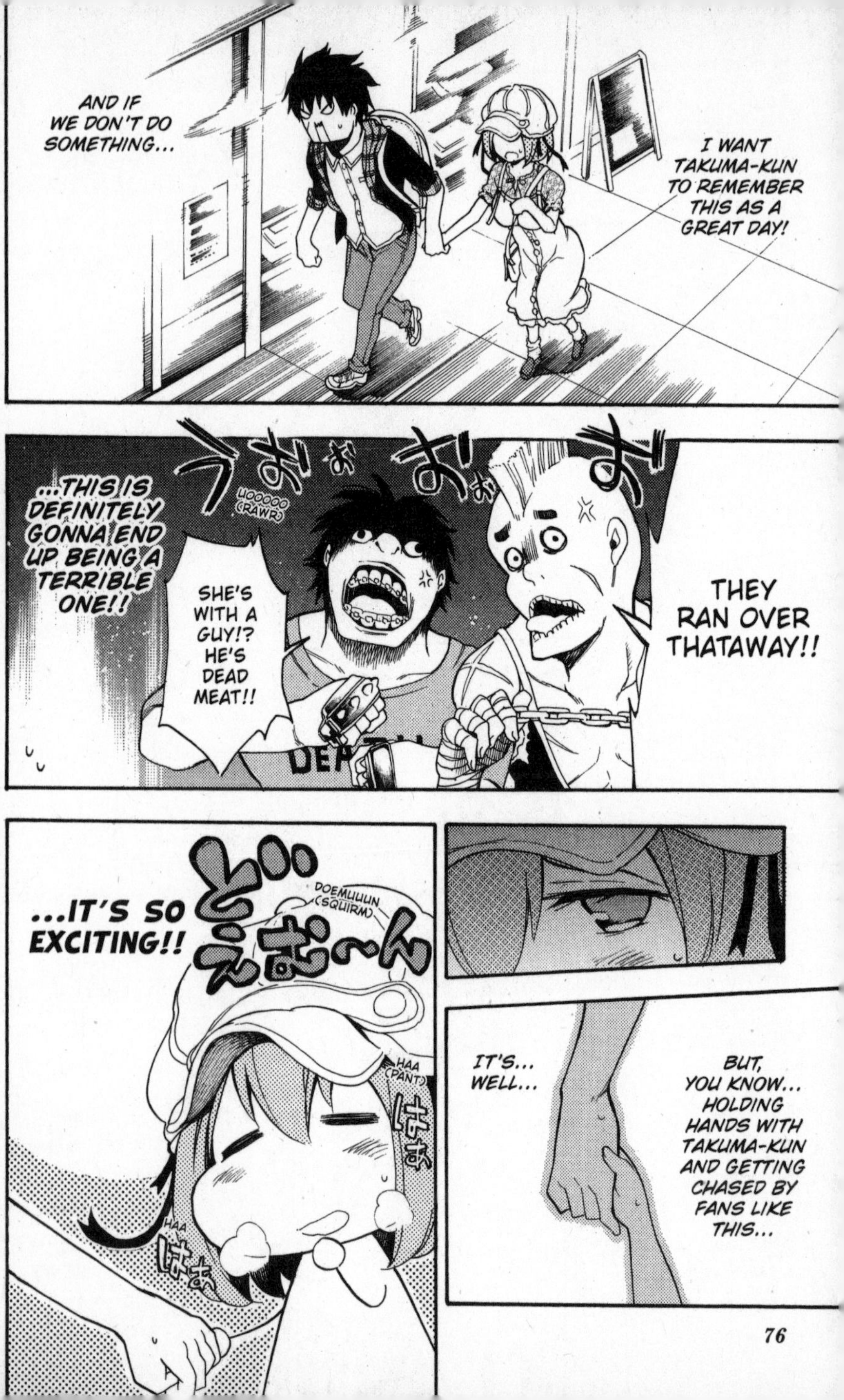
I WANT TAKUMA-KUN TO REMEMBER THIS AS A GREAT DAY!
AND IF WE DON'T DO SOMETHING...
THEY RAN OVER THATAWAY!!
UOOOOO (RAWR)
SHE'S WITH A GUY!? HE'S DEAD MEAT!!
...THIS IS DEFINITELY GONNA END UP BEING A TERRIBLE ONE!!
BUT, YOU KNOW... HOLDING HANDS WITH TAKUMA-KUN AND GETTING CHASED BY FANS LIKE THIS...
IT'S... WELL...
DOEMUUUN (SQUIRM)
...IT'S SO EXCITING!!
HAA (PANT)
HAA

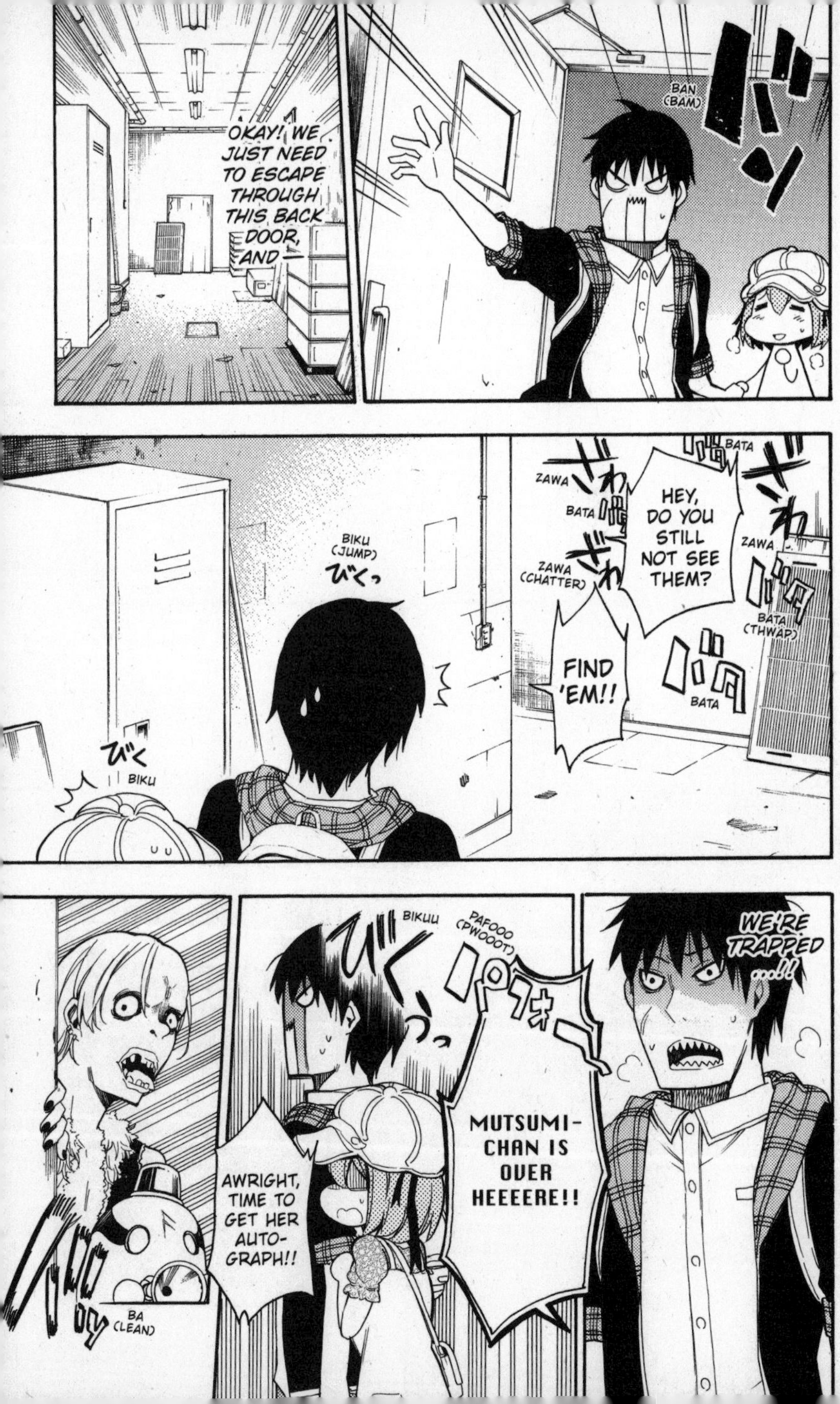

BAN (BAM)
OKAY! WE JUST NEED TO ESCAPE THROUGH THIS BACK DOOR, AND
BATA
ZAWA
HEY, DO YOU STILL NOT SEE THEM?
ZAWA
BATA
ZAWA (CHATTER)
BATA (THWAP)
FIND 'EM!!
BATA
BIKU (JUMP)
BIKU
WE'RE TRAPPED...!!
MUTSUMI-CHAN IS OVER HEEEERE!!
PAFOOO (PWOOOT)
BIKUU
AWRIGHT, TIME TO GET HER AUTO-GRAPH!!
BA (LEAN)

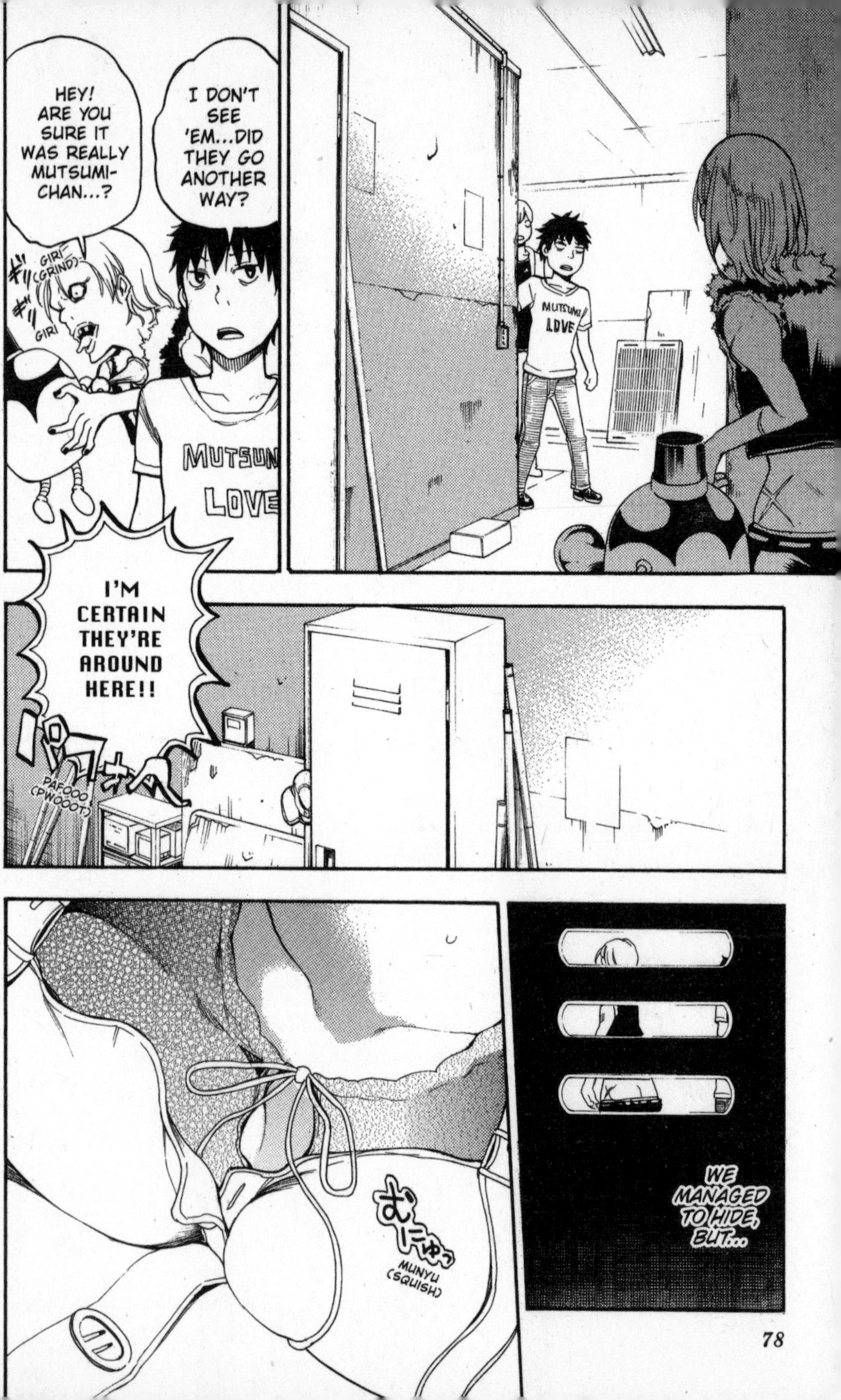
I DON'T SEE 'EM...DID THEY GO ANOTHER WAY?
HEY! ARE YOU SURE IT WAS REALLY MUTSUMI-CHAN...?
GIRI (GRIND)
GIRI
MUTSUMI LOVE
I'M CERTAIN THEY'RE AROUND HERE!!
PAFOOO (PWOOOT)
WE MANAGED TO HIDE, BUT...
むにゅっ
MUNYU (SQUISH)

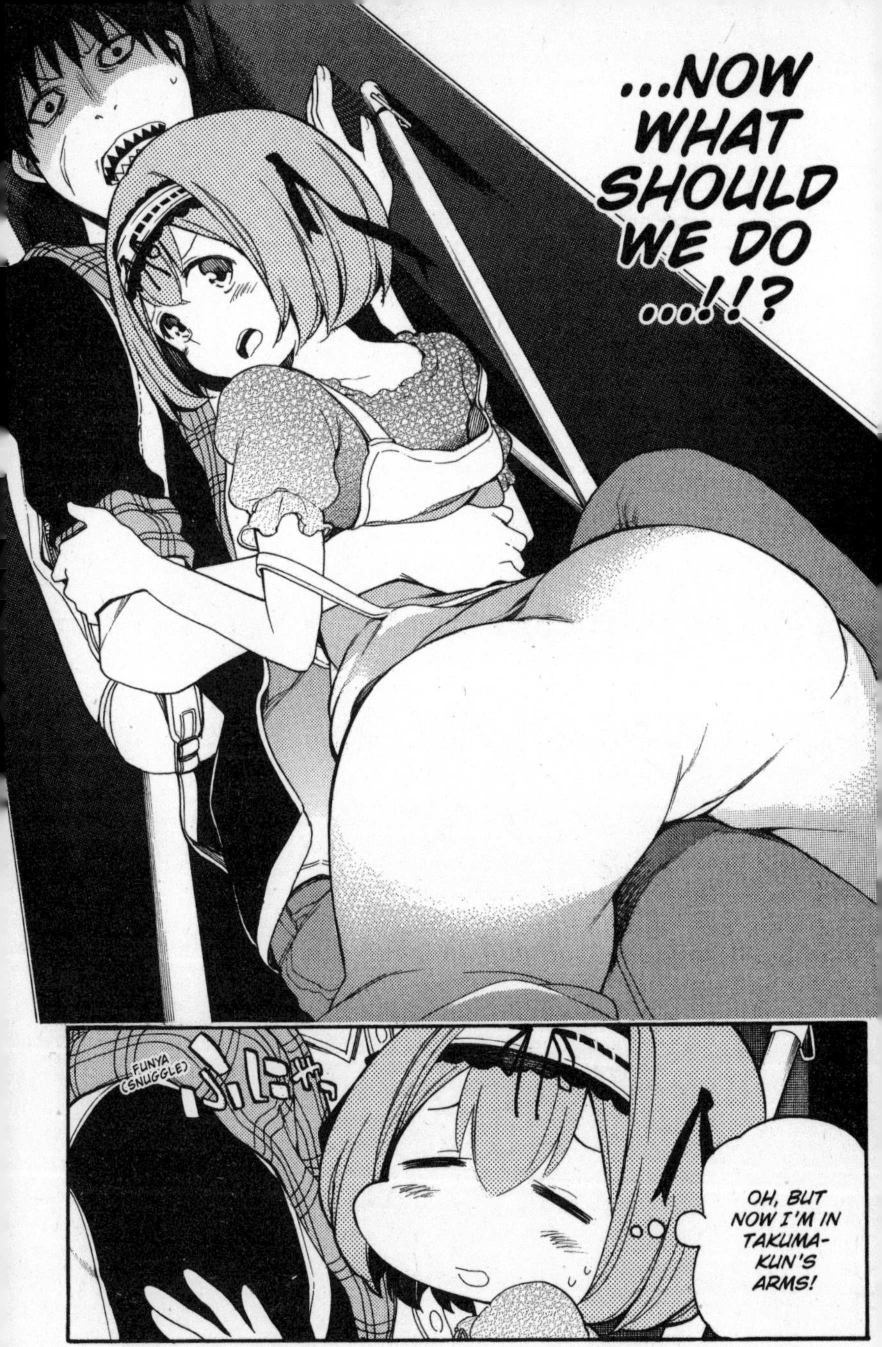
...NOW WHAT SHOULD WE DO ...!!?
OH, BUT NOW I'M IN TAKUMA-KUN'S ARMS!
FUNYA (SNUGGLE)

BY THE WAY, DO YOU THINK MUTSUMI AND TAKUMA-SAN ARE ALL RIGHT...?
YOU DON'T NEED TO WORRY SO MUCH. IT'S NOT AS IF MUTSUMI'S FANS ARE GOING TO FIND HER AND CHASE THE TWO OF THEM INTO A LOCKER LIKE SOME KIND OF SILLY ROM-COM.

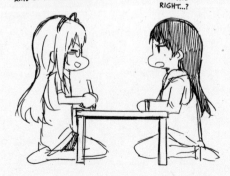

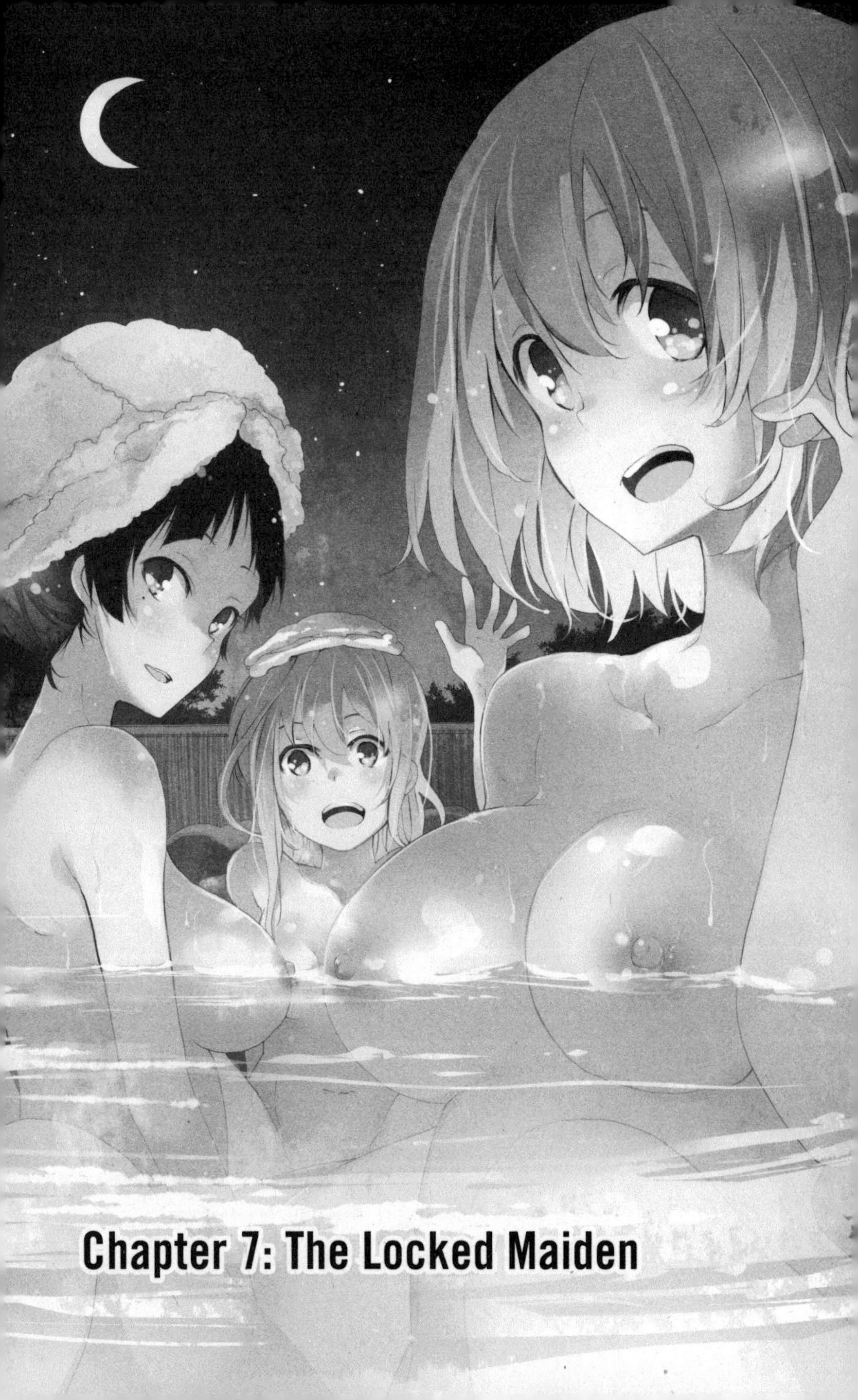

Chapter 7: The Locked Maiden

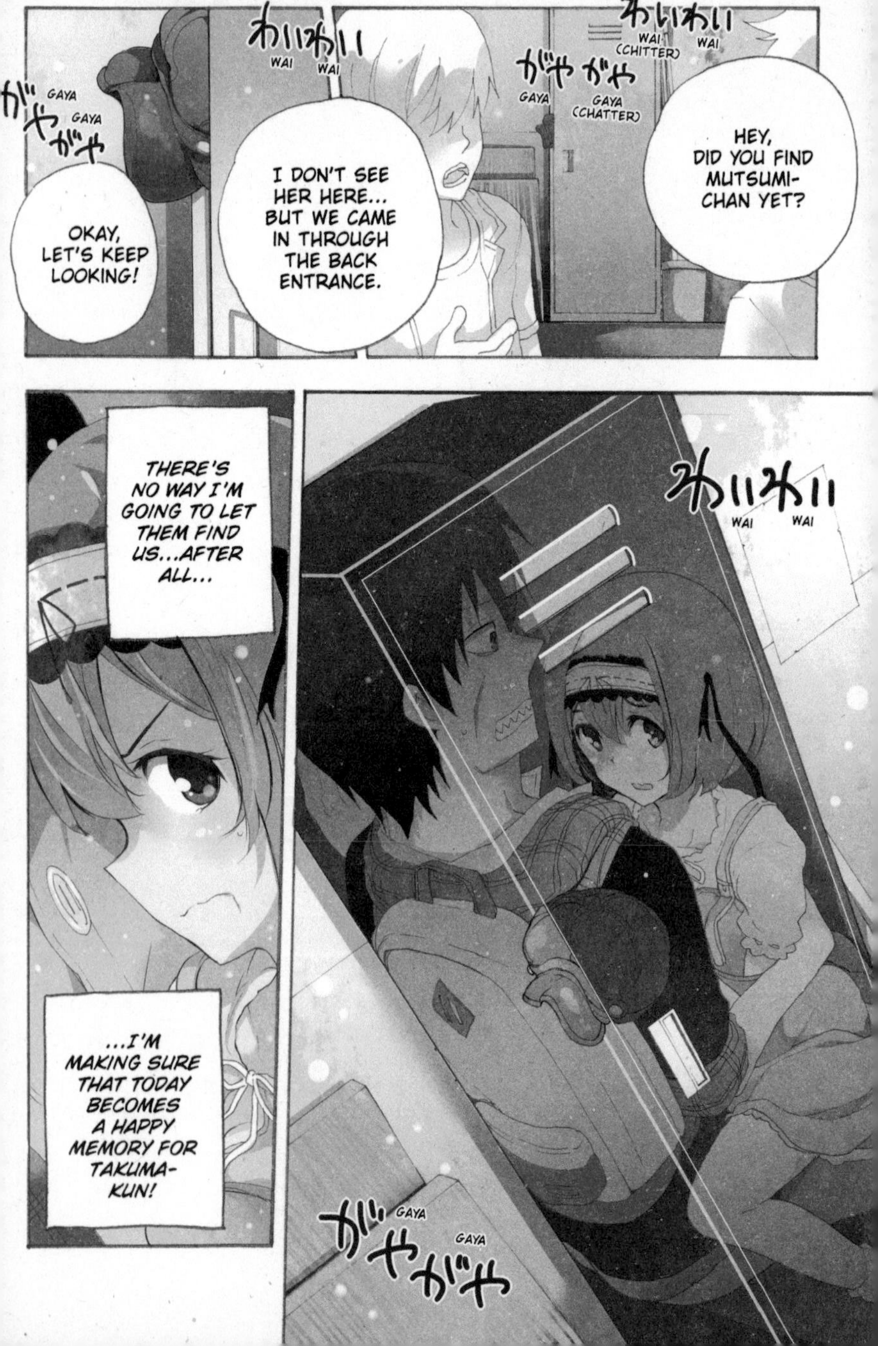
わいわい
WAI (CHITTER) WAI
がやがや
GAYA GAYA (CHATTER)
HEY, DID YOU FIND MUTSUMI-CHAN YET?
わいわい
WAI WAI
I DON'T SEE HER HERE... BUT WE CAME IN THROUGH THE BACK ENTRANCE.
がやがや
GAYA GAYA
OKAY, LET'S KEEP LOOKING!
わいわい
WAI WAI
がやがや
GAYA GAYA
THERE'S NO WAY I'M GOING TO LET THEM FIND US...AFTER ALL...
...I'M MAKING SURE THAT TODAY BECOMES A HAPPY MEMORY FOR TAKUMA-KUN!

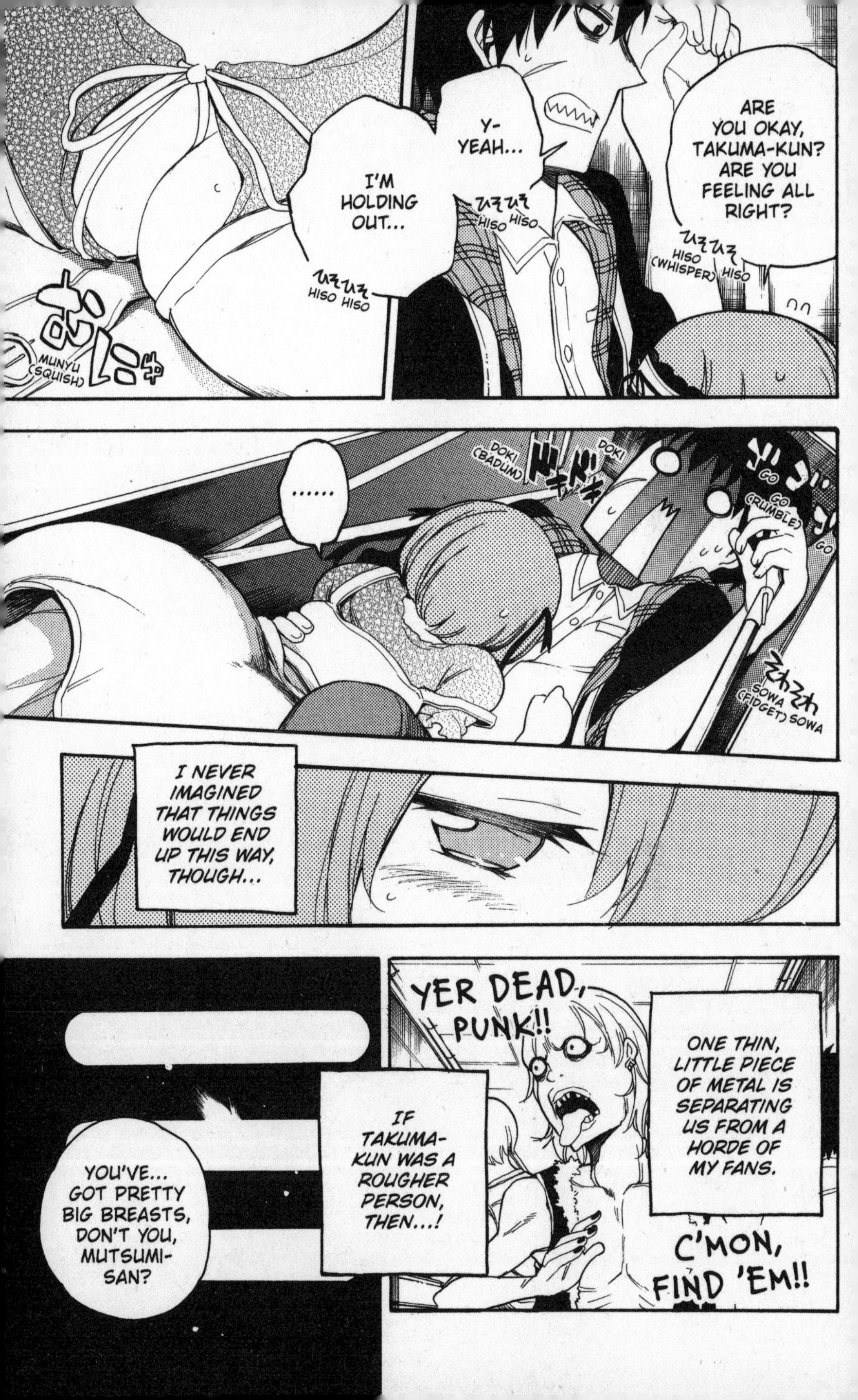
ARE YOU OKAY, TAKUMA-KUN? ARE YOU FEELING ALL RIGHT?
ひそひそ HISO (WHISPER) HISO
Y-YEAH...
ひそひそ HISO HISO
I'M HOLDING OUT...
ひそひそ HISO HISO
MUNYU (SQUISH)
DOKI (BADUM) DOKI
GO GO (RUMBLE) GO
......
SOWA (FIDGET) SOWA
I NEVER IMAGINED THAT THINGS WOULD END UP THIS WAY, THOUGH...
ONE THIN, LITTLE PIECE OF METAL IS SEPARATING US FROM A HORDE OF MY FANS.
YER DEAD, PUNK!!
C'MON, FIND 'EM!!
IF TAKUMA-KUN WAS A ROUGHER PERSON, THEN...!
YOU'VE... GOT PRETTY BIG BREASTS, DON'T YOU, MUTSUMI-SAN?

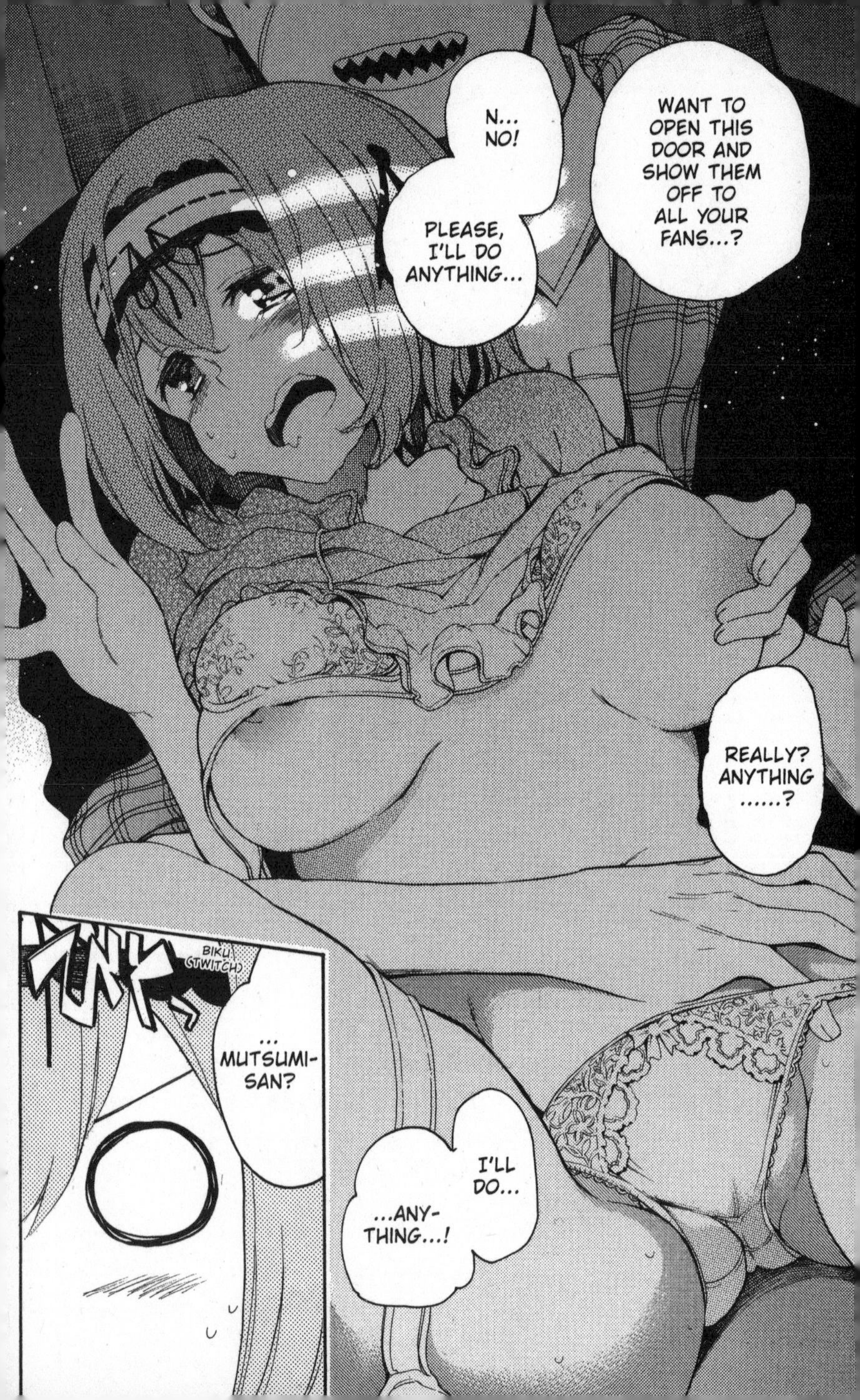
WANT TO OPEN THIS DOOR AND SHOW THEM OFF TO ALL YOUR FANS...?
N... NO!
PLEASE, I'LL DO ANYTHING...
REALLY? ANYTHING ......?
I'LL DO...
...ANY-THING...!
BIKU (TWITCH)
... MUTSUMI-SAN?

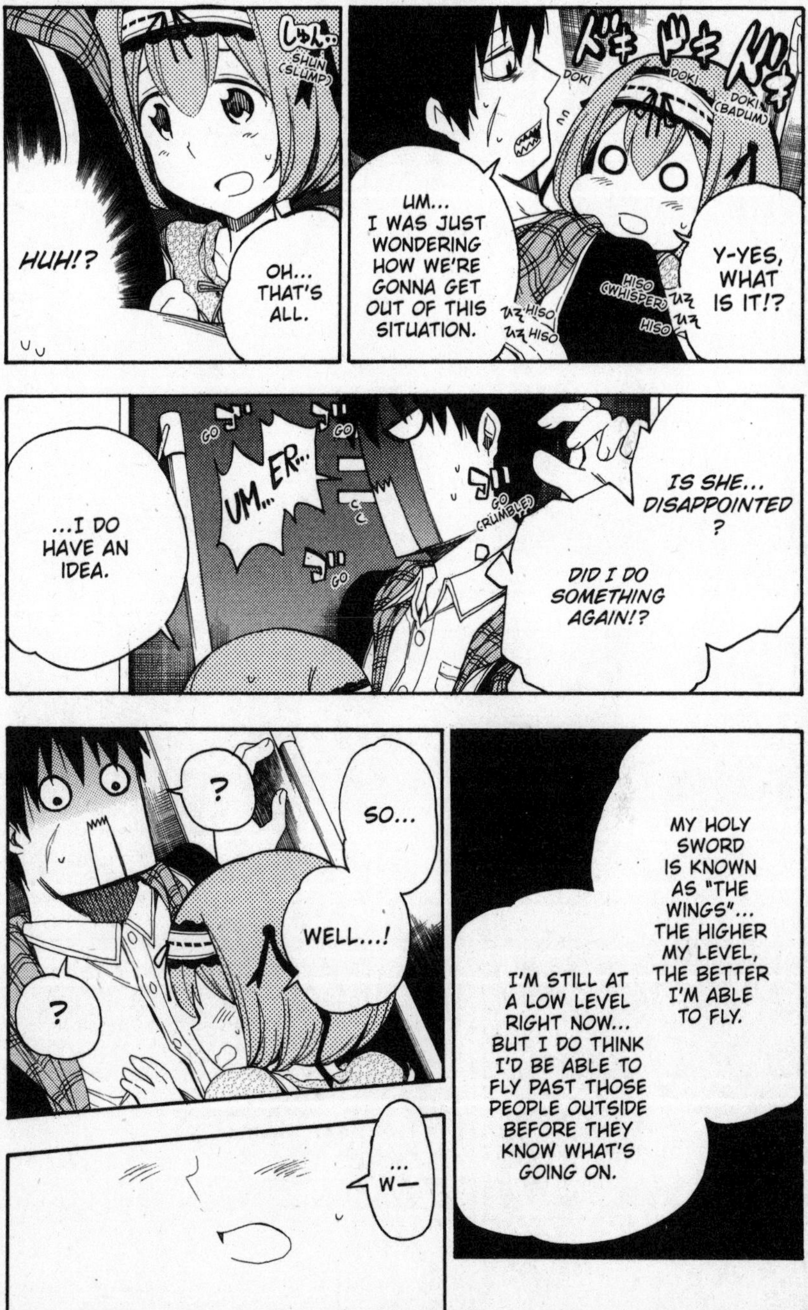
DOKI DOKI DOKI (BADUM)
Y-YES, WHAT IS IT!?
HISO (WHISPER) HISO HISO HISO
UM... I WAS JUST WONDERING HOW WE'RE GONNA GET OUT OF THIS SITUATION.
SHUN (SLUMP)
OH... THAT'S ALL.
HUH!?
IS SHE... DISAPPOINTED?
DID I DO SOMETHING AGAIN!?
GO (RUMBLE)
GO GO GO
UM... ER...
...I DO HAVE AN IDEA.
MY HOLY SWORD IS KNOWN AS "THE WINGS"... THE HIGHER MY LEVEL, THE BETTER I'M ABLE TO FLY.
I'M STILL AT A LOW LEVEL RIGHT NOW... BUT I DO THINK I'D BE ABLE TO FLY PAST THOSE PEOPLE OUTSIDE BEFORE THEY KNOW WHAT'S GOING ON.
SO...
?
WELL...!
?
...W—

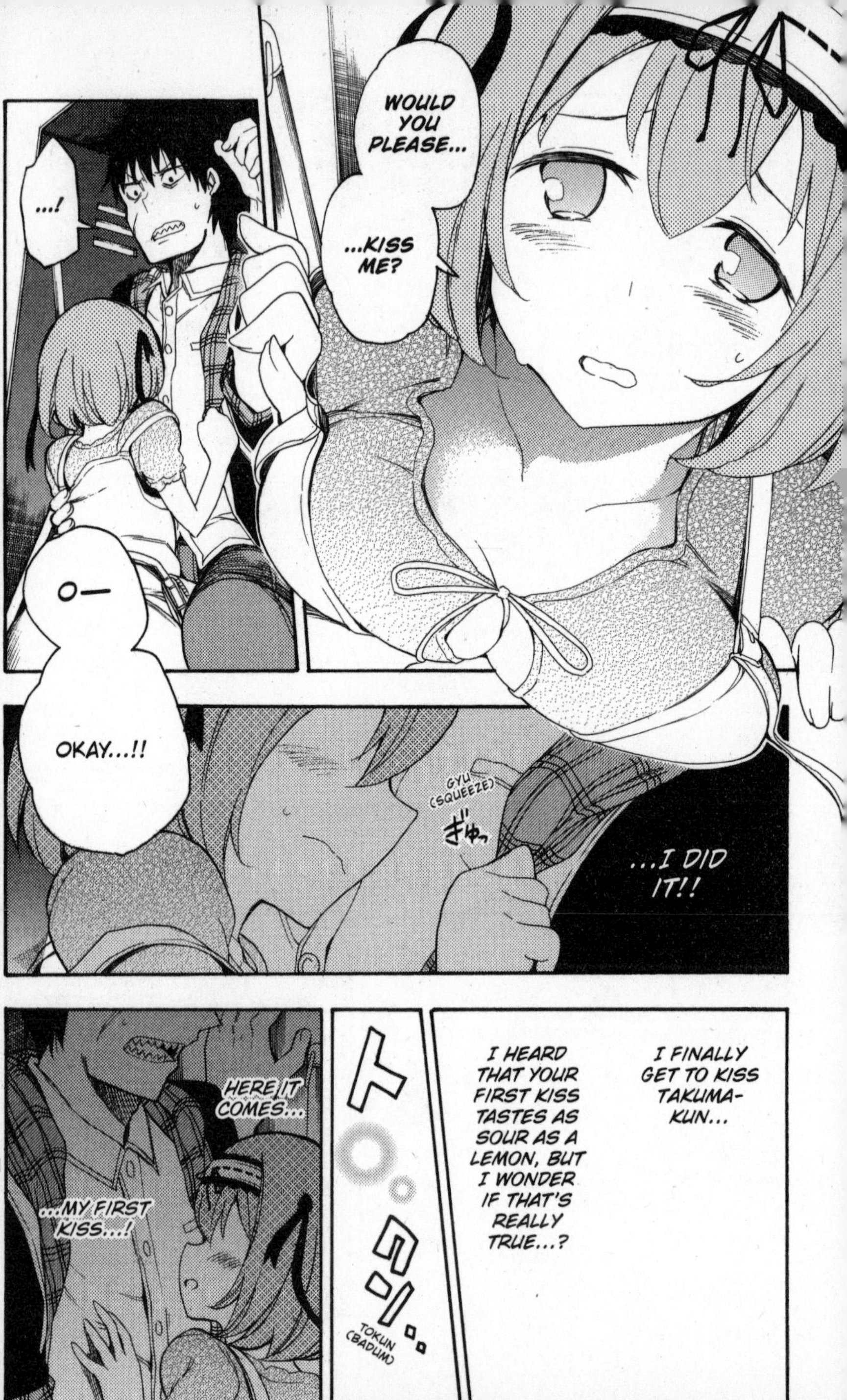

WOULD YOU PLEASE...
...KISS ME?
...!
O—
OKAY...!!
...I DID IT!!
GYU (SQUEEZE)
ぎゅっ
I FINALLY GET TO KISS TAKUMA-KUN...
I HEARD THAT YOUR FIRST KISS TASTES AS SOUR AS A LEMON, BUT I WONDER IF THAT'S REALLY TRUE...?
トクン
TOKUN (BADUM)
HERE IT COMES...
...MY FIRST KISS...!

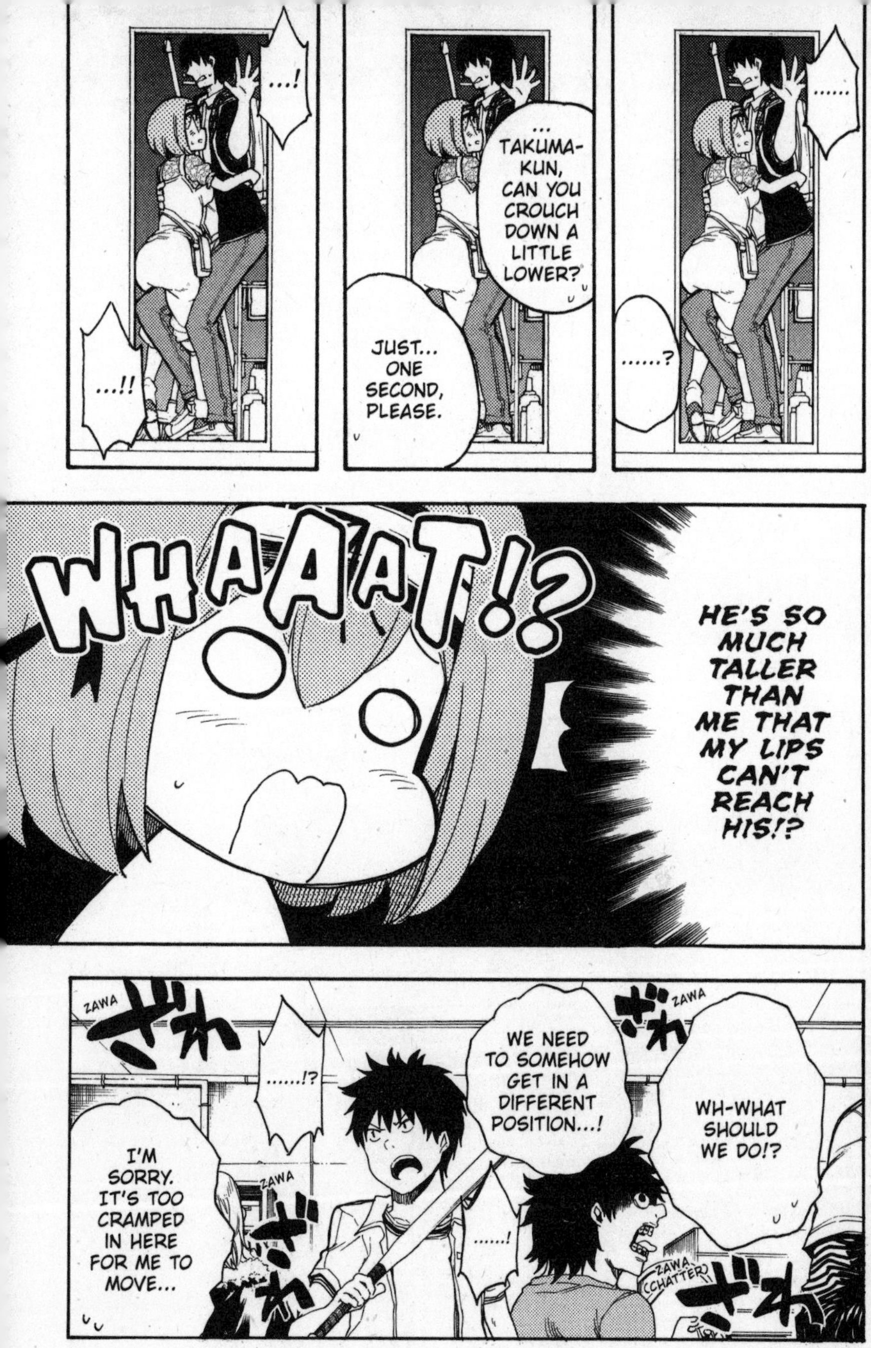
......
......?
...
TAKUMA-KUN, CAN YOU CROUCH DOWN A LITTLE LOWER?
JUST... ONE SECOND, PLEASE.
...!
...!!
WHAAAT!?
HE'S SO MUCH TALLER THAN ME THAT MY LIPS CAN'T REACH HIS!?
ZAWA
WH-WHAT SHOULD WE DO!?
WE NEED TO SOMEHOW GET IN A DIFFERENT POSITION...!
......!?
ZAWA
ZAWA
I'M SORRY. IT'S TOO CRAMPED IN HERE FOR ME TO MOVE...
......!
ZAWA (CHATTER)

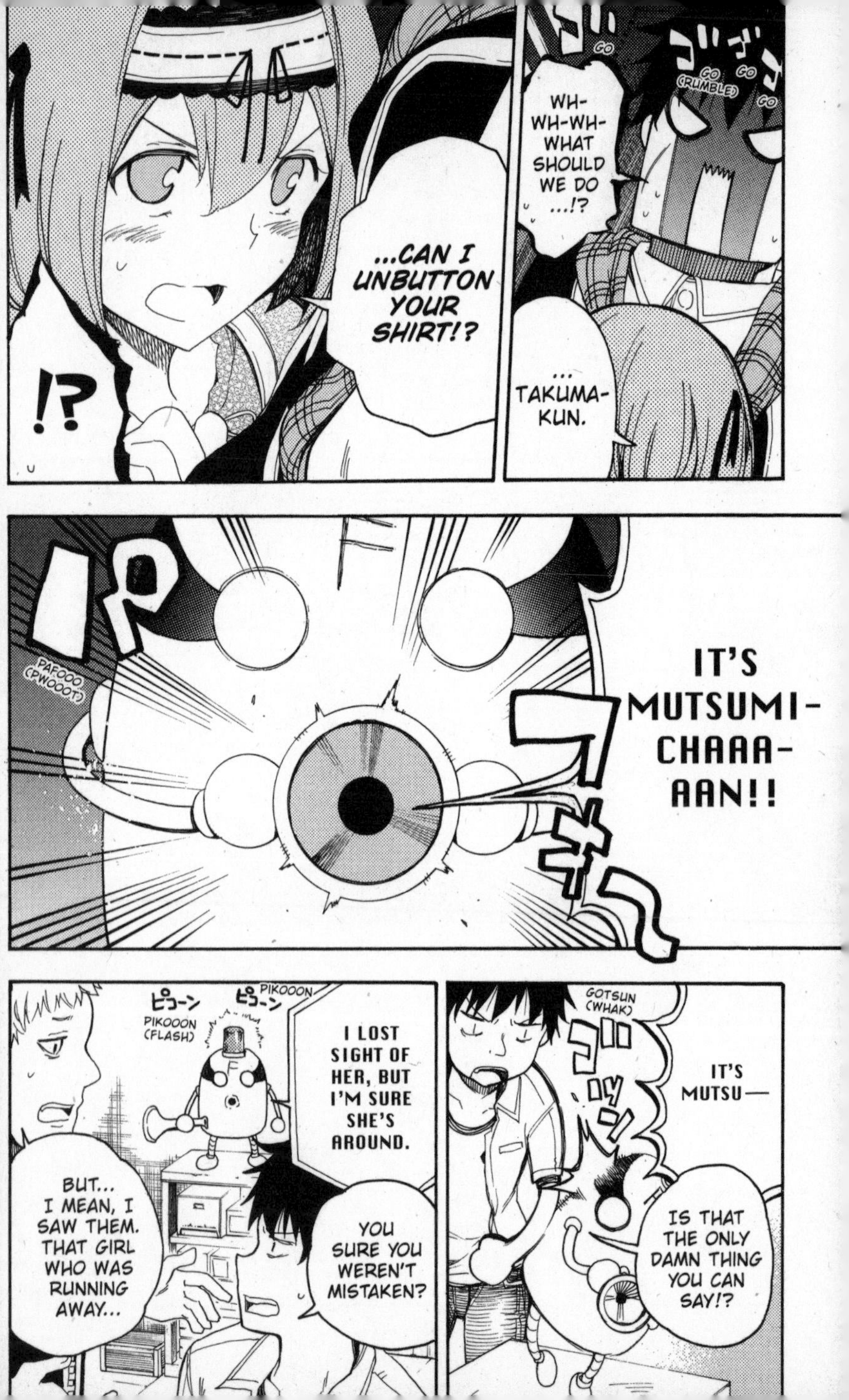
GO
GO GO (RUMBLE) GO
WH- WH-WH- WHAT SHOULD WE DO ...!?
... TAKUMA-KUN.
...CAN I UNBUTTON YOUR SHIRT!?
!?
PAFOOO (PWOOOT)
IT'S MUTSUMI-CHAAA-AAN!!
GOTSUN (WHAK)
IT'S MUTSU—
IS THAT THE ONLY DAMN THING YOU CAN SAY!?
ピコーン PIKOOON (FLASH)
ピコーン PIKOOON
I LOST SIGHT OF HER, BUT I'M SURE SHE'S AROUND.
YOU SURE YOU WEREN'T MISTAKEN?
BUT... I MEAN, I SAW THEM. THAT GIRL WHO WAS RUNNING AWAY...

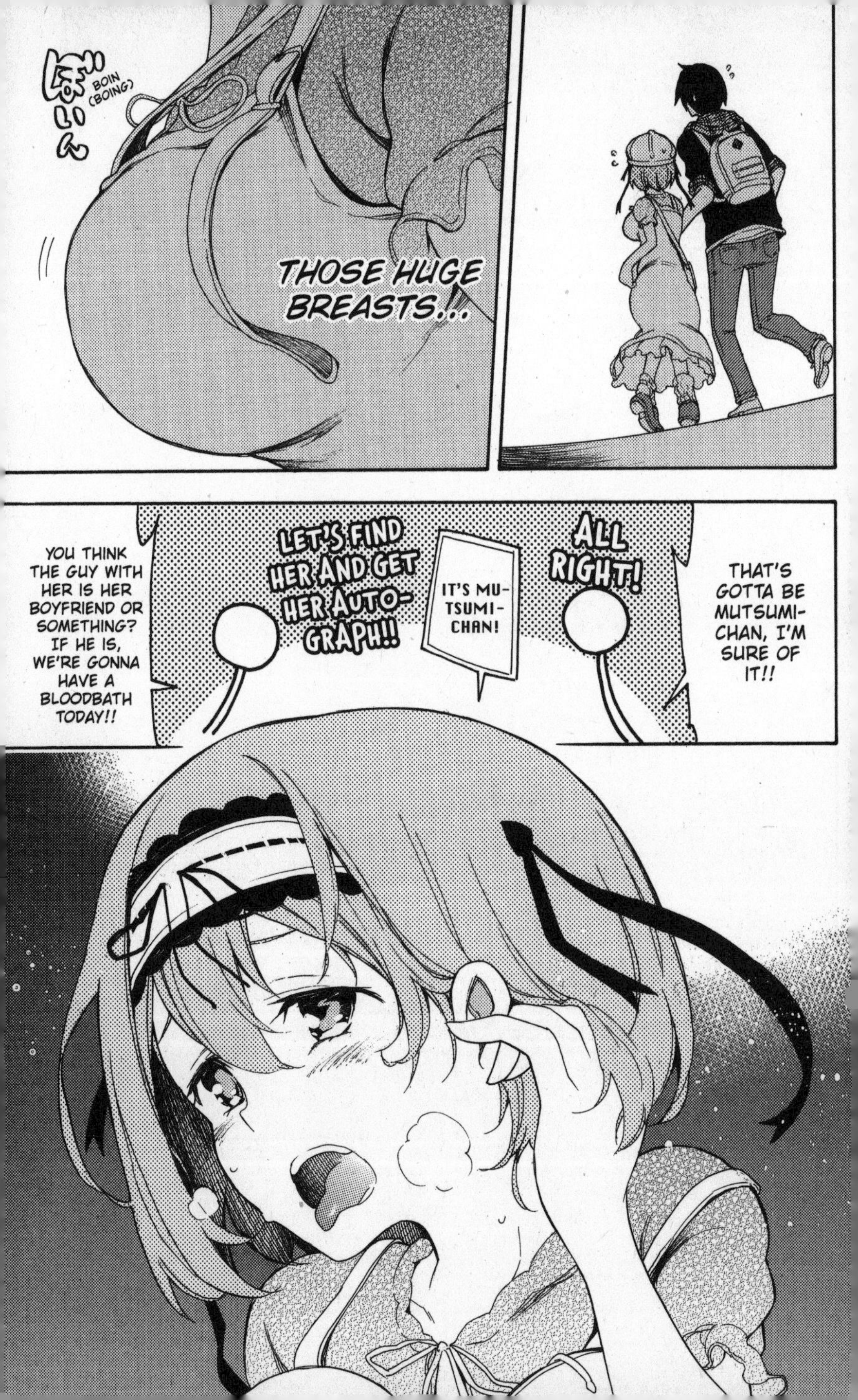
THOSE HUGE BREASTS...
BOIN (BOING)
THAT'S GOTTA BE MUTSUMI-CHAN, I'M SURE OF IT!!
ALL RIGHT!
IT'S MU-TSUMI-CHAN!
LET'S FIND HER AND GET HER AUTO-GRAPH!!
YOU THINK THE GUY WITH HER IS HER BOYFRIEND OR SOMETHING? IF HE IS, WE'RE GONNA HAVE A BLOODBATH TODAY!!

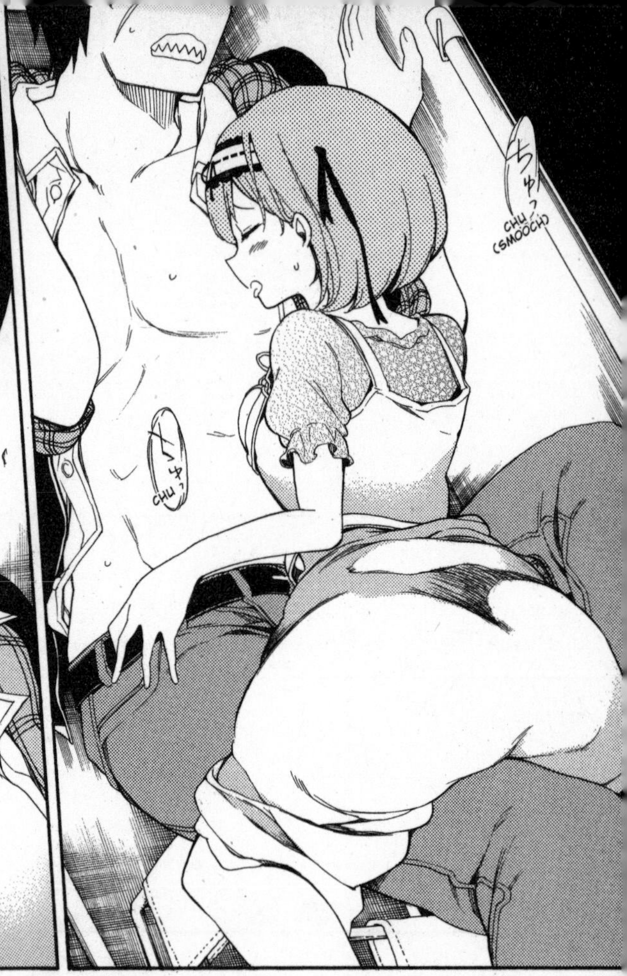
CHU (SMOOCH)
CHU

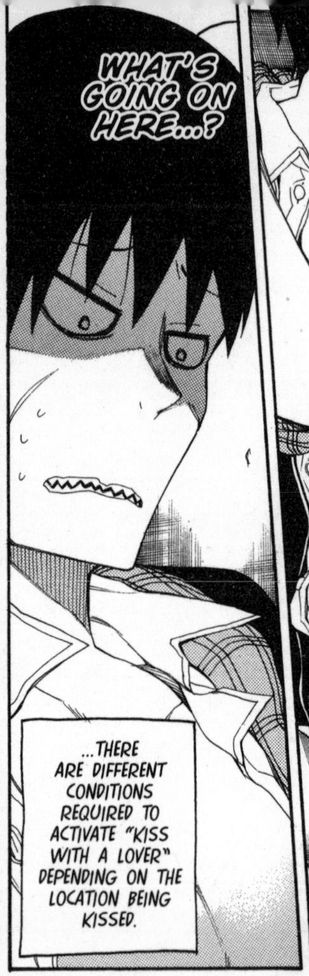
WHAT'S GOING ON HERE...?
...THERE ARE DIFFERENT CONDITIONS REQUIRED TO ACTIVATE "KISS WITH A LOVER" DEPENDING ON THE LOCATION BEING KISSED.

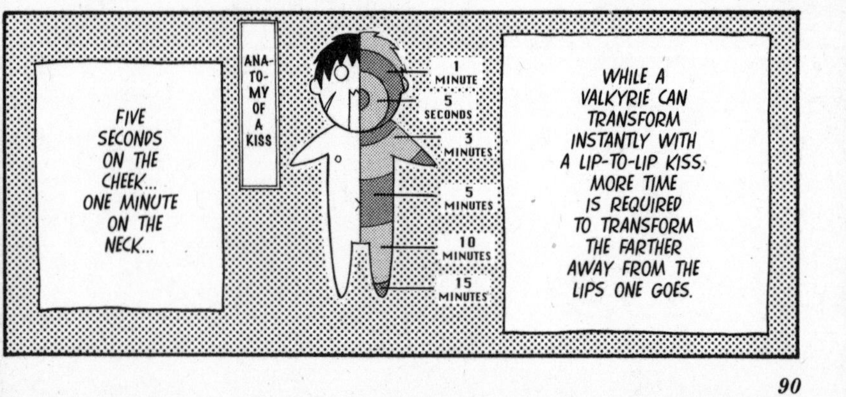
WHILE A VALKYRIE CAN TRANSFORM INSTANTLY WITH A LIP-TO-LIP KISS, MORE TIME IS REQUIRED TO TRANSFORM THE FARTHER AWAY FROM THE LIPS ONE GOES.
1 MINUTE
5 SECONDS
3 MINUTES
5 MINUTES
10 MINUTES
15 MINUTES
ANATOMY OF A KISS
FIVE SECONDS ON THE CHEEK... ONE MINUTE ON THE NECK...

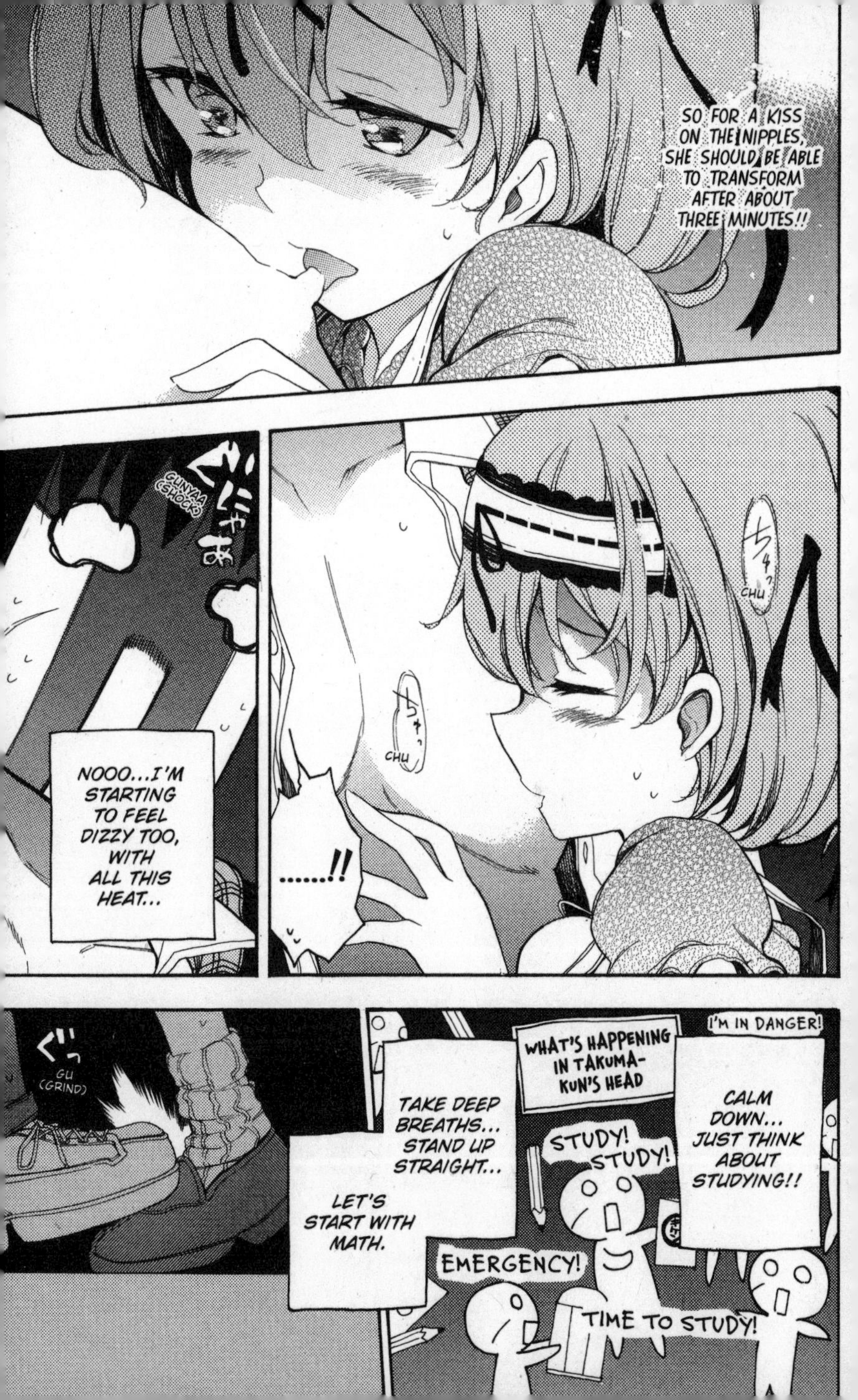
SO FOR A KISS ON THE NIPPLES, SHE SHOULD BE ABLE TO TRANSFORM AFTER ABOUT THREE MINUTES!!
CHU
CHU
......!!
GUNYAA (SHOCK)
NOOO...I'M STARTING TO FEEL DIZZY TOO, WITH ALL THIS HEAT...
I'M IN DANGER!
WHAT'S HAPPENING IN TAKUMA-KUN'S HEAD
CALM DOWN... JUST THINK ABOUT STUDYING!!
TAKE DEEP BREATHS... STAND UP STRAIGHT...
STUDY! STUDY!
LET'S START WITH MATH.
EMERGENCY!
TIME TO STUDY!
GU (GRIND)

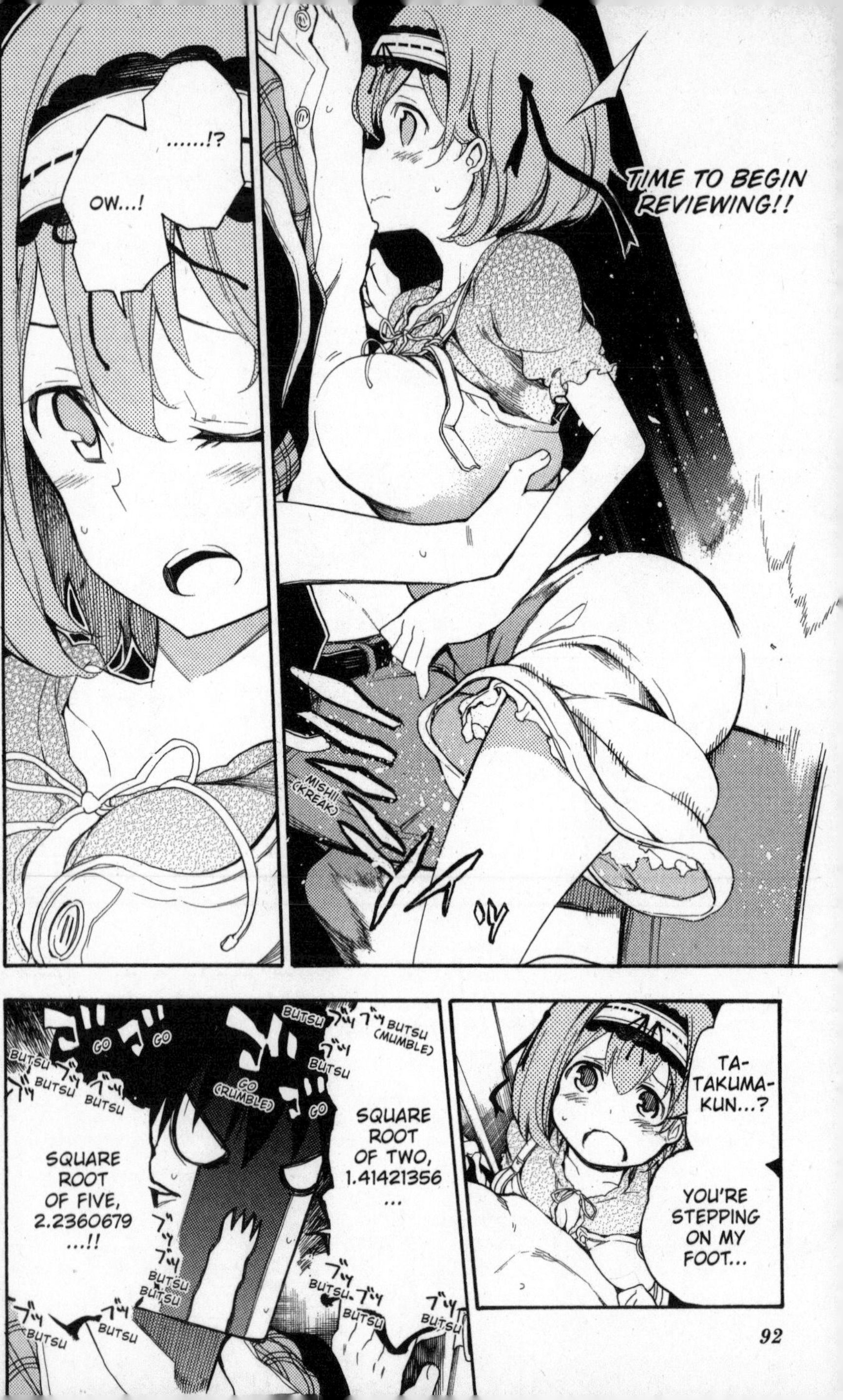

TIME TO BEGIN REVIEWING!!
MISHI! (KREAK)
......!?
OW...!
TA-TAKUMA-KUN...?
YOU'RE STEPPING ON MY FOOT...
BUTSU
BUTSU (MUMBLE)
BUTSU
GO
GO
GO (RUMBLE)
GO
BUTSU
BUTSU
BUTSU
SQUARE ROOT OF TWO, 1.41421356 ...
SQUARE ROOT OF FIVE, 2.2360679 ...!!
BUTSU
BUTSU
BUTSU
BUTSU
BUTSU
BUTSU
BUTSU

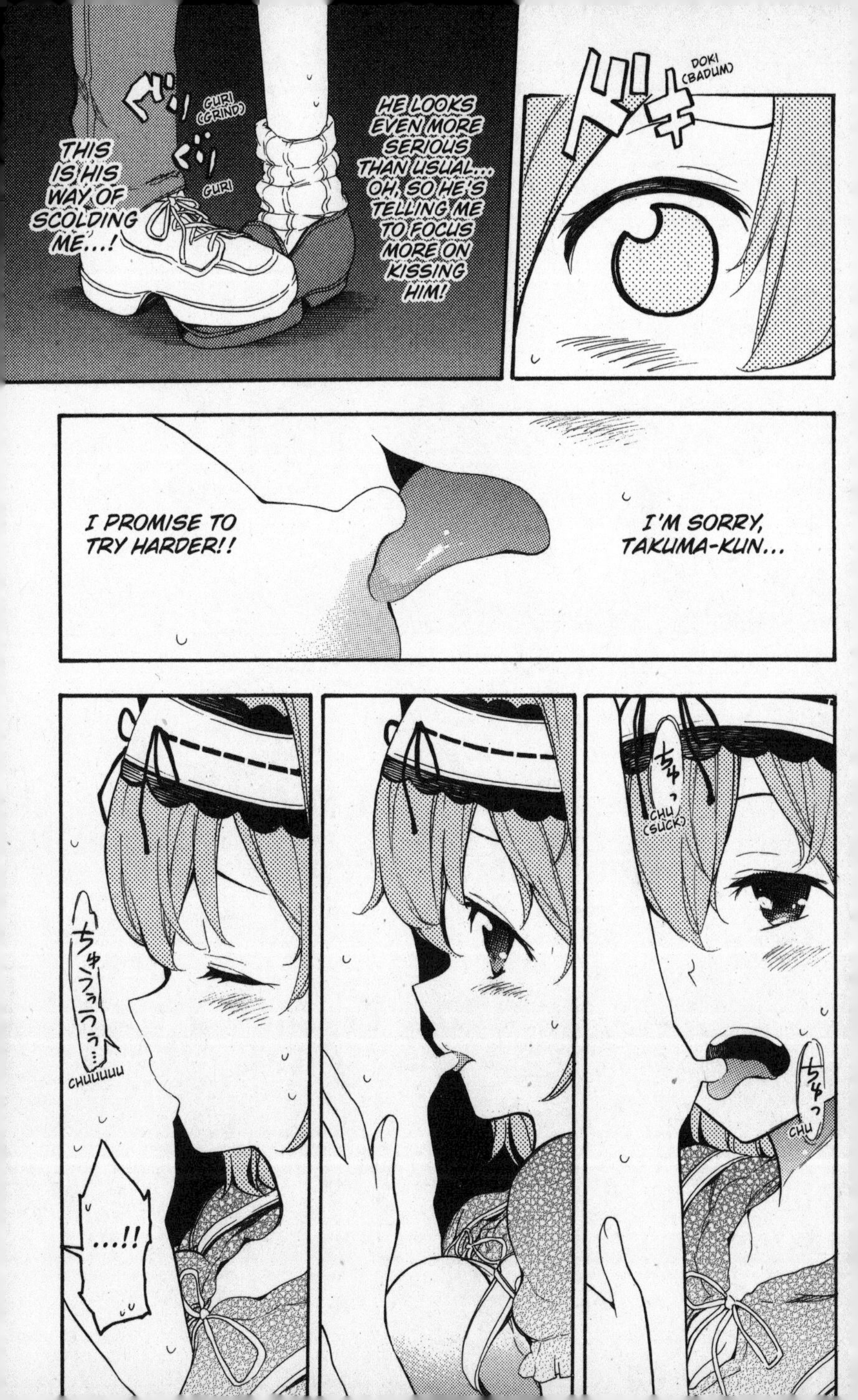
ドキ
DOKI (BADUM)
HE LOOKS EVEN MORE SERIOUS THAN USUAL... OH, SO HE'S TELLING ME TO FOCUS MORE ON KISSING HIM!
ぐり
GURI (GRIND)
ぐり
GURI
THIS IS HIS WAY OF SCOLDING ME...!
I'M SORRY, TAKUMA-KUN...
I PROMISE TO TRY HARDER!!
ちゅっ
CHU (SUCK)
ちゅっ
CHU
ちゅううう…
CHUUUUUU
...!!

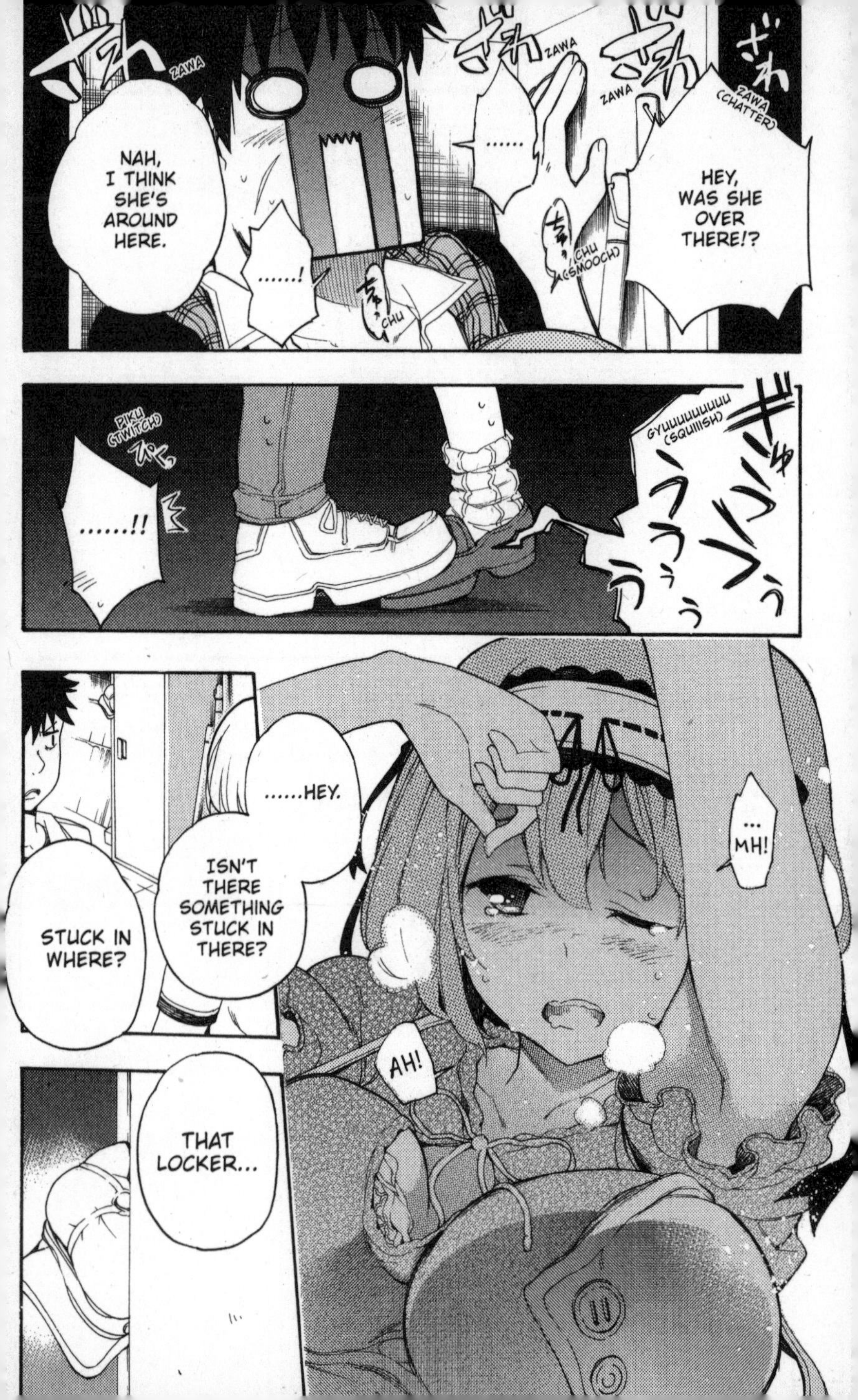
ZAWA (CHATTER)
HEY, WAS SHE OVER THERE!?
ZAWA
ZAWA
CHU (SMOOCH)
......
ZAWA
NAH, I THINK SHE'S AROUND HERE.
......!
CHU
GYUUUUUUUUU (SQUIIISH)
......!!
PIKU (TWITCH)
...MH!
......HEY.
ISN'T THERE SOMETHING STUCK IN THERE?
STUCK IN WHERE?
AH!
THAT LOCKER...

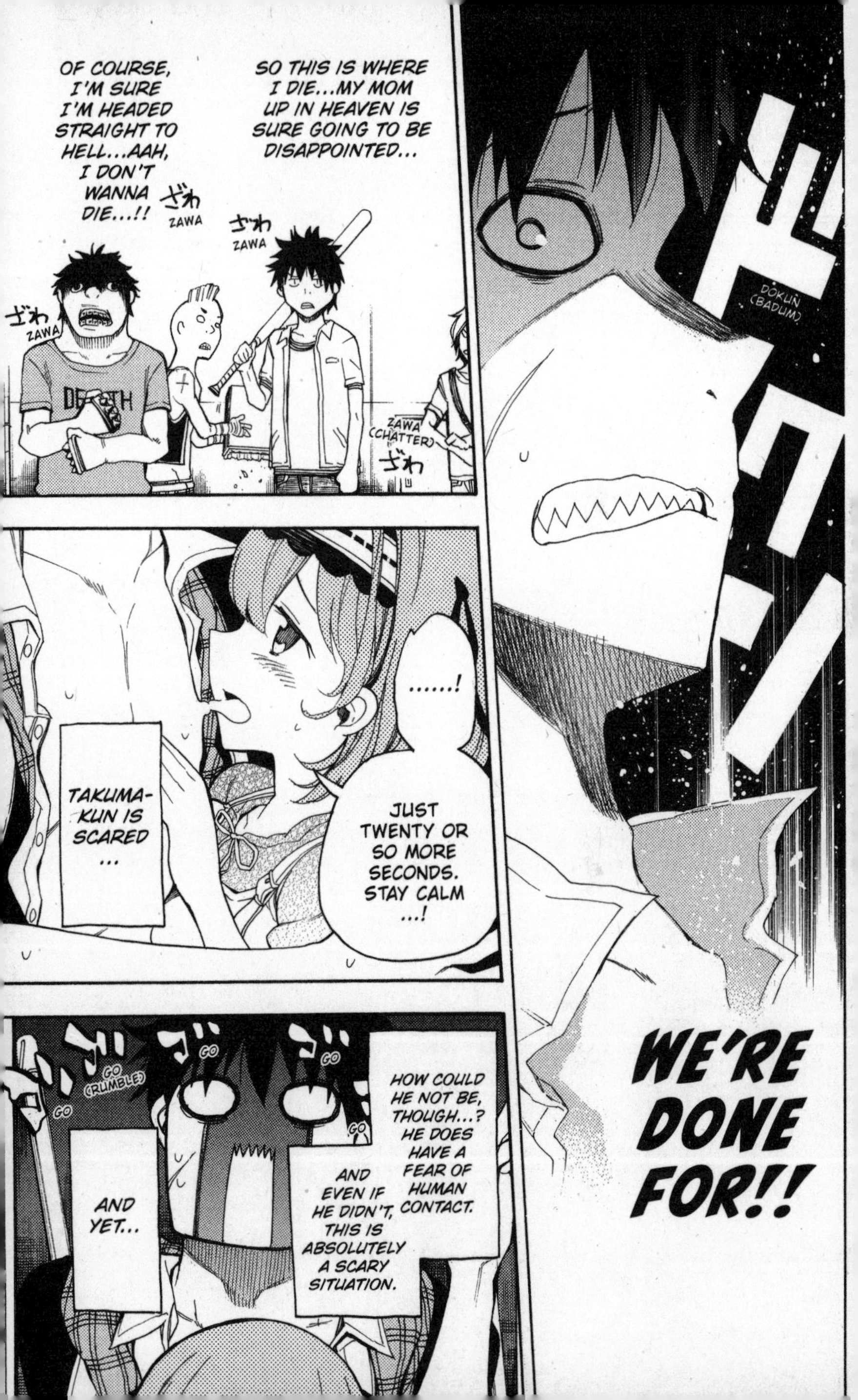
ドクン
DOKUN (BADUM)
WE'RE DONE FOR!!
SO THIS IS WHERE I DIE...MY MOM UP IN HEAVEN IS SURE GOING TO BE DISAPPOINTED...
OF COURSE, I'M SURE I'M HEADED STRAIGHT TO HELL...AAH, I DON'T WANNA DIE...!!
ざわ ZAWA
ざわ ZAWA
ざわ ZAWA
ZAWA (CHATTER) ざわ
......!
JUST TWENTY OR SO MORE SECONDS. STAY CALM ...!
TAKUMA-KUN IS SCARED ...
GO GO GO GO (RUMBLE)
HOW COULD HE NOT BE, THOUGH...? HE DOES HAVE A FEAR OF HUMAN CONTACT.
AND EVEN IF HE DIDN'T, THIS IS ABSOLUTELY A SCARY SITUATION.
AND YET...

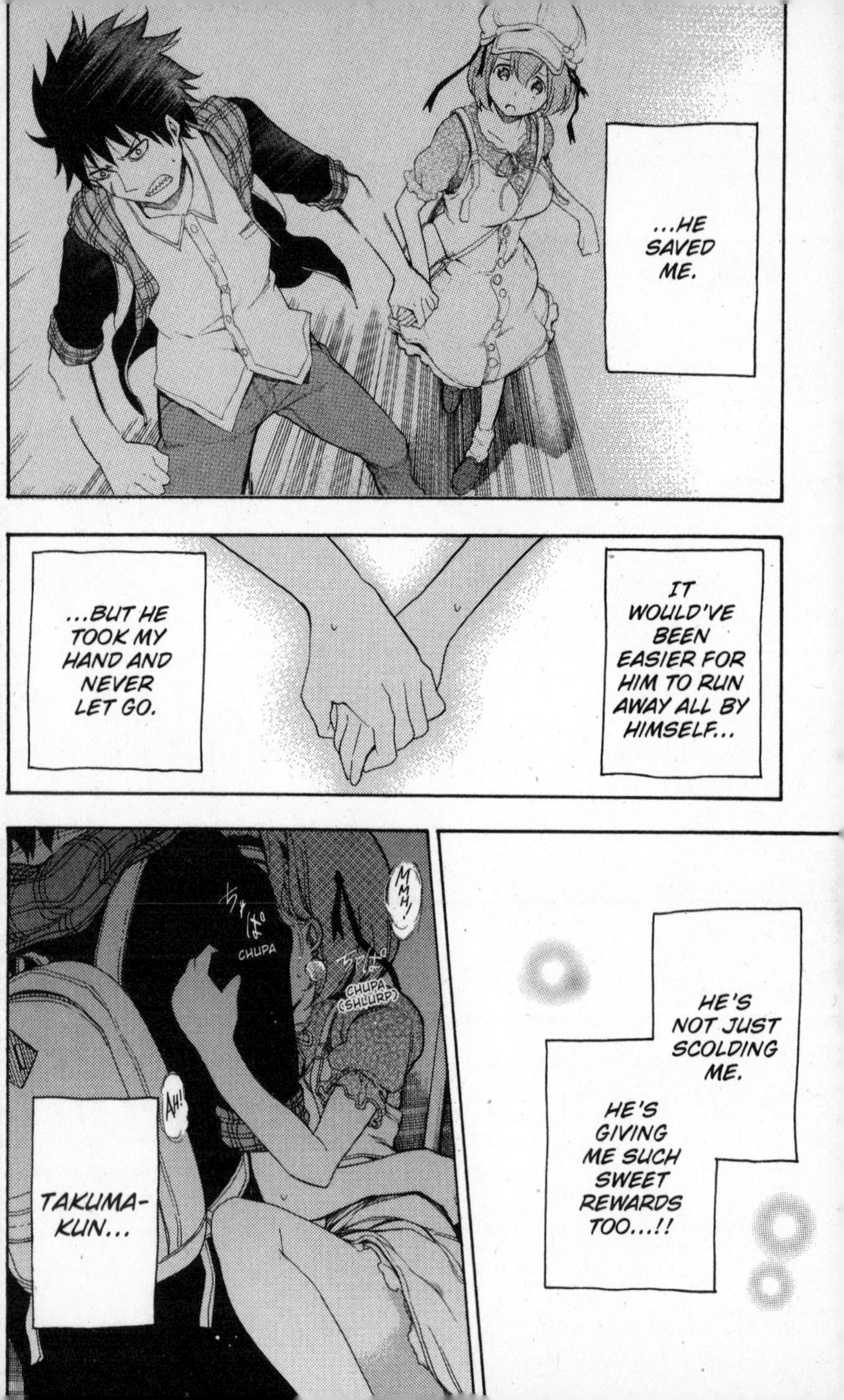
...HE SAVED ME.
IT WOULD'VE BEEN EASIER FOR HIM TO RUN AWAY ALL BY HIMSELF...
...BUT HE TOOK MY HAND AND NEVER LET GO.
HE'S NOT JUST SCOLDING ME.
HE'S GIVING ME SUCH SWEET REWARDS TOO...!!
MMH!
ちゅぱ
CHUPA
ちゅぱ
CHUPA (SHLURP)
AH!
TAKUMA-KUN...

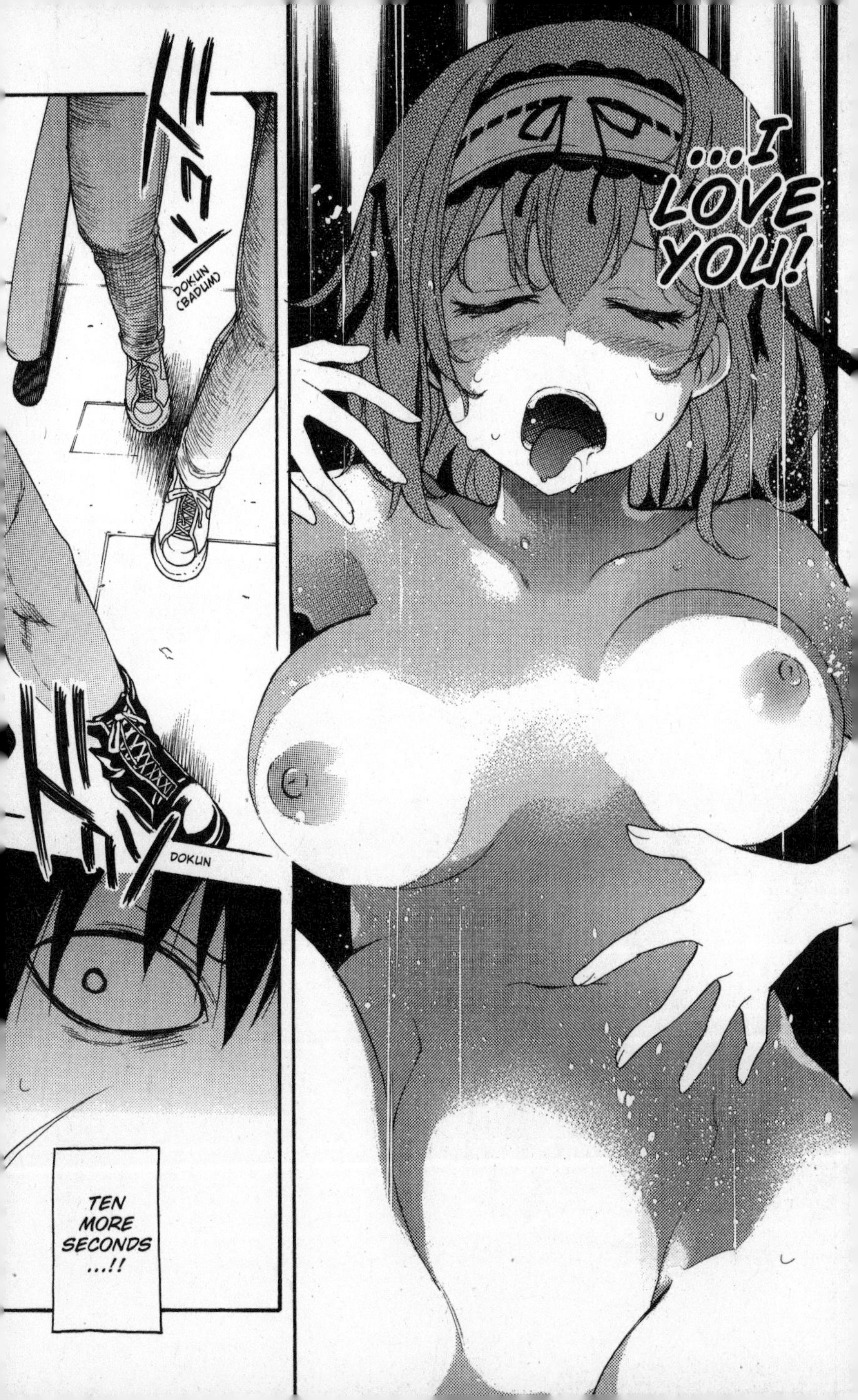
...I LOVE YOU!
DOKUN (BADUM)
DOKUN
TEN MORE SECONDS ...!!

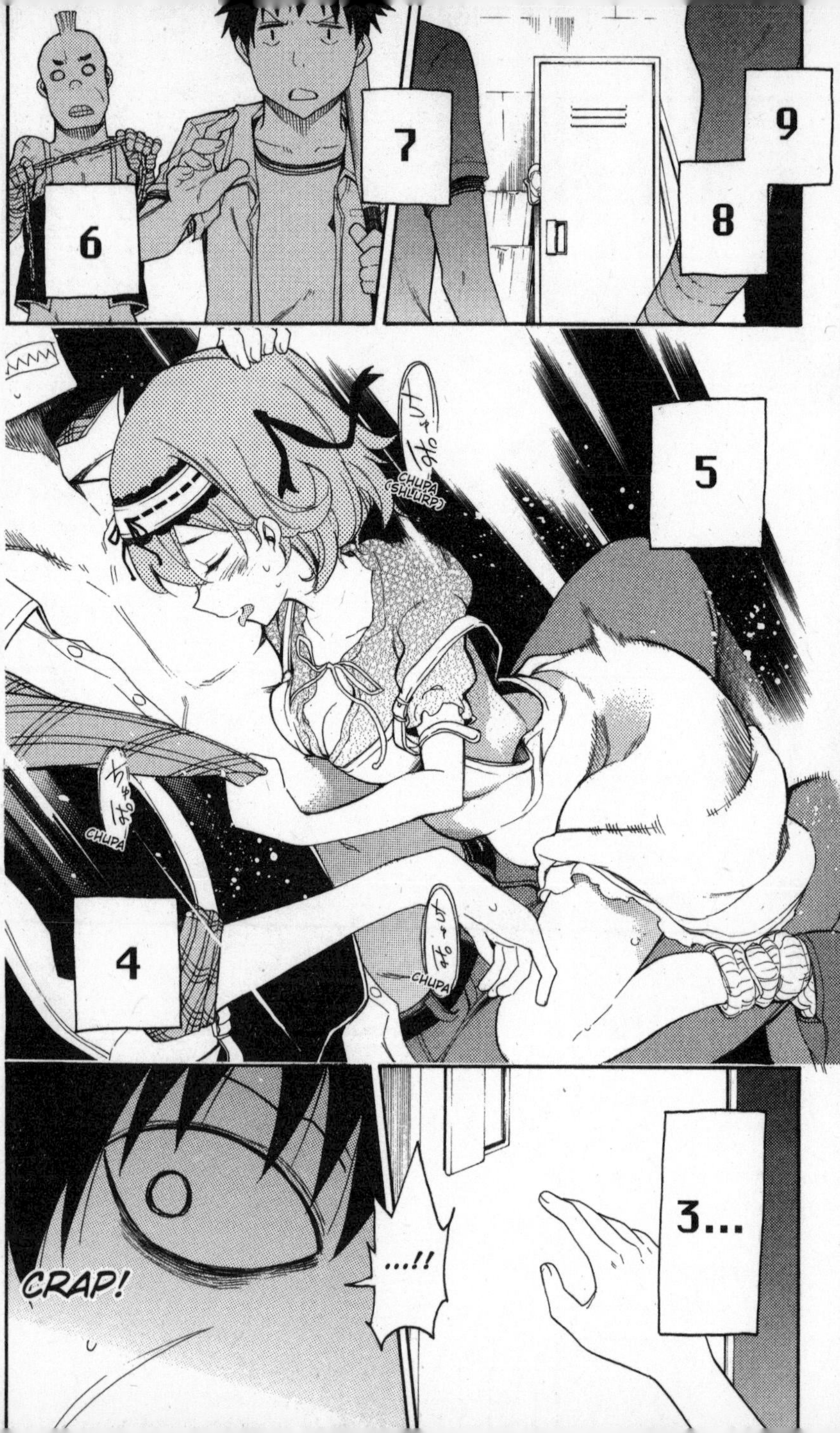

9
8
7
6
5
CHUPA (SHLURP)
CHUPA
4
CHUPA
3...
...!!
CRAP!

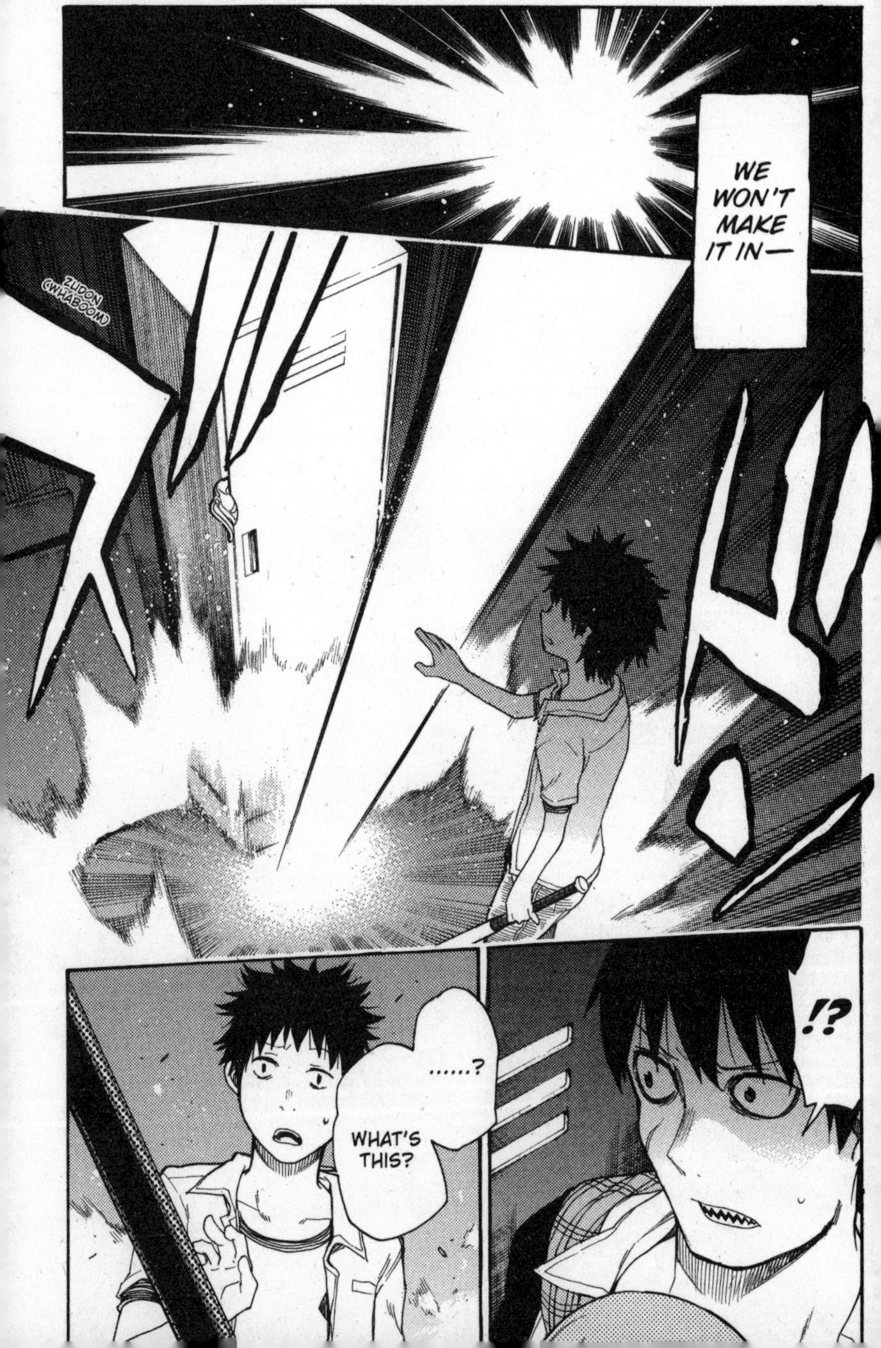
WE WON'T MAKE IT IN—
ZUDON (WHABOOM)
!?
......?
WHAT'S THIS?

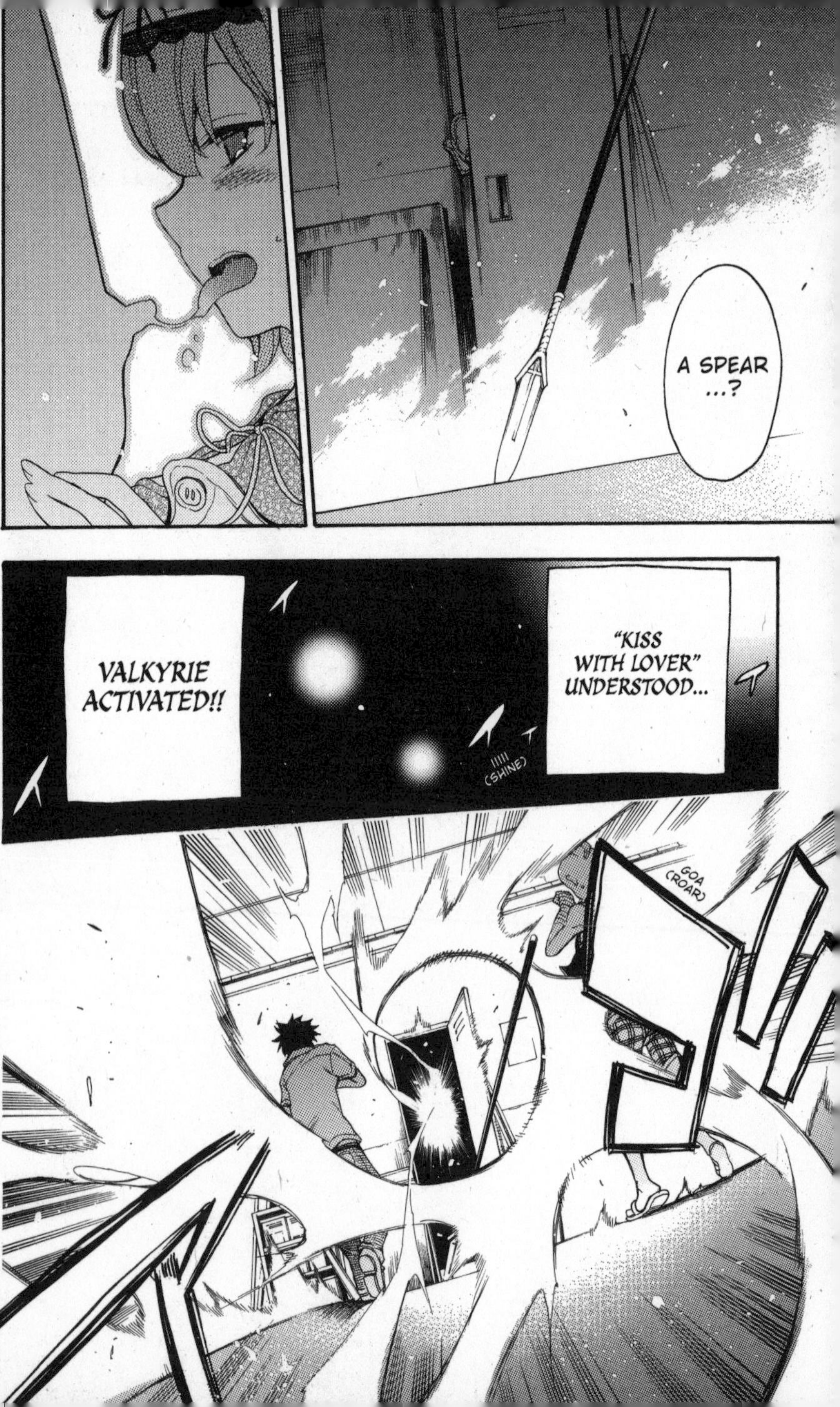
A SPEAR ...?
"KISS WITH LOVER" UNDERSTOOD...
IIIII (SHINE)
VALKYRIE ACTIVATED!!
GOA (ROAR)

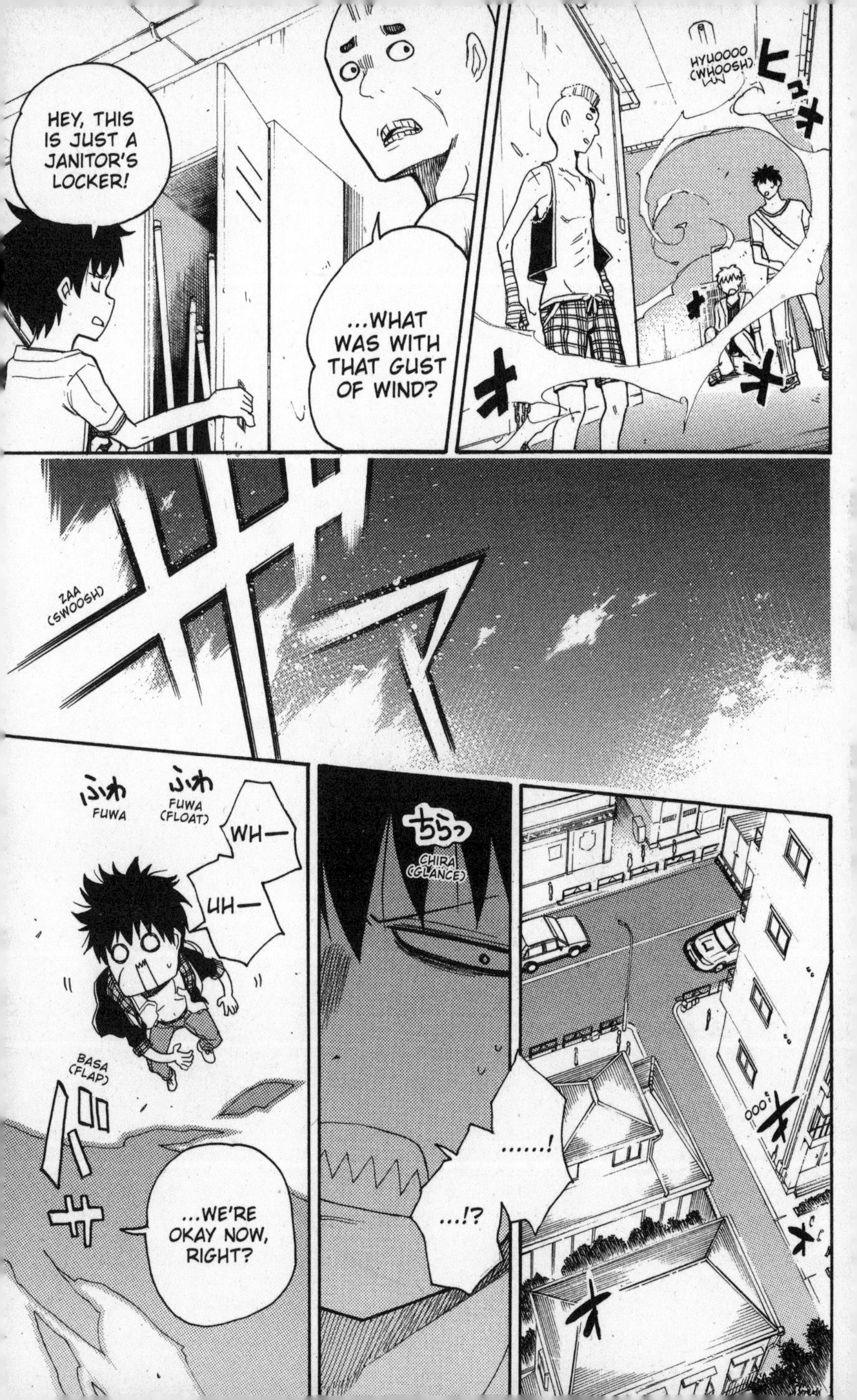
HYUOOOO (WHOOSH)
...WHAT WAS WITH THAT GUST OF WIND?
HEY, THIS IS JUST A JANITOR'S LOCKER!
ZAA (SWOOSH)
......!
ちらっ
CHIRA (GLANCE)
...!?
ふわ
FUWA (FLOAT)
ふわ
FUWA
WH—
UH—
BASA (FLAP)
...WE'RE OKAY NOW, RIGHT?

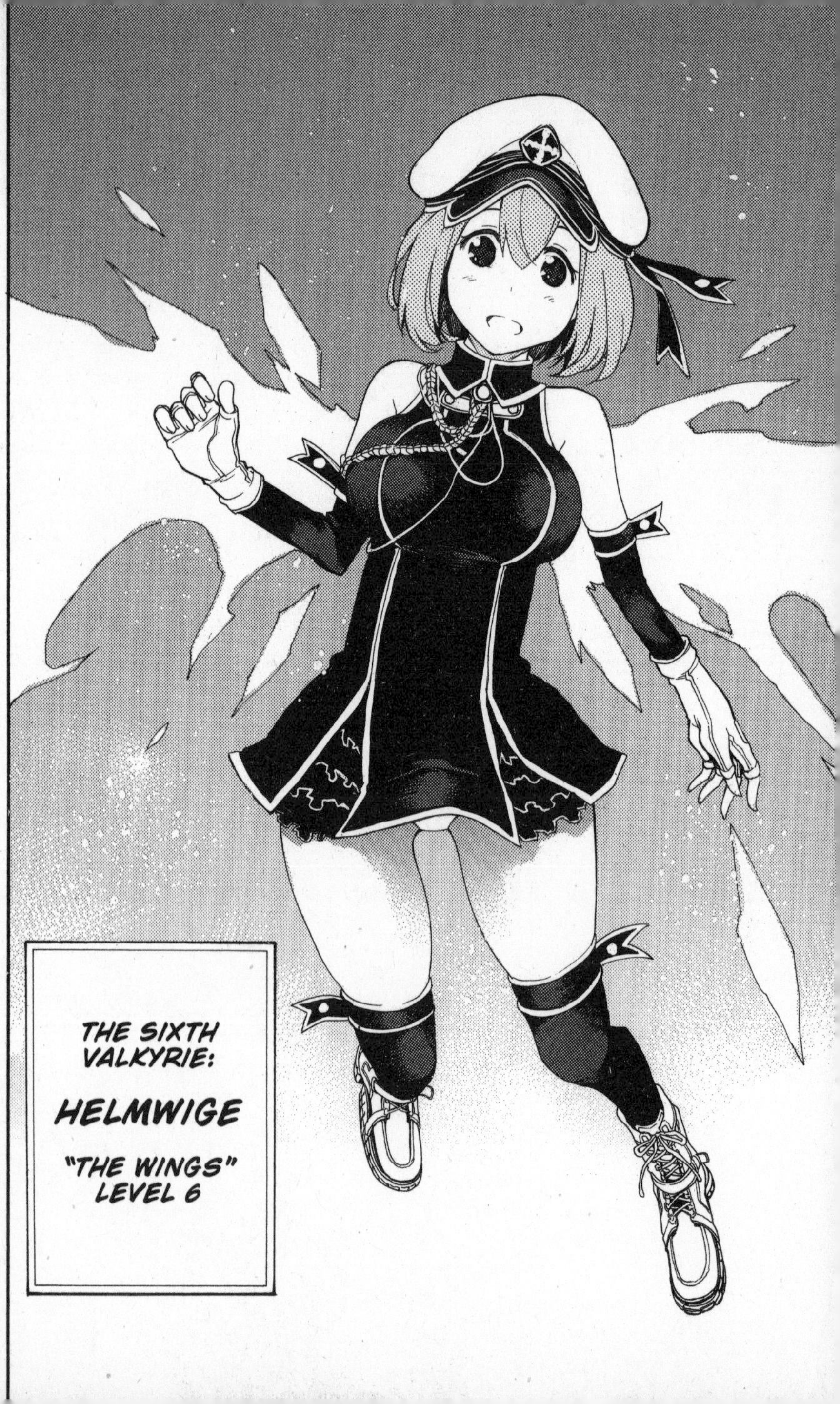
THE SIXTH VALKYRIE:
HELMWIGE
"THE WINGS" LEVEL 6

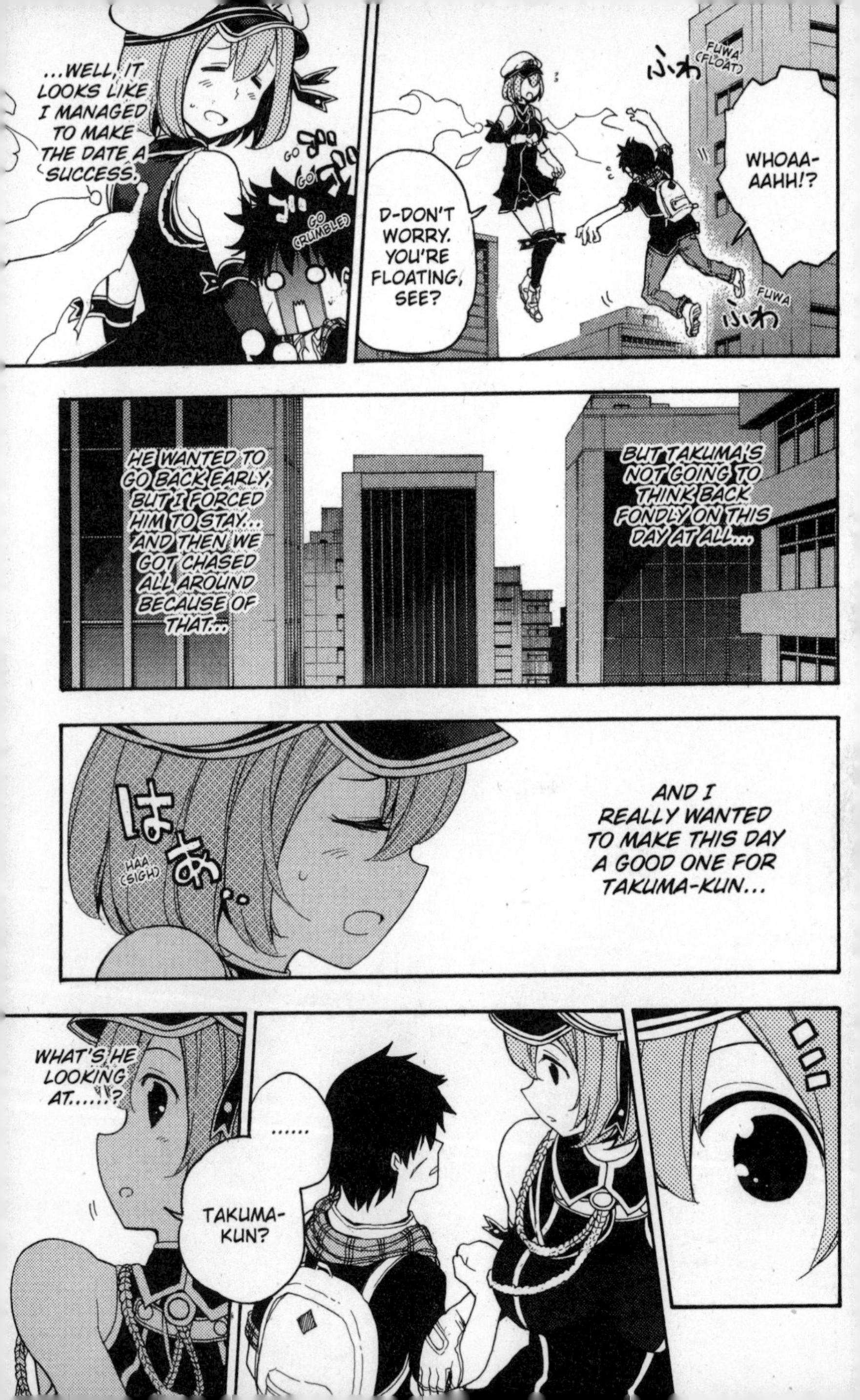
ふわ
FUWA (FLOAT)
WHOAA-AAHH!?
D-DON'T WORRY. YOU'RE FLOATING, SEE?
ふわ
FUWA
...WELL, IT LOOKS LIKE I MANAGED TO MAKE THE DATE A SUCCESS.
ゴゴゴ
GO GO GO (RUMBLE)
HE WANTED TO GO BACK EARLY, BUT I FORCED HIM TO STAY... AND THEN WE GOT CHASED ALL AROUND BECAUSE OF THAT...
BUT TAKUMA'S NOT GOING TO THINK BACK FONDLY ON THIS DAY AT ALL...
AND I REALLY WANTED TO MAKE THIS DAY A GOOD ONE FOR TAKUMA-KUN...
はぁ。。
HAA (SIGH)
......
TAKUMA-KUN?
WHAT'S HE LOOKING AT......?

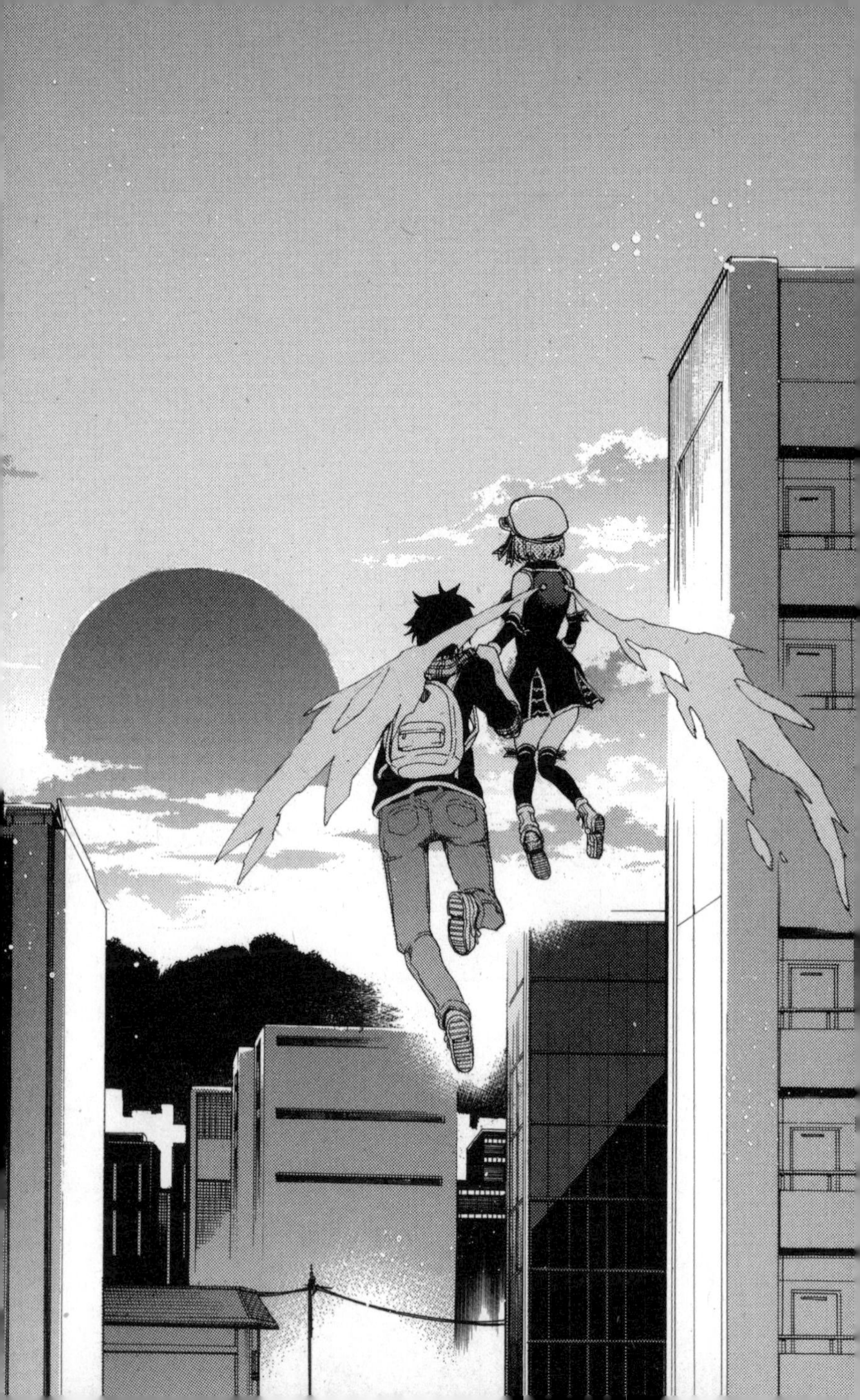

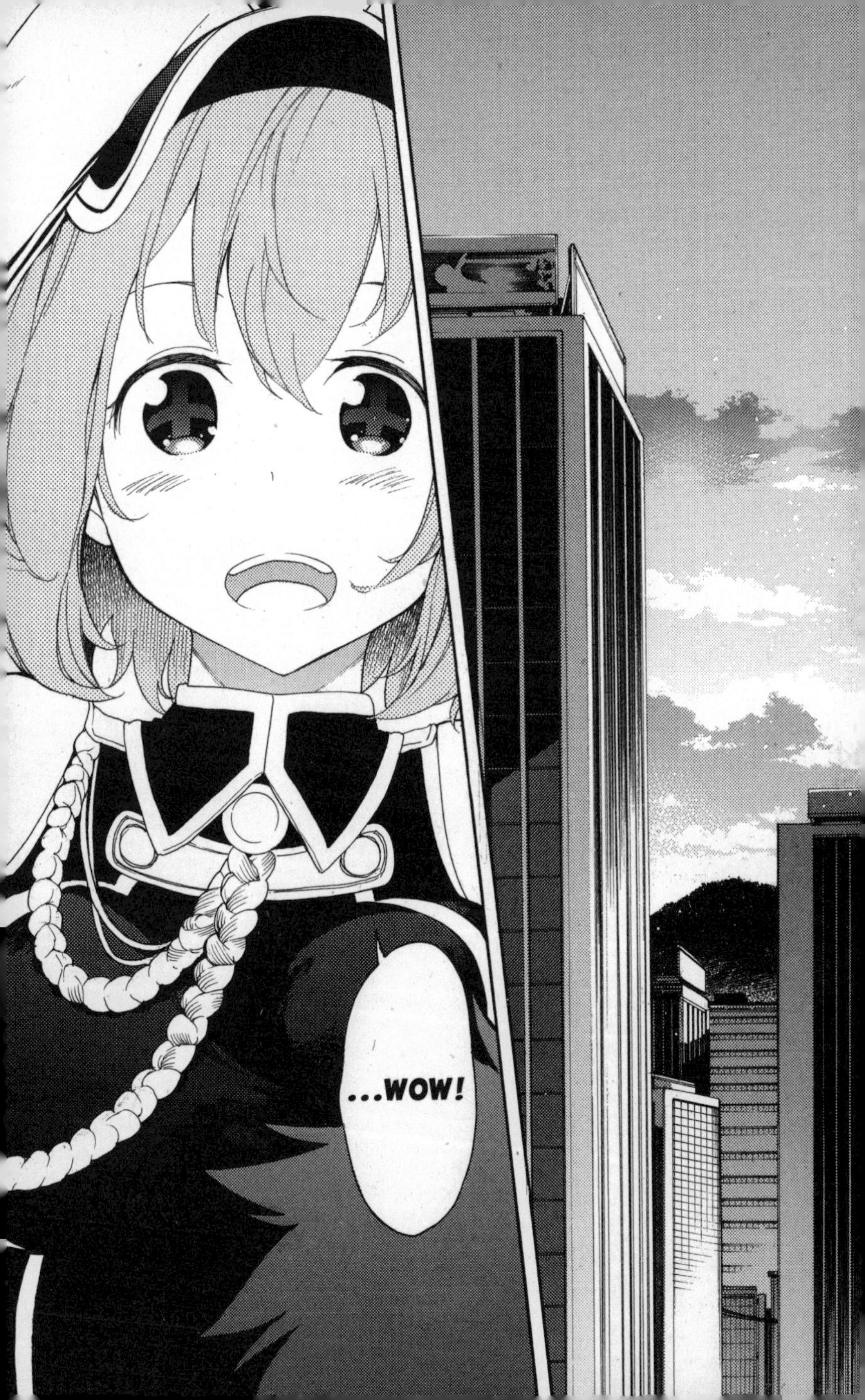
...WOW!

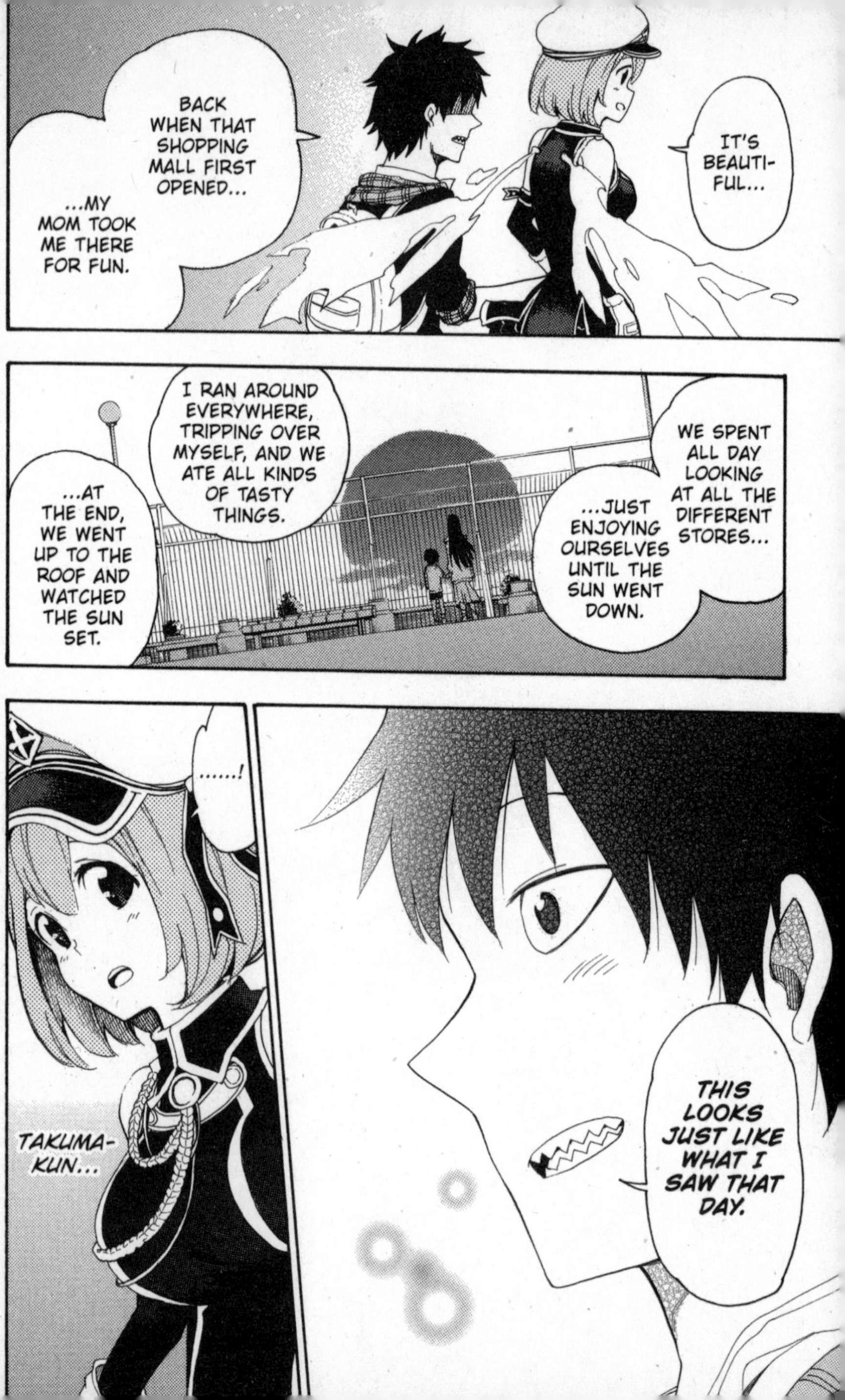
IT'S BEAUTIFUL...
BACK WHEN THAT SHOPPING MALL FIRST OPENED...
...MY MOM TOOK ME THERE FOR FUN.
WE SPENT ALL DAY LOOKING AT ALL THE DIFFERENT STORES...
...JUST ENJOYING OURSELVES UNTIL THE SUN WENT DOWN.
I RAN AROUND EVERYWHERE, TRIPPING OVER MYSELF, AND WE ATE ALL KINDS OF TASTY THINGS.
...AT THE END, WE WENT UP TO THE ROOF AND WATCHED THE SUN SET.
THIS LOOKS JUST LIKE WHAT I SAW THAT DAY.
......!
TAKUMA-KUN...

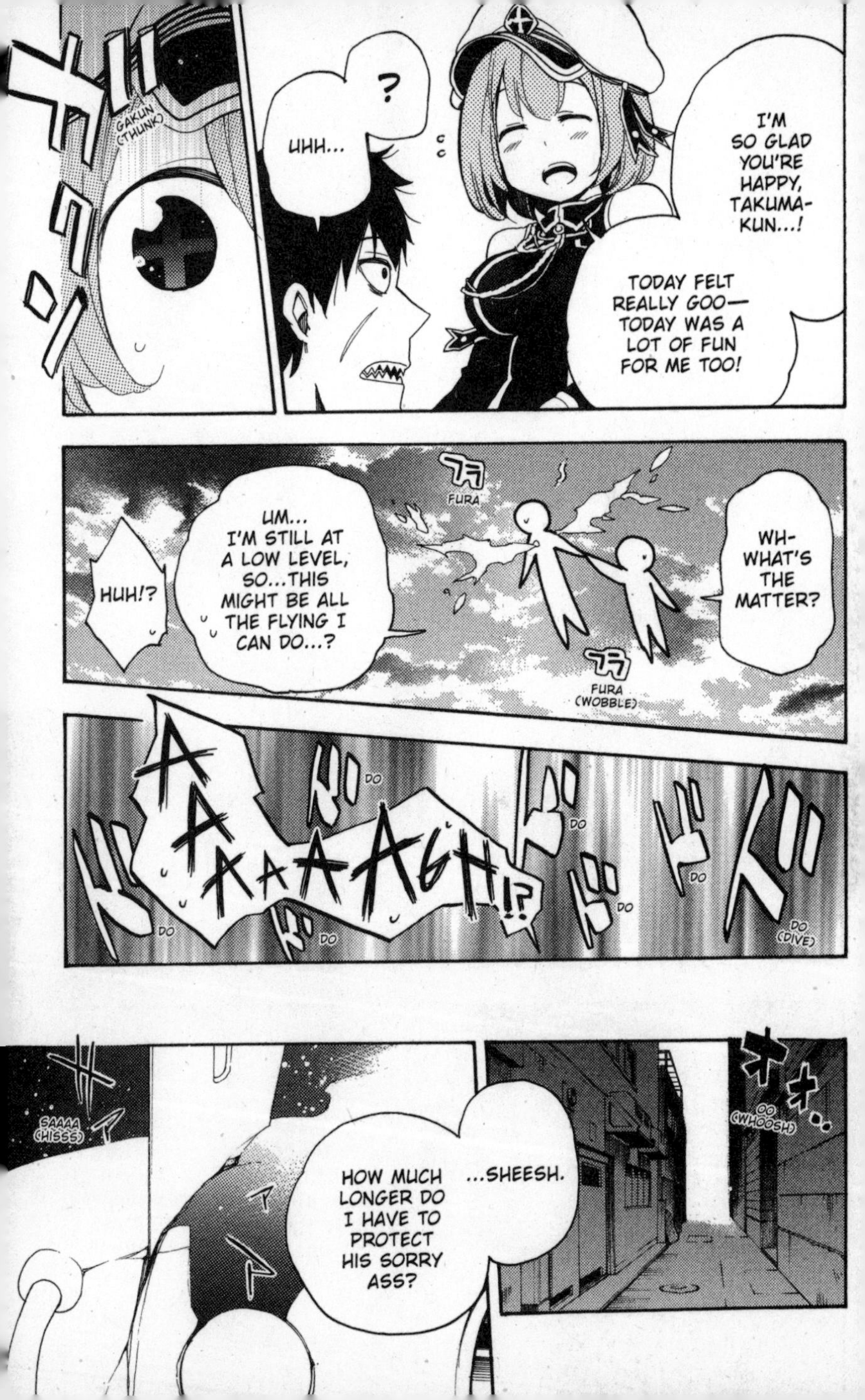
I'M SO GLAD YOU'RE HAPPY, TAKUMA-KUN...!
TODAY FELT REALLY GOO— TODAY WAS A LOT OF FUN FOR ME TOO!
?
UHH...
GAKUN (THUNK)
WH- WHAT'S THE MATTER?
FURA
FURA (WOBBLE)
UM... I'M STILL AT A LOW LEVEL, SO...THIS MIGHT BE ALL THE FLYING I CAN DO...?
HUH!?
DO (DIVE)
DO
DO
DO
AAAAAAGH!!?
DO
DO
DO
OO (WHOOSH)
...SHEESH.
HOW MUCH LONGER DO I HAVE TO PROTECT HIS SORRY ASS?
SAAAA (HISSS)

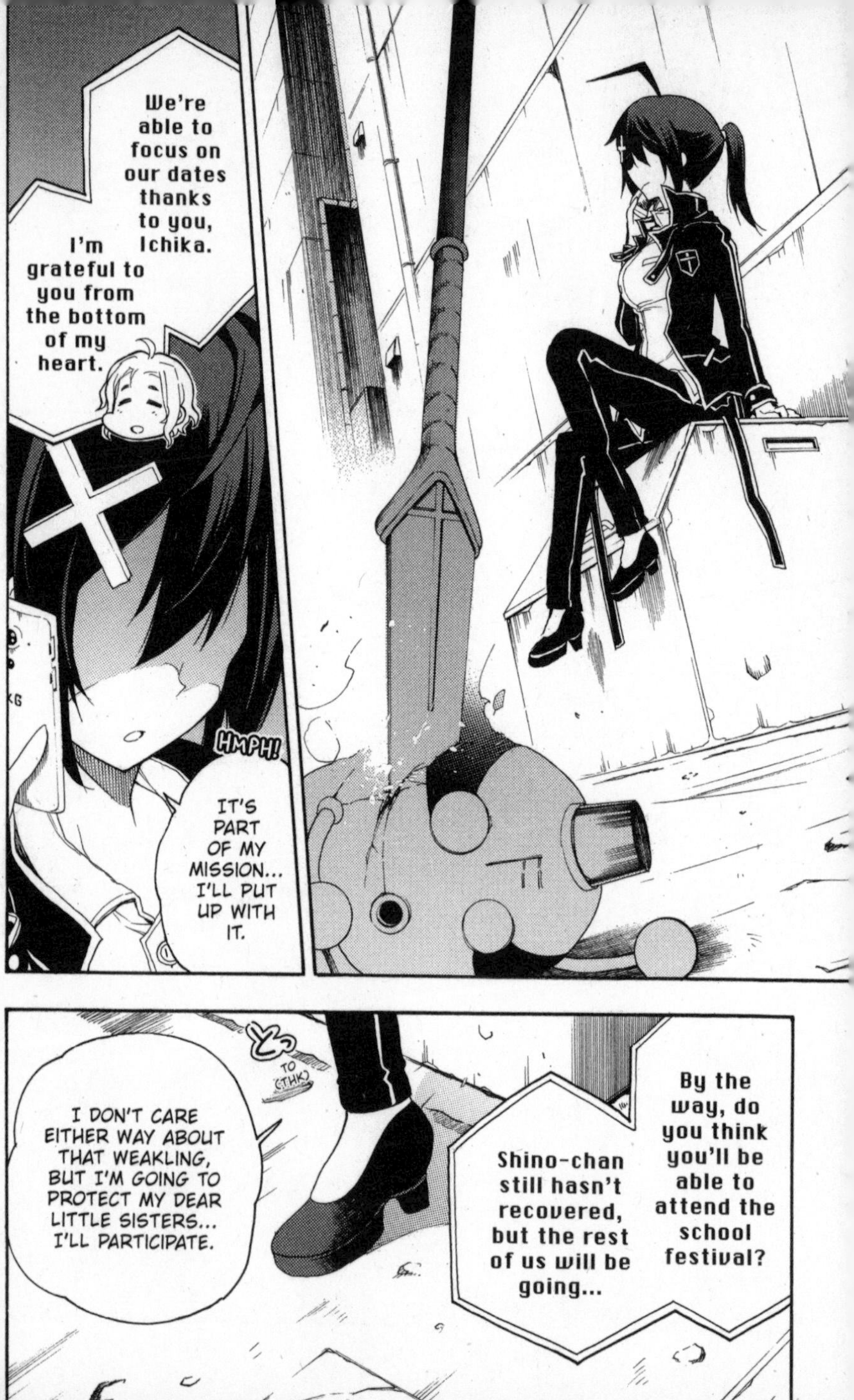
We're able to focus on our dates thanks to you, Ichika.
I'm grateful to you from the bottom of my heart.
HMPH!
IT'S PART OF MY MISSION... I'LL PUT UP WITH IT.
By the way, do you think you'll be able to attend the school festival?
Shino-chan still hasn't recovered, but the rest of us will be going...
TO (THK)
I DON'T CARE EITHER WAY ABOUT THAT WEAKLING, BUT I'M GOING TO PROTECT MY DEAR LITTLE SISTERS... I'LL PARTICIPATE.

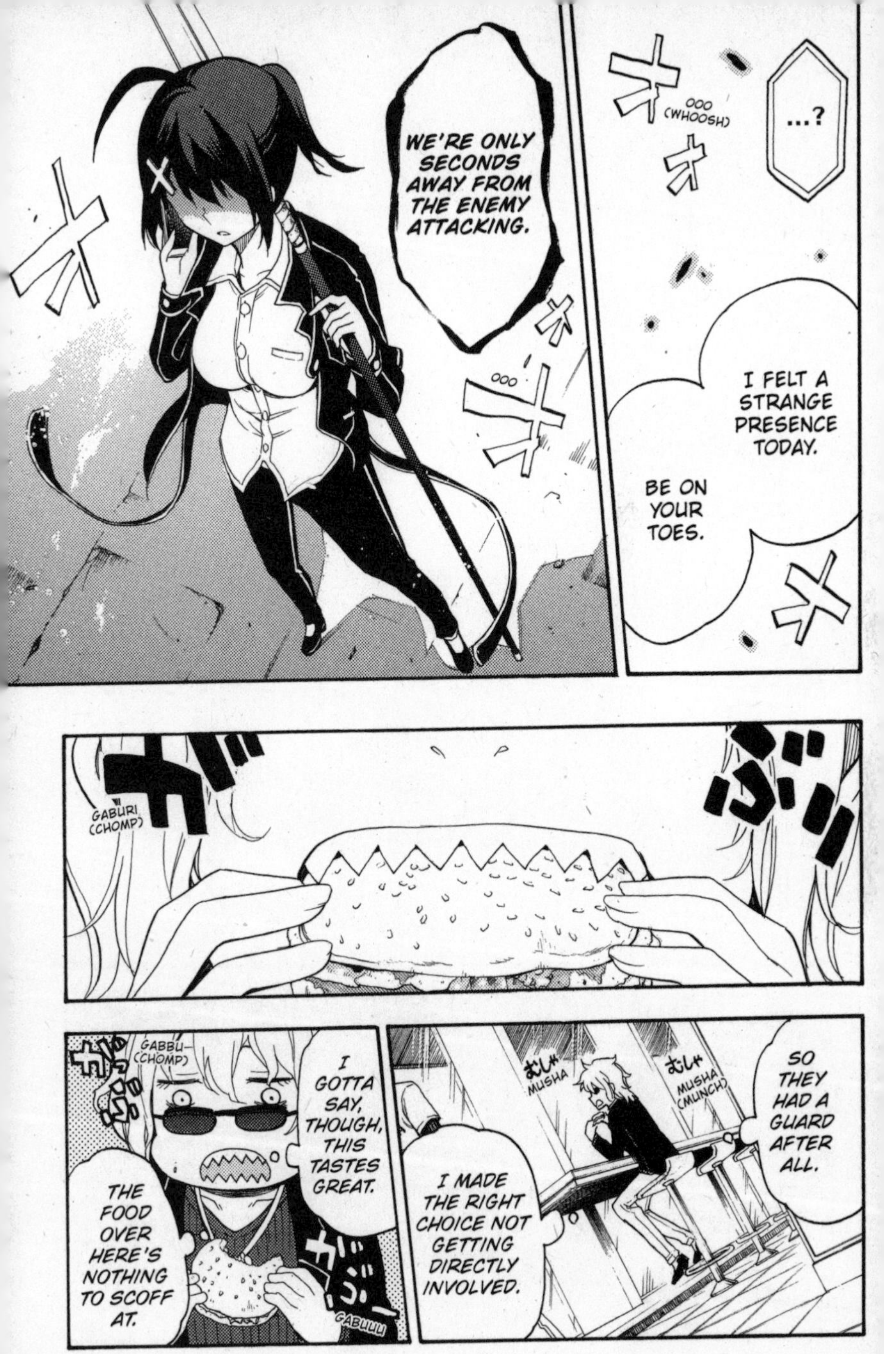
...?
OOO (WHOOSH)
I FELT A STRANGE PRESENCE TODAY.
BE ON YOUR TOES.
WE'RE ONLY SECONDS AWAY FROM THE ENEMY ATTACKING.
OOO
GABURI (CHOMP)
SO THEY HAD A GUARD AFTER ALL.
MUSHA (MUNCH)
MUSHA
I MADE THE RIGHT CHOICE NOT GETTING DIRECTLY INVOLVED.
GABBU (CHOMP)
I GOTTA SAY, THOUGH, THIS TASTES GREAT.
THE FOOD OVER HERE'S NOTHING TO SCOFF AT.
GABUUU

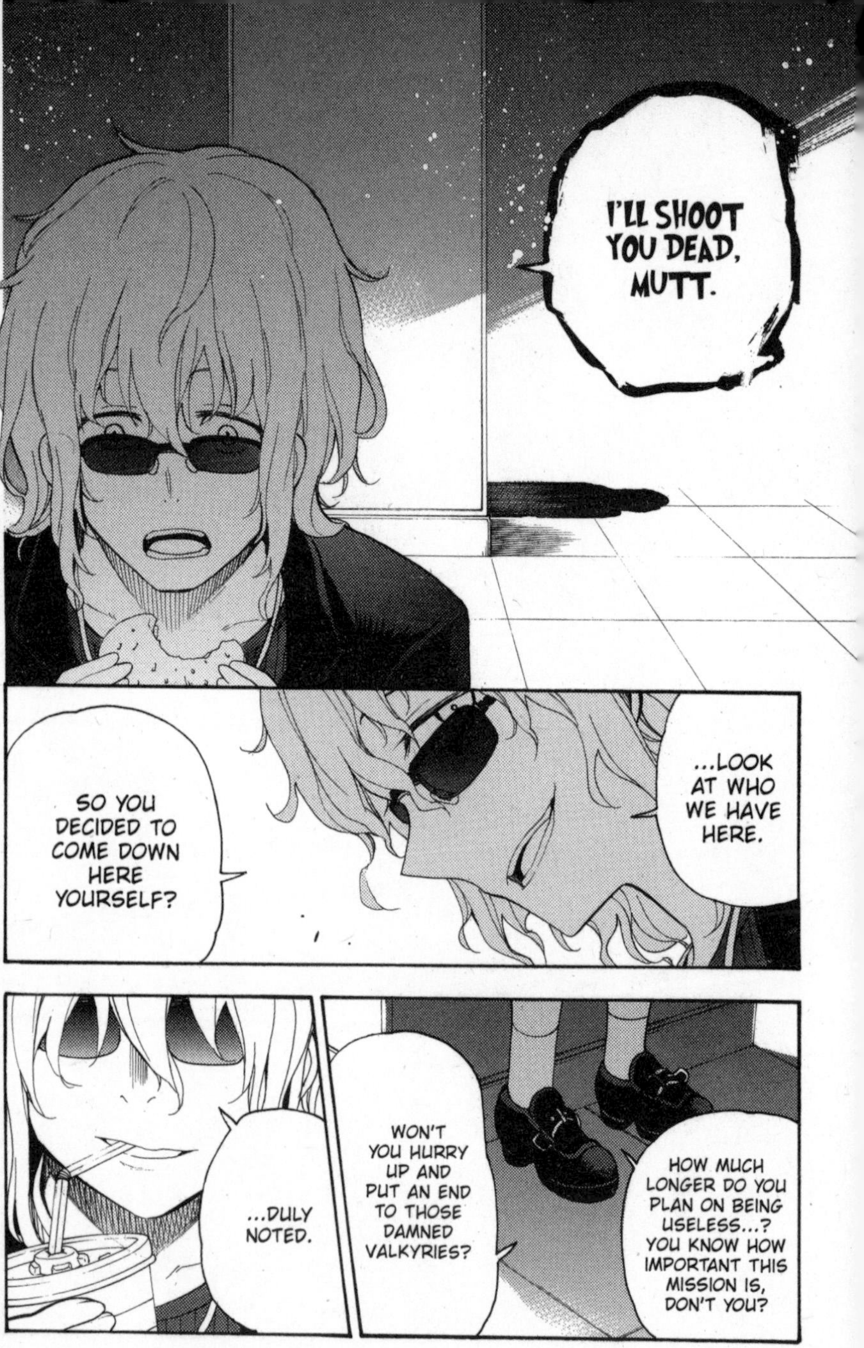
I'LL SHOOT YOU DEAD, MUTT.
...LOOK AT WHO WE HAVE HERE.
SO YOU DECIDED TO COME DOWN HERE YOURSELF?
HOW MUCH LONGER DO YOU PLAN ON BEING USELESS...? YOU KNOW HOW IMPORTANT THIS MISSION IS, DON'T YOU?
WON'T YOU HURRY UP AND PUT AN END TO THOSE DAMNED VALKYRIES?
...DULY NOTED.

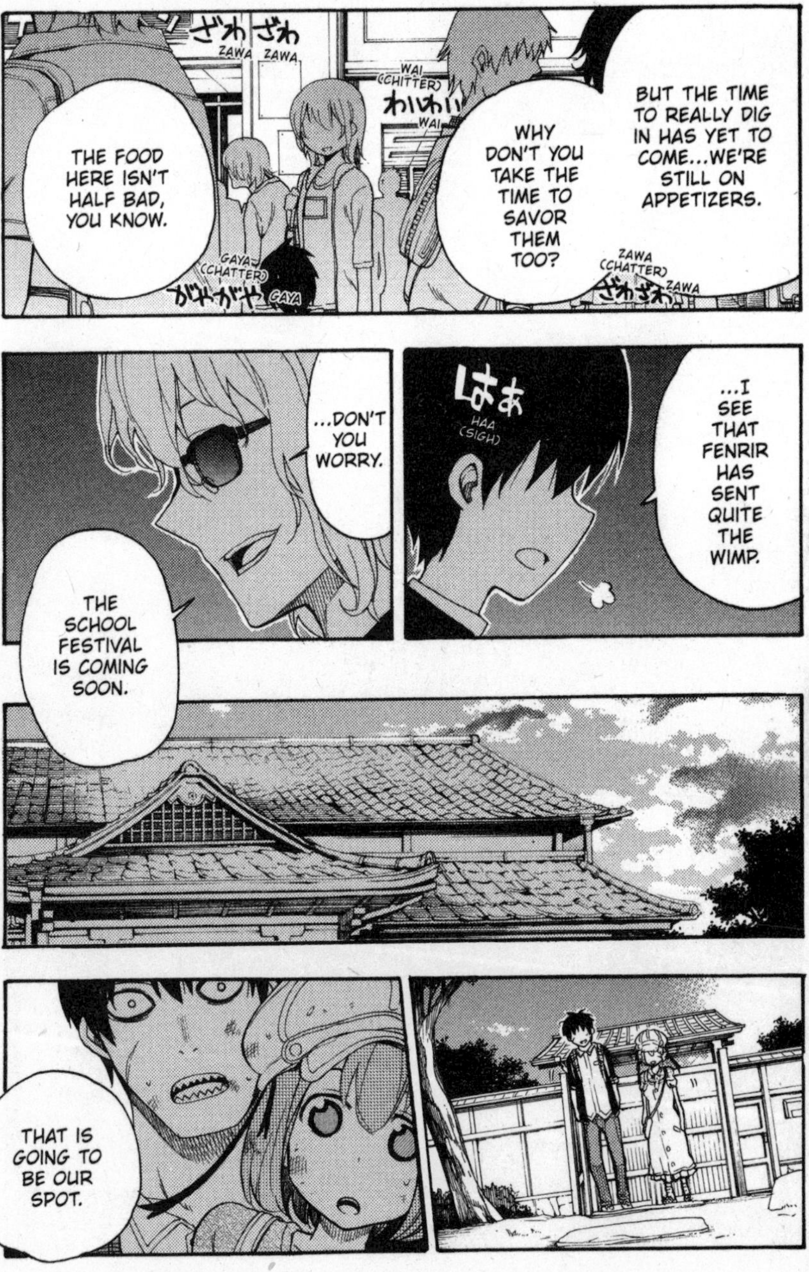
BUT THE TIME TO REALLY DIG IN HAS YET TO COME...WE'RE STILL ON APPETIZERS.
WAI (CHATTER) わいわい WAI
ざわざわ ZAWA ZAWA
WHY DON'T YOU TAKE THE TIME TO SAVOR THEM TOO?
ZAWA (CHATTER) ざわざわ ZAWA
THE FOOD HERE ISN'T HALF BAD, YOU KNOW.
GAYA (CHATTER) がやがや GAYA
...I SEE THAT FENRIR HAS SENT QUITE THE WIMP.
はあ HAA (SIGH)
...DON'T YOU WORRY.
THE SCHOOL FESTIVAL IS COMING SOON.
THAT IS GOING TO BE OUR SPOT.

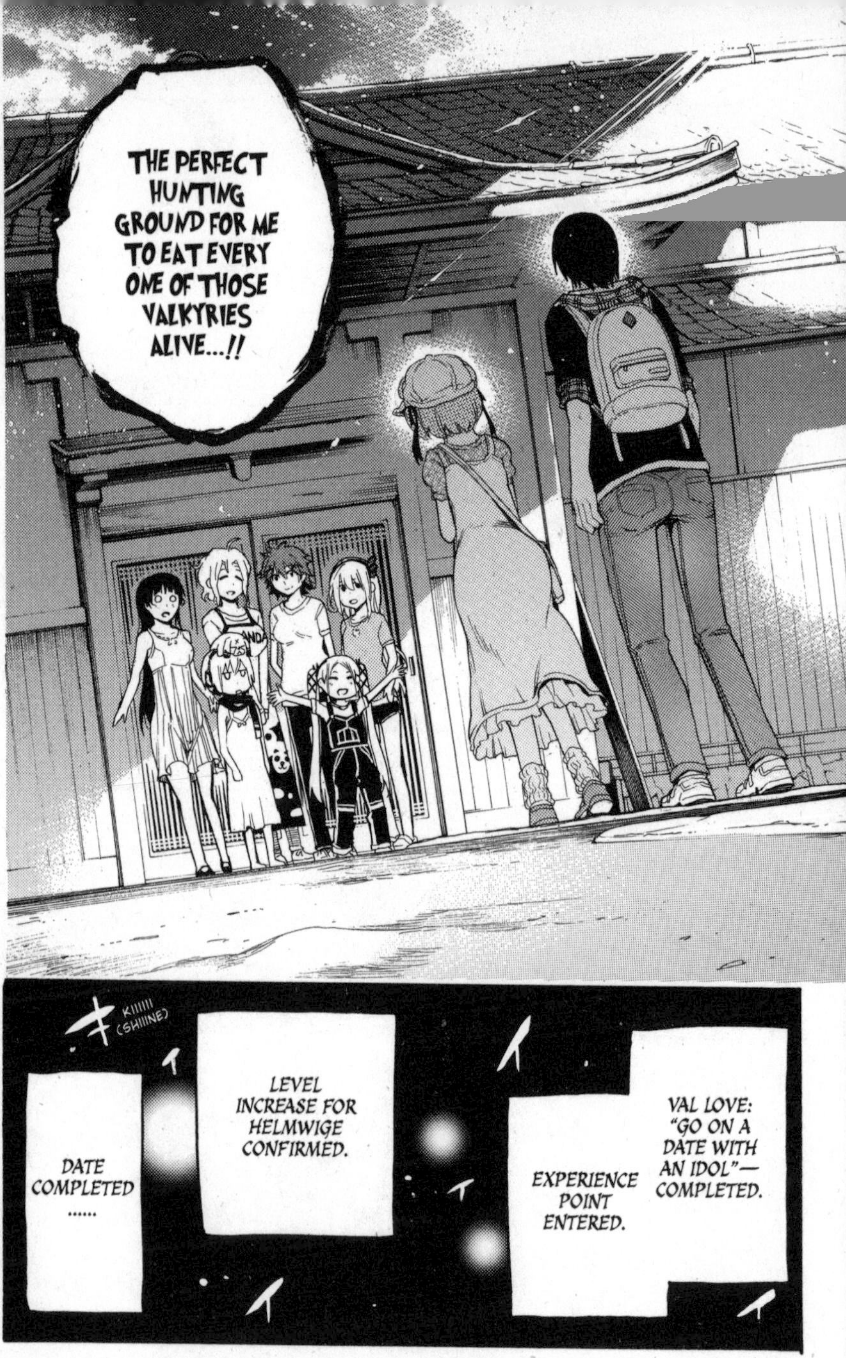
THE PERFECT HUNTING GROUND FOR ME TO EAT EVERY ONE OF THOSE VALKYRIES ALIVE...!!
VAL LOVE: "GO ON A DATE WITH AN IDOL"—COMPLETED.
EXPERIENCE POINT ENTERED.
LEVEL INCREASE FOR HELMWIGE CONFIRMED.
KIIIIII (SHIIINE)
DATE COMPLETED ......

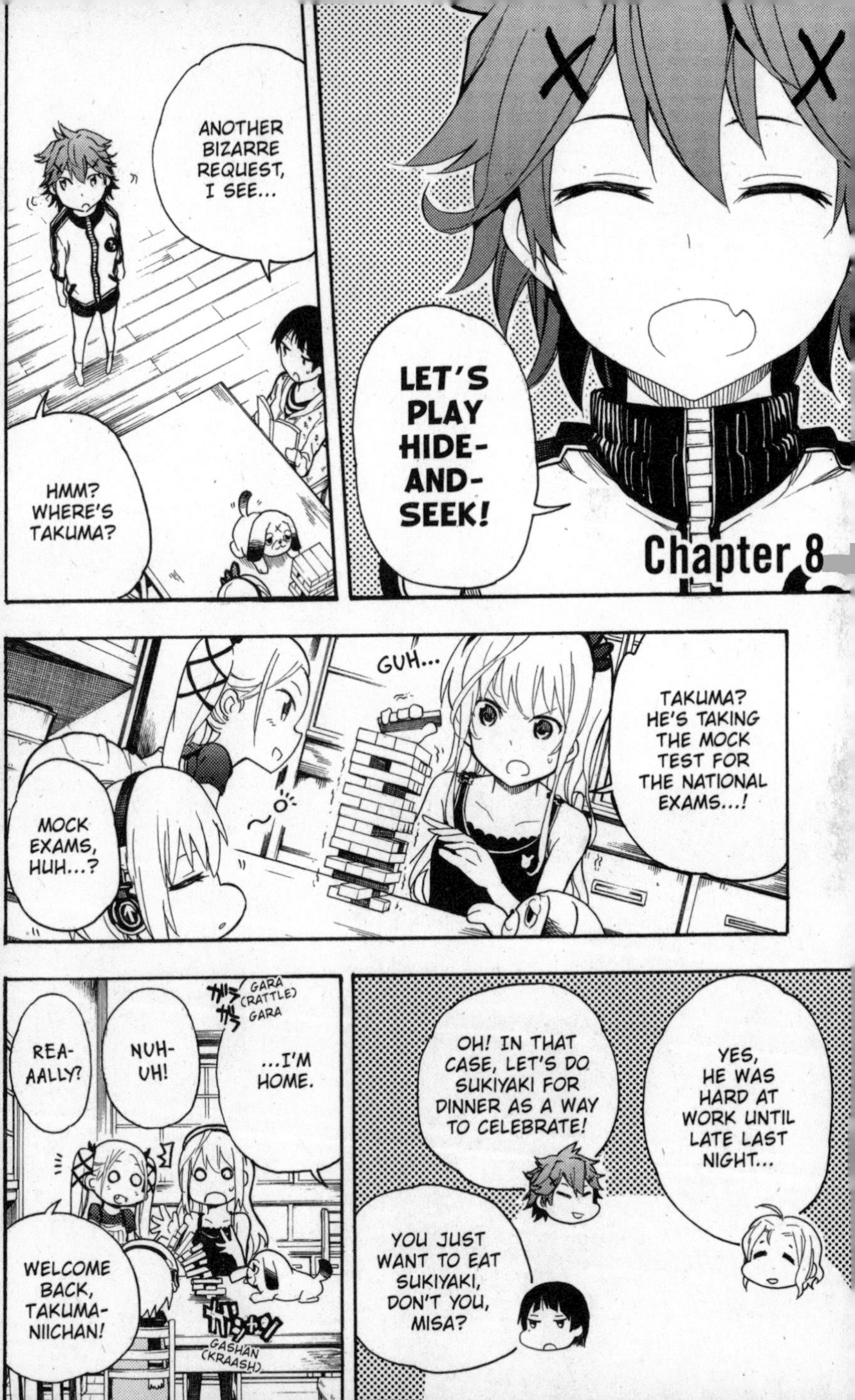
Chapter 8
LET'S PLAY HIDE-AND-SEEK!
ANOTHER BIZARRE REQUEST, I SEE...
HMM? WHERE'S TAKUMA?
TAKUMA? HE'S TAKING THE MOCK TEST FOR THE NATIONAL EXAMS...!
GUH...
MOCK EXAMS, HUH...?
YES, HE WAS HARD AT WORK UNTIL LATE LAST NIGHT...
OH! IN THAT CASE, LET'S DO SUKIYAKI FOR DINNER AS A WAY TO CELEBRATE!
YOU JUST WANT TO EAT SUKIYAKI, DON'T YOU, MISA?
GARA (RATTLE) GARA
...I'M HOME.
NUH-UH!
REA-AALLY?
WELCOME BACK, TAKUMA-NIICHAN!
GASHAN (KRAASH)

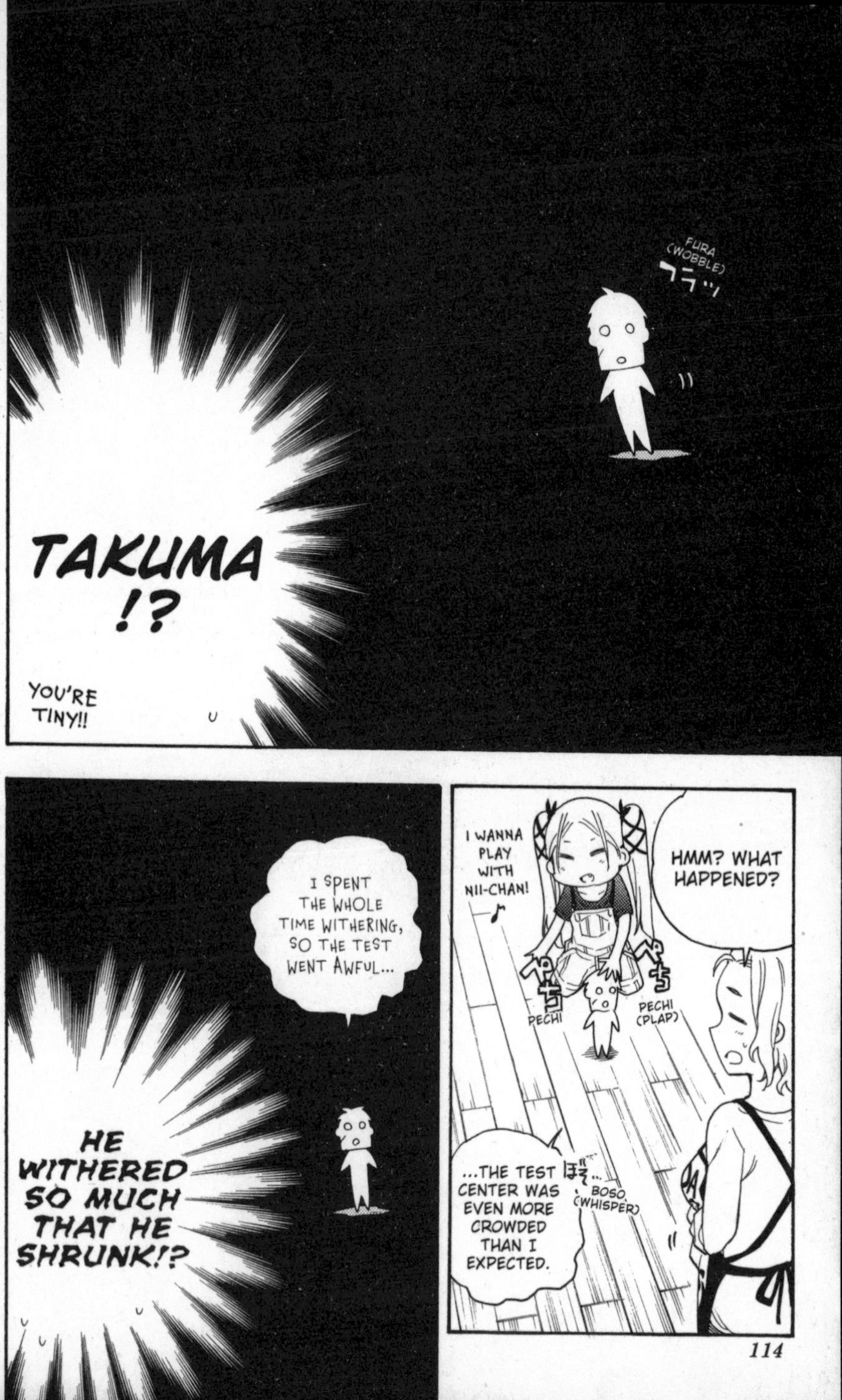
FURA (WOBBLE)
フラッ
TAKUMA !?
YOU'RE TINY!!
HMM? WHAT HAPPENED?
I WANNA PLAY WITH NII-CHAN! ♪
PECHI (PLAP)
PECHI
...THE TEST CENTER WAS EVEN MORE CROWDED THAN I EXPECTED.
BOSO (WHISPER)
I SPENT THE WHOLE TIME WITHERING, SO THE TEST WENT AWFUL...
HE WITHERED SO MUCH THAT HE SHRUNK!?

Chapter 8: The Unstoppable Maiden

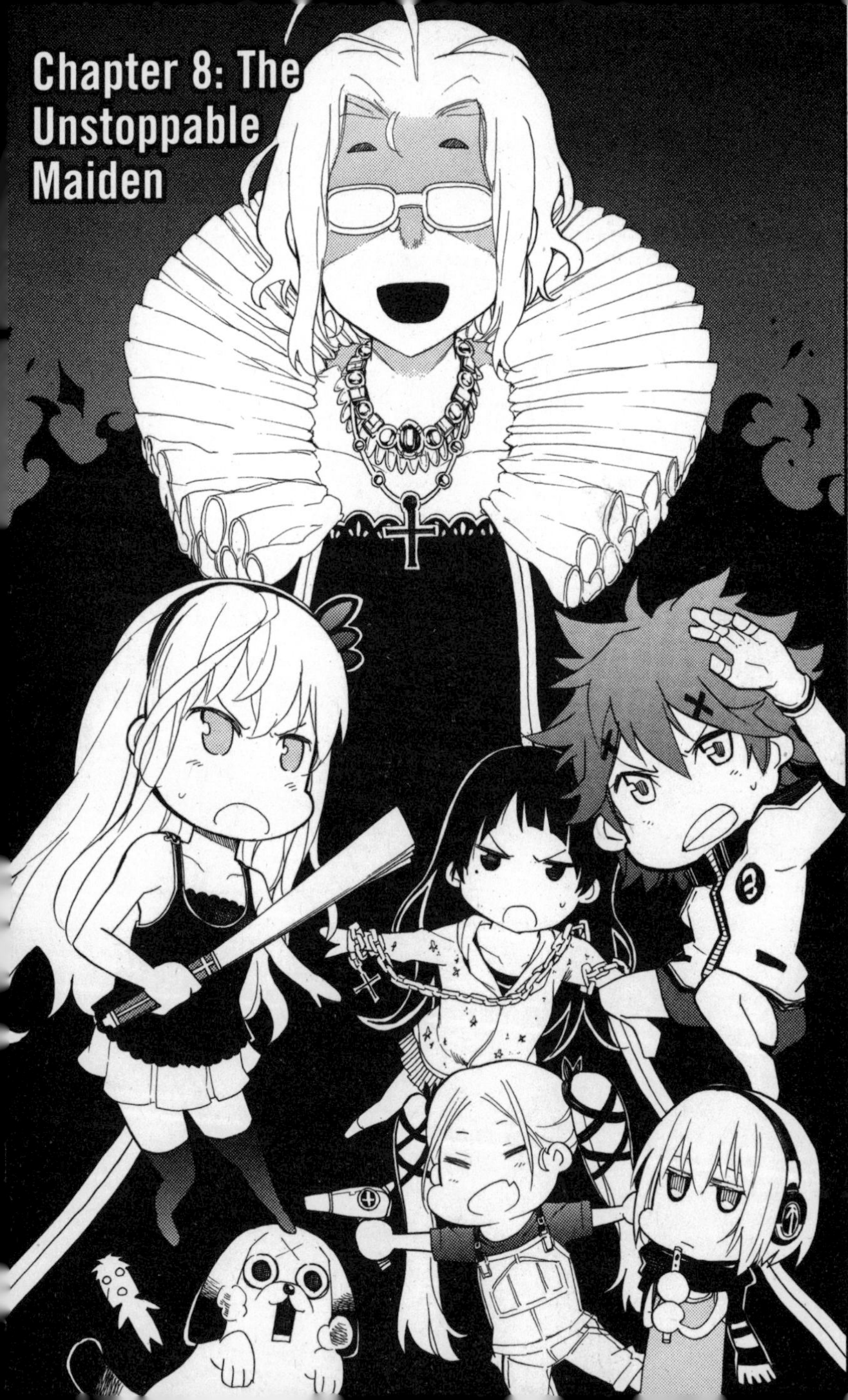

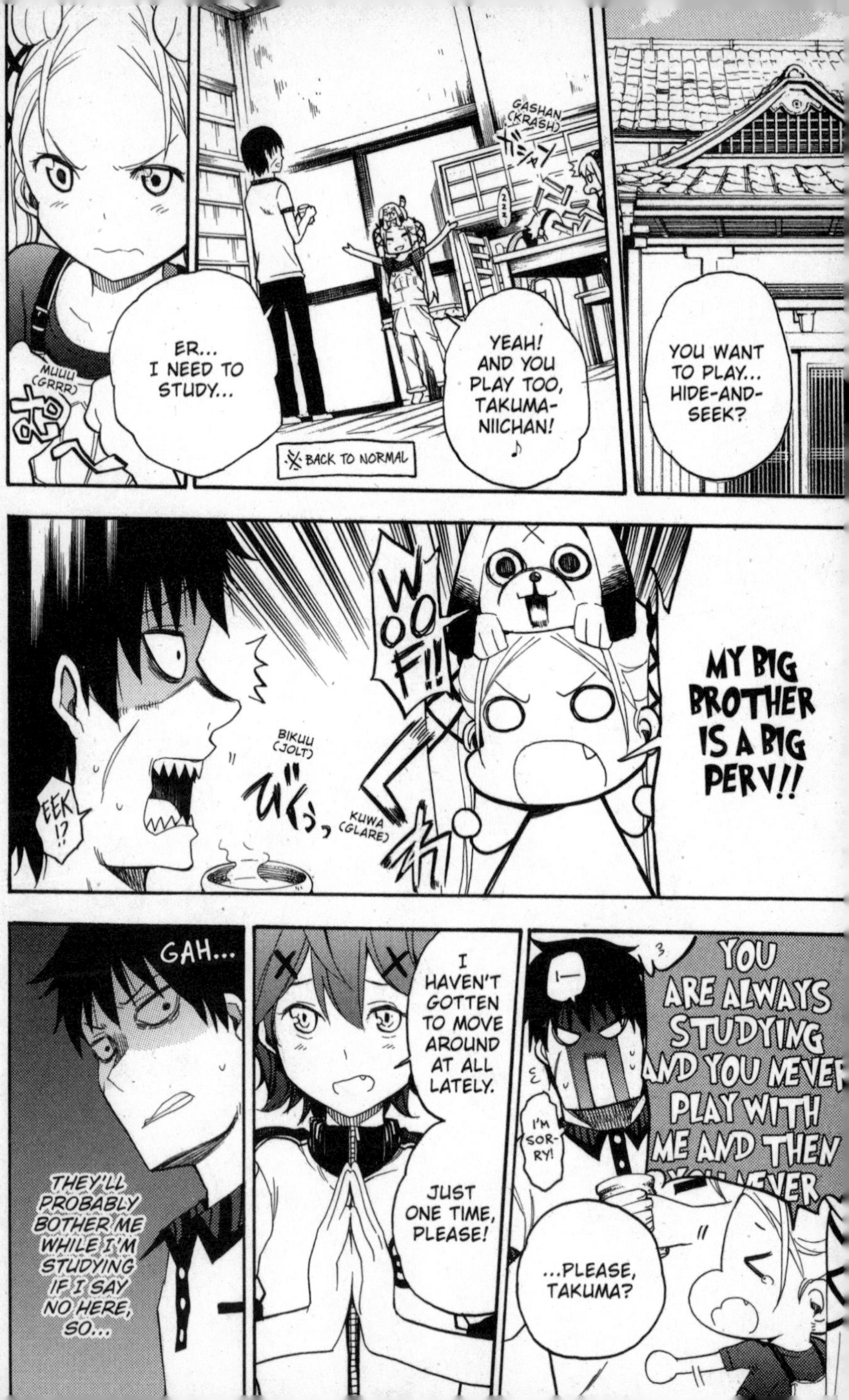
YOU WANT TO PLAY... HIDE-AND-SEEK?
GASHAN (KRASH)
ZZZ
YEAH! AND YOU PLAY TOO, TAKUMA-NIICHAN! ♪
※ BACK TO NORMAL
ER... I NEED TO STUDY...
MUUU (GRRR)
MY BIG BROTHER IS A BIG PERV!!
WOOF!!
KUWA (GLARE)
BIKUU (JOLT)
EEK!?
YOU ARE ALWAYS STUDYING AND YOU NEVER PLAY WITH ME AND THEN
...PLEASE, TAKUMA?
I'M SORRY!
I HAVEN'T GOTTEN TO MOVE AROUND AT ALL LATELY.
JUST ONE TIME, PLEASE!
GAH...
THEY'LL PROBABLY BOTHER ME WHILE I'M STUDYING IF I SAY NO HERE, SO...

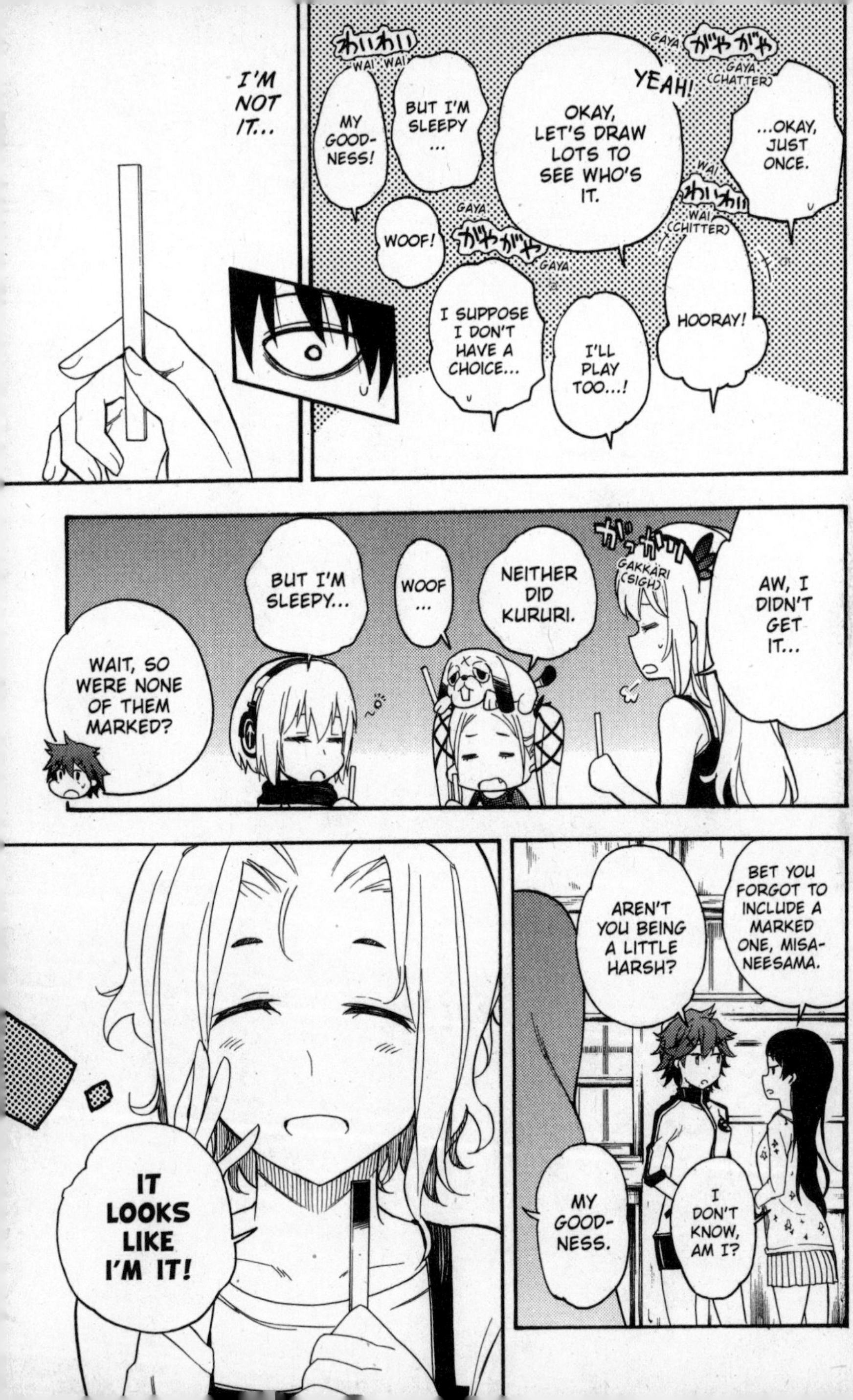
GAYA がやがや GAYA (CHATTER)
...OKAY, JUST ONCE.
YEAH!
OKAY, LET'S DRAW LOTS TO SEE WHO'S IT.
WAI わいわい WAI (CHITTER)
HOORAY!
BUT I'M SLEEPY...
わいわい WAI WAI
MY GOODNESS!
I'LL PLAY TOO...!
GAYA がやがや GAYA
WOOF!
I SUPPOSE I DON'T HAVE A CHOICE...
I'M NOT IT...
AW, I DIDN'T GET IT...
GAKKARI (SIGH)
NEITHER DID KURURI.
WOOF...
BUT I'M SLEEPY...
WAIT, SO WERE NONE OF THEM MARKED?
BET YOU FORGOT TO INCLUDE A MARKED ONE, MISA-NEESAMA.
AREN'T YOU BEING A LITTLE HARSH?
I DON'T KNOW, AM I?
MY GOOD-NESS.
IT LOOKS LIKE I'M IT!

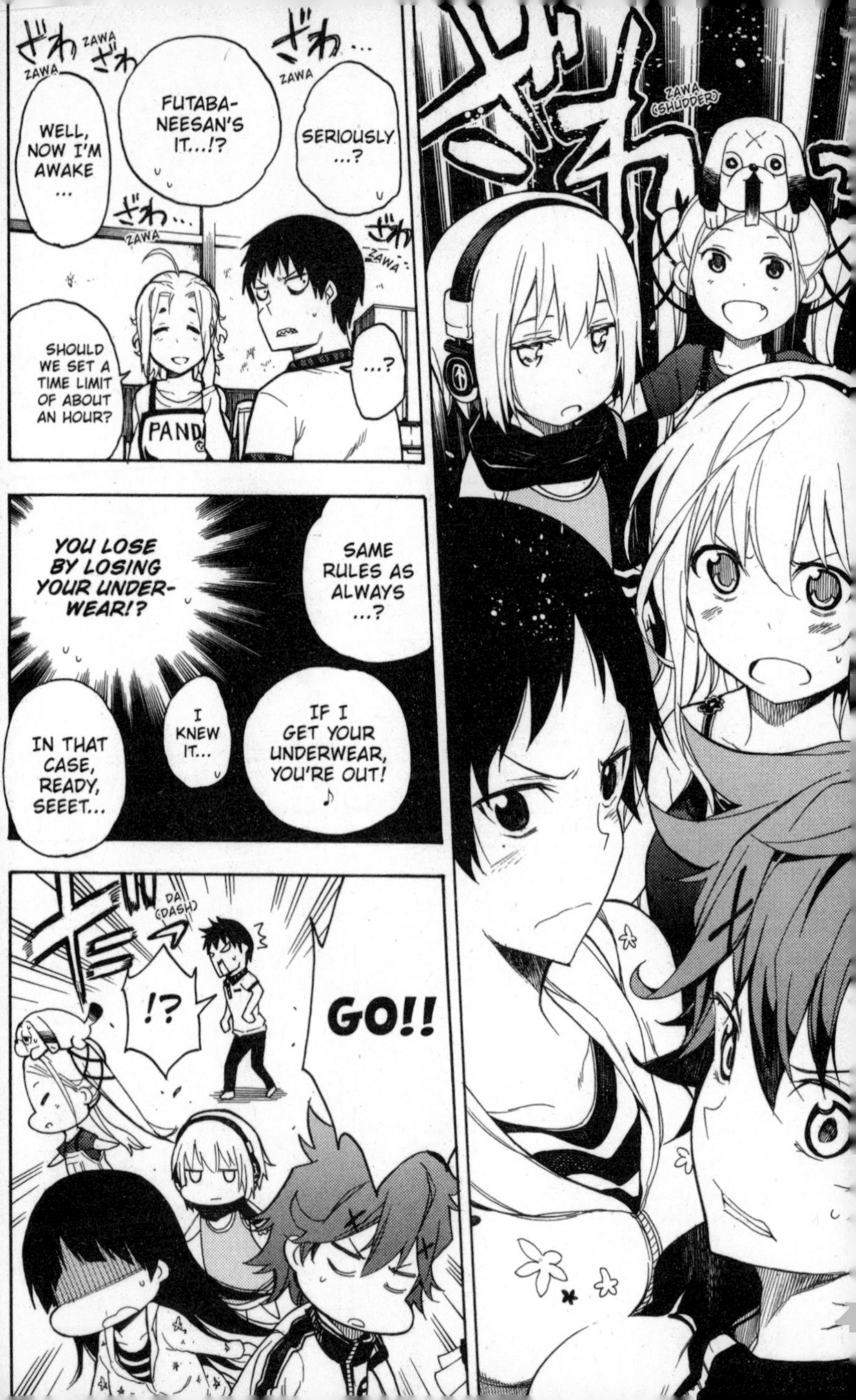
ZAWA (SHUDDER)
ZAWA
SERIOUSLY ...?
ZAWA
FUTABA-NEESAN'S IT...!?
ZAWA
WELL, NOW I'M AWAKE ...
ZAWA
ZAWA
...?
SHOULD WE SET A TIME LIMIT OF ABOUT AN HOUR?
PAND
SAME RULES AS ALWAYS ...?
YOU LOSE BY LOSING YOUR UNDER-WEAR!?
IF I GET YOUR UNDERWEAR, YOU'RE OUT! ♪
I KNEW IT...
IN THAT CASE, READY, SEEET...
GO!!
DA (DASH)
!?

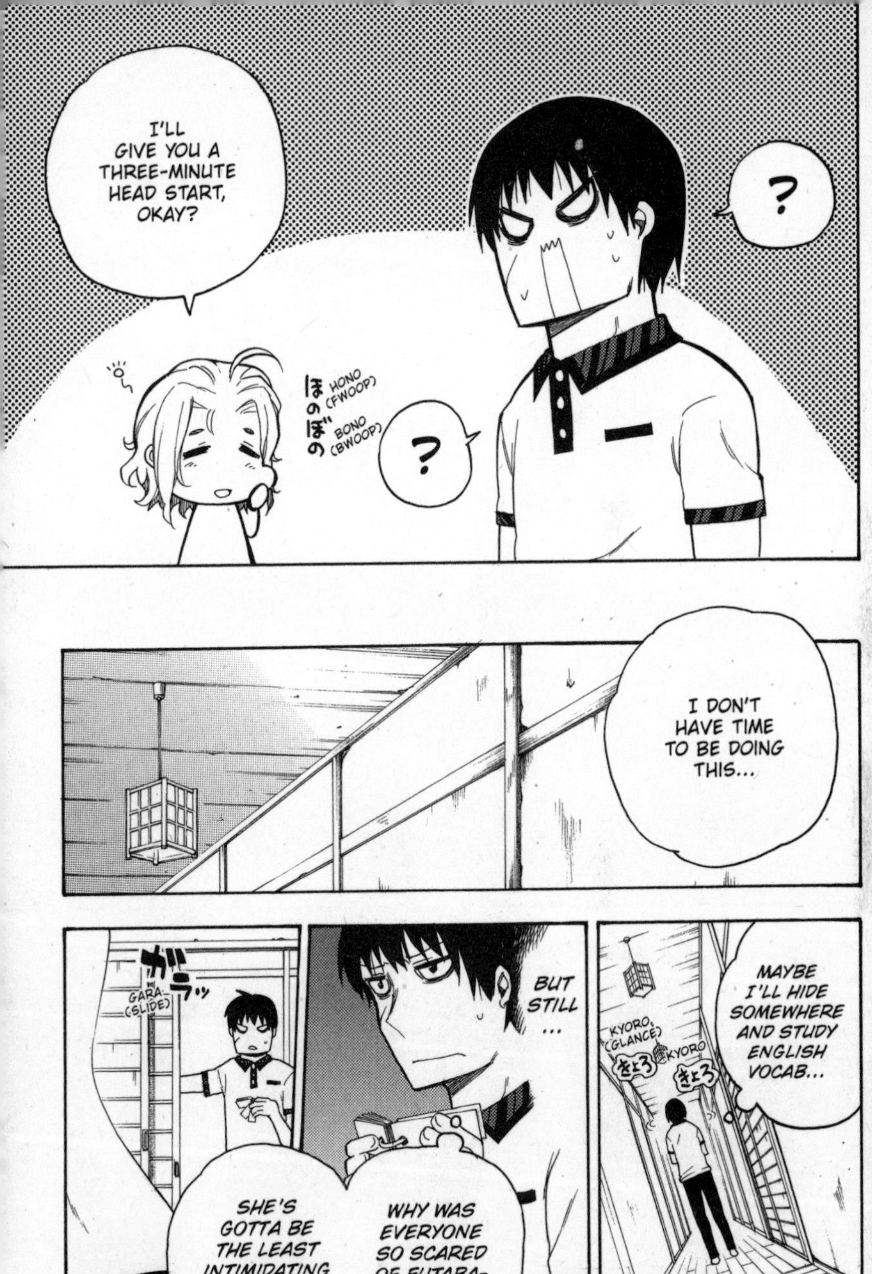
?
I'LL GIVE YOU A THREE-MINUTE HEAD START, OKAY?
ほの HONO (FWOOP)
ぼの BONO (BWOOP)
?
I DON'T HAVE TIME TO BE DOING THIS...
MAYBE I'LL HIDE SOMEWHERE AND STUDY ENGLISH VOCAB...
きょろ KYORO (GLANCE)
きょろ KYORO
BUT STILL...
WHY WAS EVERYONE SO SCARED OF FUTABA-SAN?
ガラッ GARA (SLIDE)
SHE'S GOTTA BE THE LEAST INTIMIDATING OF THE BUNCH...

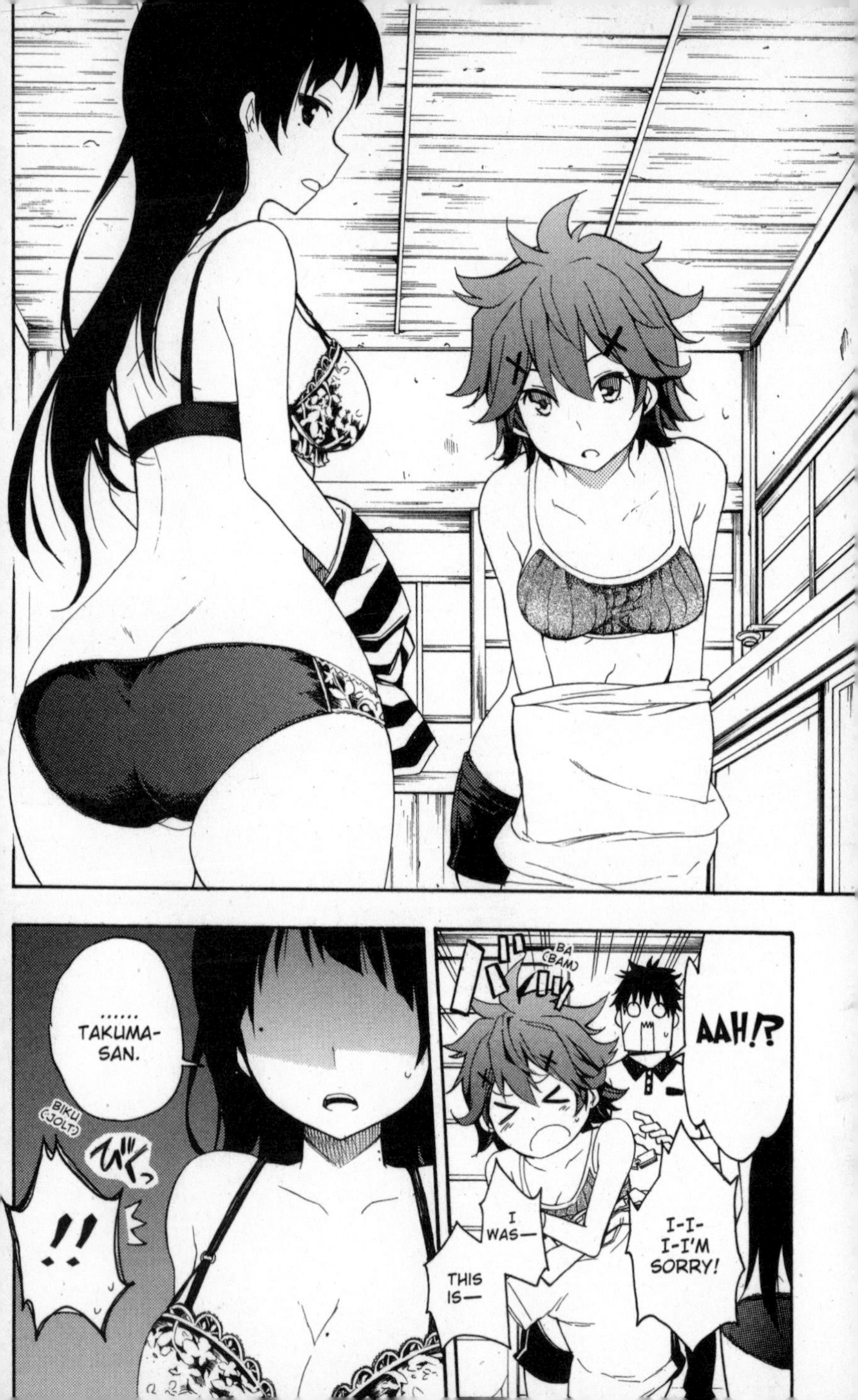
BA (BAM)
AAH!?
I-I- I-I'M SORRY!
I WAS—
THIS IS—
...... TAKUMA-SAN.
BIKU (JOLT)
びくっ
!!

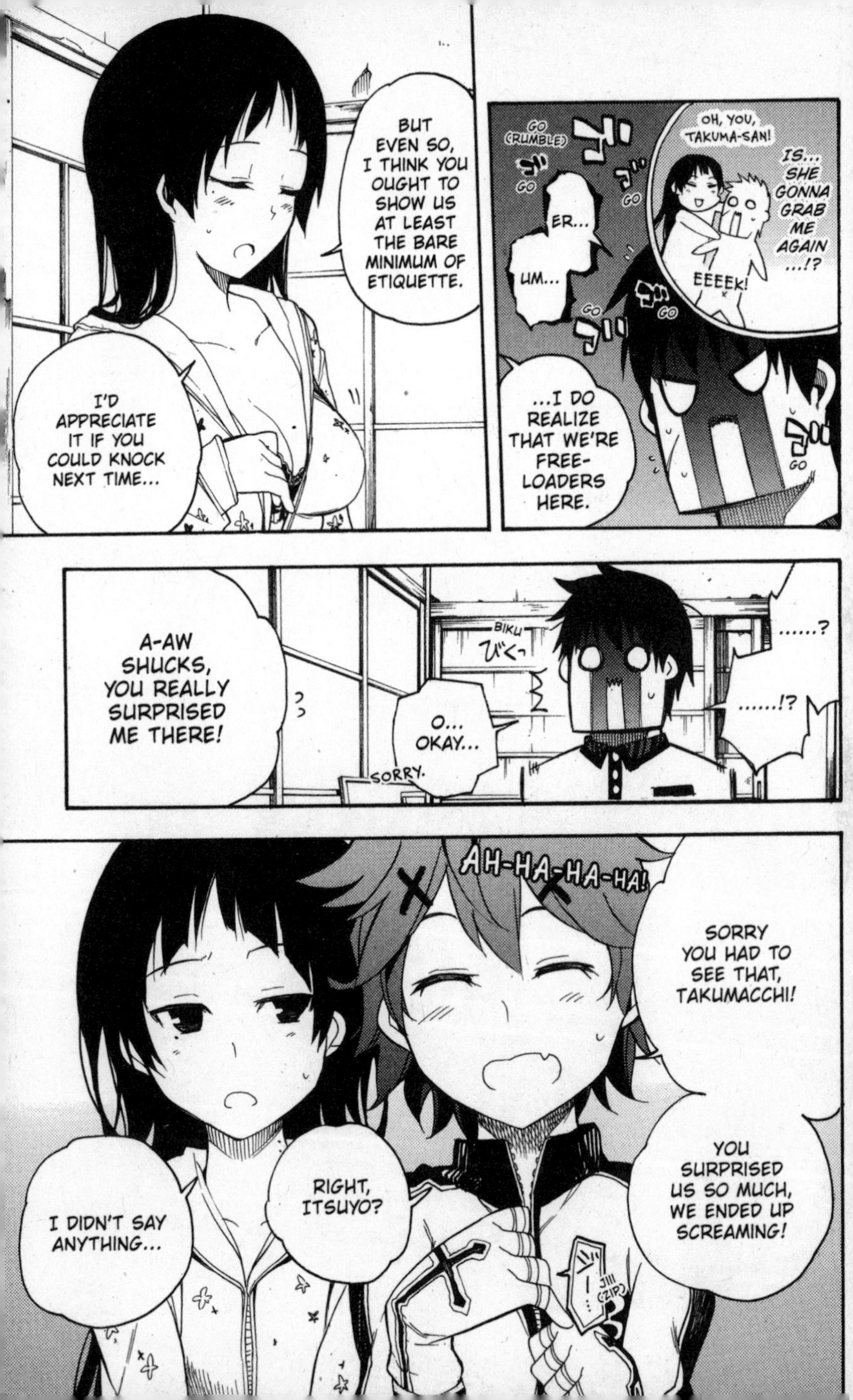
GO (RUMBLE)
GO
GO
OH, YOU, TAKUMA-SAN!
IS... SHE GONNA GRAB ME AGAIN ...!?
EEEEK!
ER...
UM...
GO
GO
GO
...I DO REALIZE THAT WE'RE FREE-LOADERS HERE.
BUT EVEN SO, I THINK YOU OUGHT TO SHOW US AT LEAST THE BARE MINIMUM OF ETIQUETTE.
I'D APPRECIATE IT IF YOU COULD KNOCK NEXT TIME...
......?
......!?
BIKU
O... OKAY...
SORRY.
A-AW SHUCKS, YOU REALLY SURPRISED ME THERE!
AH-HA-HA-HA!
SORRY YOU HAD TO SEE THAT, TAKUMACCHI!
YOU SURPRISED US SO MUCH, WE ENDED UP SCREAMING!
JIII (ZIP)
RIGHT, ITSUYO?
I DIDN'T SAY ANYTHING...

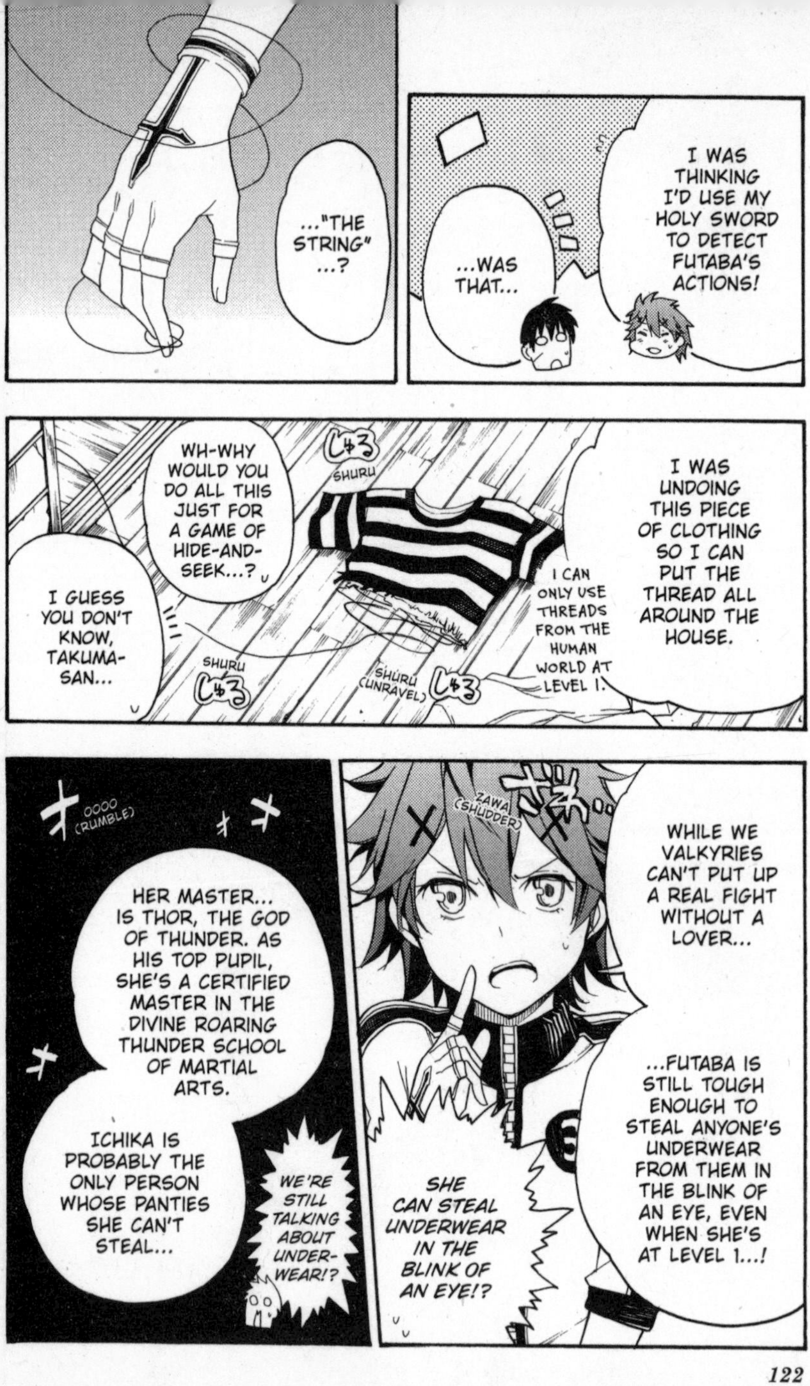
I WAS THINKING I'D USE MY HOLY SWORD TO DETECT FUTABA'S ACTIONS!
...WAS THAT...
..."THE STRING"...?
I WAS UNDOING THIS PIECE OF CLOTHING SO I CAN PUT THE THREAD ALL AROUND THE HOUSE.
I CAN ONLY USE THREADS FROM THE HUMAN WORLD AT LEVEL 1.
SHURU (UNRAVEL)
SHURU
WH-WHY WOULD YOU DO ALL THIS JUST FOR A GAME OF HIDE-AND-SEEK...?
SHURU
I GUESS YOU DON'T KNOW, TAKUMA-SAN...
ZAWA (SHUDDER)
WHILE WE VALKYRIES CAN'T PUT UP A REAL FIGHT WITHOUT A LOVER...
...FUTABA IS STILL TOUGH ENOUGH TO STEAL ANYONE'S UNDERWEAR FROM THEM IN THE BLINK OF AN EYE, EVEN WHEN SHE'S AT LEVEL 1...!
SHE CAN STEAL UNDERWEAR IN THE BLINK OF AN EYE!?
OOOO (RUMBLE)
HER MASTER... IS THOR, THE GOD OF THUNDER. AS HIS TOP PUPIL, SHE'S A CERTIFIED MASTER IN THE DIVINE ROARING THUNDER SCHOOL OF MARTIAL ARTS.
ICHIKA IS PROBABLY THE ONLY PERSON WHOSE PANTIES SHE CAN'T STEAL...
WE'RE STILL TALKING ABOUT UNDER-WEAR!?

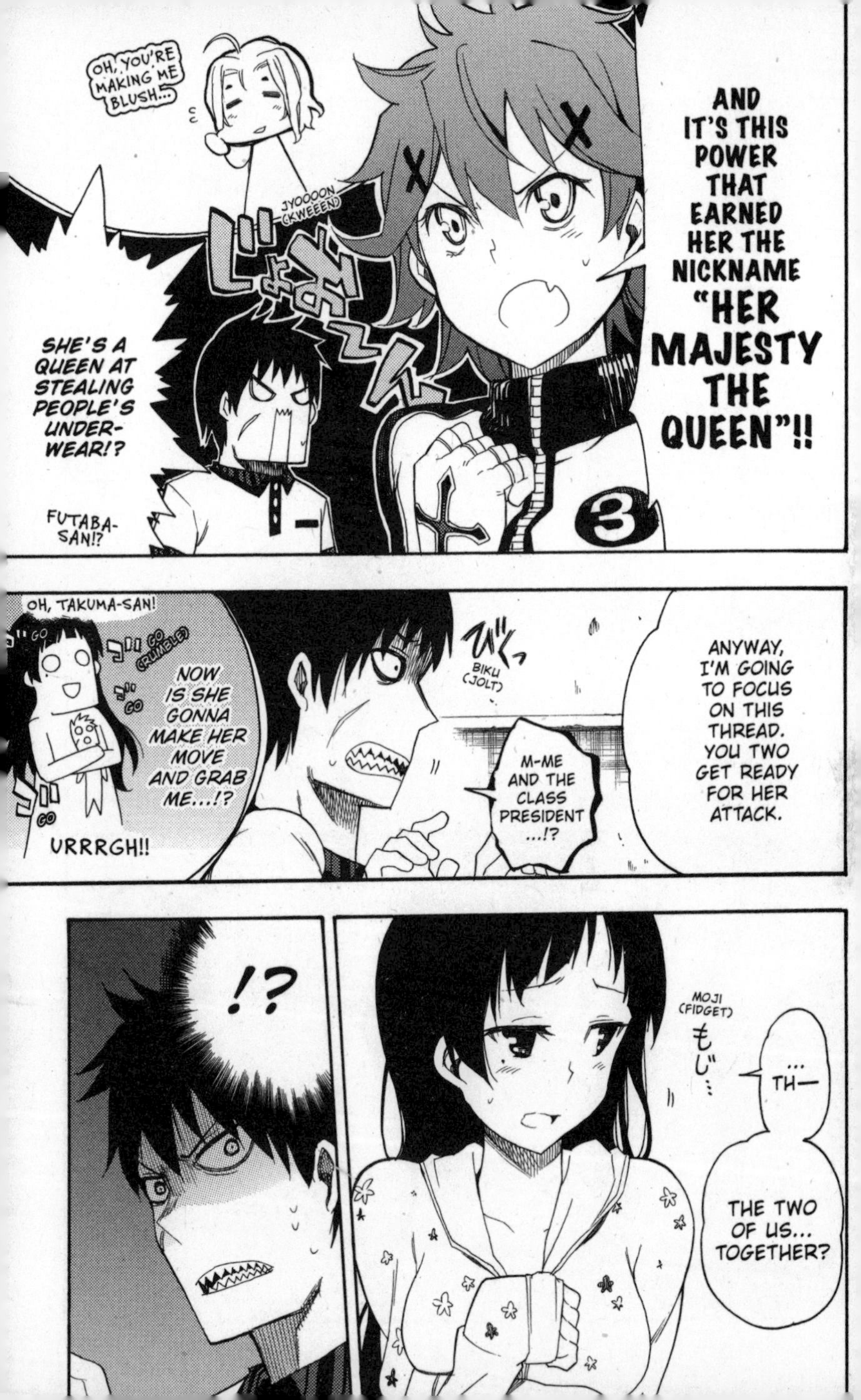
AND IT'S THIS POWER THAT EARNED HER THE NICKNAME "HER MAJESTY THE QUEEN"!!
JYOOOON (KWEEEN)
OH, YOU'RE MAKING ME BLUSH...
SHE'S A QUEEN AT STEALING PEOPLE'S UNDER-WEAR!?
FUTABA-SAN!?
ANYWAY, I'M GOING TO FOCUS ON THIS THREAD. YOU TWO GET READY FOR HER ATTACK.
M-ME AND THE CLASS PRESIDENT ...!?
BIKU (JOLT)
NOW IS SHE GONNA MAKE HER MOVE AND GRAB ME...!?
OH, TAKUMA-SAN!
GO (RUMBLE)
GO
GO
URRRGH!!
MOJI (FIDGET)
... TH—
THE TWO OF US... TOGETHER?
!?

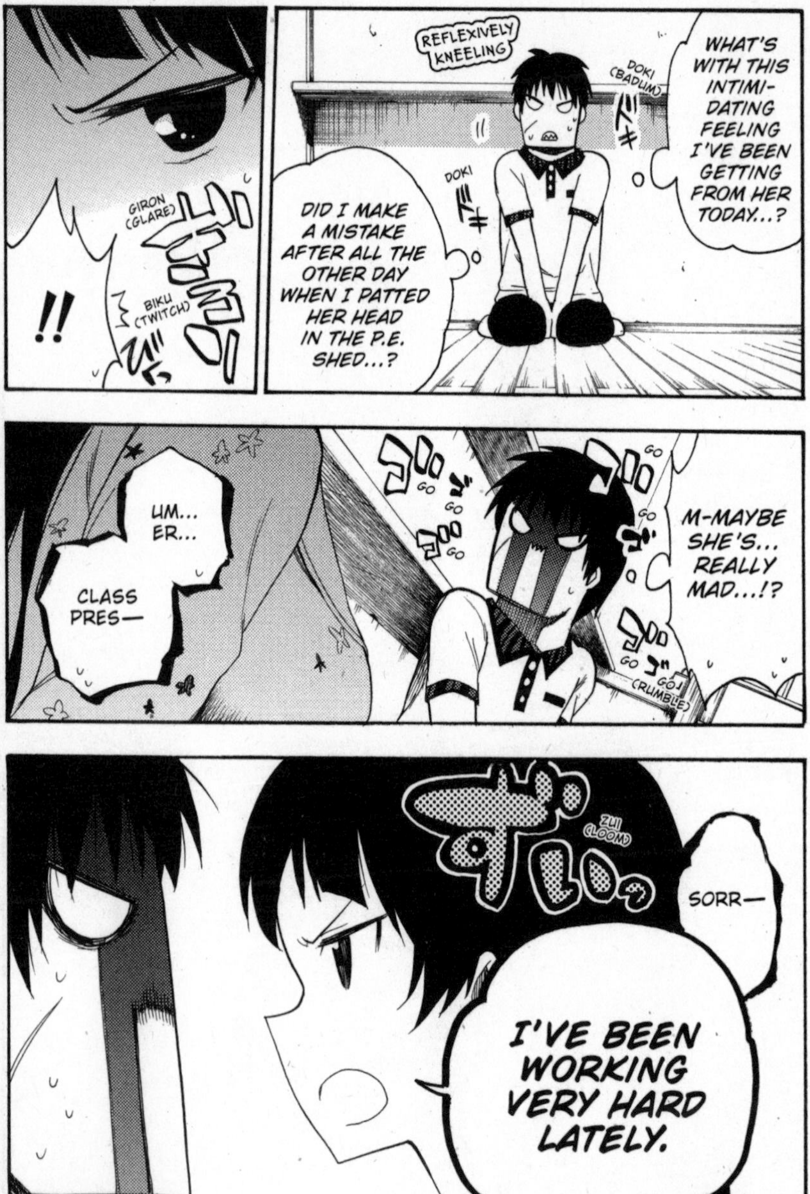
WHAT'S WITH THIS INTIMIDATING FEELING I'VE BEEN GETTING FROM HER TODAY...?
DOKI (BADUM)
REFLEXIVELY KNEELING
DOKI
DID I MAKE A MISTAKE AFTER ALL THE OTHER DAY WHEN I PATTED HER HEAD IN THE P.E. SHED...?
GIRON (GLARE)
BIKU (TWITCH)
!!
M-MAYBE SHE'S... REALLY MAD...!?
GO GO GO GO GO GO GO GO (RUMBLE)
UM... ER...
CLASS PRES—
SORR—
ZUI (LOOM)
I'VE BEEN WORKING VERY HARD LATELY.

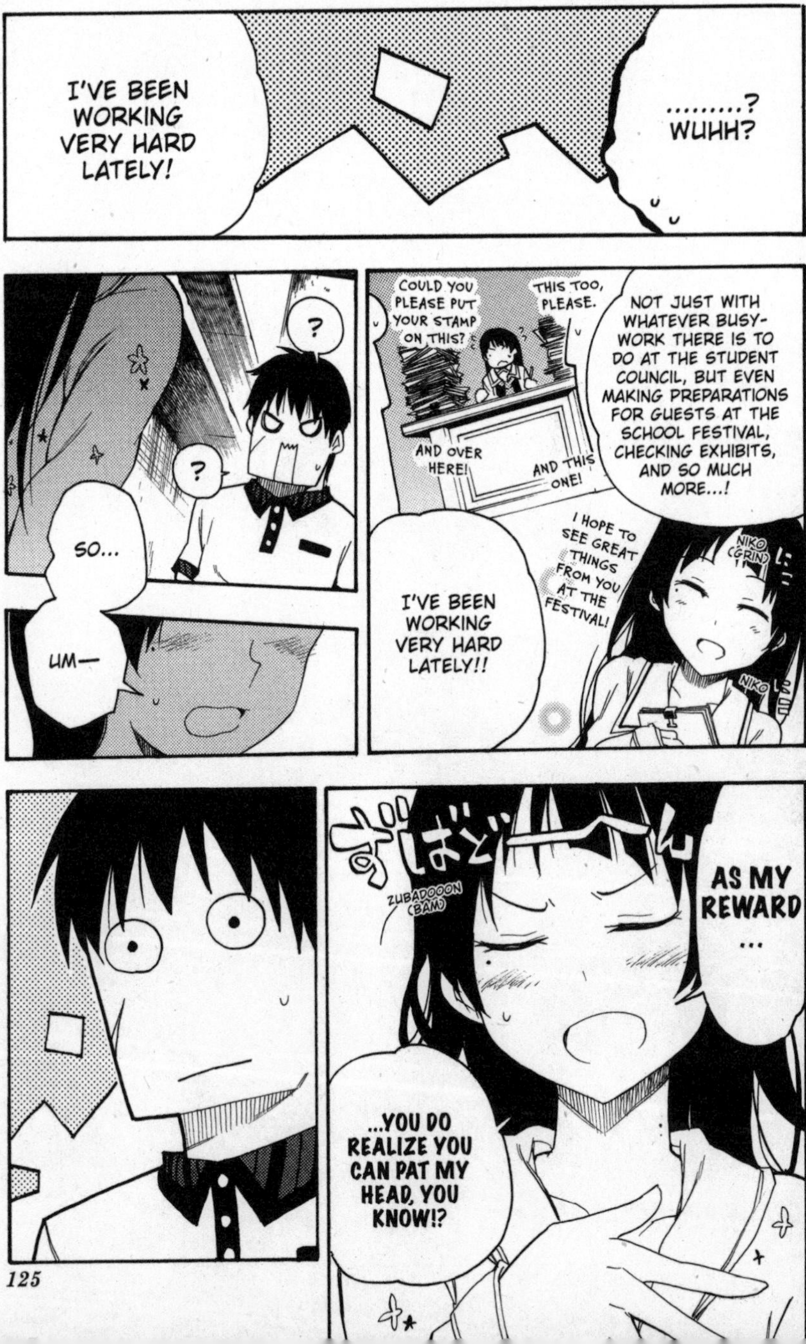
........?
WUHH?
I'VE BEEN WORKING VERY HARD LATELY!
NOT JUST WITH WHATEVER BUSY-WORK THERE IS TO DO AT THE STUDENT COUNCIL, BUT EVEN MAKING PREPARATIONS FOR GUESTS AT THE SCHOOL FESTIVAL, CHECKING EXHIBITS, AND SO MUCH MORE...!
THIS TOO, PLEASE.
COULD YOU PLEASE PUT YOUR STAMP ON THIS?
AND THIS ONE!
AND OVER HERE!
にこ
NIKO (GRIN)
I HOPE TO SEE GREAT THINGS FROM YOU AT THE FESTIVAL!
にこ
NIKO
I'VE BEEN WORKING VERY HARD LATELY!!
SO...
UM—
AS MY REWARD ...
ずばどーーん
ZUBADOOON (BAM)
...YOU DO REALIZE YOU CAN PAT MY HEAD, YOU KNOW!?

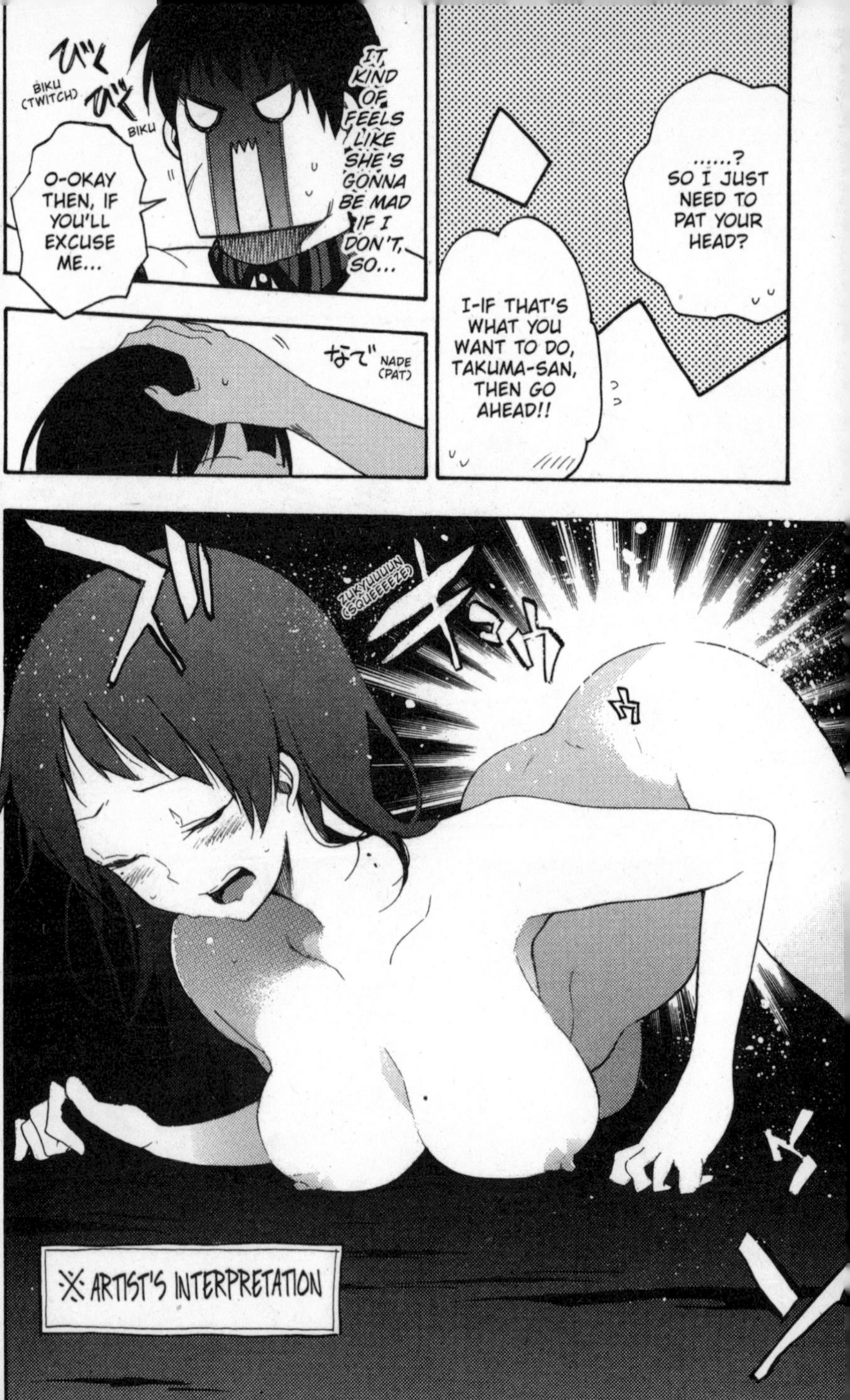
......? SO I JUST NEED TO PAT YOUR HEAD?
I-IF THAT'S WHAT YOU WANT TO DO, TAKUMA-SAN, THEN GO AHEAD!!
びく BIKU (TWITCH)
びく BIKU
IT KIND OF FEELS LIKE SHE'S GONNA BE MAD IF I DON'T, SO...
O-OKAY THEN, IF YOU'LL EXCUSE ME...
なで NADE (PAT)
ZUKYUUUUUN (SQUEEEEZE)
※ARTIST'S INTERPRETATION

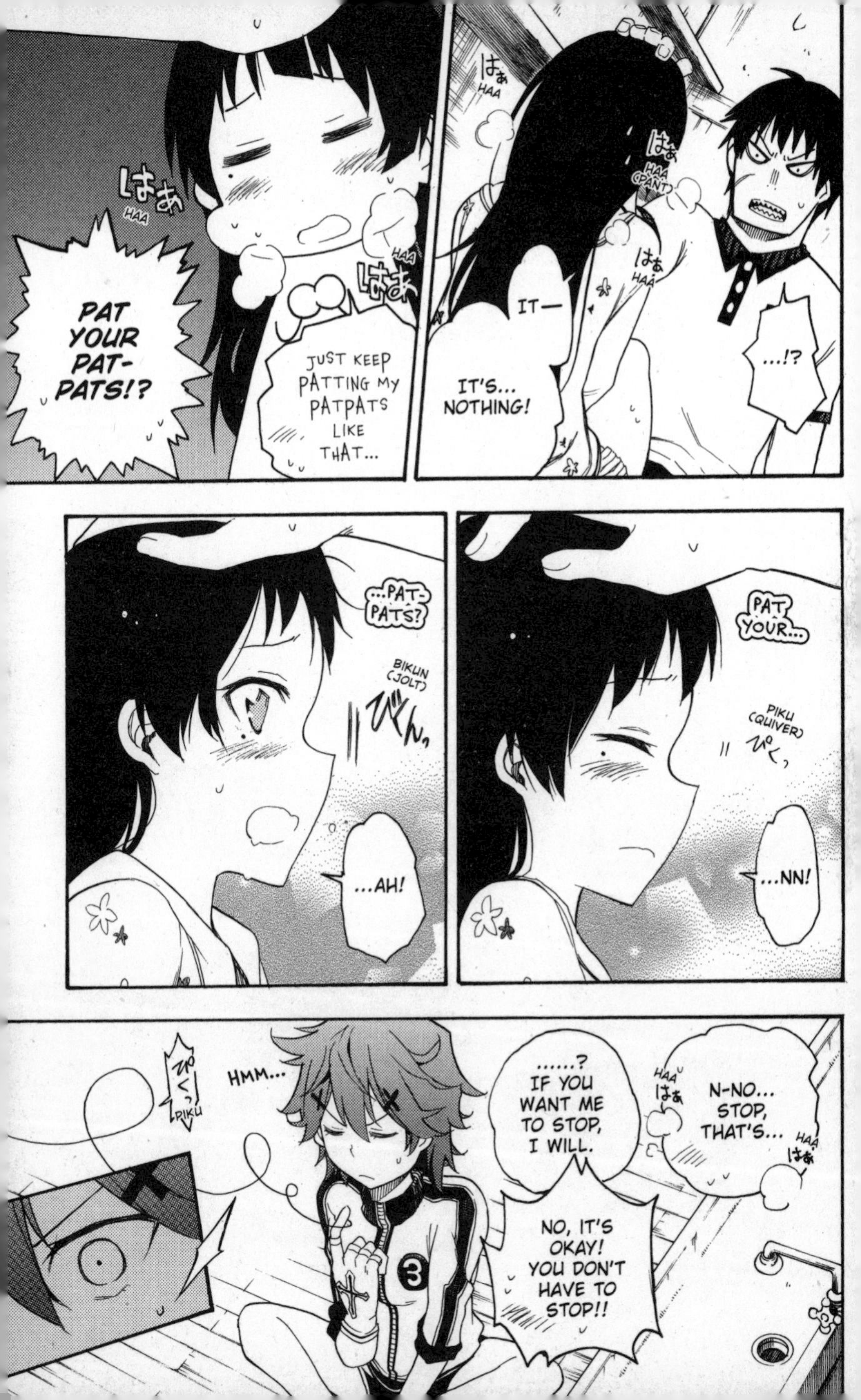
はぁ HAA
はぁ HAA (PANT)
はぁ HAA
IT—
IT'S... NOTHING!
...!?
はぁ HAA
はぁ HAA
JUST KEEP PATTING MY PATPATS LIKE THAT...
PAT YOUR PAT-PATS!?
PAT YOUR...
ぴくっ PIKU (QUIVER)
...NN!
...PAT-PATS?
びくんっ BIKUN (JOLT)
...AH!
はぁ HAA
N-NO... STOP, THAT'S...
はぁ HAA
......? IF YOU WANT ME TO STOP, I WILL.
NO, IT'S OKAY! YOU DON'T HAVE TO STOP!!
HMM...
ぴくっ PIKU

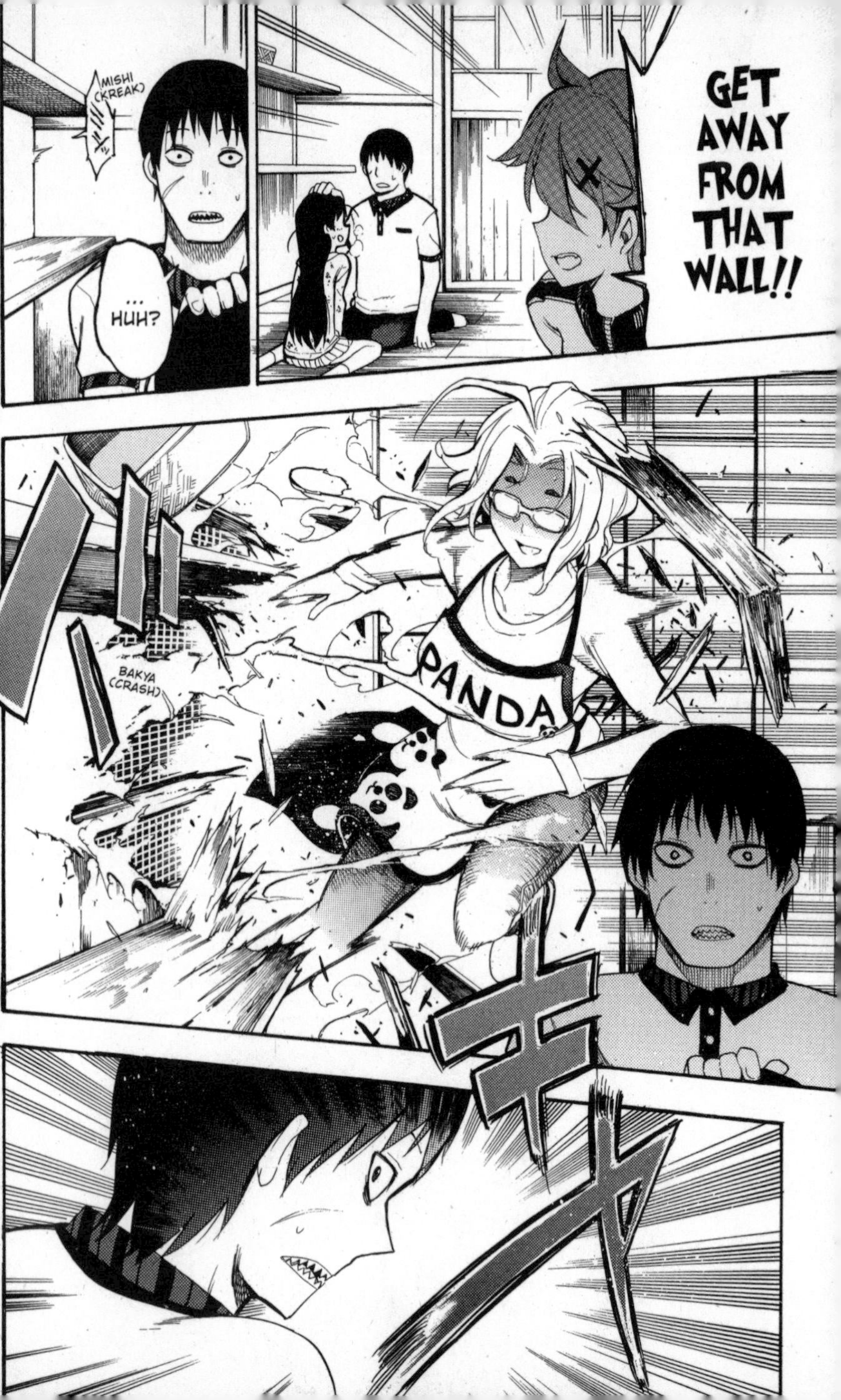
GET AWAY FROM THAT WALL!!
MISHI (KREAK)
... HUH?
BAKYA (CRASH)

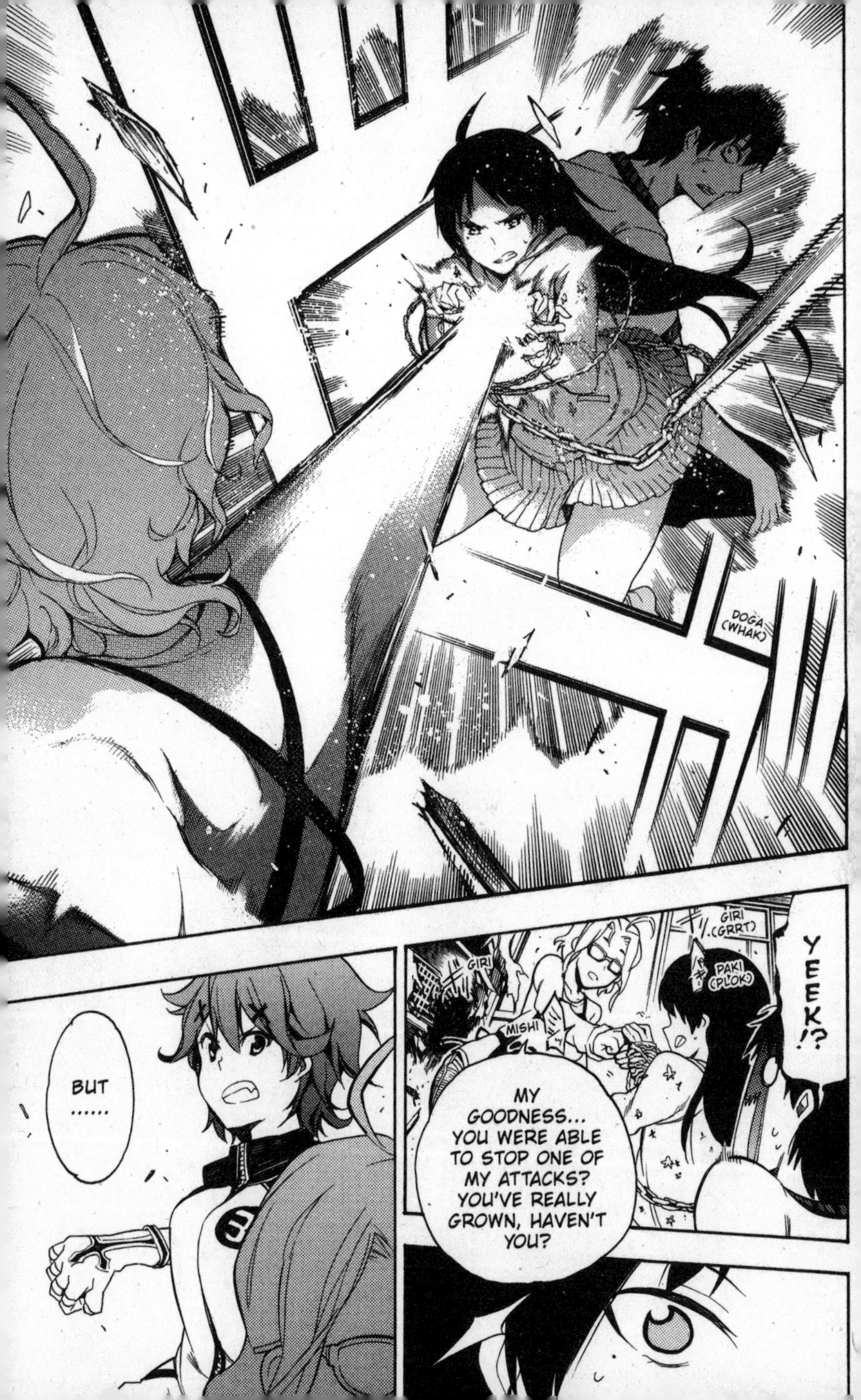

DOGA (WHAK)
YEEK!?
GIRI (GRRT)
PAKI (PLOK)
GIRI
MISHI
MY GOODNESS... YOU WERE ABLE TO STOP ONE OF MY ATTACKS? YOU'VE REALLY GROWN, HAVEN'T YOU?
BUT ......

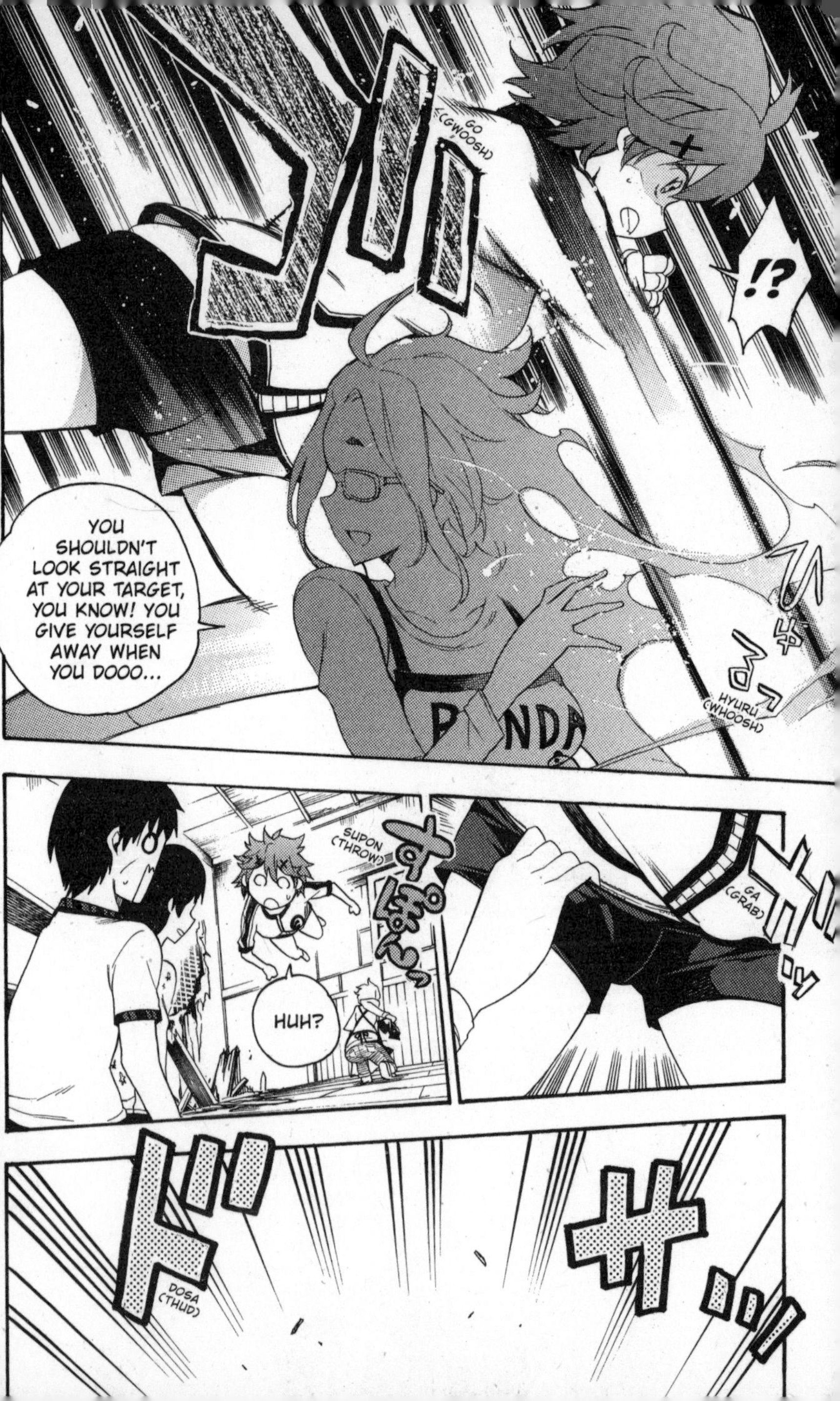
GO (GWOOSH)
!?
YOU SHOULDN'T LOOK STRAIGHT AT YOUR TARGET, YOU KNOW! YOU GIVE YOURSELF AWAY WHEN YOU DOOO...
HYURU (WHOOSH)
GA (GRAB)
SUPON (THROW)
HUH?
DOSA (THUD)

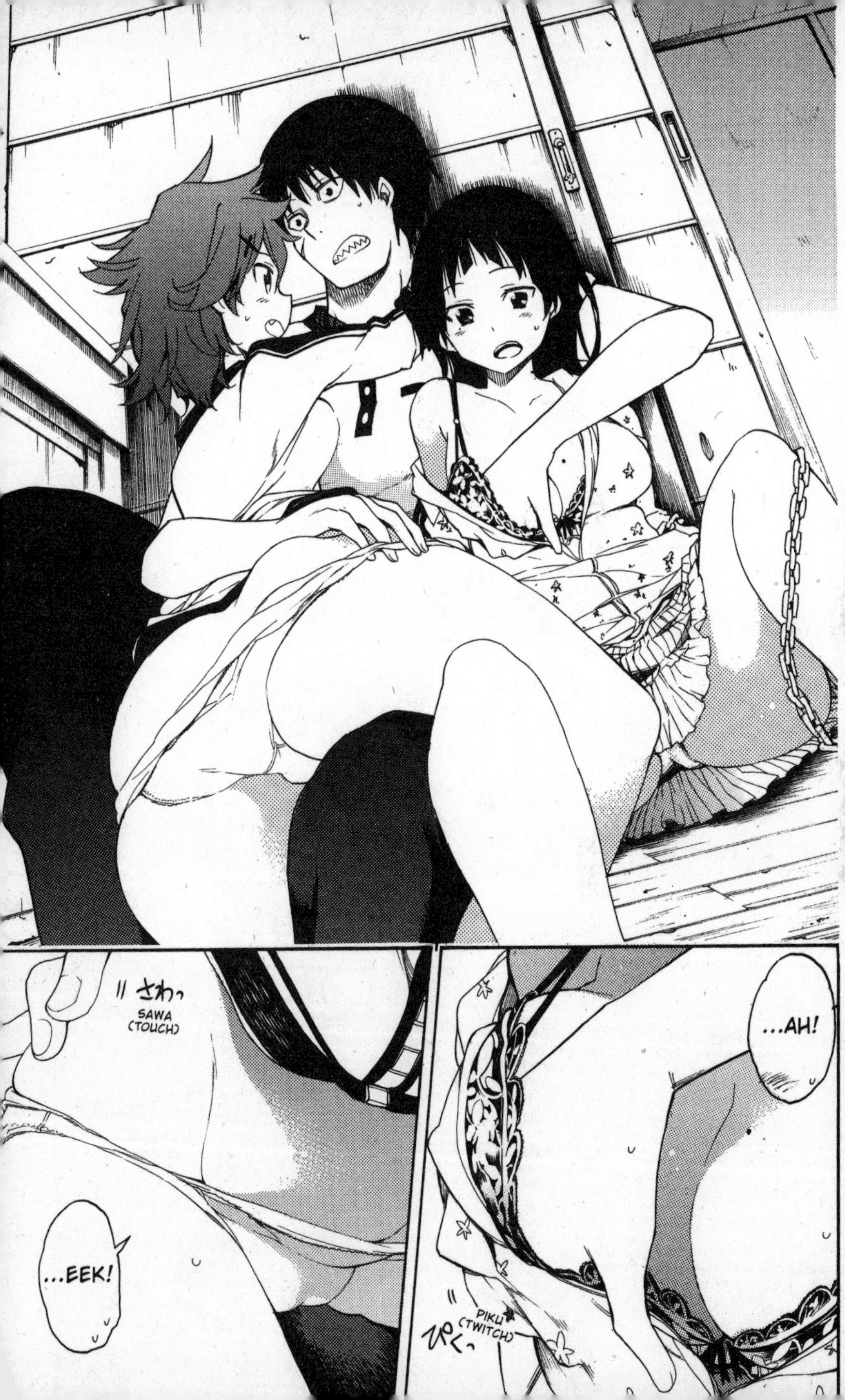
...AH!
ぴくっ
PIKU (TWITCH)
さわっ
SAWA (TOUCH)
...EEK!

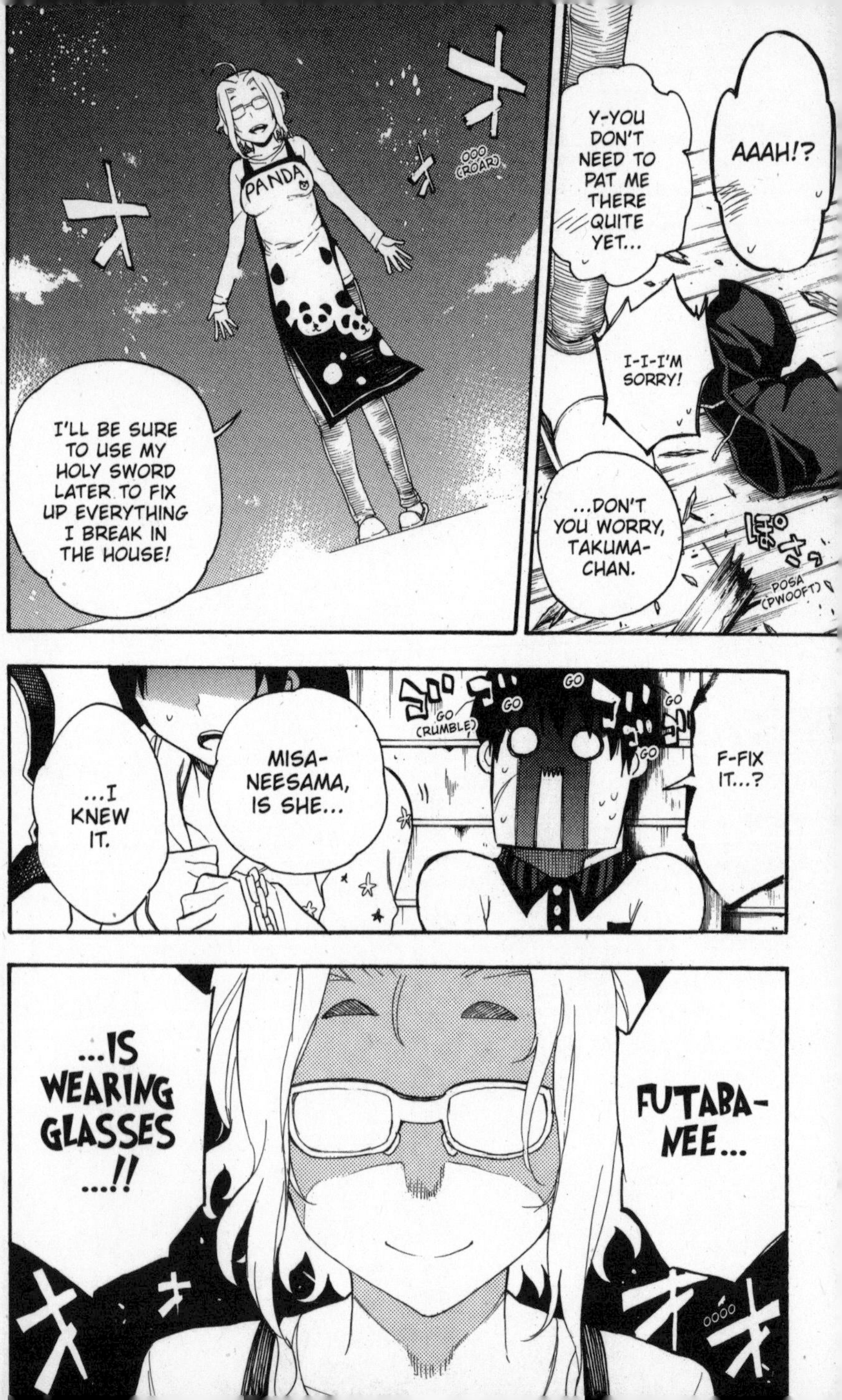
AAAH!?
Y-YOU DON'T NEED TO PAT ME THERE QUITE YET...
I-I-I'M SORRY!
...DON'T YOU WORRY, TAKUMA-CHAN.
POSA (PWOOFT)
OOO (ROAR)
I'LL BE SURE TO USE MY HOLY SWORD LATER TO FIX UP EVERYTHING I BREAK IN THE HOUSE!
F-FIX IT...?
GO GO GO GO
GO (RUMBLE)
MISA-NEESAMA, IS SHE...
...I KNEW IT.
FUTABA-NEE...
...IS WEARING GLASSES ...!!
OOOO

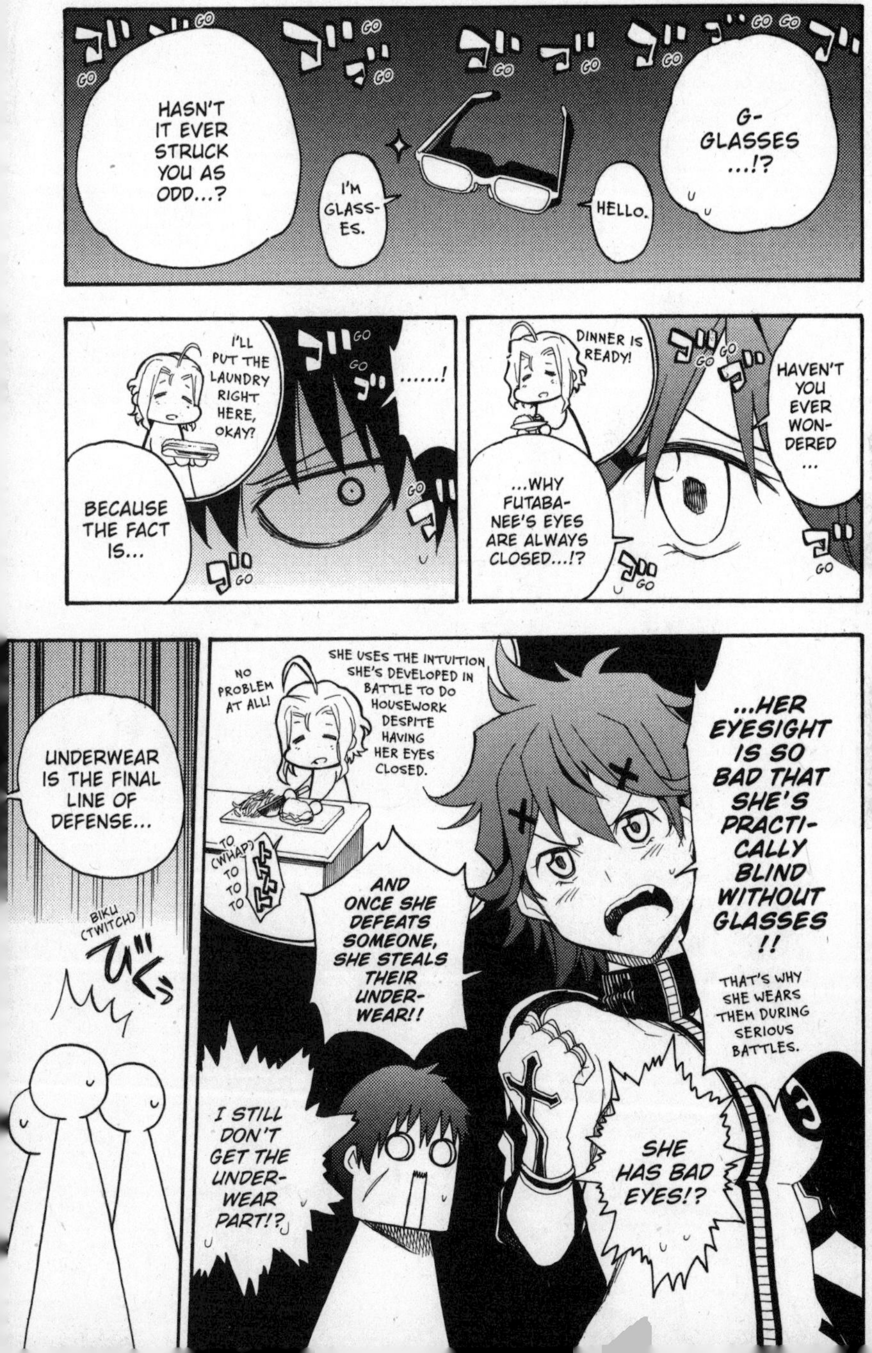
GO GO GO GO GO GO GO GO GO GO
G-GLASSES...!?
HELLO.
I'M GLASSES-ES.
HASN'T IT EVER STRUCK YOU AS ODD...?
HAVEN'T YOU EVER WONDERED...
GO GO GO
DINNER IS READY!
...WHY FUTABA-NEE'S EYES ARE ALWAYS CLOSED...!?
GO
......!
GO GO
I'LL PUT THE LAUNDRY RIGHT HERE, OKAY?
BECAUSE THE FACT IS...
GO GO
...HER EYESIGHT IS SO BAD THAT SHE'S PRACTICALLY BLIND WITHOUT GLASSES!!
THAT'S WHY SHE WEARS THEM DURING SERIOUS BATTLES.
SHE USES THE INTUITION SHE'S DEVELOPED IN BATTLE TO DO HOUSEWORK DESPITE HAVING HER EYES CLOSED.
NO PROBLEM AT ALL!
TO (WHAP) TO TO TO
SHE HAS BAD EYES!?
AND ONCE SHE DEFEATS SOMEONE, SHE STEALS THEIR UNDERWEAR!!
I STILL DON'T GET THE UNDERWEAR PART!?
UNDERWEAR IS THE FINAL LINE OF DEFENSE...
BIKU (TWITCH)

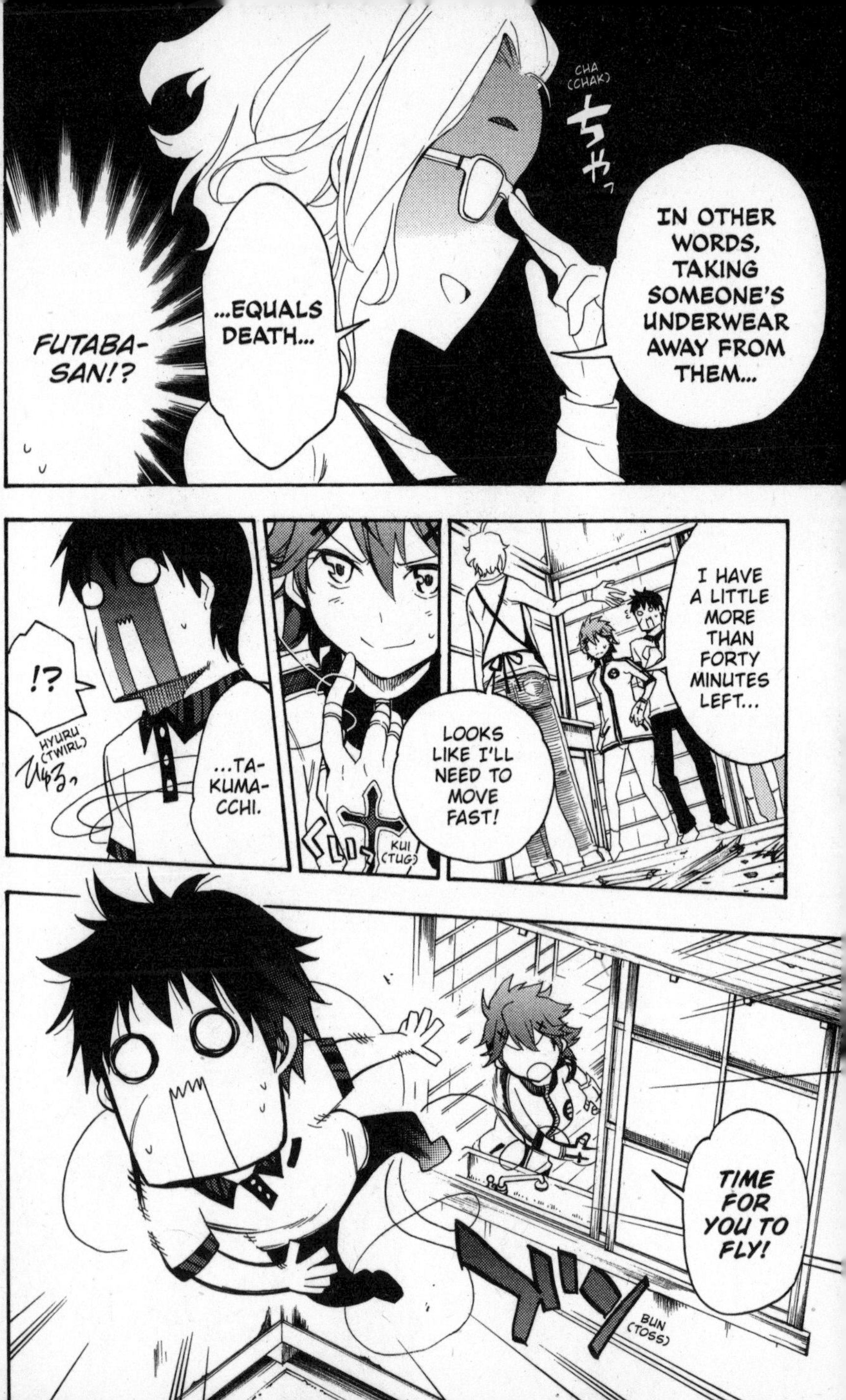
CHA (CHAK)
ちゃっ
IN OTHER WORDS, TAKING SOMEONE'S UNDERWEAR AWAY FROM THEM...
...EQUALS DEATH...
FUTABA-SAN!?
I HAVE A LITTLE MORE THAN FORTY MINUTES LEFT...
LOOKS LIKE I'LL NEED TO MOVE FAST!
KUI (TUG)
...TA-KUMA-CCHI.
!?
HYURU (TWIRL)
ひゅるっ
TIME FOR YOU TO FLY!
BUN (TOSS)

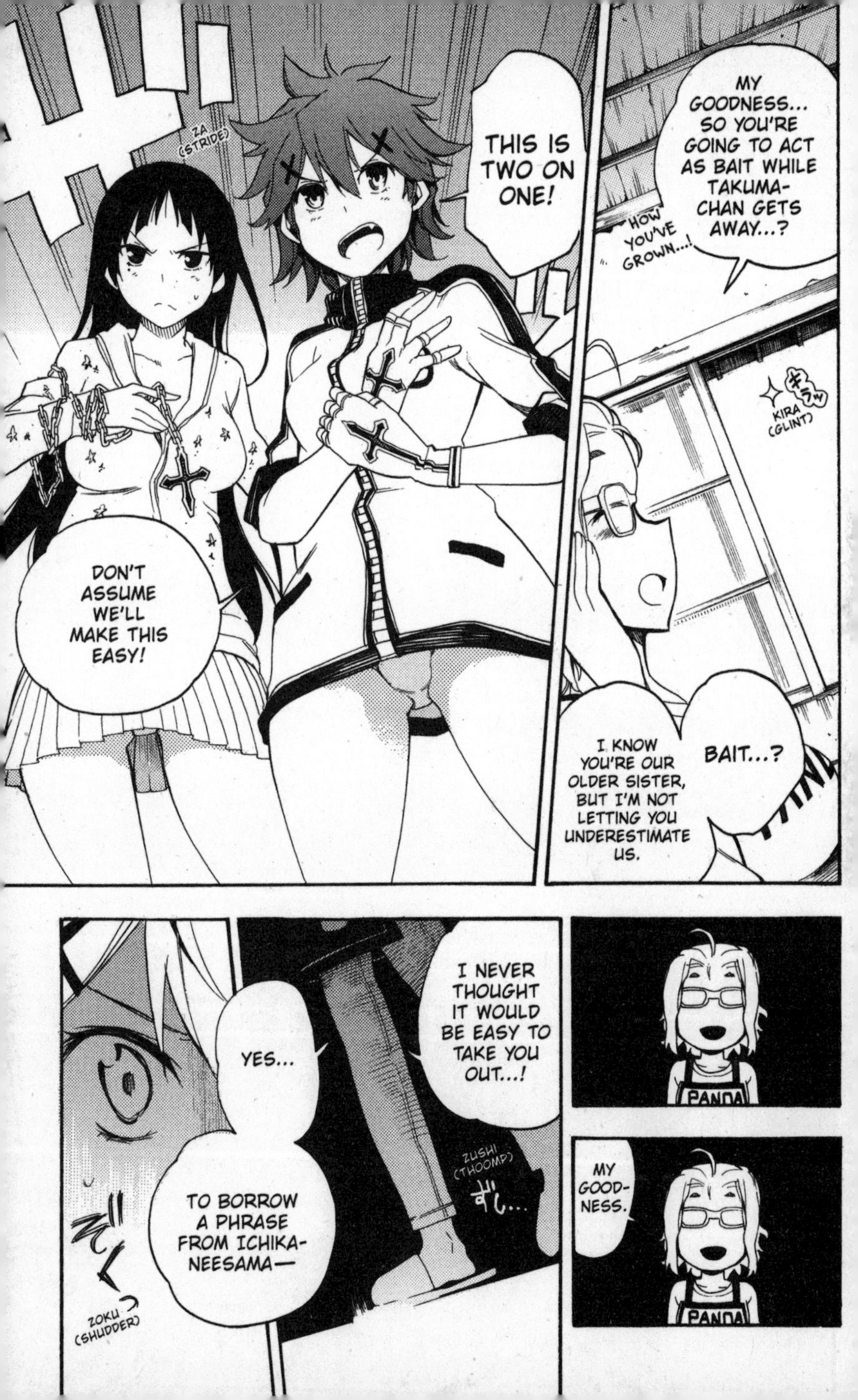
MY GOODNESS... SO YOU'RE GOING TO ACT AS BAIT WHILE TAKUMA-CHAN GETS AWAY...?
HOW YOU'VE GROWN...!
KIRA (GLINT)
BAIT...?
I KNOW YOU'RE OUR OLDER SISTER, BUT I'M NOT LETTING YOU UNDERESTIMATE US.
ZA (STRIDE)
THIS IS TWO ON ONE!
DON'T ASSUME WE'LL MAKE THIS EASY!
PANDA
MY GOOD-NESS.
PANDA
I NEVER THOUGHT IT WOULD BE EASY TO TAKE YOU OUT...!
YES...
ZUSHI (THOOMP)
TO BORROW A PHRASE FROM ICHIKA-NEESAMA—
ZOKU (SHUDDER)

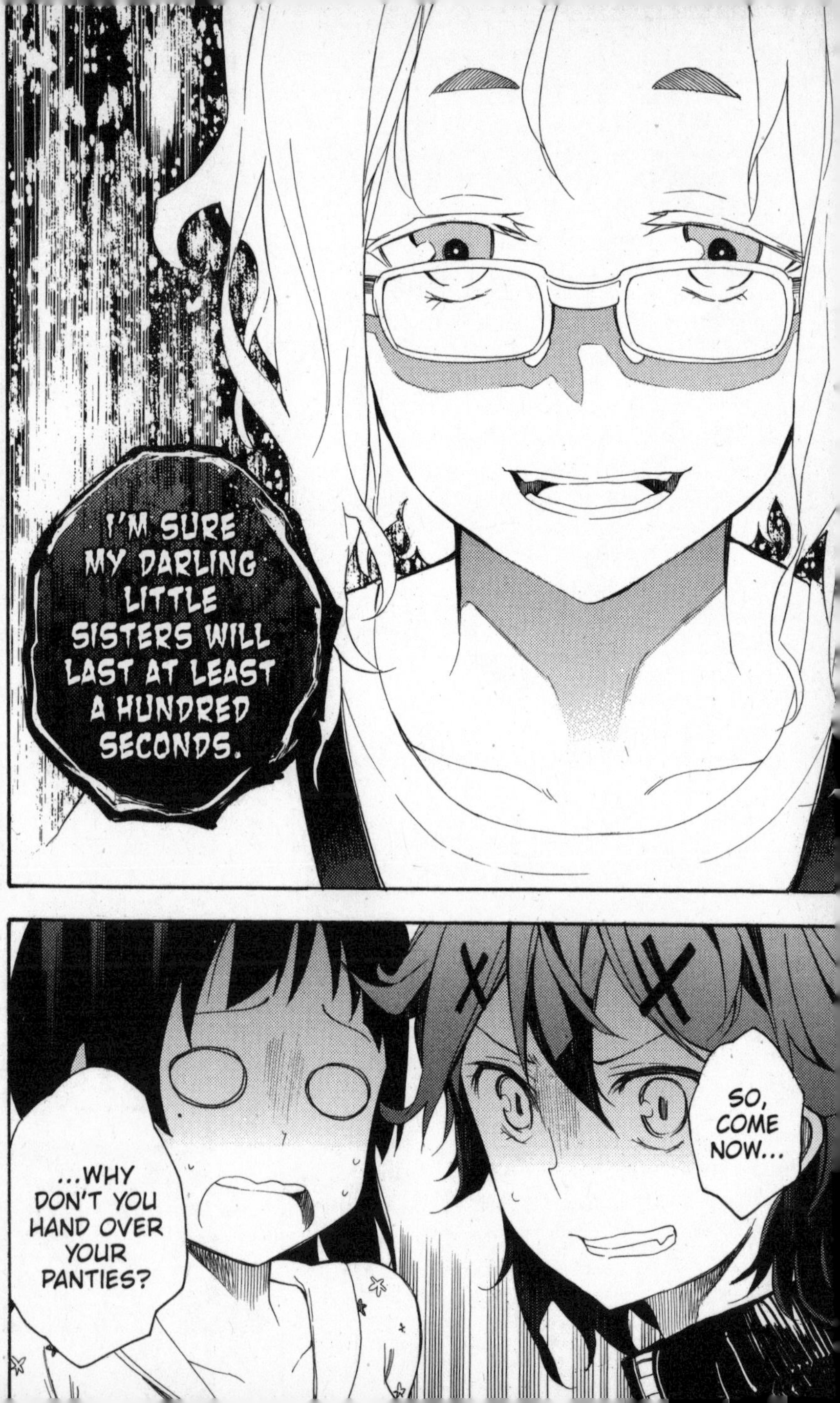
I'M SURE MY DARLING LITTLE SISTERS WILL LAST AT LEAST A HUNDRED SECONDS.
SO, COME NOW...
...WHY DON'T YOU HAND OVER YOUR PANTIES?

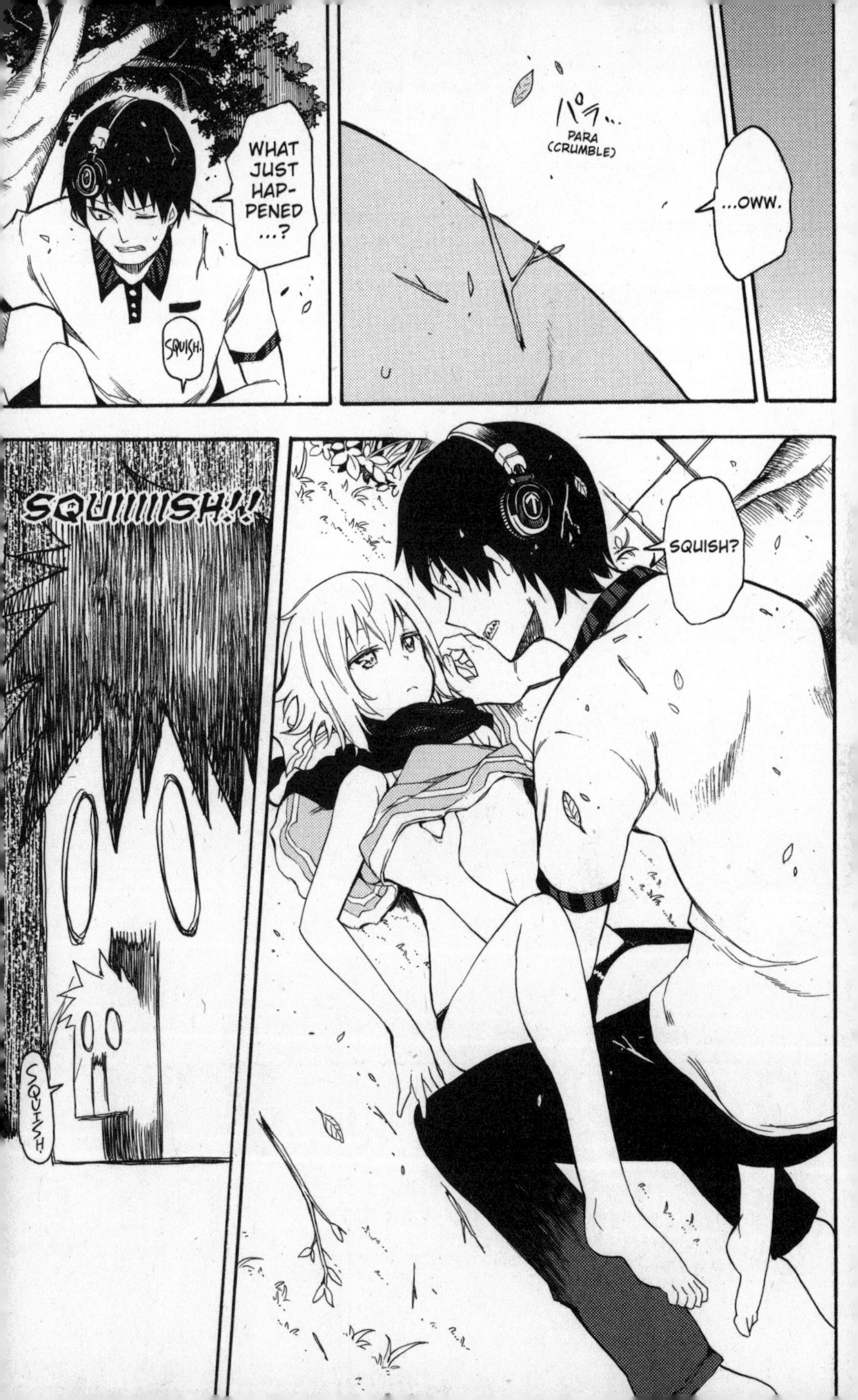
...OWW.
パラ...
PARA (CRUMBLE)
WHAT JUST HAPPENED...?
SQUISH.
SQUISH?
SQUIIIIISH!!
SQUISH.

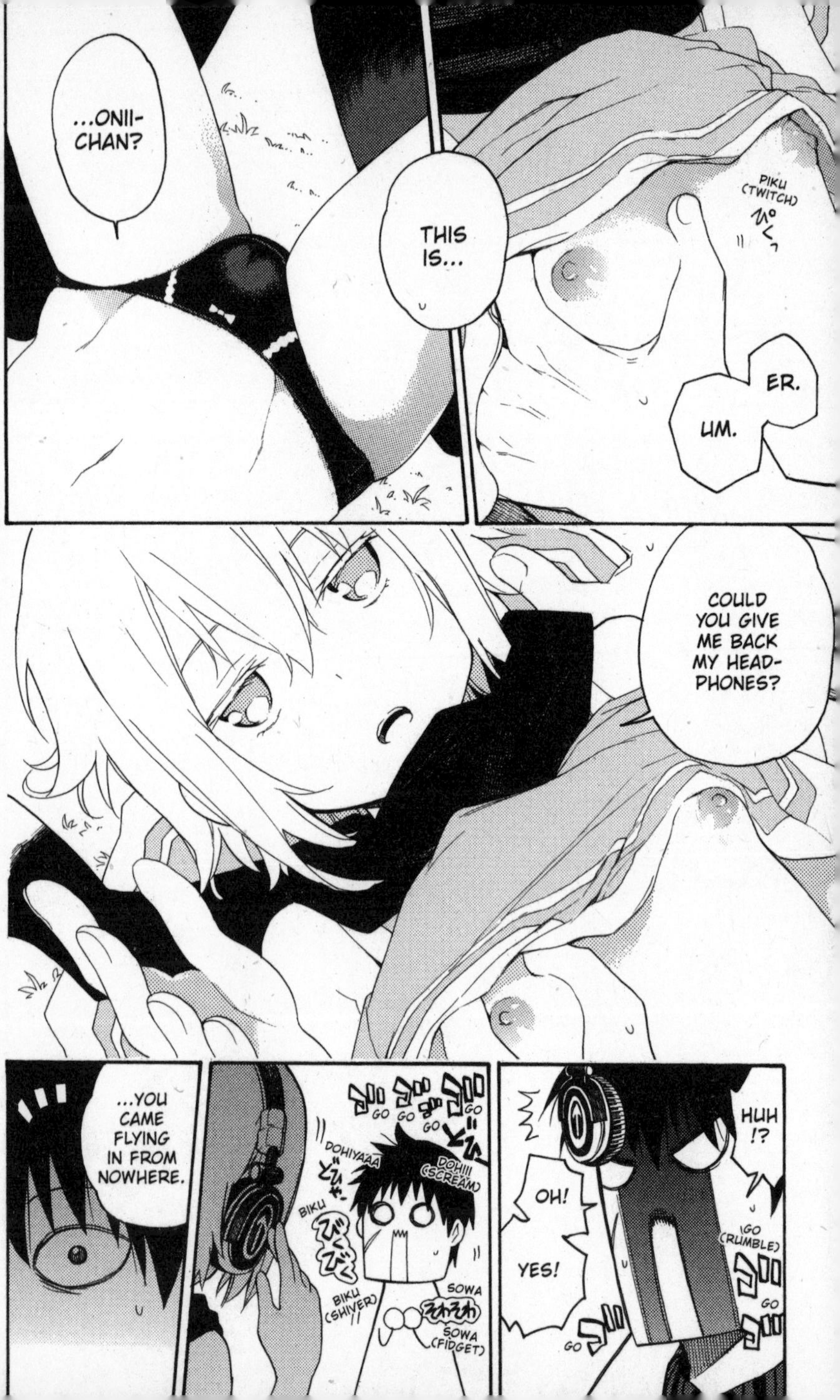
PIKU (TWITCH)
ER.
UM.
THIS IS...
...ONII-CHAN?
COULD YOU GIVE ME BACK MY HEAD-PHONES?
HUH !?
OH!
YES!
GO (RUMBLE)
GO
GO
GO
GO
GO
DOHIII (SCREAM)
DOHIYAAA
BIKU
BIKU (SHIVER)
SOWA
SOWA (FIDGET)
...YOU CAME FLYING IN FROM NOWHERE.

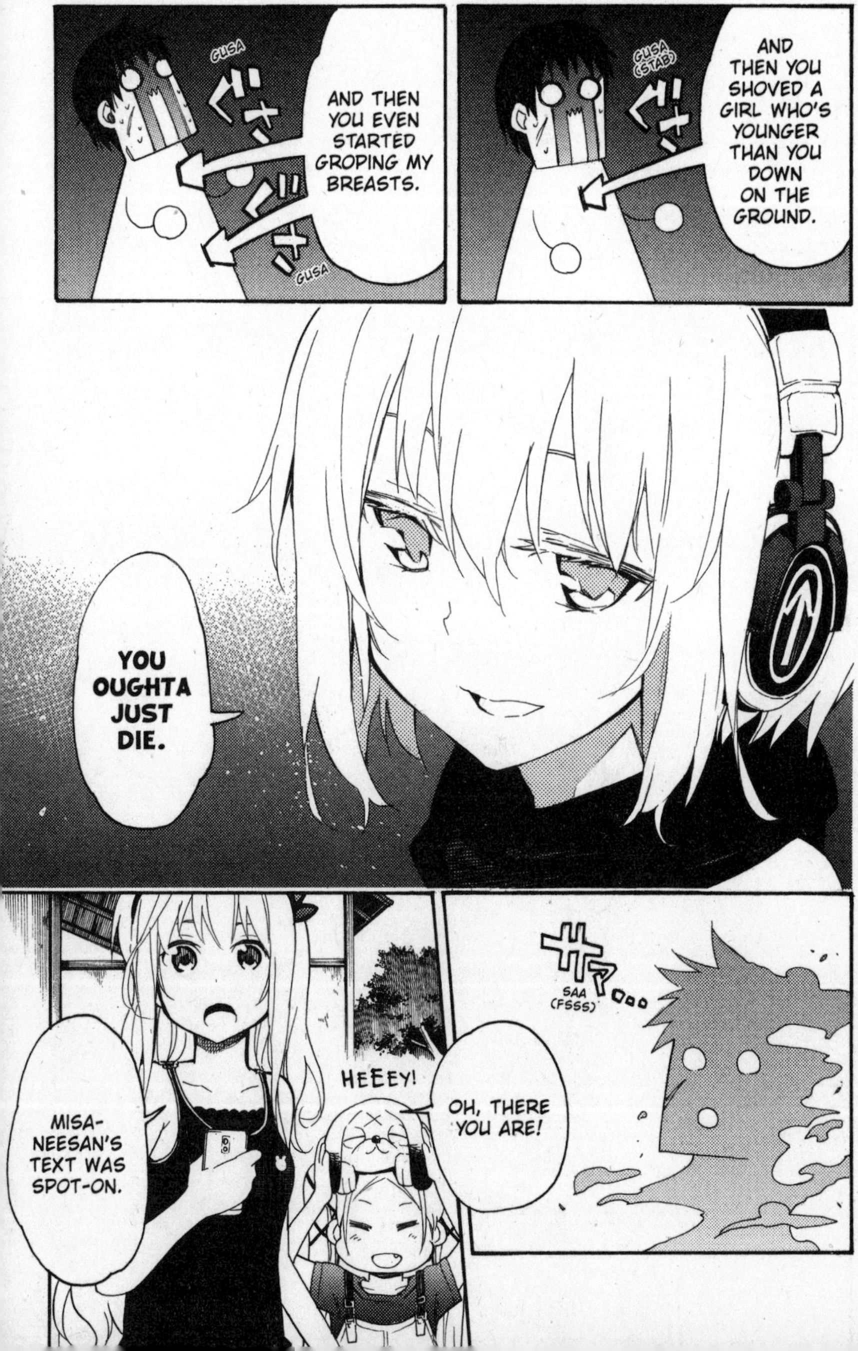
GUSA (STAB)
AND THEN YOU SHOVED A GIRL WHO'S YOUNGER THAN YOU DOWN ON THE GROUND.
GUSA
AND THEN YOU EVEN STARTED GROPING MY BREASTS.
GUSA
YOU OUGHTA JUST DIE.
SAA (FSSS)
HEEEY!
OH, THERE YOU ARE!
MISA-NEESAN'S TEXT WAS SPOT-ON.

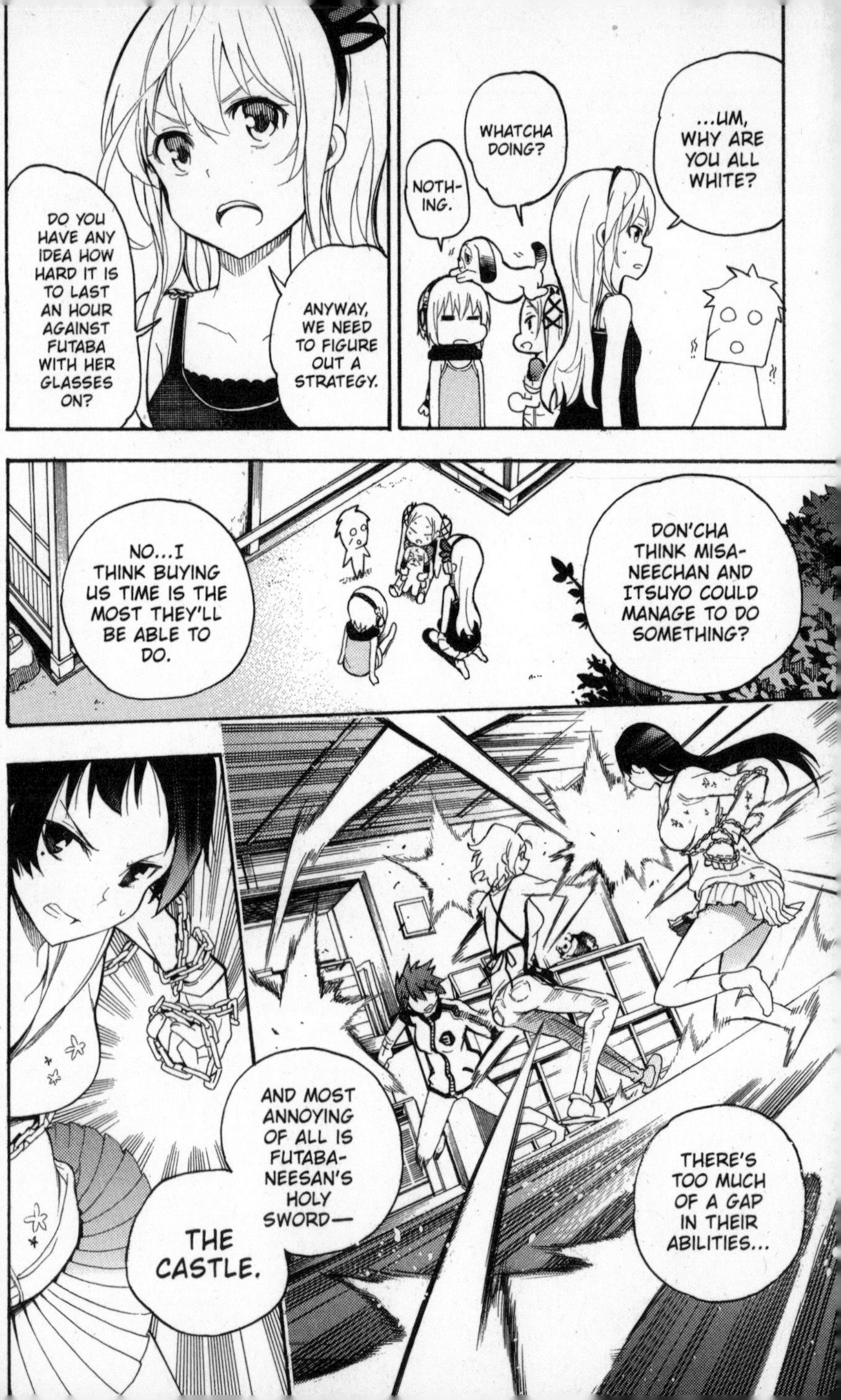
...UM, WHY ARE YOU ALL WHITE?
WHATCHA DOING?
NOTH-ING.
ANYWAY, WE NEED TO FIGURE OUT A STRATEGY.
DO YOU HAVE ANY IDEA HOW HARD IT IS TO LAST AN HOUR AGAINST FUTABA WITH HER GLASSES ON?
DON'CHA THINK MISA-NEECHAN AND ITSUYO COULD MANAGE TO DO SOMETHING?
NO...I THINK BUYING US TIME IS THE MOST THEY'LL BE ABLE TO DO.
THERE'S TOO MUCH OF A GAP IN THEIR ABILITIES...
AND MOST ANNOYING OF ALL IS FUTABA-NEESAN'S HOLY SWORD—
THE CASTLE.

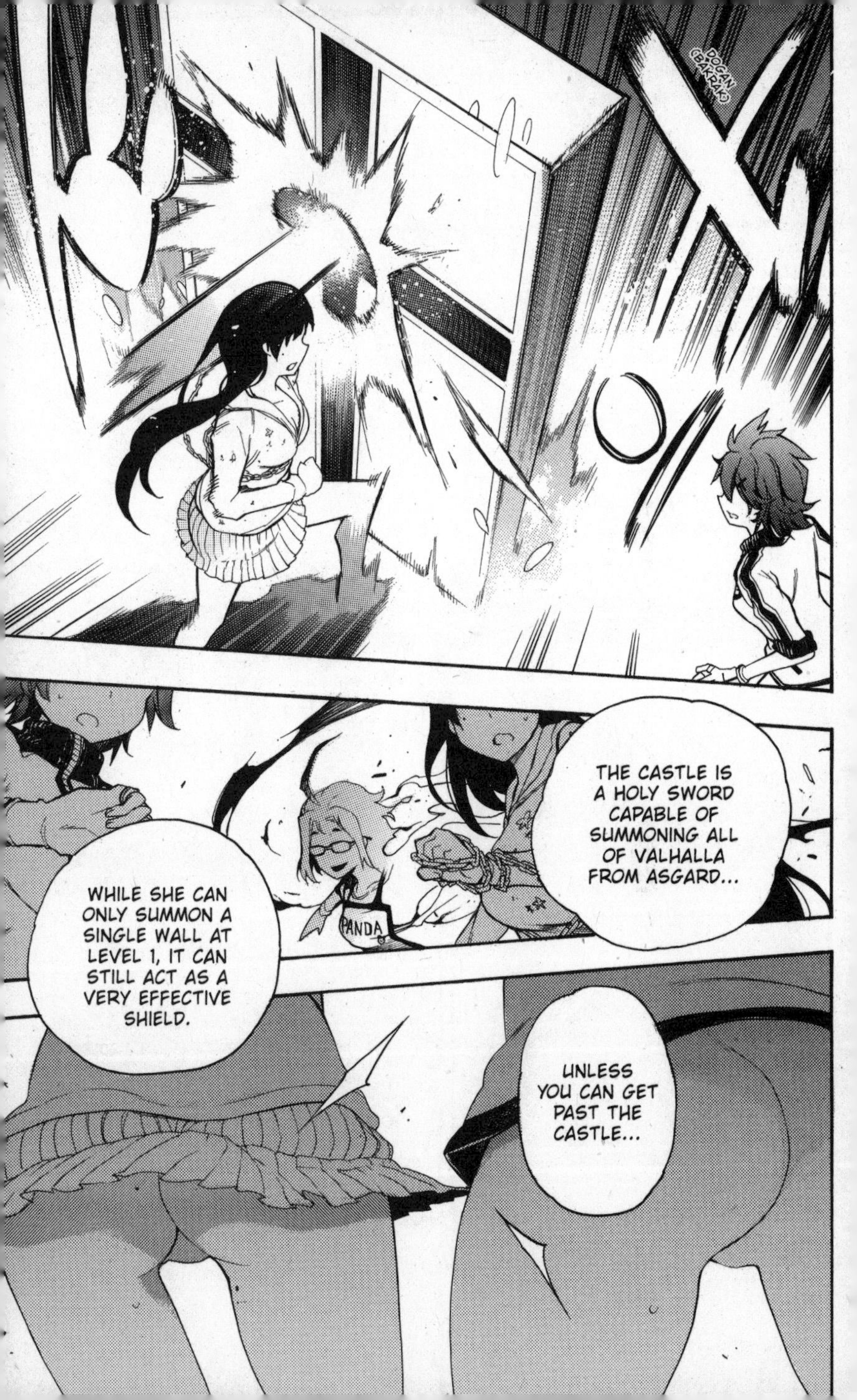
DOGAN (BAKRAK)
THE CASTLE IS A HOLY SWORD CAPABLE OF SUMMONING ALL OF VALHALLA FROM ASGARD...
WHILE SHE CAN ONLY SUMMON A SINGLE WALL AT LEVEL 1, IT CAN STILL ACT AS A VERY EFFECTIVE SHIELD.
UNLESS YOU CAN GET PAST THE CASTLE...

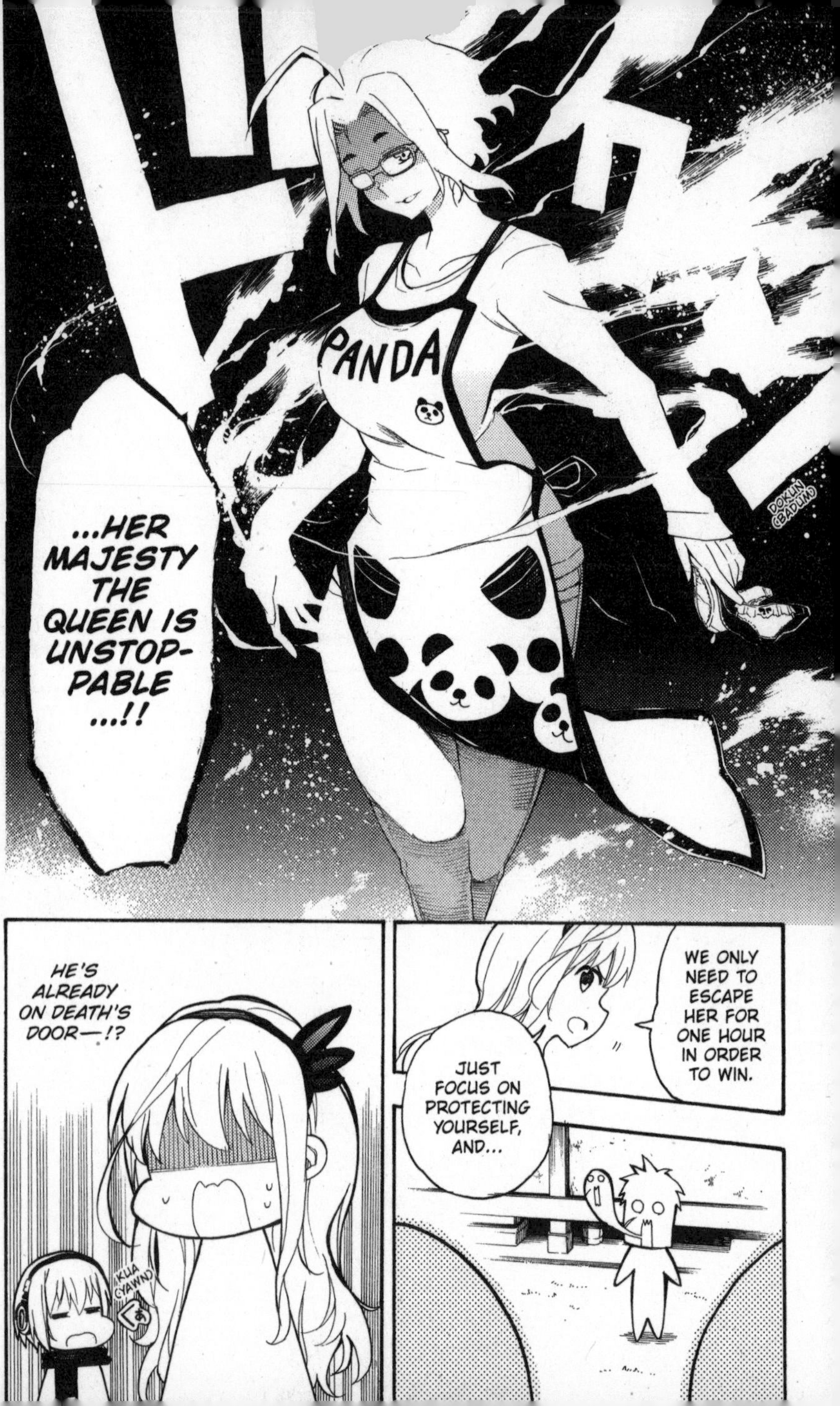

PANDA
DOKUN (BADUM)
...HER MAJESTY THE QUEEN IS UNSTOP-PABLE ...!!
WE ONLY NEED TO ESCAPE HER FOR ONE HOUR IN ORDER TO WIN.
JUST FOCUS ON PROTECTING YOURSELF, AND...
HE'S ALREADY ON DEATH'S DOOR—!?
KUA (YAWN)

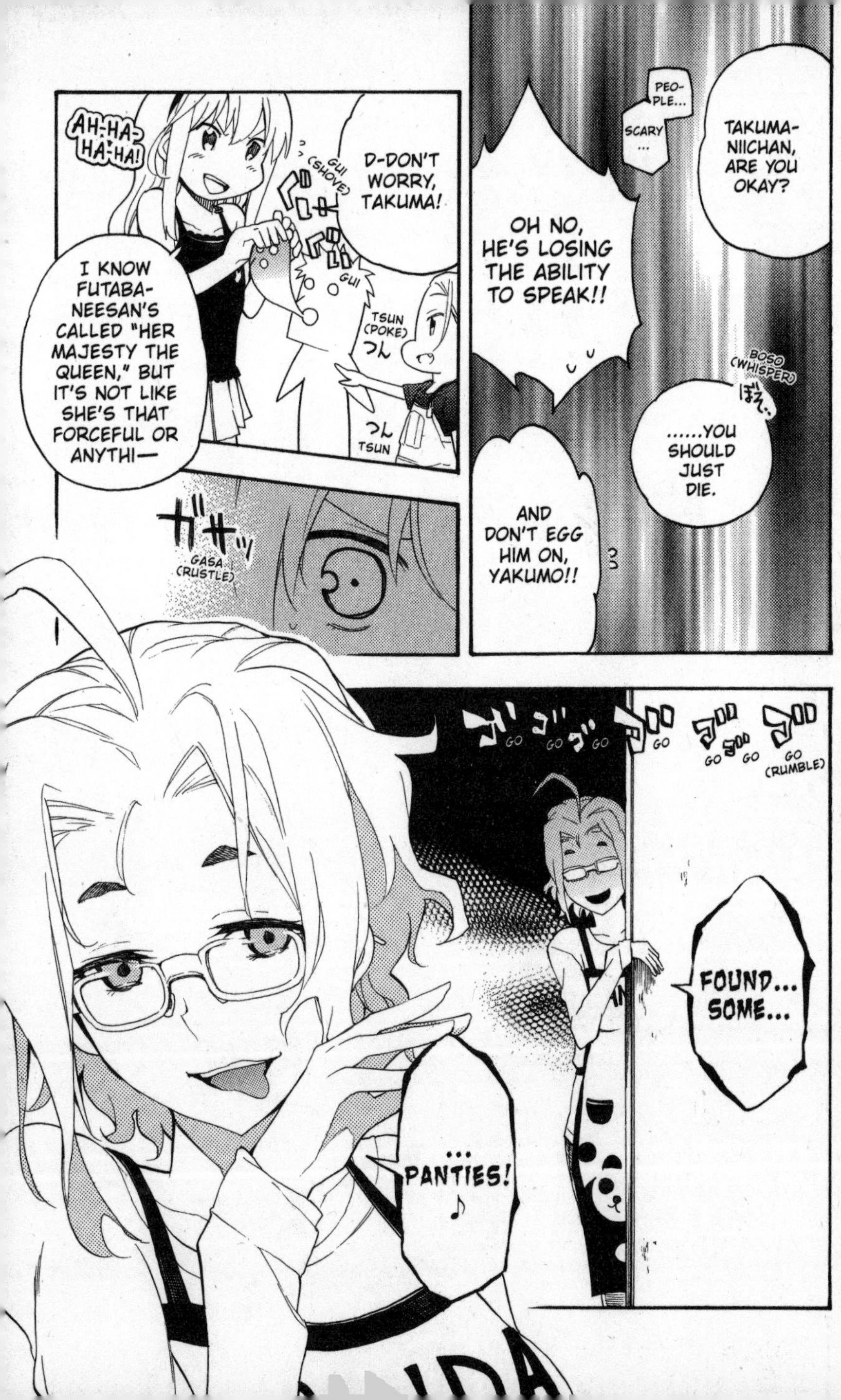

TAKUMA-NIICHAN, ARE YOU OKAY?
PEO-PLE...
SCARY...
OH NO, HE'S LOSING THE ABILITY TO SPEAK!!
BOSO (WHISPER)
ぼそ…
......YOU SHOULD JUST DIE.
AND DON'T EGG HIM ON, YAKUMO!!
D-DON'T WORRY, TAKUMA!
GUI (SHOVE)
GUI
AH-HA-HA-HA!
TSUN (POKE)
つん
つん
TSUN
I KNOW FUTABA-NEESAN'S CALLED "HER MAJESTY THE QUEEN," BUT IT'S NOT LIKE SHE'S THAT FORCEFUL OR ANYTHI—
ガサッ
GASA (RUSTLE)
GO GO GO GO GO GO GO GO GO (RUMBLE)
FOUND... SOME...
...PANTIES! ♪

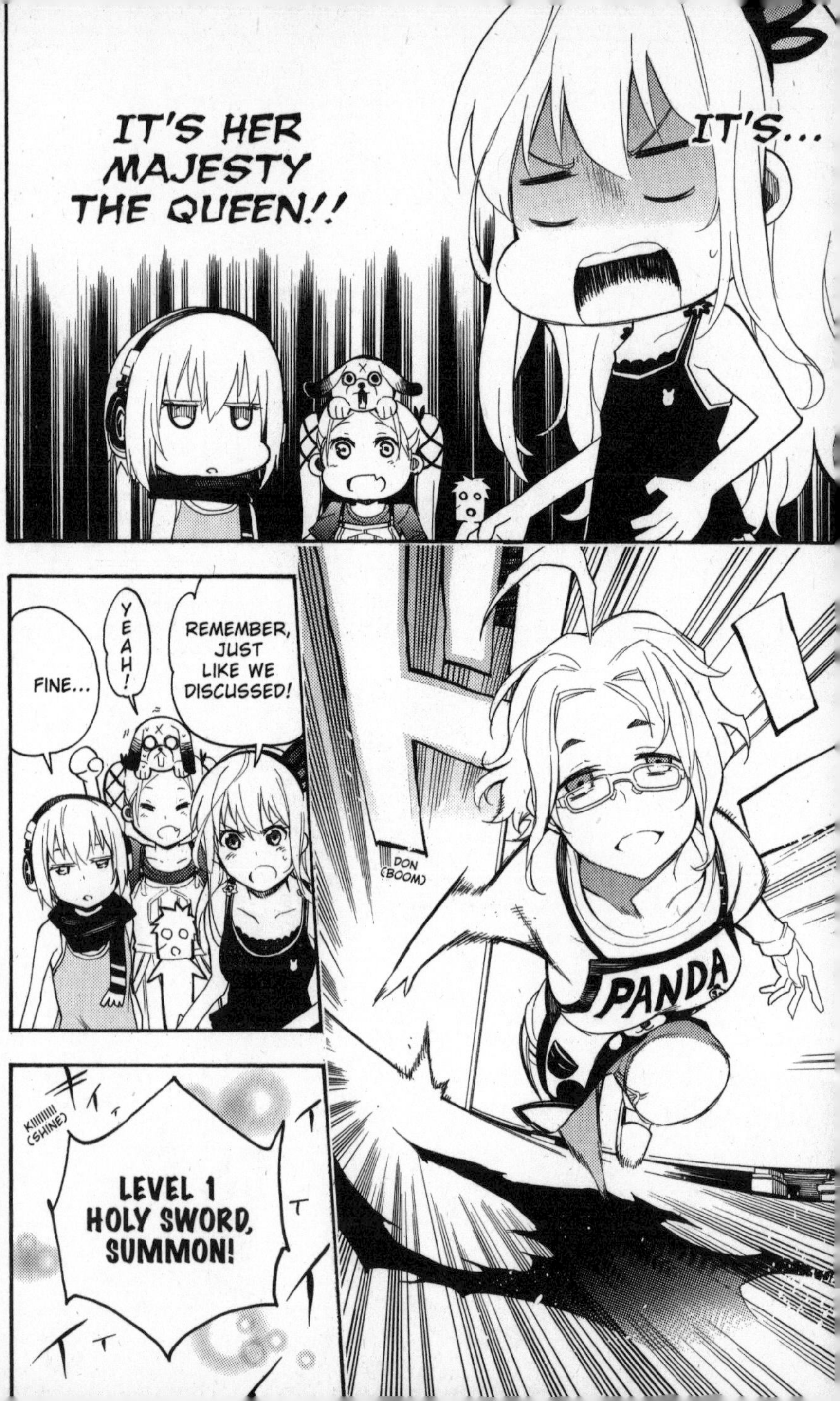
IT'S...
IT'S HER MAJESTY THE QUEEN!!
DON (BOOM)
REMEMBER, JUST LIKE WE DISCUSSED!
YEAH!
FINE...
KIIIIIII (SHINE)
LEVEL 1 HOLY SWORD, SUMMON!

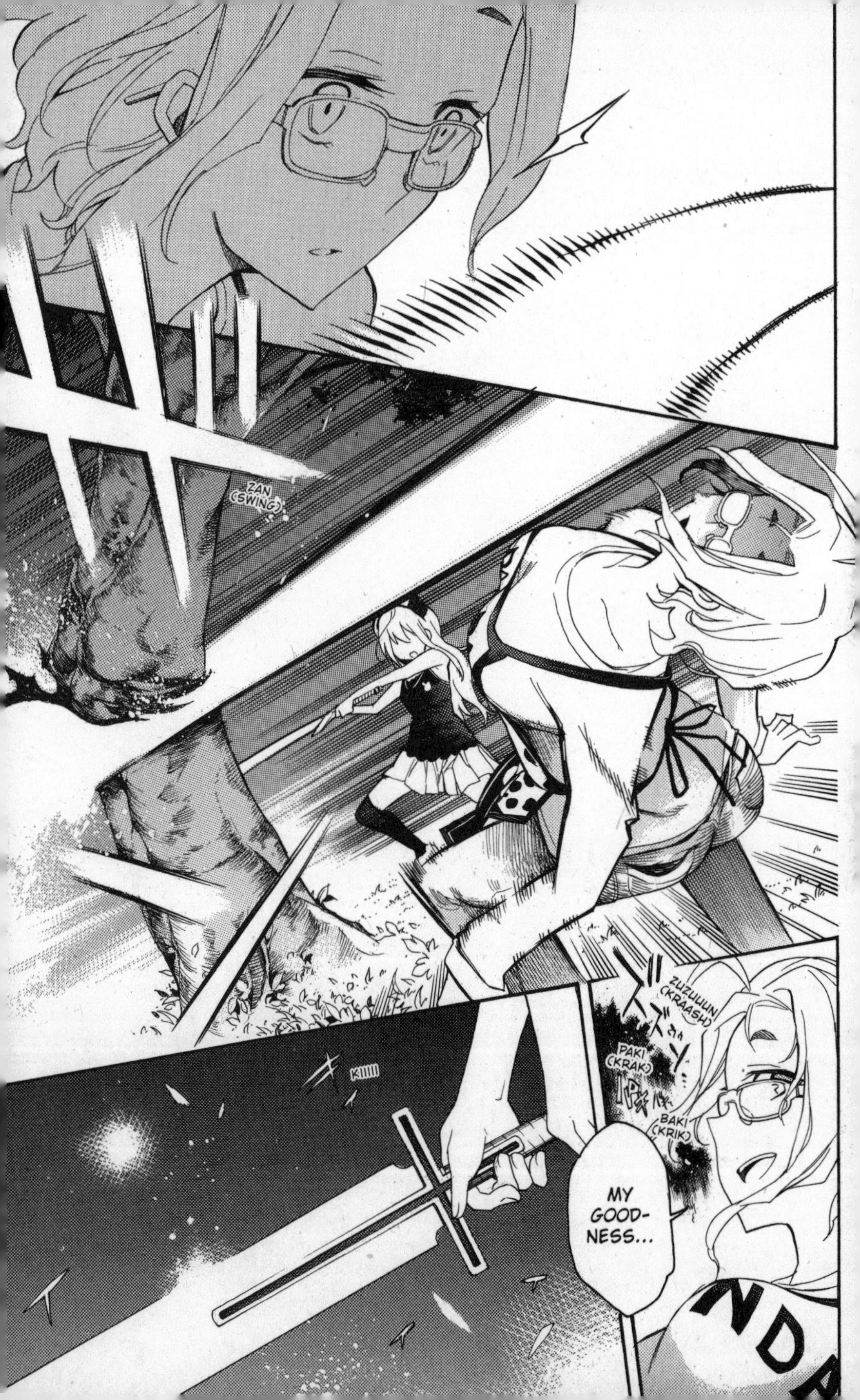
ZAN (SWING)
ZUZUUUN (KRAASH)
PAKI (KRAK)
BAKI (KRIK)
MY GOOD-NESS...
KIIIII

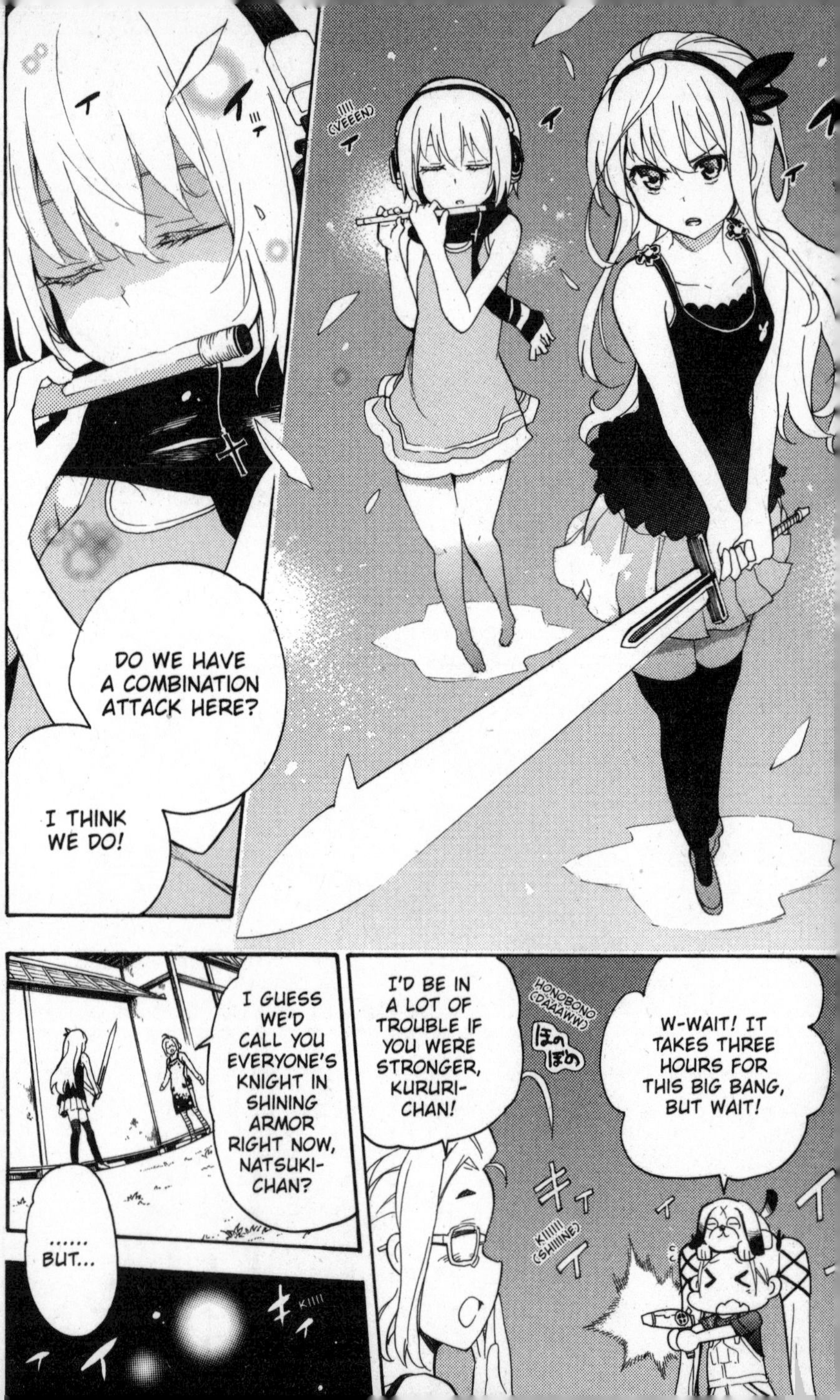
IIII (VEEEN)
DO WE HAVE A COMBINATION ATTACK HERE?
I THINK WE DO!
W-WAIT! IT TAKES THREE HOURS FOR THIS BIG BANG, BUT WAIT!
KIIIII (SHIIINE)
HONOBONO (DAAAWW)
I'D BE IN A LOT OF TROUBLE IF YOU WERE STRONGER, KURURI-CHAN!
I GUESS WE'D CALL YOU EVERYONE'S KNIGHT IN SHINING ARMOR RIGHT NOW, NATSUKI-CHAN?
...... BUT...
KIIII

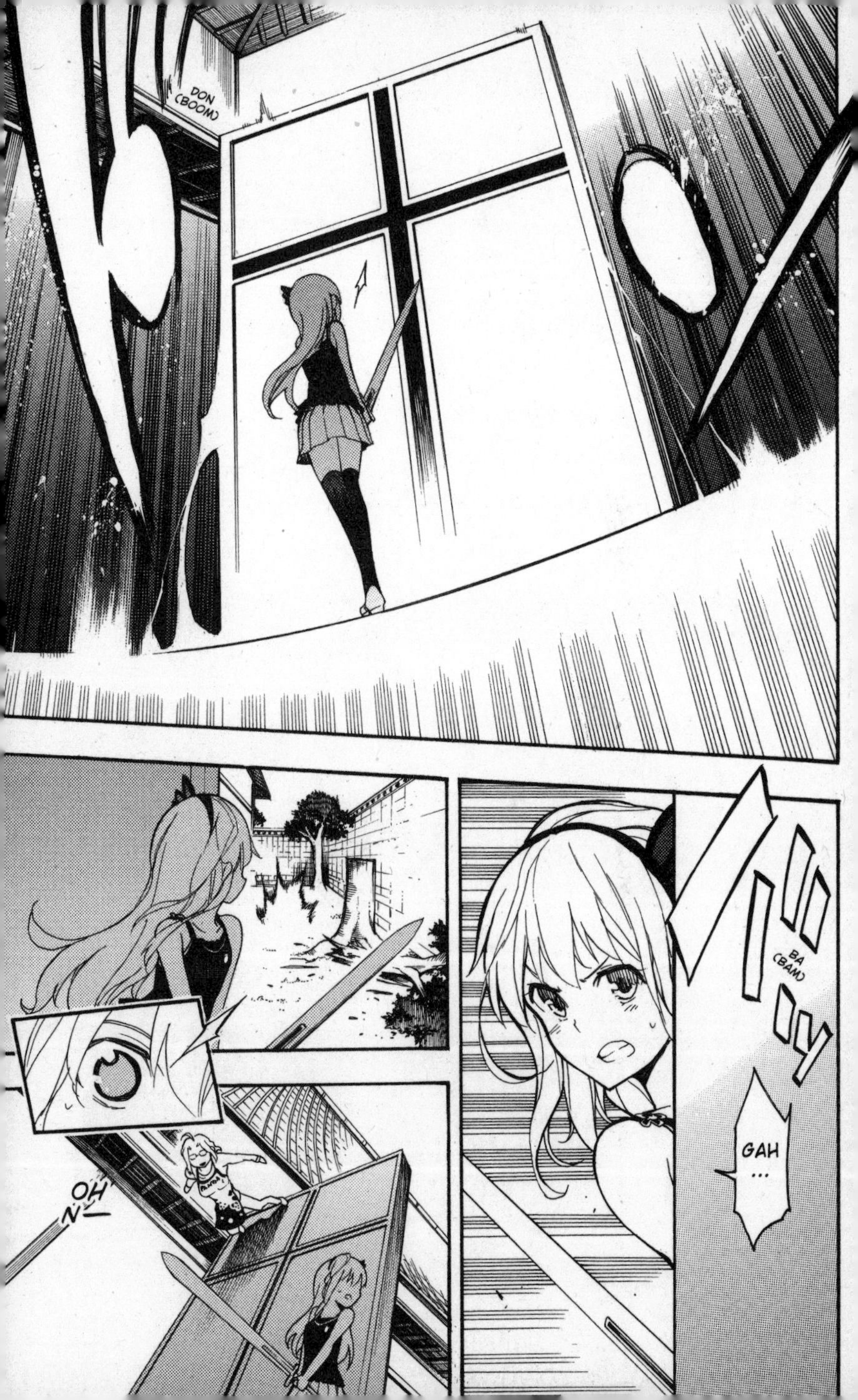
DON (BOOM)
BA (BAM)
GAH ...
OH N-

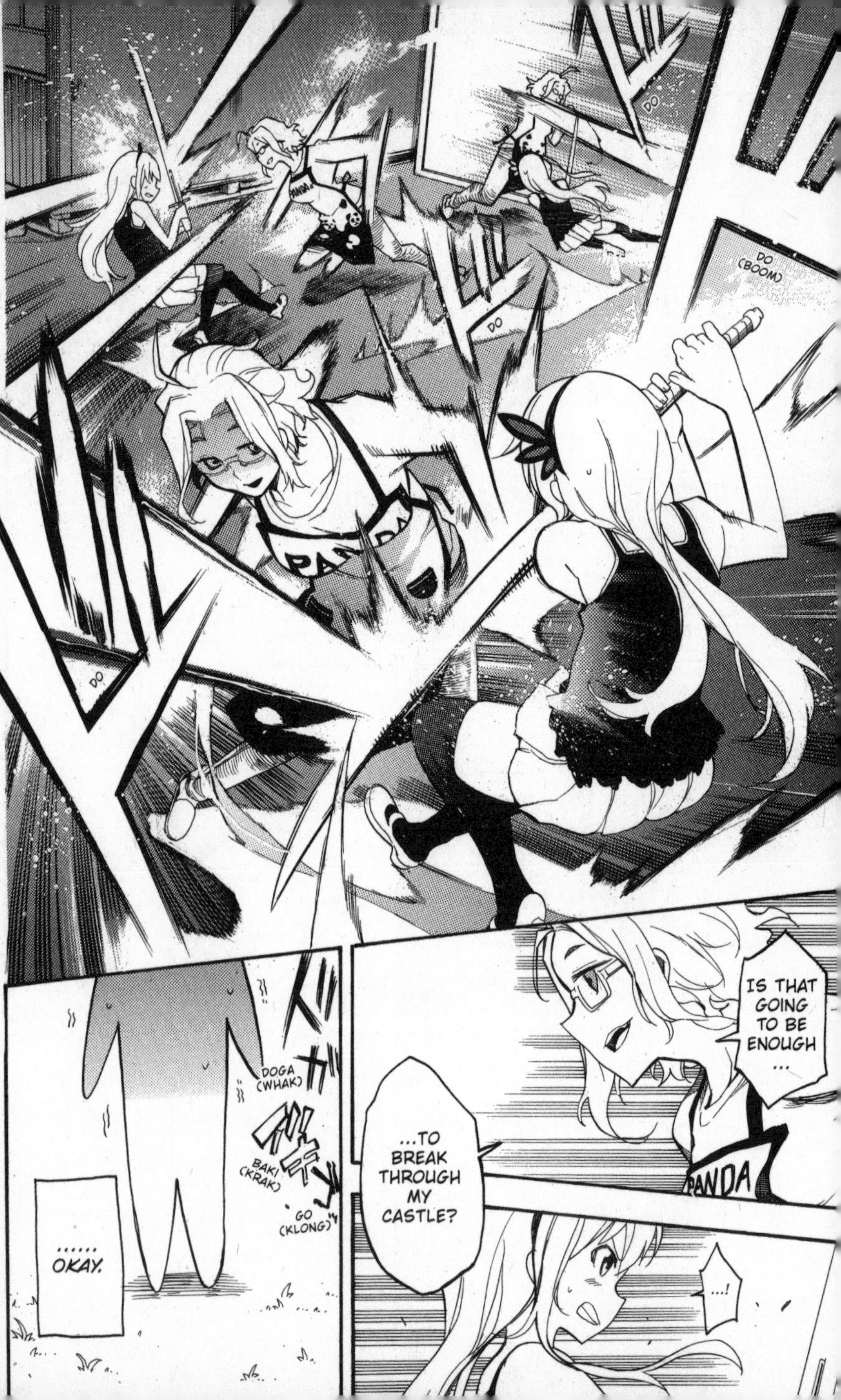
DO
DO
(BOOM)
DO
DO
IS THAT GOING TO BE ENOUGH ...
...TO BREAK THROUGH MY CASTLE?
PANDA
...!
DOGA
(WHAK)
BAKI
(KRAK)
GO
(KLONG)
.... OKAY.

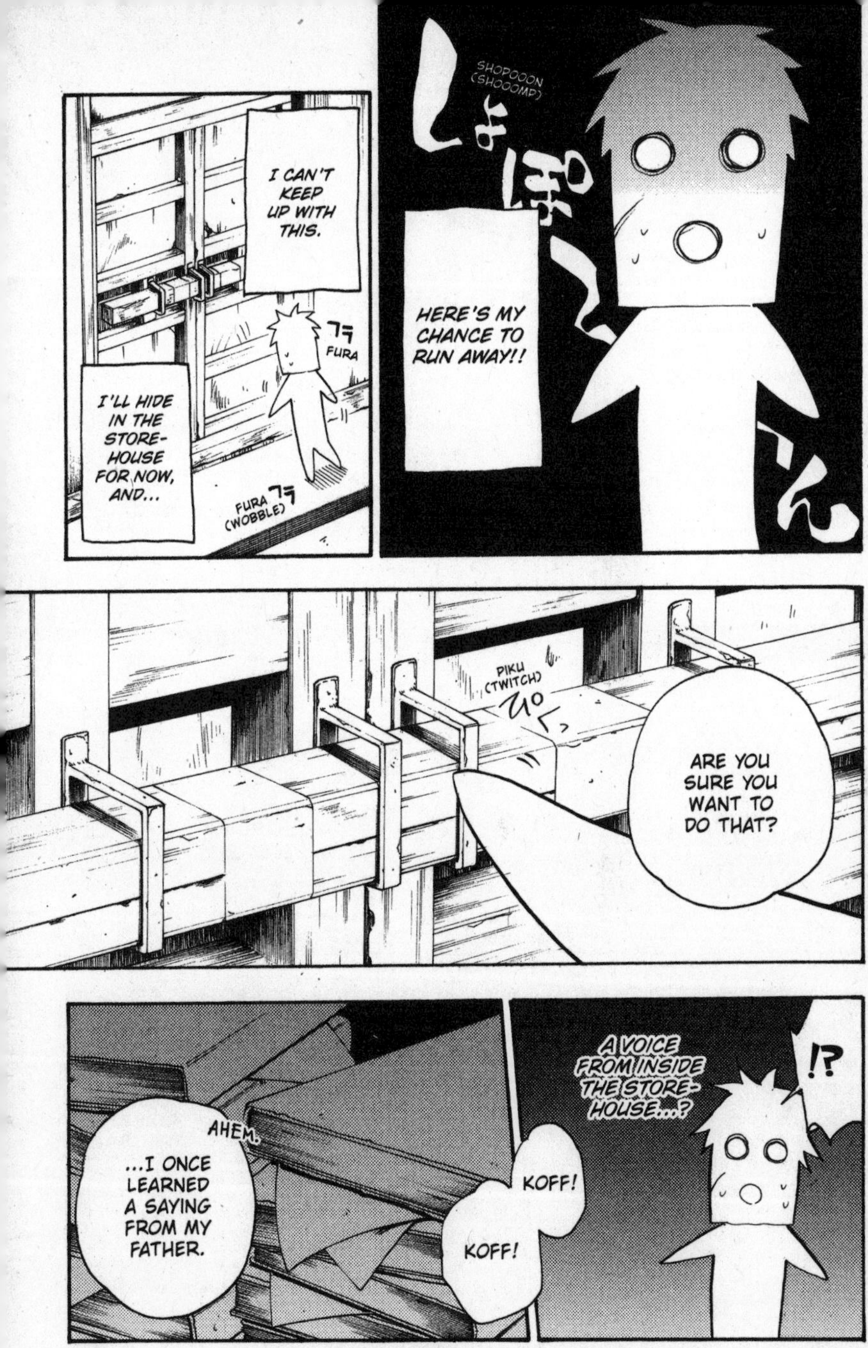
SHOPOOON (SHOOOMP)
HERE'S MY CHANCE TO RUN AWAY!!
I CAN'T KEEP UP WITH THIS.
フラ FURA
I'LL HIDE IN THE STOREHOUSE FOR NOW, AND...
FURA フラ (WOBBLE)
PIKU (TWITCH)
ARE YOU SURE YOU WANT TO DO THAT?
!?
A VOICE FROM INSIDE THE STOREHOUSE...?
KOFF!
KOFF!
AHEM.
...I ONCE LEARNED A SAYING FROM MY FATHER.

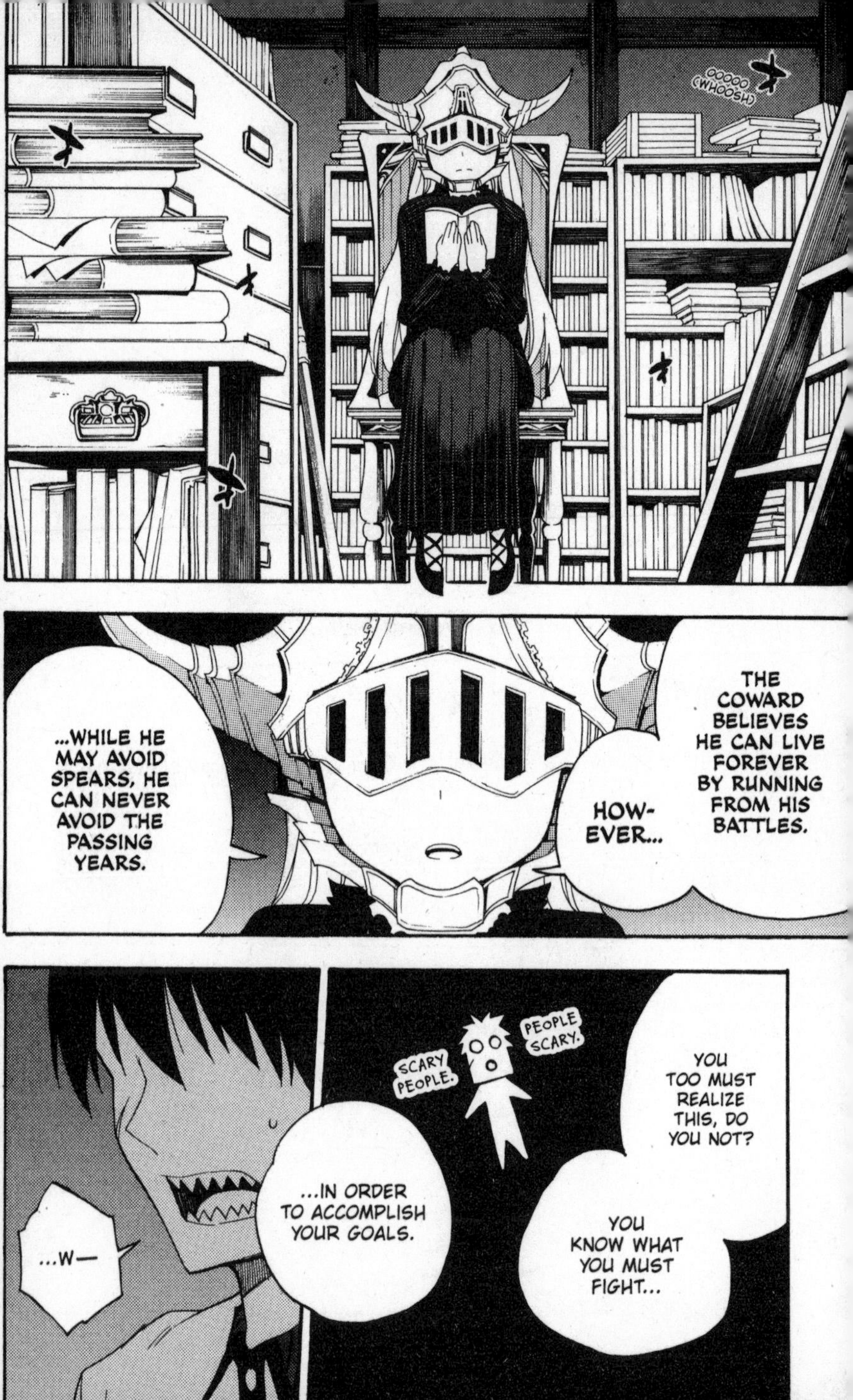
OOOOO (WHOOSH)
THE COWARD BELIEVES HE CAN LIVE FOREVER BY RUNNING FROM HIS BATTLES.
HOW-EVER...
...WHILE HE MAY AVOID SPEARS, HE CAN NEVER AVOID THE PASSING YEARS.
YOU TOO MUST REALIZE THIS, DO YOU NOT?
PEOPLE SCARY.
SCARY PEOPLE.
YOU KNOW WHAT YOU MUST FIGHT...
...IN ORDER TO ACCOMPLISH YOUR GOALS.
...W—

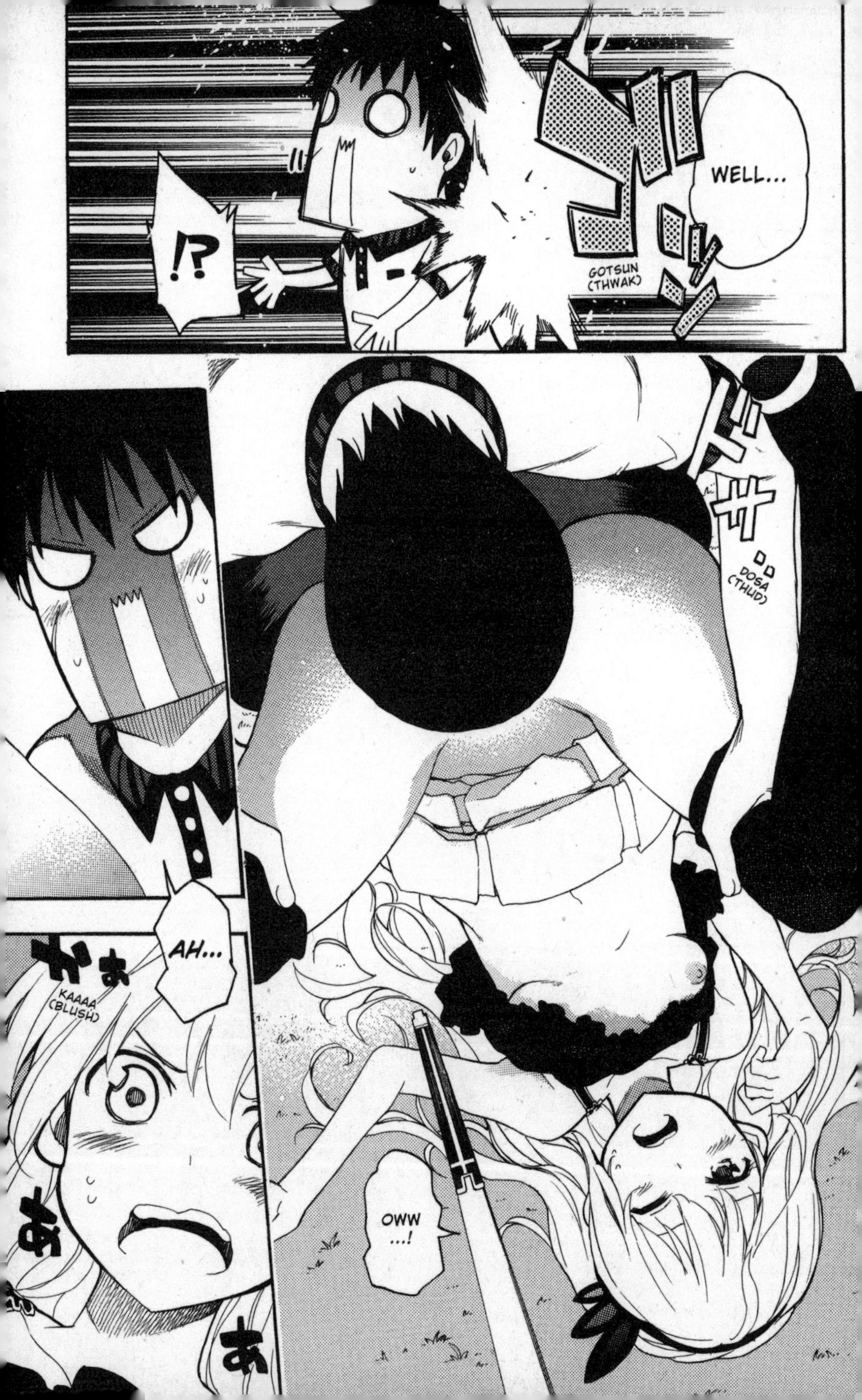
WELL...
GOTSUN (THWAK)
!?
DOSA (THUD)
OWW ...!
AH...
KAAAA (BLUSH)

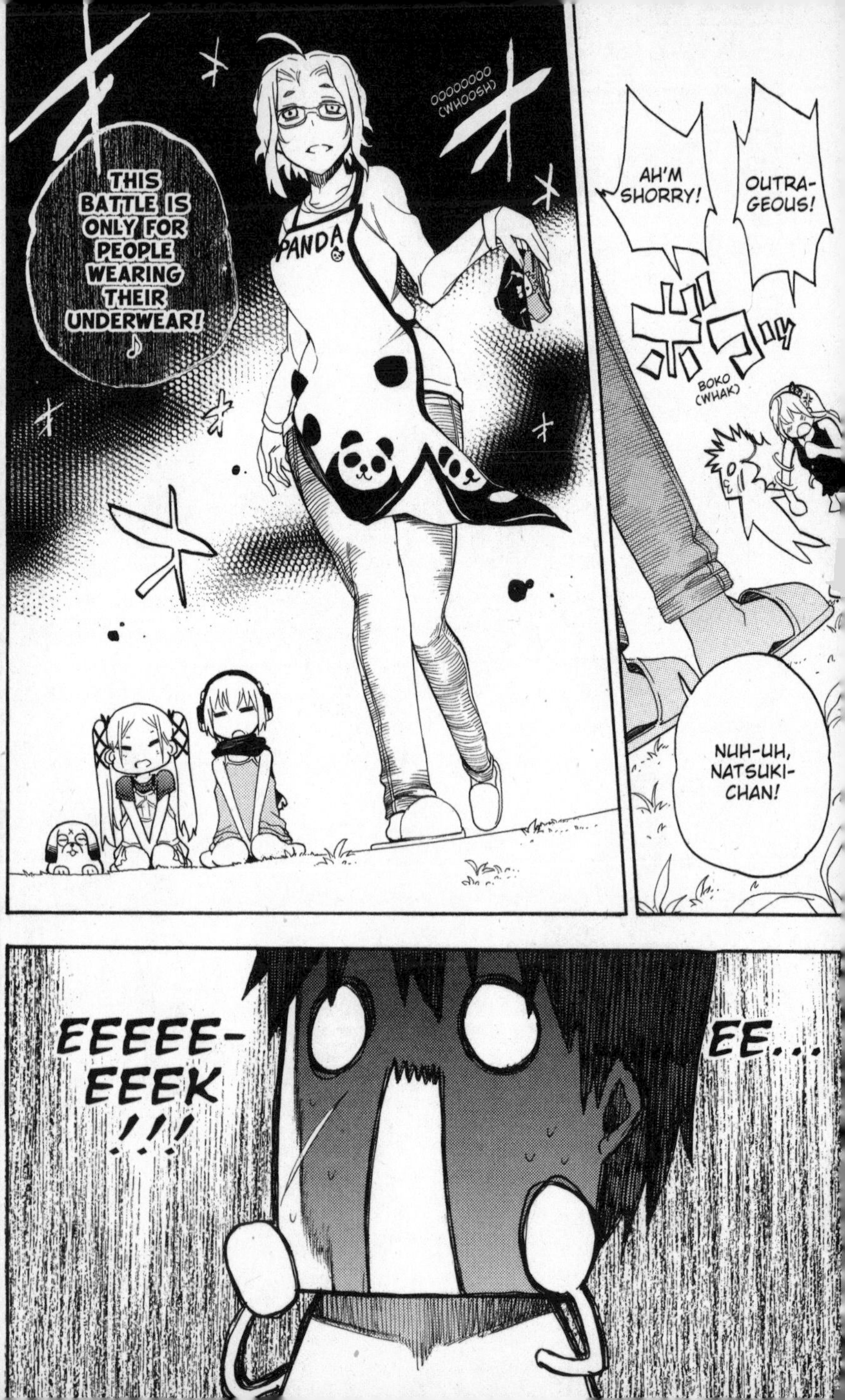
OUTRA-GEOUS!
AH'M SHORRY!
BOKO (WHAK)
NUH-UH, NATSUKI-CHAN!
OOOOOOOO (WHOOSH)
THIS BATTLE IS ONLY FOR PEOPLE WEARING THEIR UNDERWEAR! ♪
EE...
EEEEE-EEEK!!!!

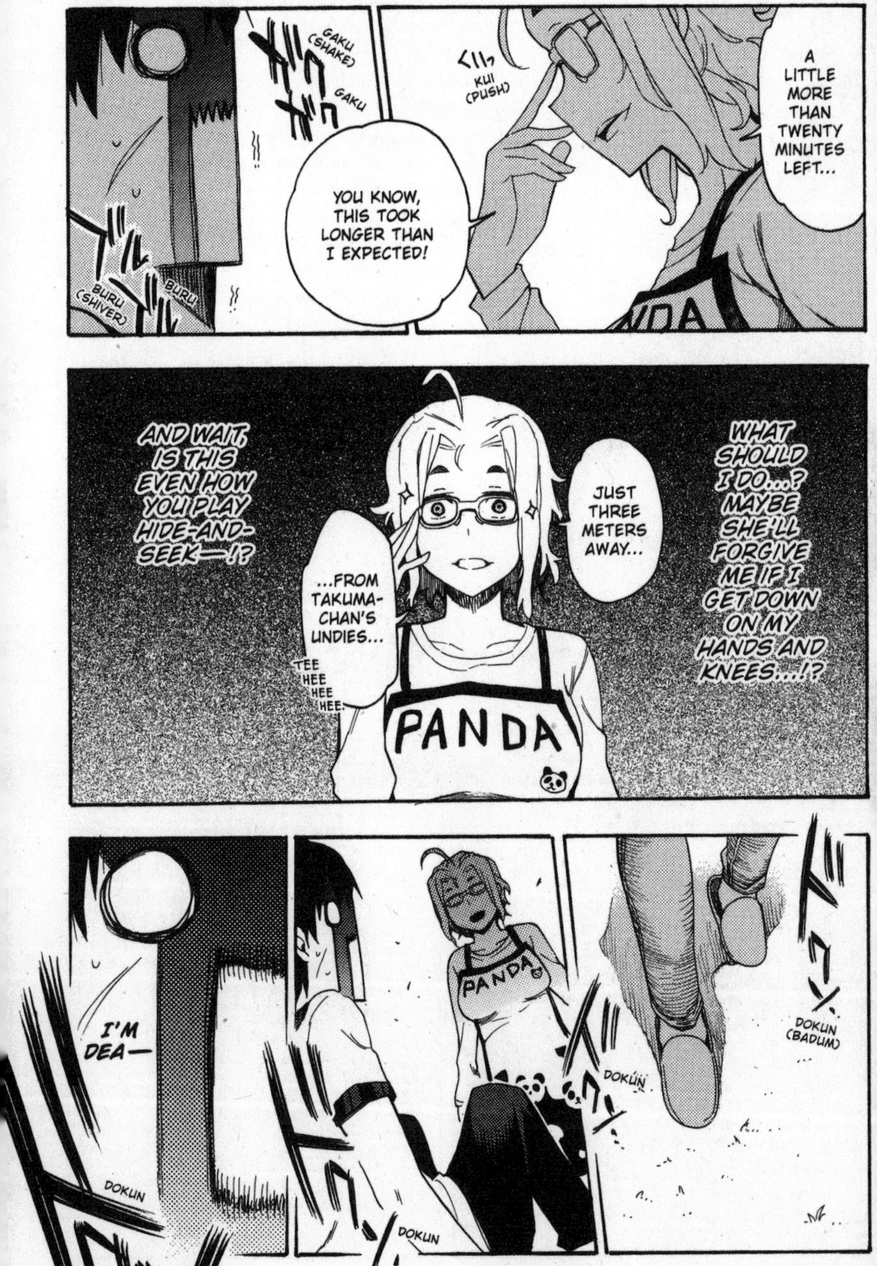
A LITTLE MORE THAN TWENTY MINUTES LEFT...
KUI (PUSH)
YOU KNOW, THIS TOOK LONGER THAN I EXPECTED!
GAKU (SHAKE)
GAKU
BURU (SHIVER)
BURU
WHAT SHOULD I DO...? MAYBE SHE'LL FORGIVE ME IF I GET DOWN ON MY HANDS AND KNEES...!?
JUST THREE METERS AWAY...
...FROM TAKUMA-CHAN'S UNDIES...
TEE HEE HEE HEE.
AND WAIT, IS THIS EVEN HOW YOU PLAY HIDE-AND-SEEK—!?
DOKUN (BADUM)
DOKUN
DOKUN
I'M DEA—
DOKUN

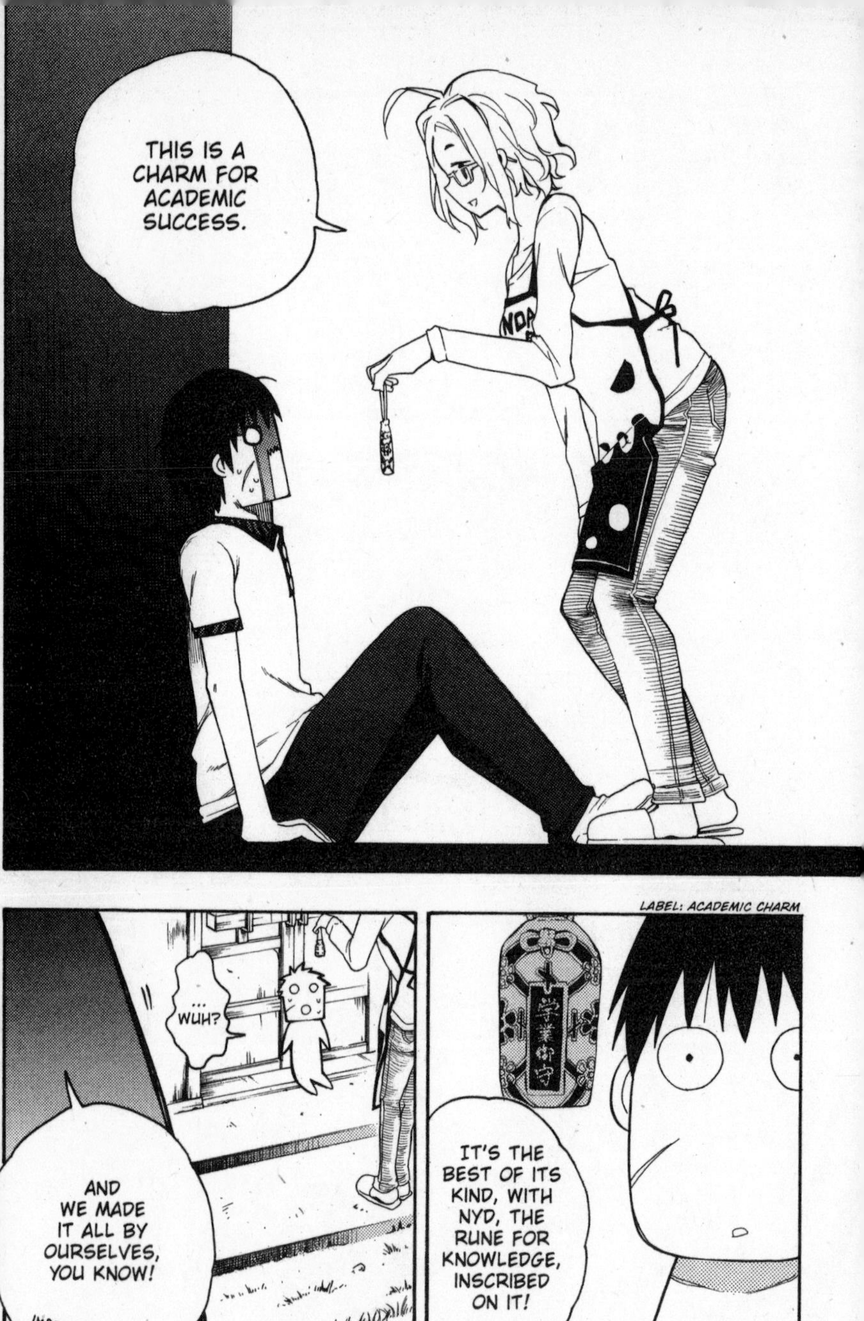
THIS IS A CHARM FOR ACADEMIC SUCCESS.
LABEL: ACADEMIC CHARM
学業御守
IT'S THE BEST OF ITS KIND, WITH NYD, THE RUNE FOR KNOWLEDGE, INSCRIBED ON IT!
...WUH?
AND WE MADE IT ALL BY OURSELVES, YOU KNOW!
IMPRESSIVE, RIGHT?

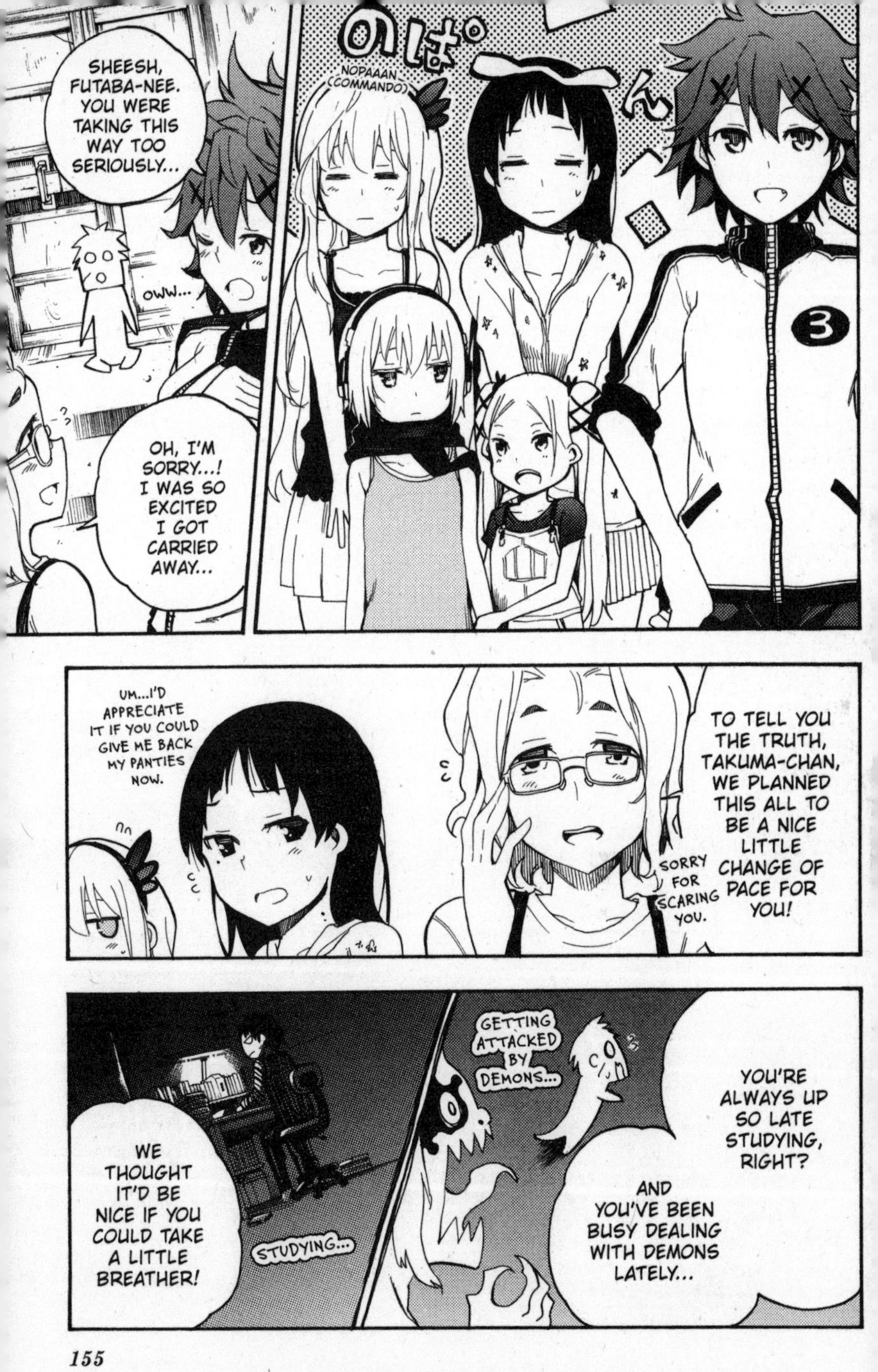
のぱん
NOPAAAN (COMMANDO)
SHEESH, FUTABA-NEE. YOU WERE TAKING THIS WAY TOO SERIOUSLY...
OWW...
OH, I'M SORRY...! I WAS SO EXCITED I GOT CARRIED AWAY...
TO TELL YOU THE TRUTH, TAKUMA-CHAN, WE PLANNED THIS ALL TO BE A NICE LITTLE CHANGE OF PACE FOR YOU!
SORRY FOR SCARING YOU.
UM...I'D APPRECIATE IT IF YOU COULD GIVE ME BACK MY PANTIES NOW.
YOU'RE ALWAYS UP SO LATE STUDYING, RIGHT?
AND YOU'VE BEEN BUSY DEALING WITH DEMONS LATELY...
GETTING ATTACKED BY DEMONS...
STUDYING...
WE THOUGHT IT'D BE NICE IF YOU COULD TAKE A LITTLE BREATHER!

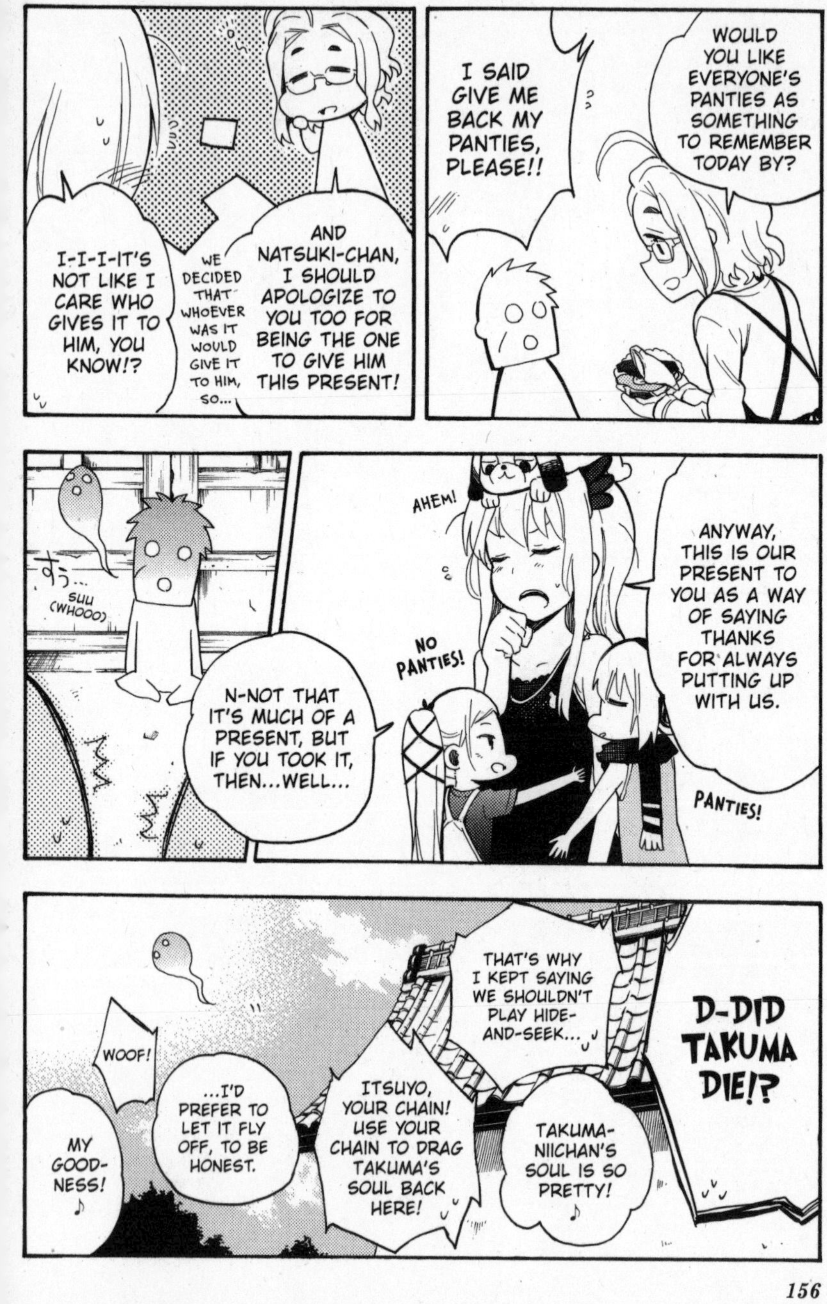
WOULD YOU LIKE EVERYONE'S PANTIES AS SOMETHING TO REMEMBER TODAY BY?
I SAID GIVE ME BACK MY PANTIES, PLEASE!!
AND NATSUKI-CHAN, I SHOULD APOLOGIZE TO YOU TOO FOR BEING THE ONE TO GIVE HIM THIS PRESENT!
WE DECIDED THAT WHOEVER WAS IT WOULD GIVE IT TO HIM, SO...
I-I-I-IT'S NOT LIKE I CARE WHO GIVES IT TO HIM, YOU KNOW!?
ANYWAY, THIS IS OUR PRESENT TO YOU AS A WAY OF SAYING THANKS FOR ALWAYS PUTTING UP WITH US.
AHEM!
NO PANTIES!
PANTIES!
N-NOT THAT IT'S MUCH OF A PRESENT, BUT IF YOU TOOK IT, THEN...WELL...
すぅ...
SUU (WHOOO)
D-DID TAKUMA DIE!?
THAT'S WHY I KEPT SAYING WE SHOULDN'T PLAY HIDE-AND-SEEK...
TAKUMA-NIICHAN'S SOUL IS SO PRETTY! ♪
ITSUYO, YOUR CHAIN! USE YOUR CHAIN TO DRAG TAKUMA'S SOUL BACK HERE!
...I'D PREFER TO LET IT FLY OFF, TO BE HONEST.
WOOF!
MY GOODNESS! ♪

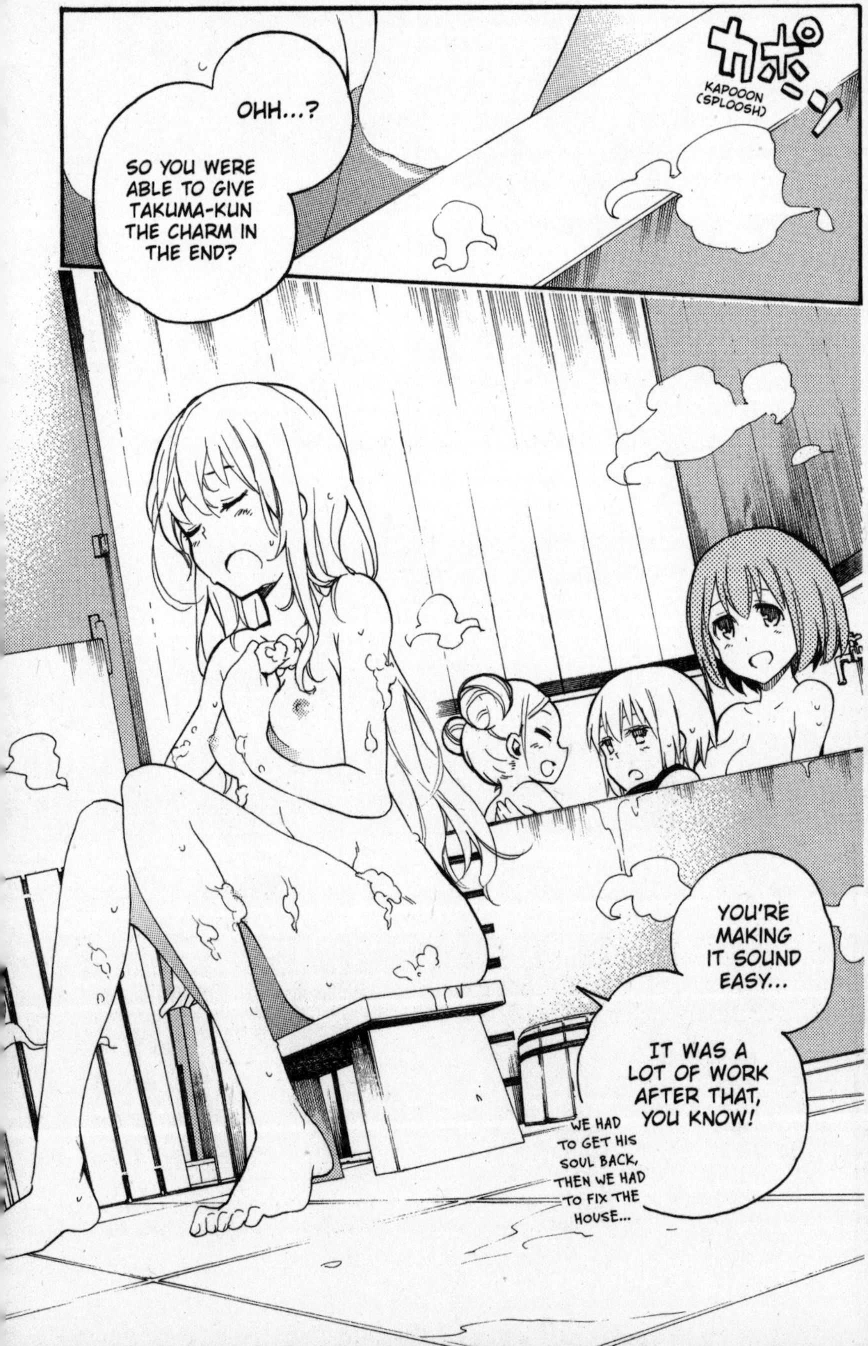
カポーン
KAPOOON (SPLOOSH)
OHH...?
SO YOU WERE ABLE TO GIVE TAKUMA-KUN THE CHARM IN THE END?
YOU'RE MAKING IT SOUND EASY...
IT WAS A LOT OF WORK AFTER THAT, YOU KNOW!
WE HAD TO GET HIS SOUL BACK, THEN WE HAD TO FIX THE HOUSE...

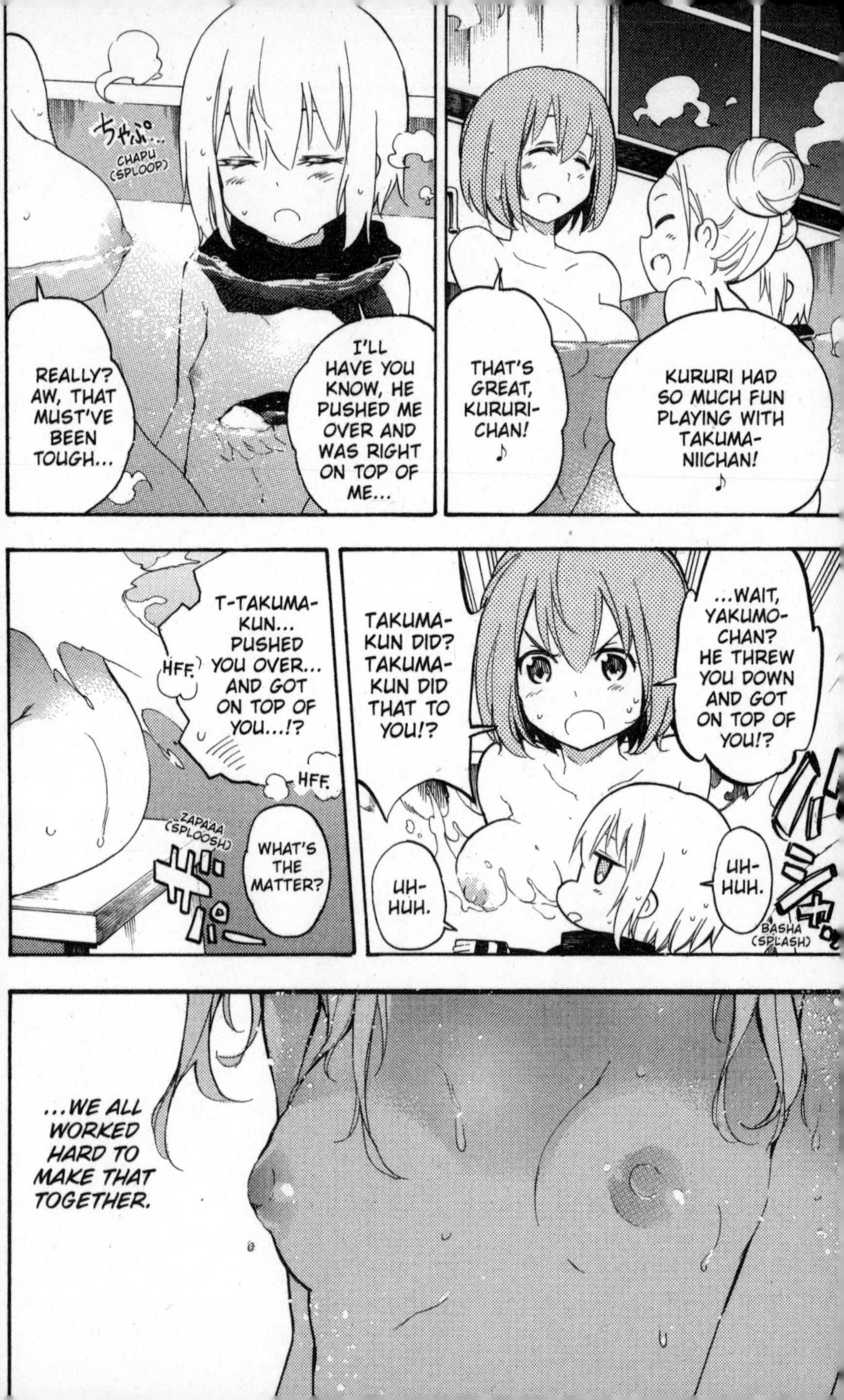
KURURI HAD SO MUCH FUN PLAYING WITH TAKUMA-NIICHAN! ♪
THAT'S GREAT, KURURI-CHAN! ♪
ちゃぷ… CHAPU (SPLOOP)
I'LL HAVE YOU KNOW, HE PUSHED ME OVER AND WAS RIGHT ON TOP OF ME…
REALLY? AW, THAT MUST'VE BEEN TOUGH…
…WAIT, YAKUMO-CHAN? HE THREW YOU DOWN AND GOT ON TOP OF YOU!?
TAKUMA-KUN DID? TAKUMA-KUN DID THAT TO YOU!?
UH-HUH.
BASHA (SPLASH)
UH-HUH.
T-TAKUMA-KUN… PUSHED YOU OVER… AND GOT ON TOP OF YOU…!?
HFF.
HFF.
ZAPAAA (SPLOOSH)
WHAT'S THE MATTER?
…WE ALL WORKED HARD TO MAKE THAT TOGETHER.

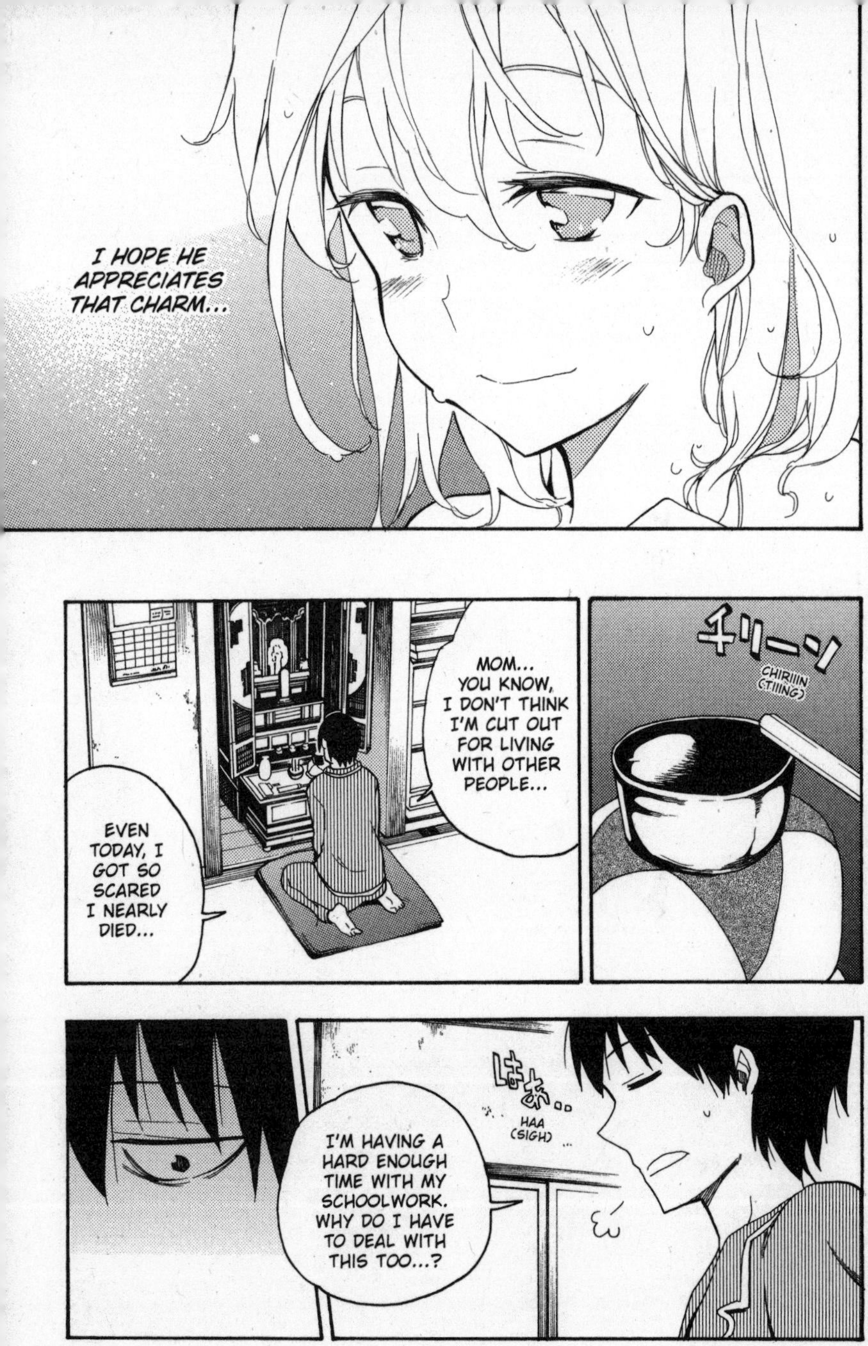
I HOPE HE APPRECIATES THAT CHARM...
チリーン
CHIRIIN (TIIING)
MOM... YOU KNOW, I DON'T THINK I'M CUT OUT FOR LIVING WITH OTHER PEOPLE...
EVEN TODAY, I GOT SO SCARED I NEARLY DIED...
はぁ..
HAA (SIGH)
I'M HAVING A HARD ENOUGH TIME WITH MY SCHOOLWORK. WHY DO I HAVE TO DEAL WITH THIS TOO...?

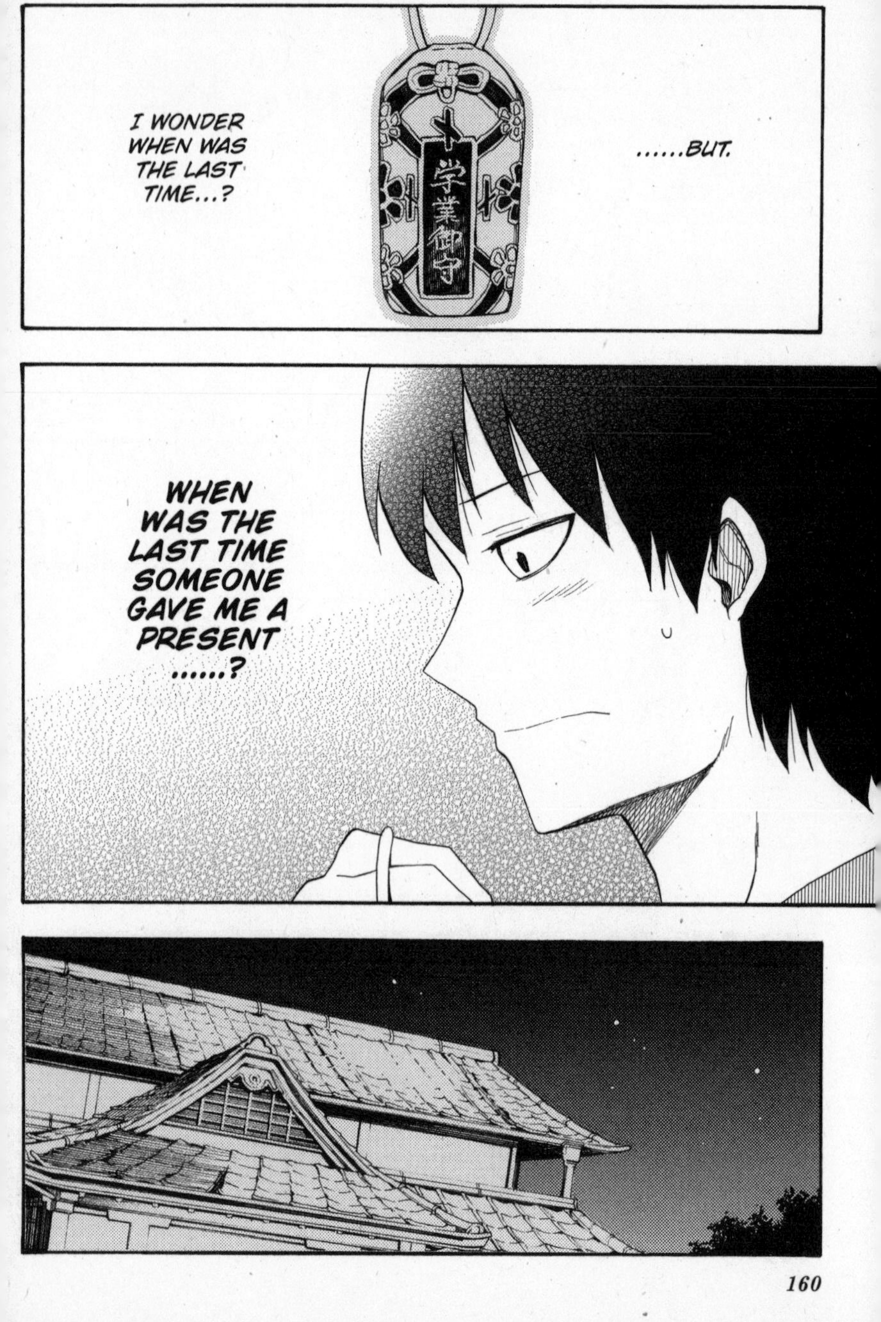
......BUT.
学業御守
I WONDER WHEN WAS THE LAST TIME...?
WHEN WAS THE LAST TIME SOMEONE GAVE ME A PRESENT ......?

Val X Love

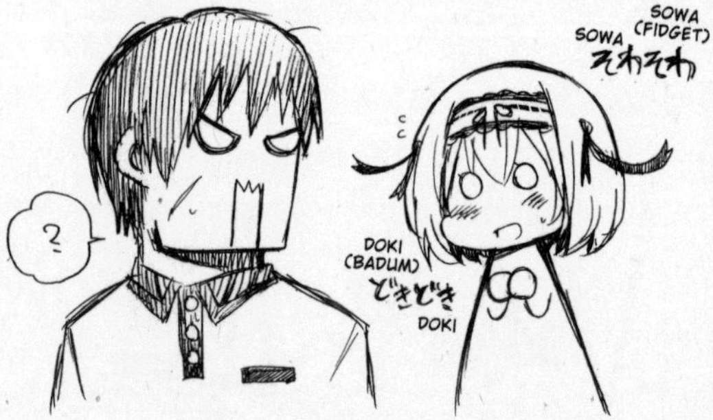
SOWA
SOWA (FIDGET)
そわそわ
DOKI (BADUM)
どきどき
DOKI
?

Chapter 9: The Wet Maiden

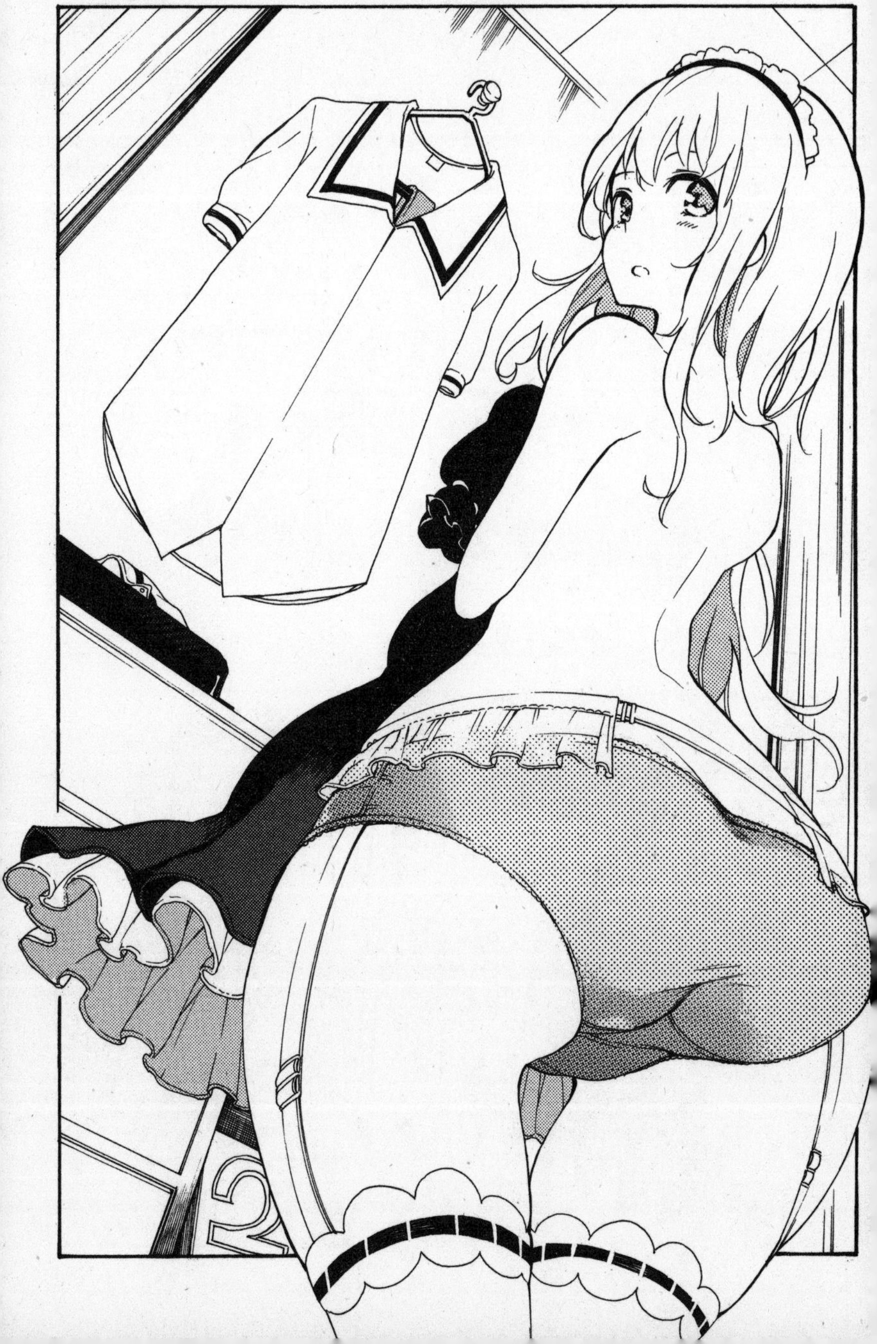

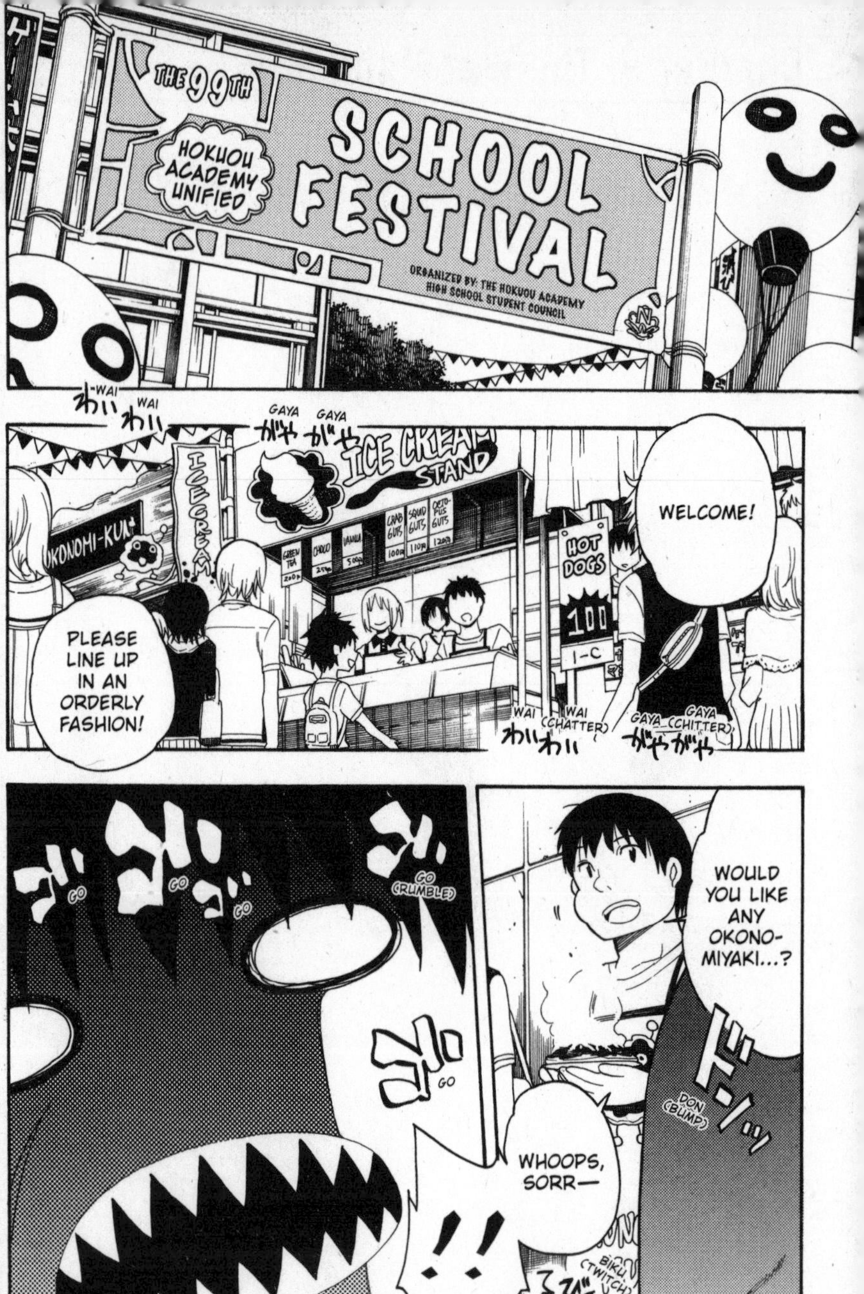
THE 99TH
HOKUOU ACADEMY UNIFIED
SCHOOL FESTIVAL
ORGANIZED BY: THE HOKUOU ACADEMY HIGH SCHOOL STUDENT COUNCIL
わいわい WAI WAI
がやがや GAYA GAYA
ICE CREAM STAND
ICE CREAM
OKONOMI-KUN
GREEN TEA
CHOCO
VANILLA
CRAB GUTS
SQUID GUTS
OCTOPUS GUTS
HOT DOGS
100
1-C
WELCOME!
PLEASE LINE UP IN AN ORDERLY FASHION!
わいわい WAI WAI (CHATTER)
がやがや GAYA GAYA (CHITTER)
WOULD YOU LIKE ANY OKONOMIYAKI...?
ドンッ DON (BUMP)
WHOOPS, SORR—
!!
びくっ BIKU (TWITCH)
ゴゴゴゴ GO GO GO GO (RUMBLE)
ゴ GO

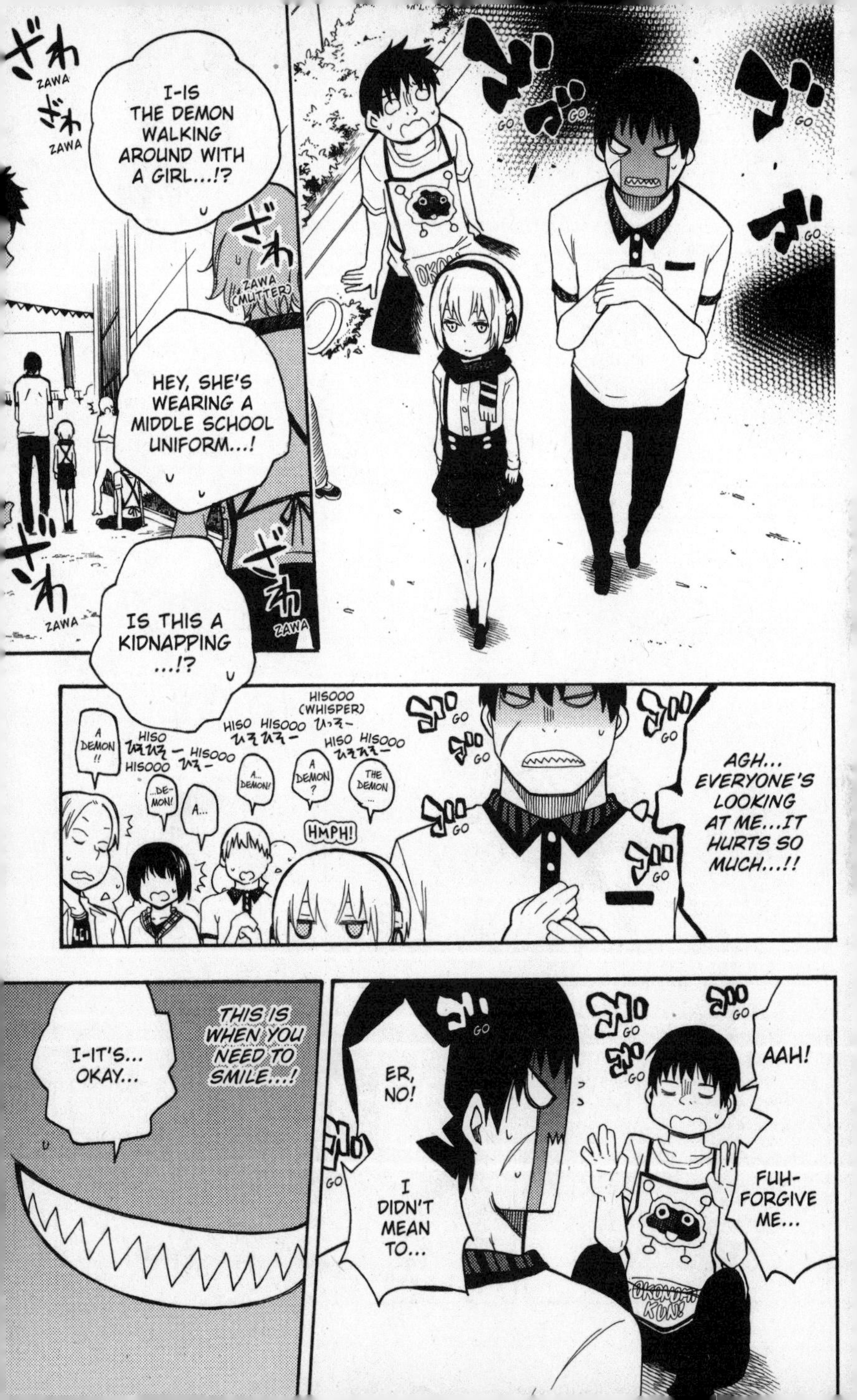
ゴ GO
ゴ GO
ゴ GO
ゴ GO
ざわ ZAWA
ざわ ZAWA
I-IS THE DEMON WALKING AROUND WITH A GIRL...!?
ざわ ZAWA (MUTTER)
HEY, SHE'S WEARING A MIDDLE SCHOOL UNIFORM...!
ざわ ZAWA
ざわ ZAWA
IS THIS A KIDNAPPING...!?
ゴゴゴ GO
AGH... EVERYONE'S LOOKING AT ME...IT HURTS SO MUCH...!!
HISOOO (WHISPER) ひっそー
HISO HISOOO ひそひそー
HISO HISOOO ひそひそー
HISO ひそひそー HISOOO ひそー HISOOO ひそー
A DEMON!!
...DE-MON!
A...
A... DEMON!
A DEMON?
THE DEMON...
HMPH!
ゴ GO
AAH!
FUH-FORGIVE ME...
ER, NO!
I DIDN'T MEAN TO...
THIS IS WHEN YOU NEED TO SMILE...!
I-IT'S... OKAY...

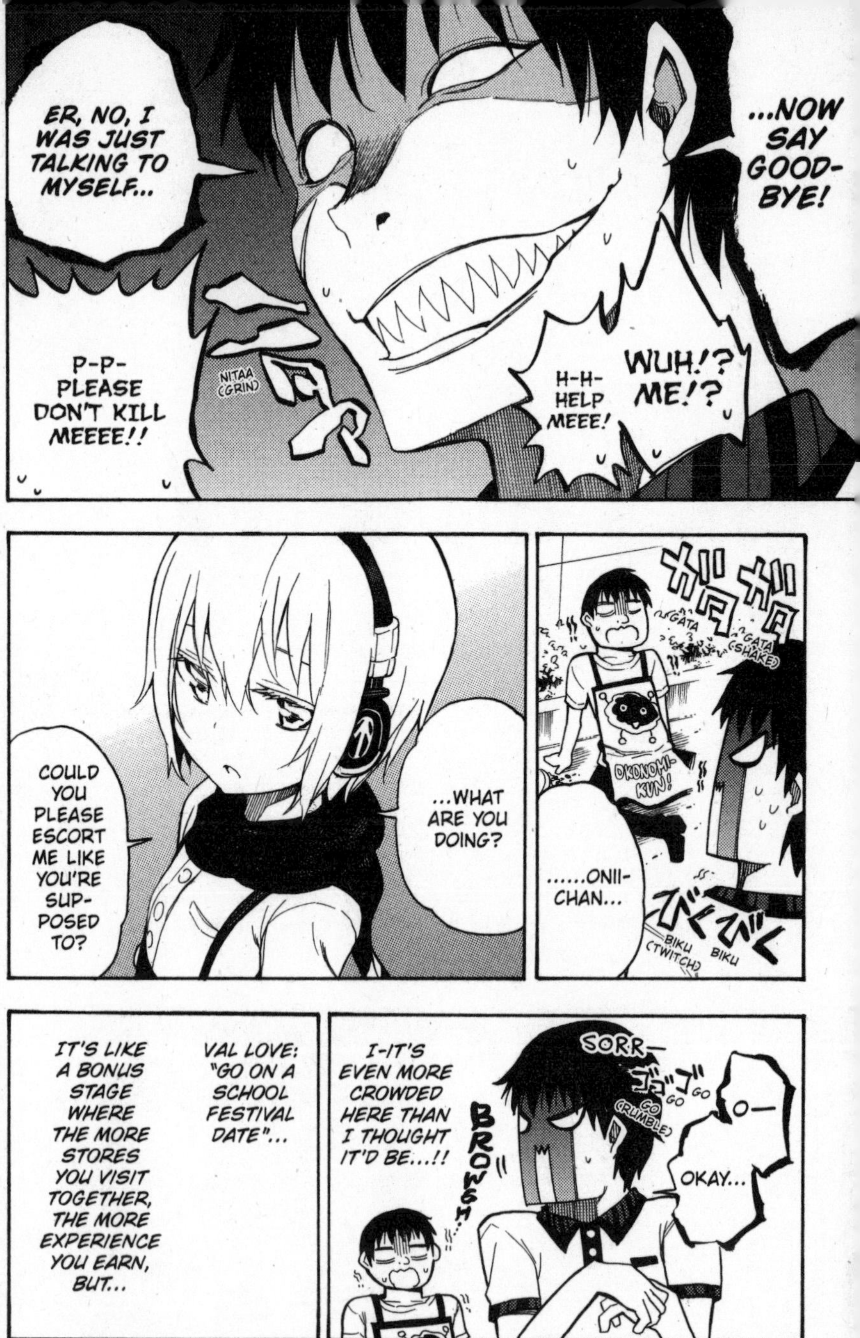
...NOW SAY GOOD-BYE!
WUH!? ME!?
H-H-HELP MEEE!
NITAA (GRIN)
P-P-PLEASE DON'T KILL MEEEE!!
ER, NO, I WAS JUST TALKING TO MYSELF...
ガタガタ
GATA GATA (SHAKE)
......ONII-CHAN...
びくびく
BIKU BIKU (TWITCH)
...WHAT ARE YOU DOING?
COULD YOU PLEASE ESCORT ME LIKE YOU'RE SUPPOSED TO?
SORR—
O—
ゴゴ
GO GO (RUMBLE)
OKAY...
BROWSH...
I-IT'S EVEN MORE CROWDED HERE THAN I THOUGHT IT'D BE...!!
VAL LOVE: "GO ON A SCHOOL FESTIVAL DATE"...
IT'S LIKE A BONUS STAGE WHERE THE MORE STORES YOU VISIT TOGETHER, THE MORE EXPERIENCE YOU EARN, BUT...

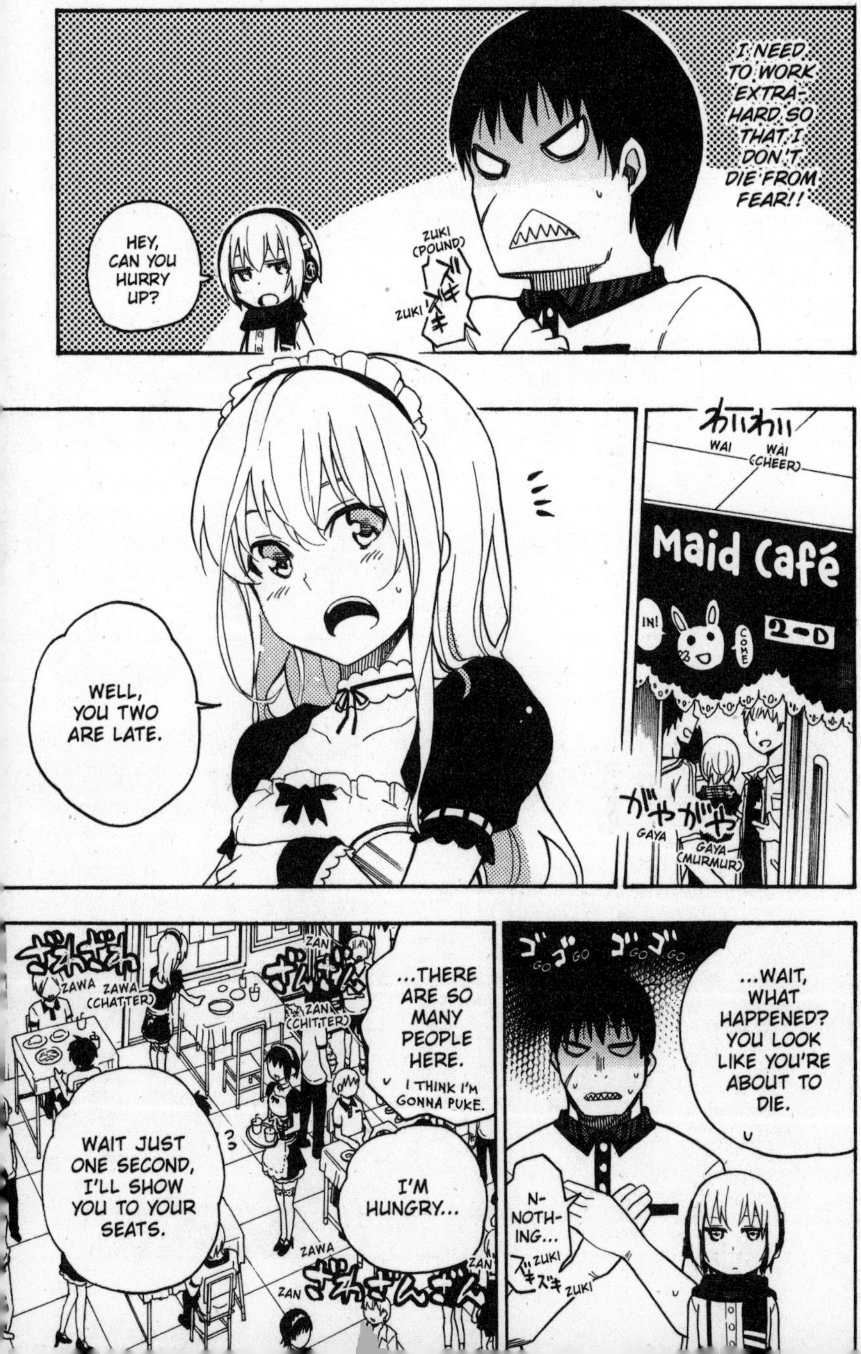
I NEED TO WORK EXTRA-HARD SO THAT I DON'T DIE FROM FEAR!!
ズキズキ
ZUKI (POUND)
ZUKI
HEY, CAN YOU HURRY UP?
わいわい
WAI WAI (CHEER)
Maid Café
2-D
COME
IN!
がやがや
GAYA GAYA (MURMUR)
WELL, YOU TWO ARE LATE.
ゴゴゴゴ
GO GO GO GO
...WAIT, WHAT HAPPENED? YOU LOOK LIKE YOU'RE ABOUT TO DIE.
N-NOTHING...
ズキズキ
ZUKI ZUKI
...THERE ARE SO MANY PEOPLE HERE.
I THINK I'M GONNA PUKE.
ざんざん
ZAN ZAN (CHITTER)
ざわざわ
ZAWA ZAWA (CHATTER)
I'M HUNGRY...
WAIT JUST ONE SECOND, I'LL SHOW YOU TO YOUR SEATS.
ざわざんざん
ZAWA ZAN ZAN

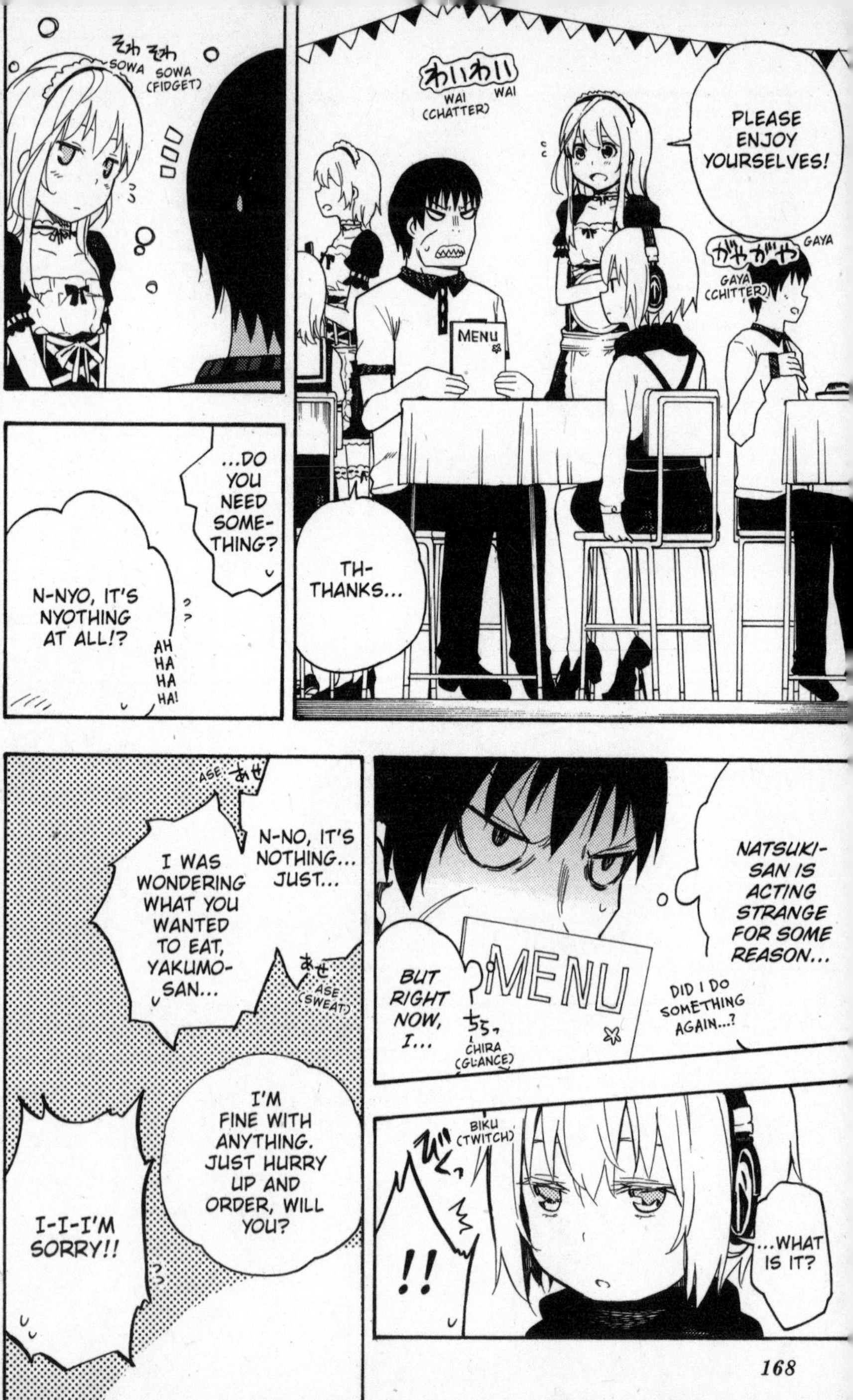
PLEASE ENJOY YOURSELVES!
がやがや GAYA GAYA (CHITTER)
わいわい WAI WAI (CHATTER)
TH-THANKS...
そわそわ SOWA SOWA (FIDGET)
...DO YOU NEED SOME-THING?
N-NYO, IT'S NYOTHING AT ALL!?
AH HA HA HA!
NATSUKI-SAN IS ACTING STRANGE FOR SOME REASON...
DID I DO SOMETHING AGAIN...?
MENU
BUT RIGHT NOW, I...
ちらっ CHIRA (GLANCE)
...WHAT IS IT?
びくっ BIKU (TWITCH)
!!
あせ ASE
N-NO, IT'S NOTHING... JUST...
I WAS WONDERING WHAT YOU WANTED TO EAT, YAKUMO-SAN...
あせ ASE (SWEAT)
I'M FINE WITH ANYTHING. JUST HURRY UP AND ORDER, WILL YOU?
I-I-I'M SORRY!!

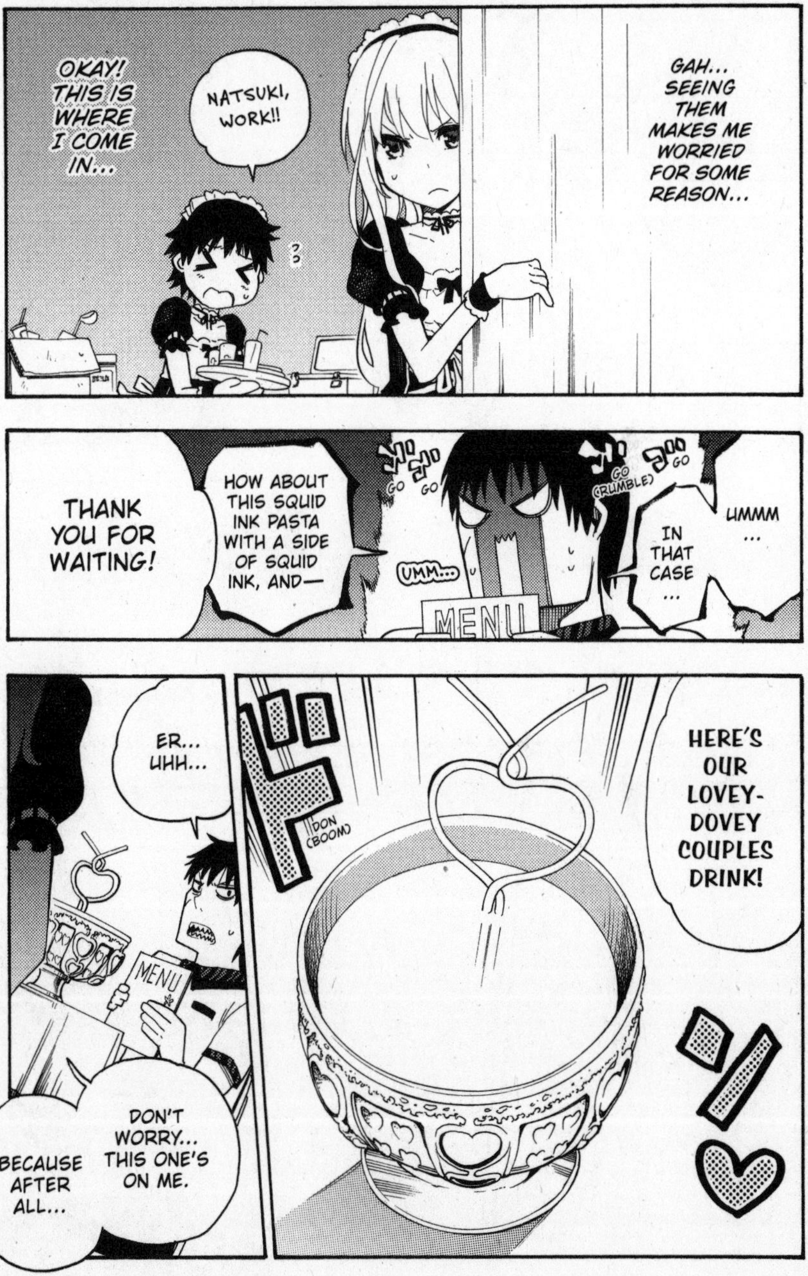
GAH... SEEING THEM MAKES ME WORRIED FOR SOME REASON...
NATSUKI, WORK!!
OKAY! THIS IS WHERE I COME IN...
UMMM ...
IN THAT CASE ...
GO GO (RUMBLE)
GO GO
UMM...
MENU
HOW ABOUT THIS SQUID INK PASTA WITH A SIDE OF SQUID INK, AND—
THANK YOU FOR WAITING!
HERE'S OUR LOVEY-DOVEY COUPLES DRINK!
DON (BOOM)
ER... UHH...
MENU
DON'T WORRY... THIS ONE'S ON ME.
BECAUSE AFTER ALL...

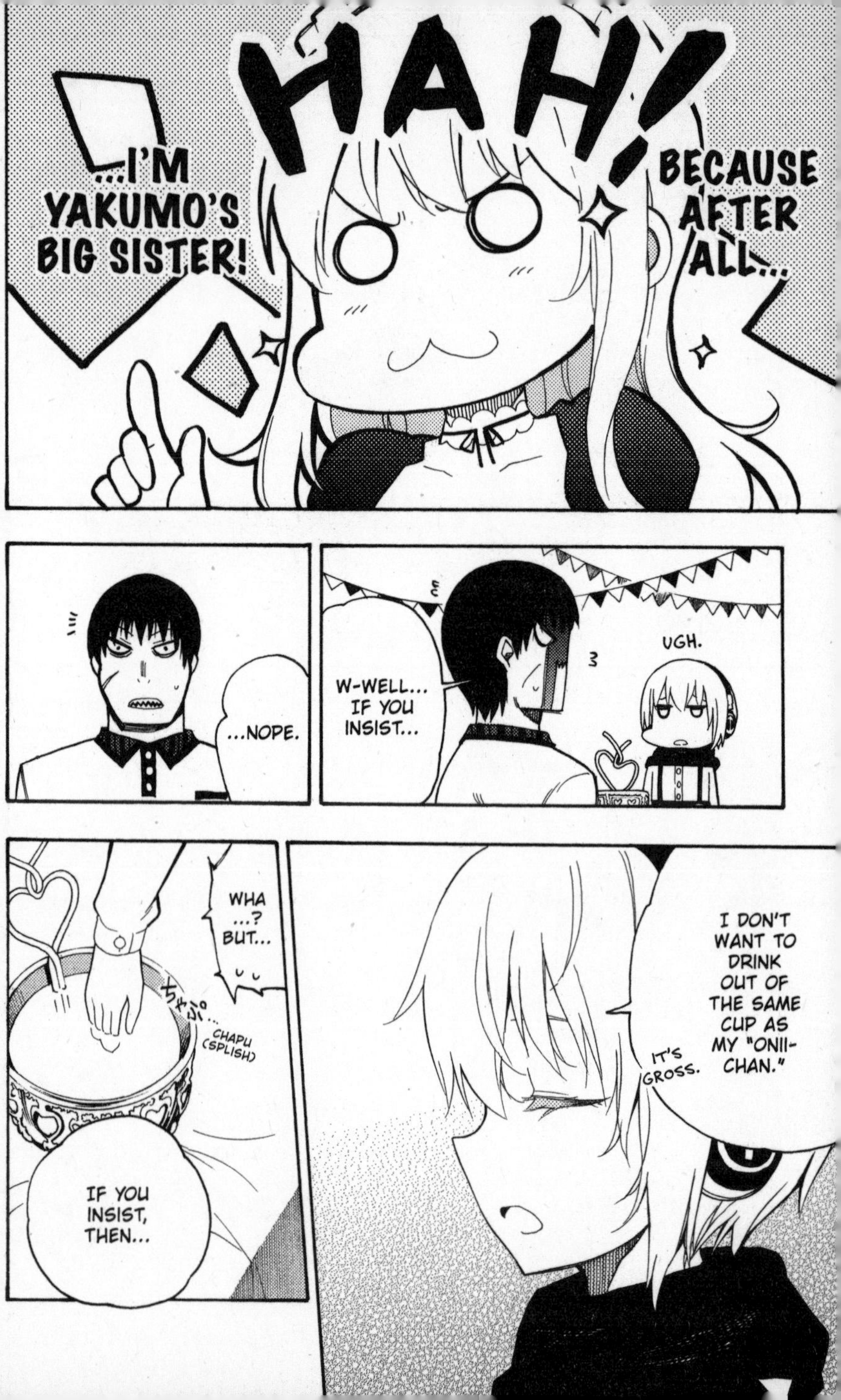
BECAUSE AFTER ALL...
HAH!
...I'M YAKUMO'S BIG SISTER!
W-WELL... IF YOU INSIST...
UGH.
...NOPE.
I DON'T WANT TO DRINK OUT OF THE SAME CUP AS MY "ONII-CHAN."
IT'S GROSS.
WHA ...? BUT...
ちゃぷ...
CHAPU (SPLISH)
IF YOU INSIST, THEN...

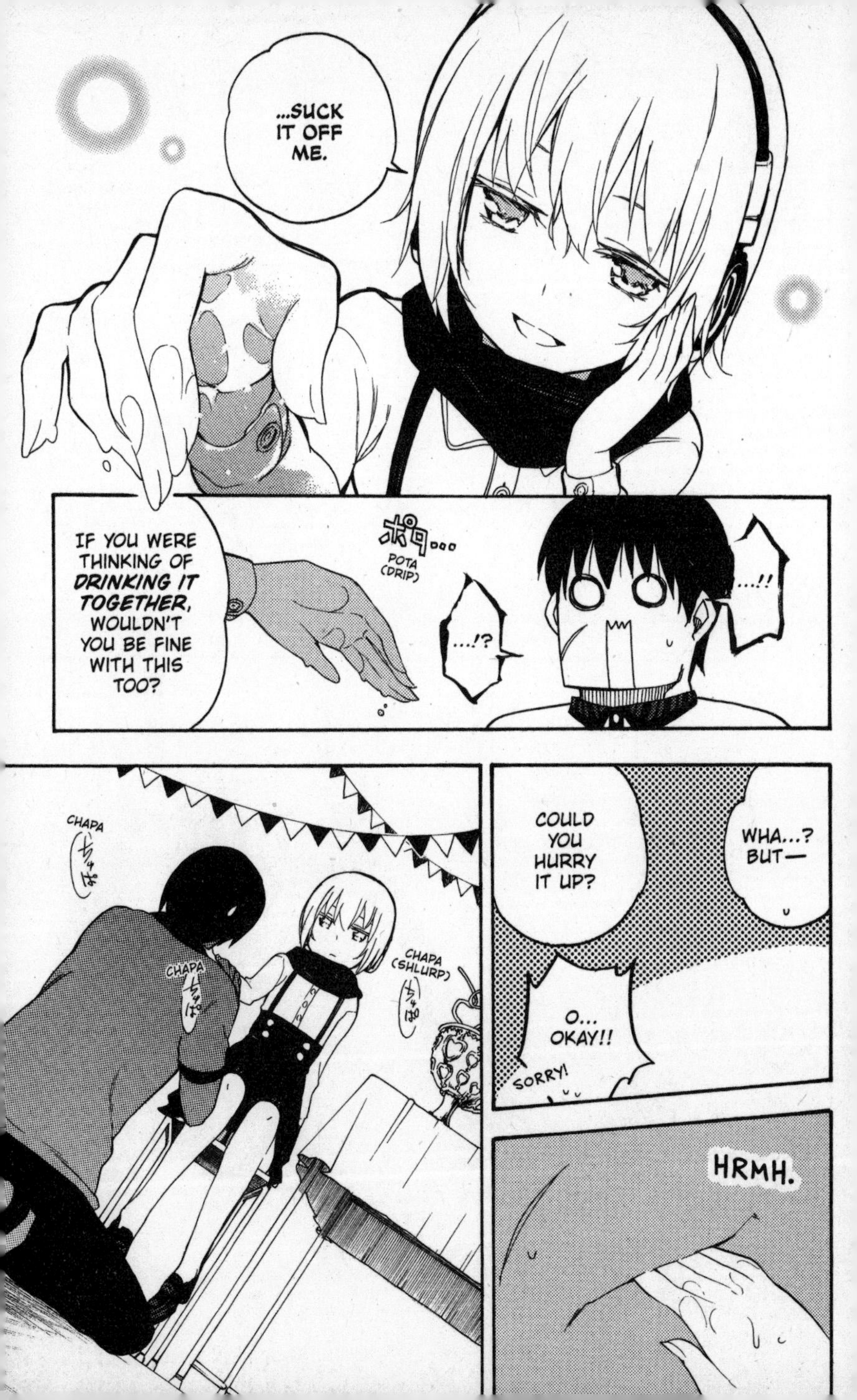
...SUCK IT OFF ME.
...!!
...!?
ポタ...
POTA (DRIP)
IF YOU WERE THINKING OF *DRINKING IT TOGETHER*, WOULDN'T YOU BE FINE WITH THIS TOO?
WHA...? BUT—
COULD YOU HURRY IT UP?
O... OKAY!!
SORRY!
HRMH.
ちゅぱ
CHAPA (SHLURP)
ちゅぱ
CHAPA
ちゅぱ
CHAPA

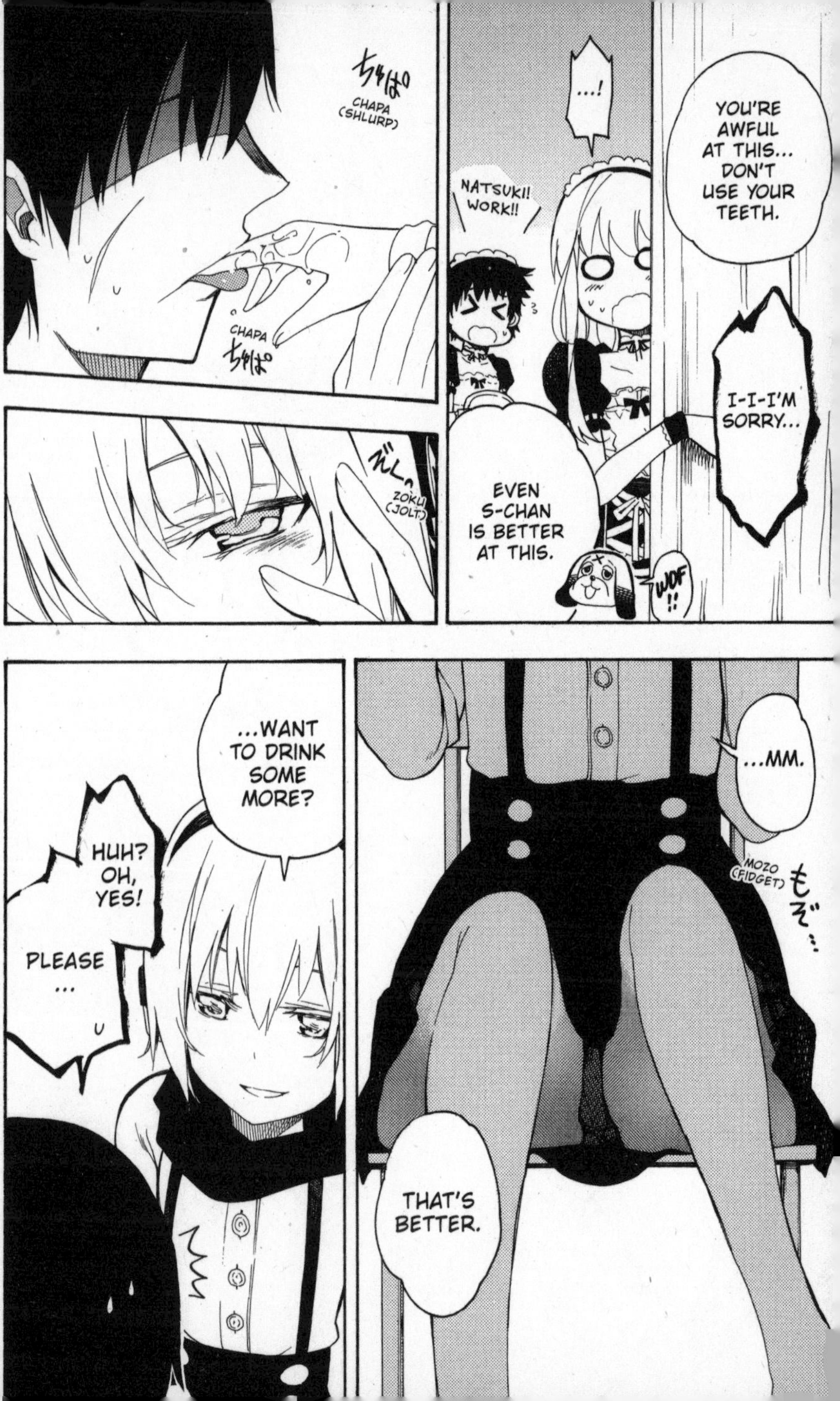
YOU'RE AWFUL AT THIS... DON'T USE YOUR TEETH.
...!
NATSUKI!! WORK!!
I-I-I'M SORRY...
EVEN S-CHAN IS BETTER AT THIS.
WOF !!
ちゅぱ
CHAPA (SHLURP)
CHAPA
ちゅぱ
ぞくっ
ZOKU (JOLT)
...MM.
MOZO (FIDGET)
もぞ…
THAT'S BETTER.
...WANT TO DRINK SOME MORE?
HUH? OH, YES!
PLEASE ...

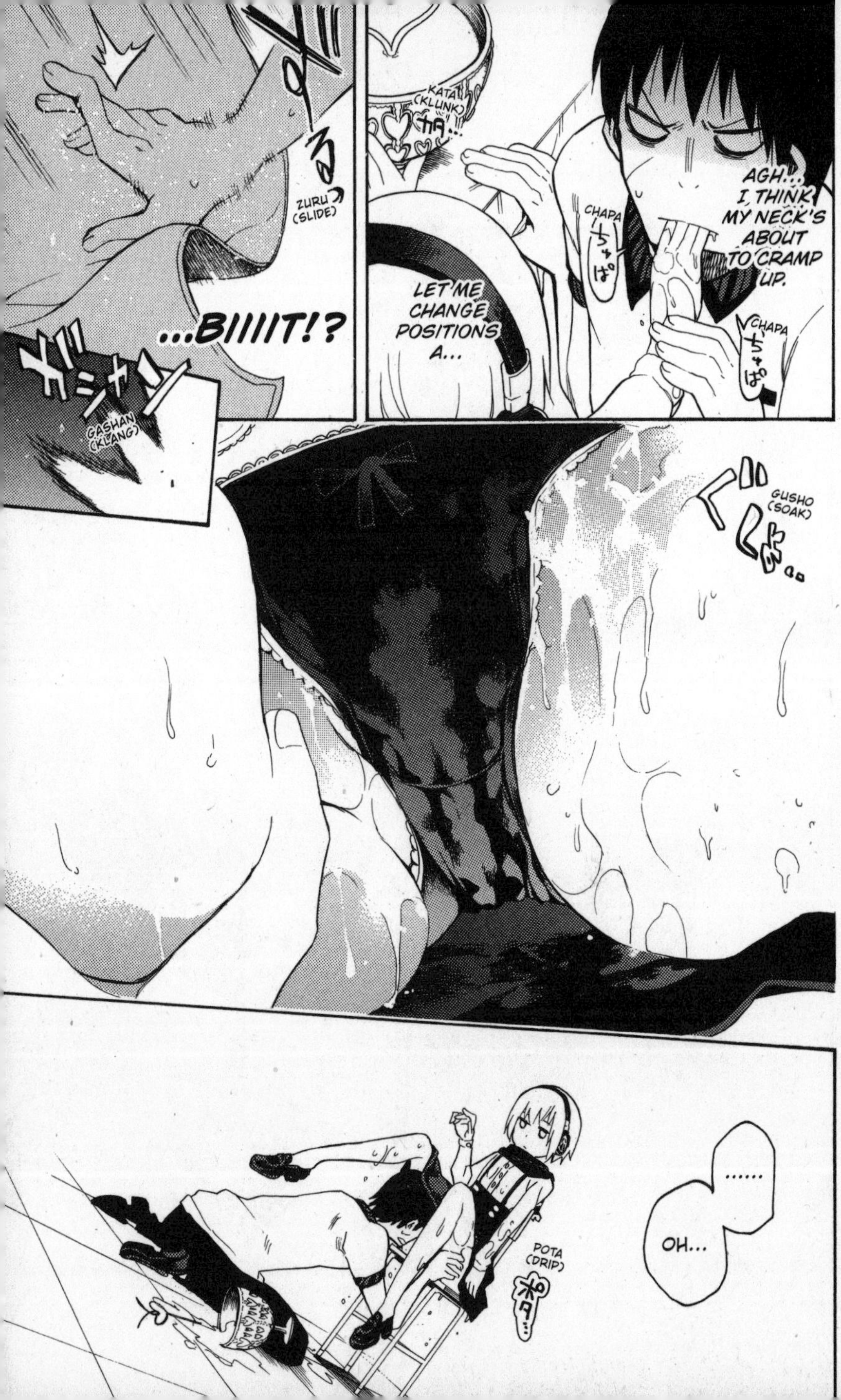
AGH... I THINK MY NECK'S ABOUT TO CRAMP UP.
CHAPA
ちゅぱ
KATA (KLUNK)
LET ME CHANGE POSITIONS A...
CHAPA
ちゅぱ
ZURU (SLIDE)
...BIIIIT!?
GASHAN (KLANG)
GUSHO (SOAK)
......
OH...
POTA (DRIP)

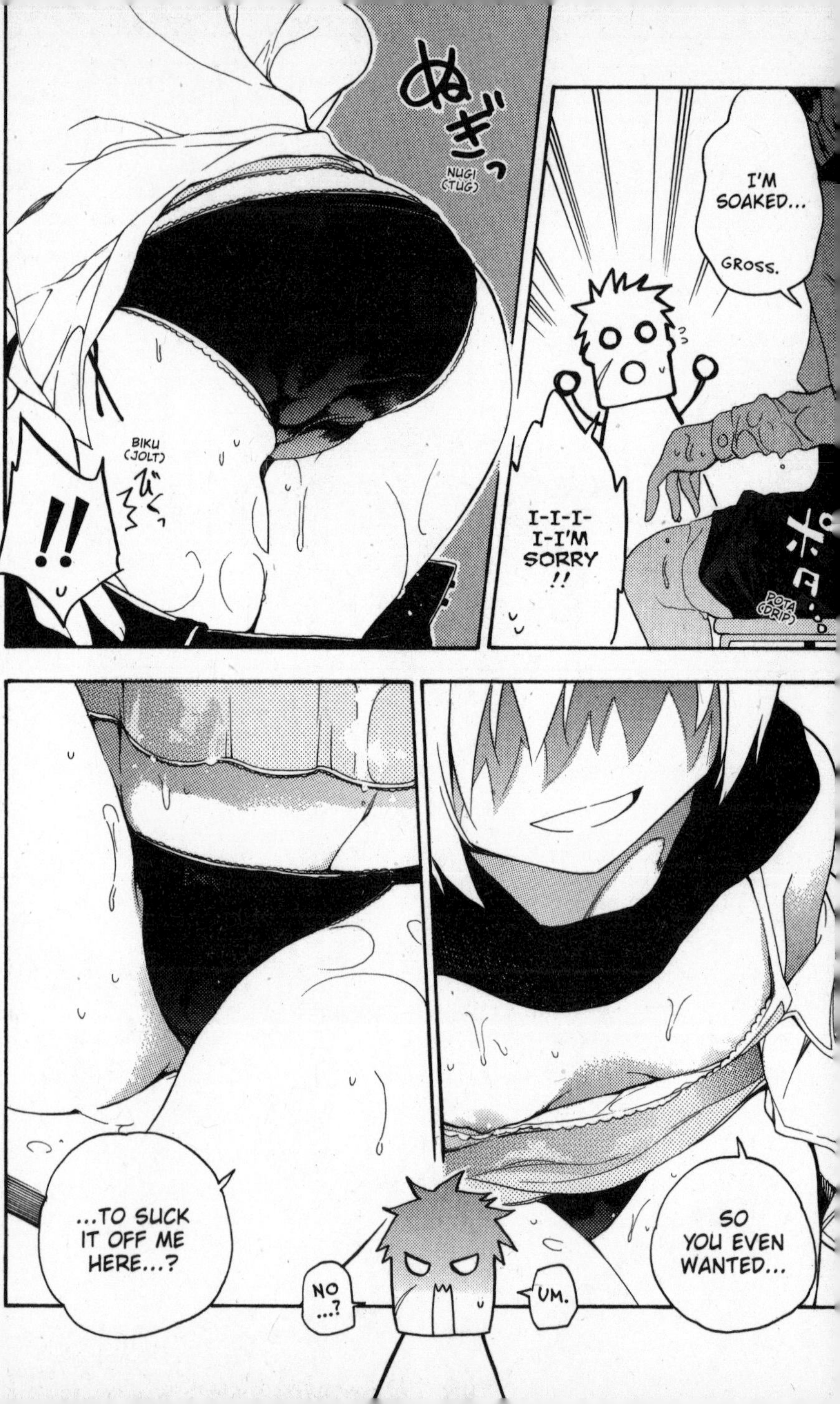

I'M SOAKED...
GROSS.
ポタ…
POTA (DRIP)
I-I-I-I-I'M SORRY!!
ぬぎっ
NUGI (TUG)
びくっ
BIKU (JOLT)
!!
SO YOU EVEN WANTED...
UM.
NO ...?
...TO SUCK IT OFF ME HERE...?

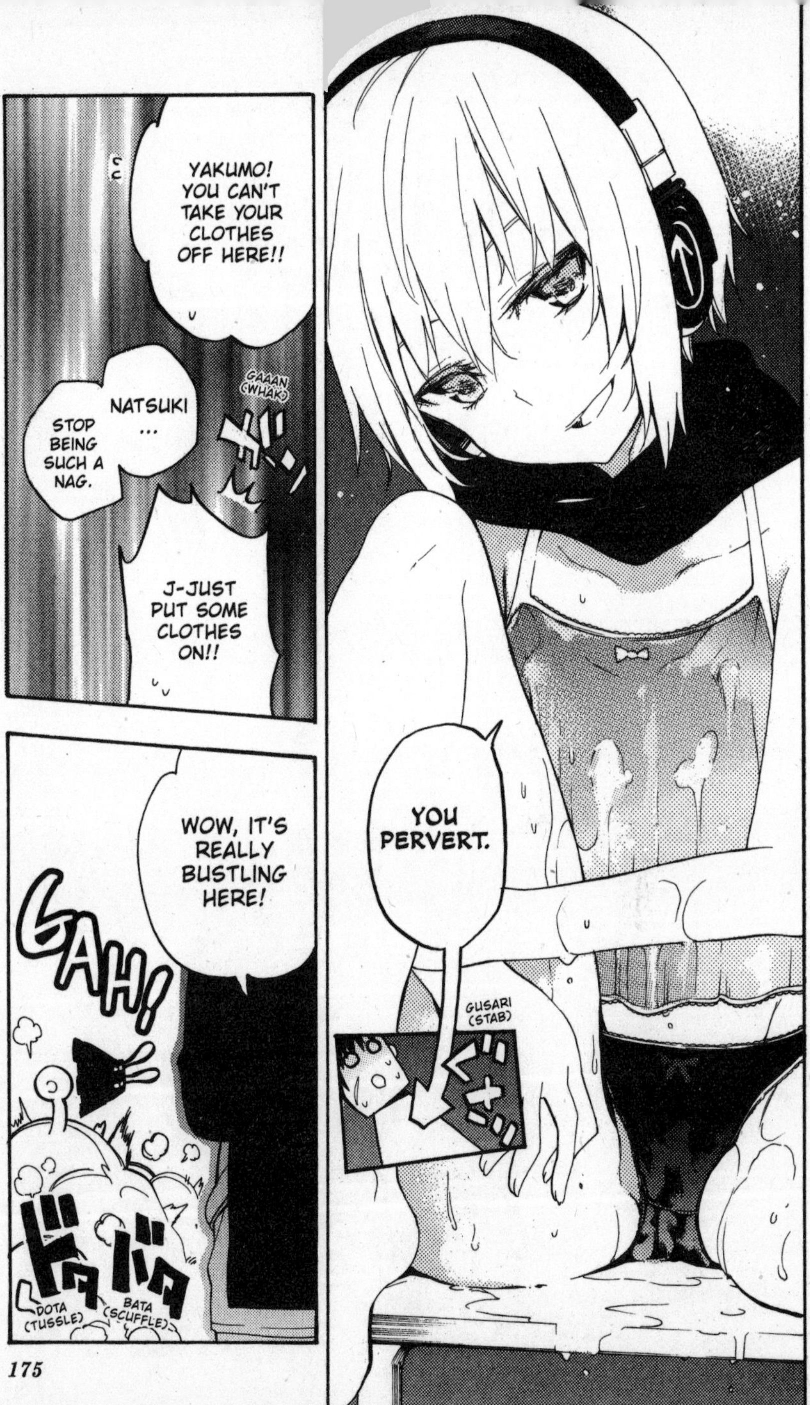
YOU PERVERT.
GUSARI (STAB)
YAKUMO! YOU CAN'T TAKE YOUR CLOTHES OFF HERE!!
GAAAN (WHAK)
NATSUKI...
STOP BEING SUCH A NAG.
J-JUST PUT SOME CLOTHES ON!!
WOW, IT'S REALLY BUSTLING HERE!
GAH!
BATA (SCUFFLE)
DOTA (TUSSLE)

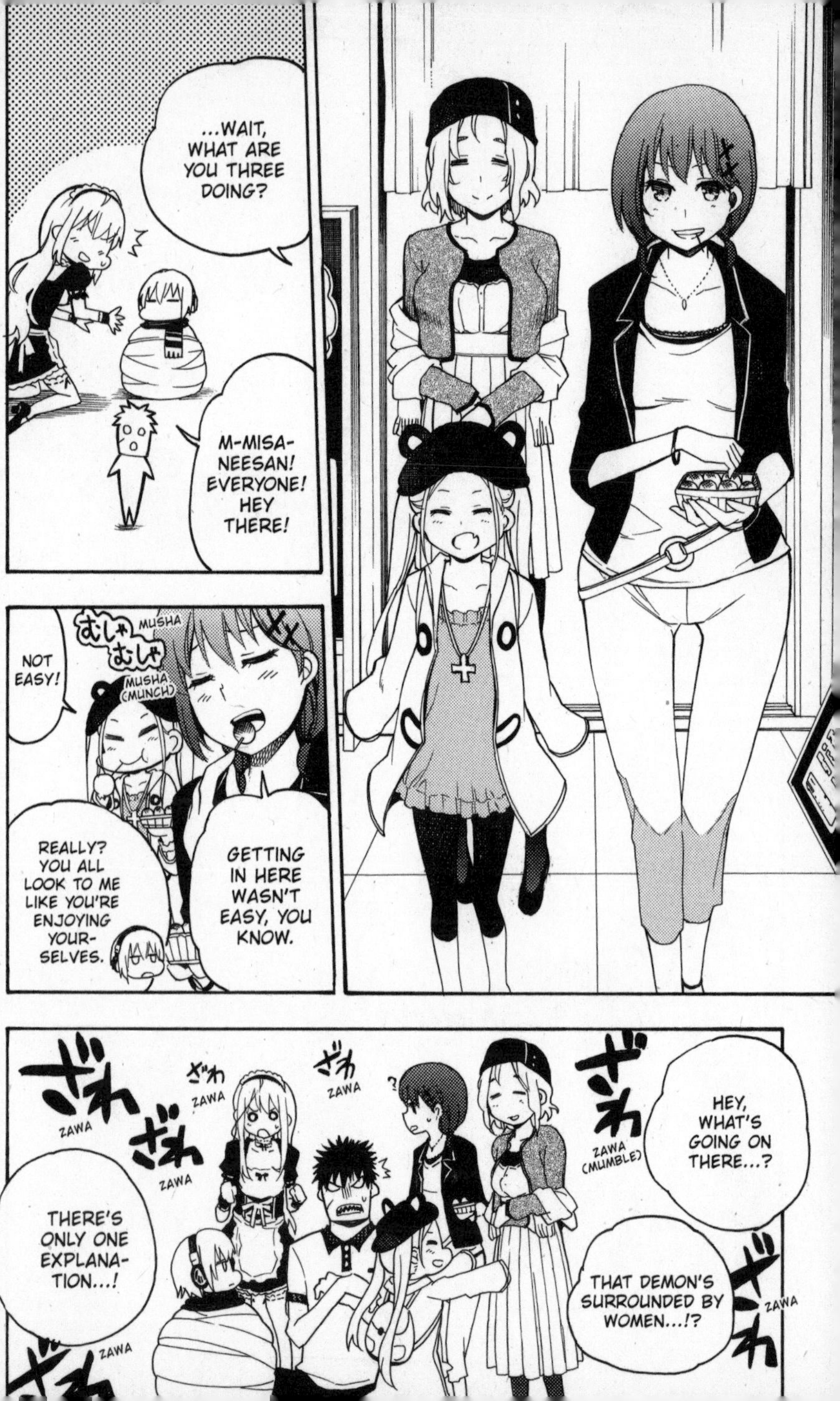
...WAIT, WHAT ARE YOU THREE DOING?
M-MISA-NEESAN! EVERYONE! HEY THERE!
むしゃむしゃ MUSHA MUSHA (MUNCH)
GETTING IN HERE WASN'T EASY, YOU KNOW.
NOT EASY!
REALLY? YOU ALL LOOK TO ME LIKE YOU'RE ENJOYING YOUR-SELVES.
ざわ ZAWA (MUMBLE)
HEY, WHAT'S GOING ON THERE...?
ざわ ZAWA
THAT DEMON'S SURROUNDED BY WOMEN...!?
ざわ ZAWA
ざわ ZAWA
ざわ ZAWA
ざわ ZAWA
THERE'S ONLY ONE EXPLANATION...!
ざわ ZAWA

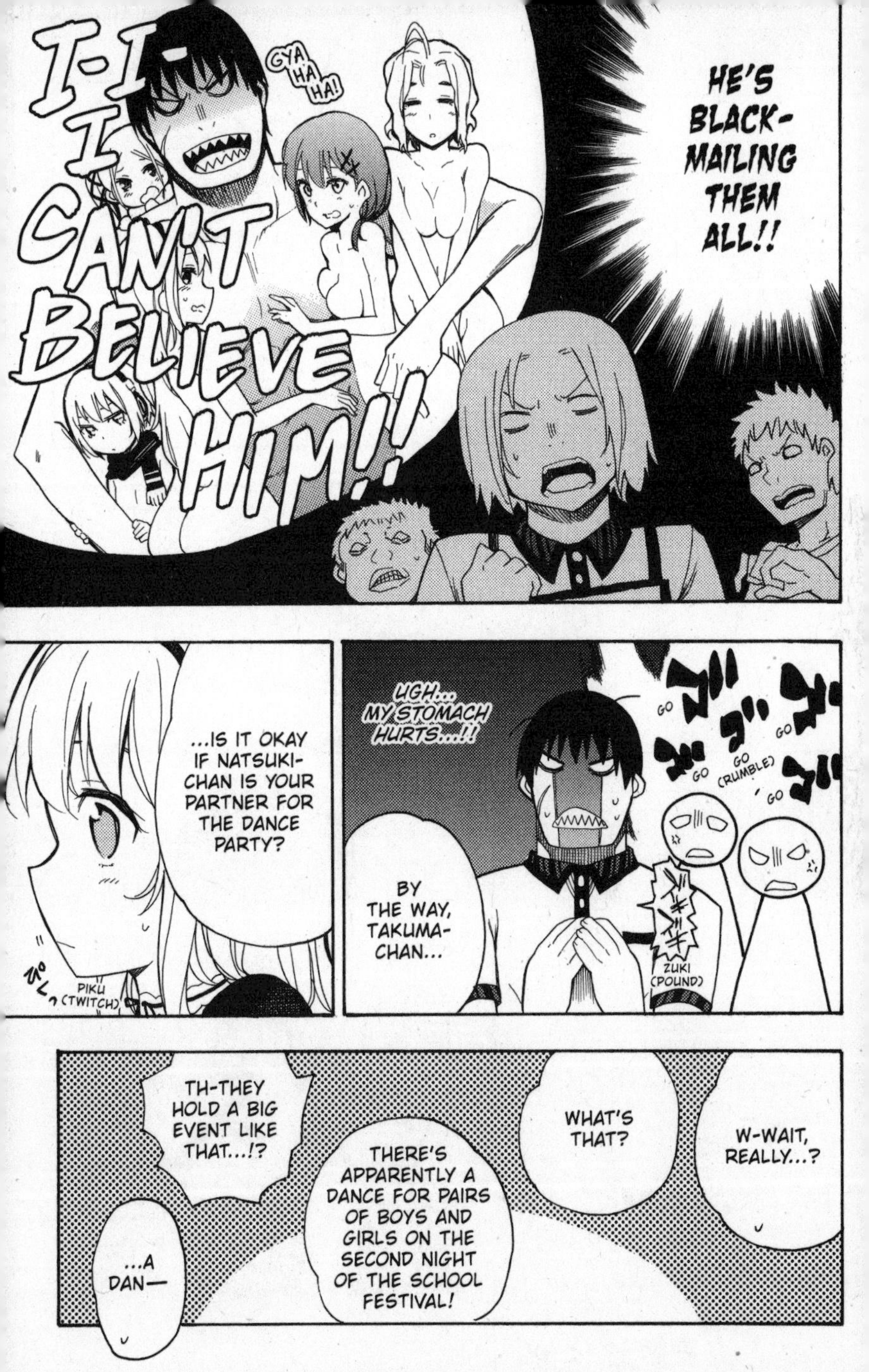
HE'S BLACK-MAILING THEM ALL!!
GYA HA HA!
I-I-I CAN'T BELIEVE HIM!!
UGH... MY STOMACH HURTS...!!
GO GO GO GO (RUMBLE) GO GO
BY THE WAY, TAKUMA-CHAN...
ZUKI (POUND)
...IS IT OKAY IF NATSUKI-CHAN IS YOUR PARTNER FOR THE DANCE PARTY?
PIKU (TWITCH)
W-WAIT, REALLY...?
WHAT'S THAT?
THERE'S APPARENTLY A DANCE FOR PAIRS OF BOYS AND GIRLS ON THE SECOND NIGHT OF THE SCHOOL FESTIVAL!
TH-THEY HOLD A BIG EVENT LIKE THAT...!?
...A DAN—

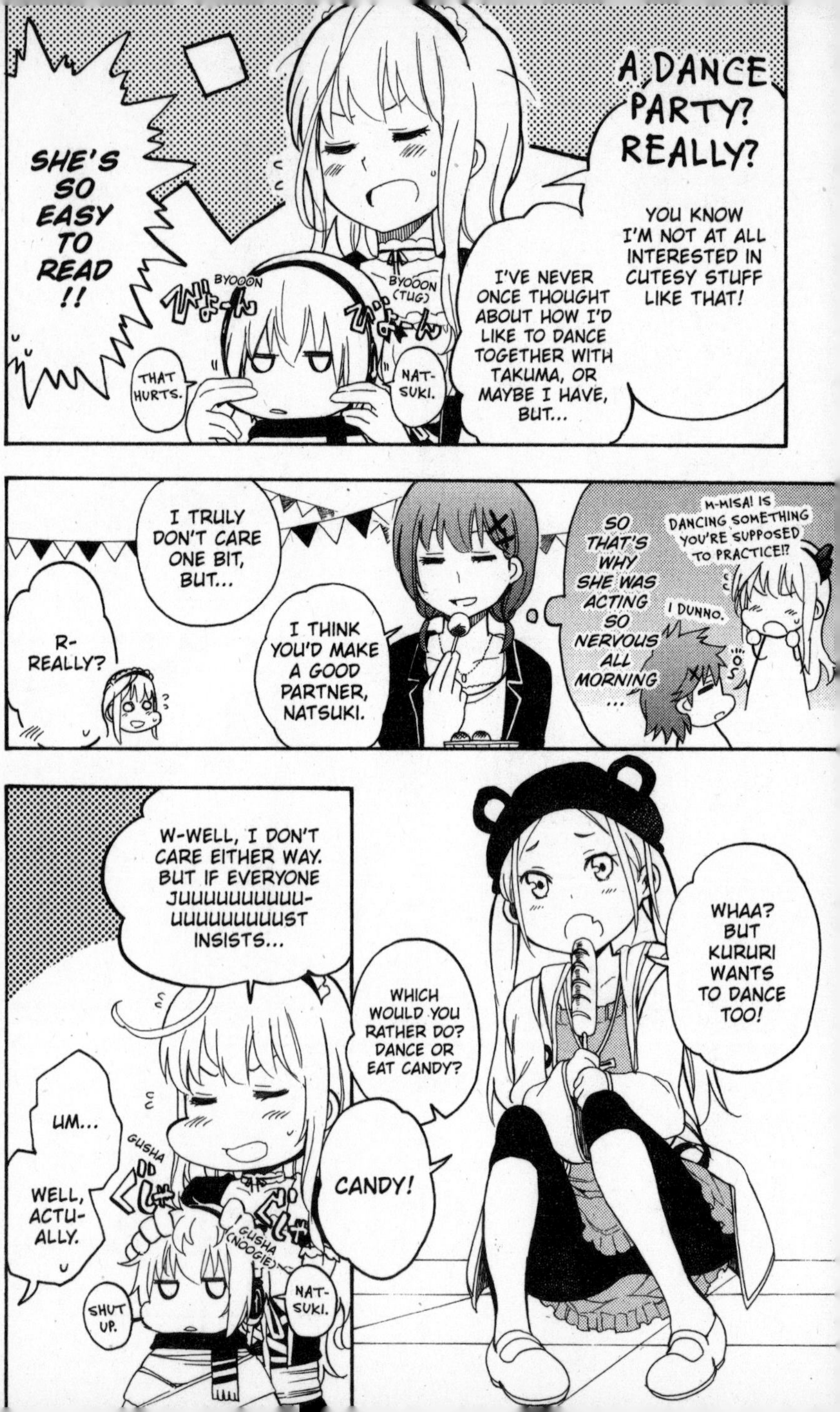
A DANCE PARTY? REALLY?
YOU KNOW I'M NOT AT ALL INTERESTED IN CUTESY STUFF LIKE THAT!
I'VE NEVER ONCE THOUGHT ABOUT HOW I'D LIKE TO DANCE TOGETHER WITH TAKUMA, OR MAYBE I HAVE, BUT...
BYOOON (TUG)
NAT-SUKI.
BYOOON
SHE'S SO EASY TO READ!!
THAT HURTS.
M-MISA! IS DANCING SOMETHING YOU'RE SUPPOSED TO PRACTICE!?
I DUNNO.
SO THAT'S WHY SHE WAS ACTING SO NERVOUS ALL MORNING...
I TRULY DON'T CARE ONE BIT, BUT...
I THINK YOU'D MAKE A GOOD PARTNER, NATSUKI.
R-REALLY?
WHAA? BUT KURURI WANTS TO DANCE TOO!
WHICH WOULD YOU RATHER DO? DANCE OR EAT CANDY?
CANDY!
W-WELL, I DON'T CARE EITHER WAY. BUT IF EVERYONE JUUUUUUUUUU-UUUUUUUUUST INSISTS...
UM...
WELL, ACTU-ALLY.
GUSHA
GUSHA (NOOGIE)
NAT-SUKI.
SHUT UP.

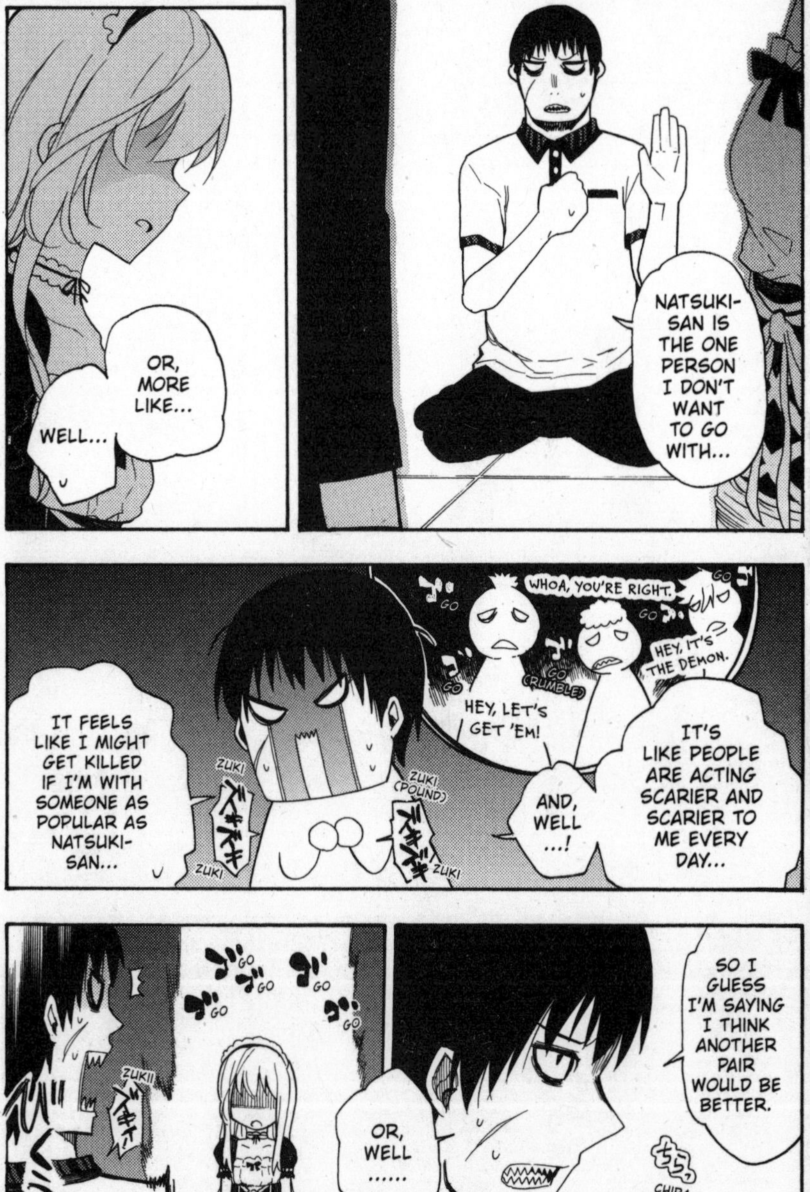
NATSUKI-SAN IS THE ONE PERSON I DON'T WANT TO GO WITH...
OR, MORE LIKE...
WELL...
WHOA, YOU'RE RIGHT.
GO
GO
HEY, IT'S THE DEMON.
GO
GO
GO (RUMBLE)
IT'S LIKE PEOPLE ARE ACTING SCARIER AND SCARIER TO ME EVERY DAY...
HEY, LET'S GET 'EM!
AND, WELL ...!
ZUKI (POUND)
ZUKI
ZUKI
ZUKI
IT FEELS LIKE I MIGHT GET KILLED IF I'M WITH SOMEONE AS POPULAR AS NATSUKI-SAN...
SO I GUESS I'M SAYING I THINK ANOTHER PAIR WOULD BE BETTER.
ちらっ
CHIRA (GLANCE)
OR, WELL ......
GO
GO
GO
GO
GO
ZUKII
BIKUU (JOLT)

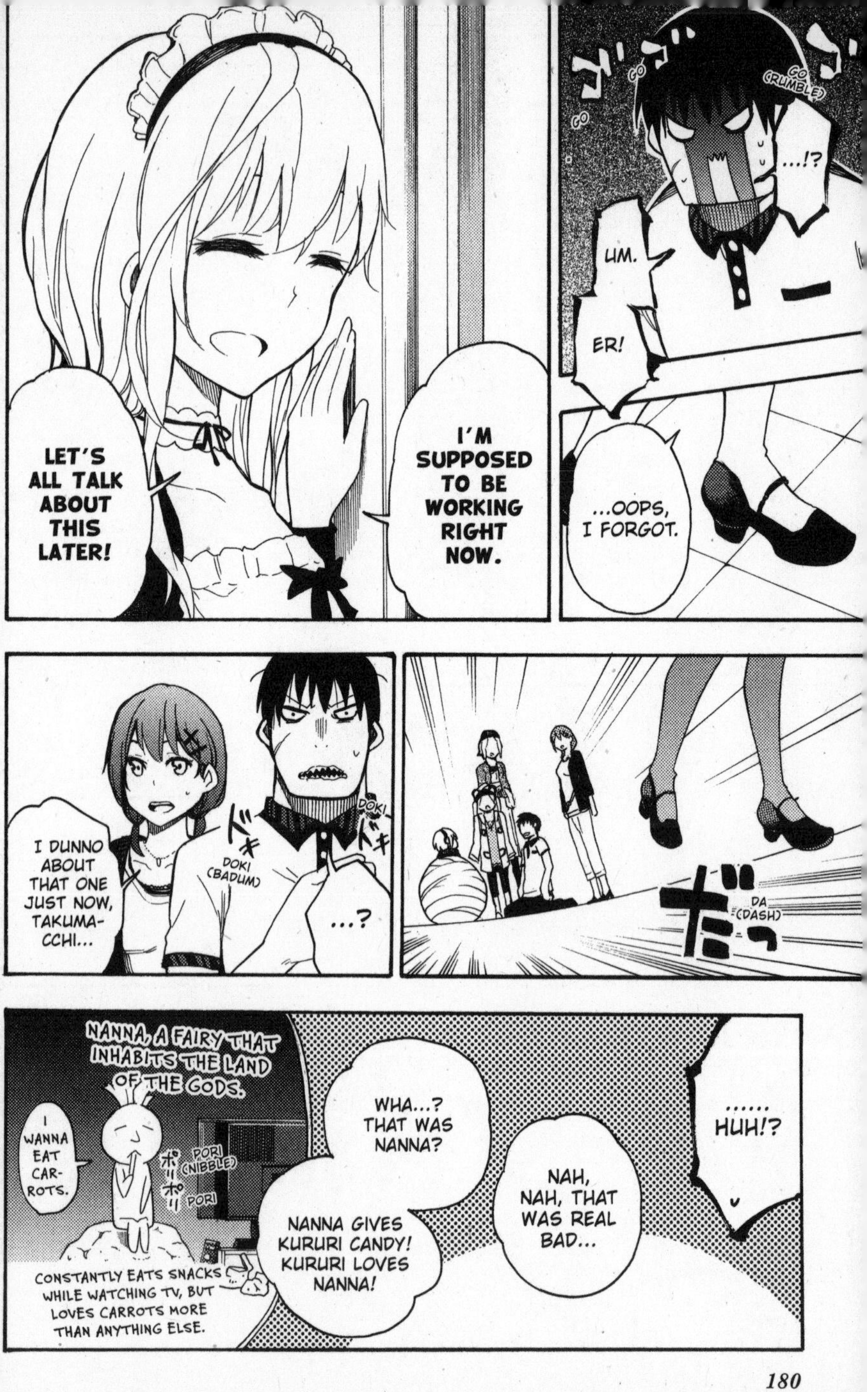
GO
GO
GO (RUMBLE)
...!?
UM.
ER!
...OOPS, I FORGOT.
I'M SUPPOSED TO BE WORKING RIGHT NOW.
LET'S ALL TALK ABOUT THIS LATER!
DA (DASH)
DOKI
DOKI (BADUM)
...?
I DUNNO ABOUT THAT ONE JUST NOW, TAKUMA-CCHI...
......HUH!?
WHA...? THAT WAS NANNA?
NAH, NAH, THAT WAS REAL BAD...
NANNA GIVES KURURI CANDY! KURURI LOVES NANNA!
NANNA, A FAIRY THAT INHABITS THE LAND OF THE GODS.
I WANNA EAT CAR-ROTS.
PORI (NIBBLE)
PORI
CONSTANTLY EATS SNACKS WHILE WATCHING TV, BUT LOVES CARROTS MORE THAN ANYTHING ELSE.

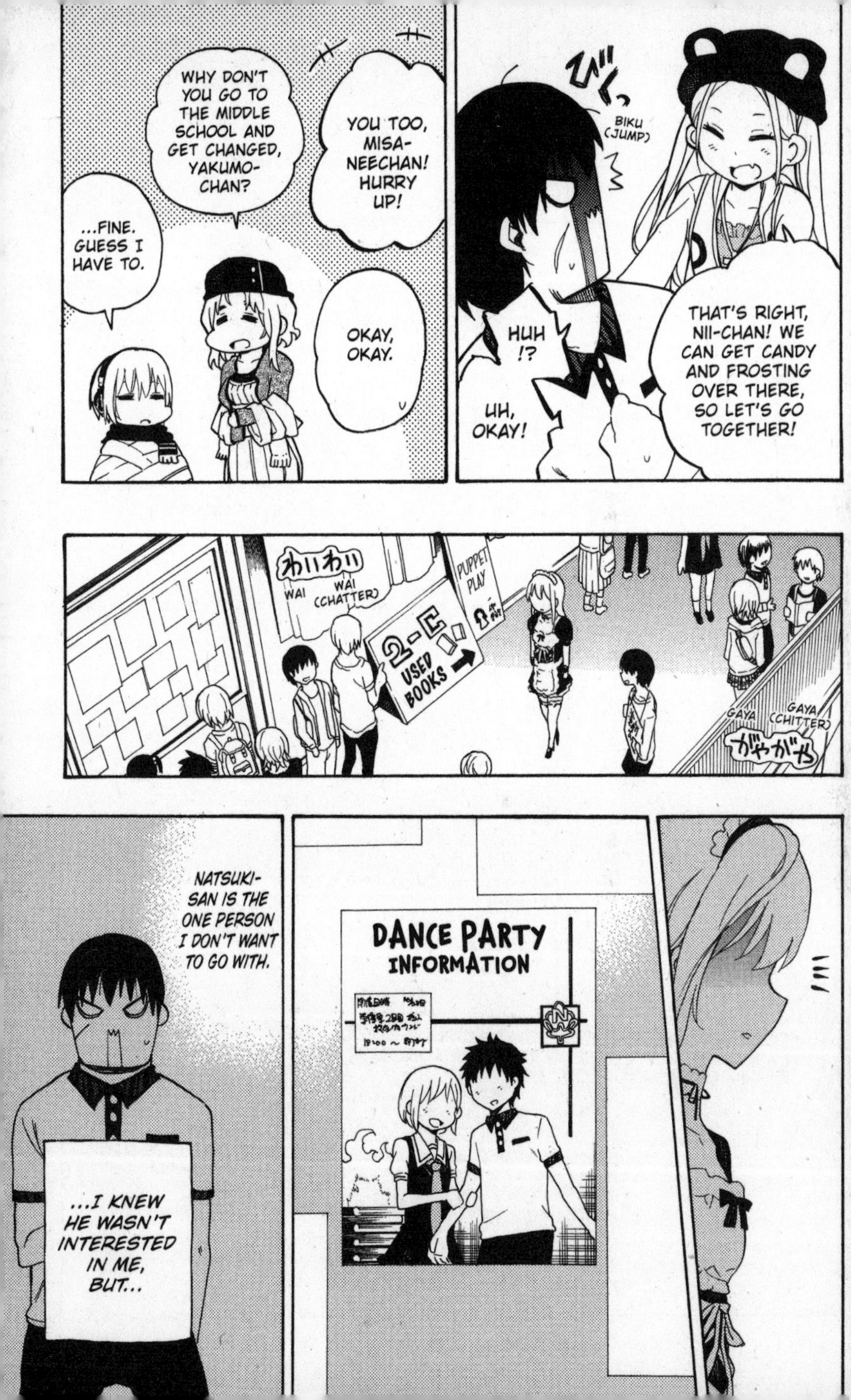
BIKU (JUMP)
THAT'S RIGHT, NII-CHAN! WE CAN GET CANDY AND FROSTING OVER THERE, SO LET'S GO TOGETHER!
HUH !?
UH, OKAY!
WHY DON'T YOU GO TO THE MIDDLE SCHOOL AND GET CHANGED, YAKUMO-CHAN?
...FINE. GUESS I HAVE TO.
YOU TOO, MISA-NEECHAN! HURRY UP!
OKAY, OKAY.
GAYA GAYA (CHITTER)
がやがや
PUPPET PLAY
2-C USED BOOKS
WAI WAI (CHATTER)
わいわい
DANCE PARTY INFORMATION
NATSUKI-SAN IS THE ONE PERSON I DON'T WANT TO GO WITH.
...I KNEW HE WASN'T INTERESTED IN ME, BUT...

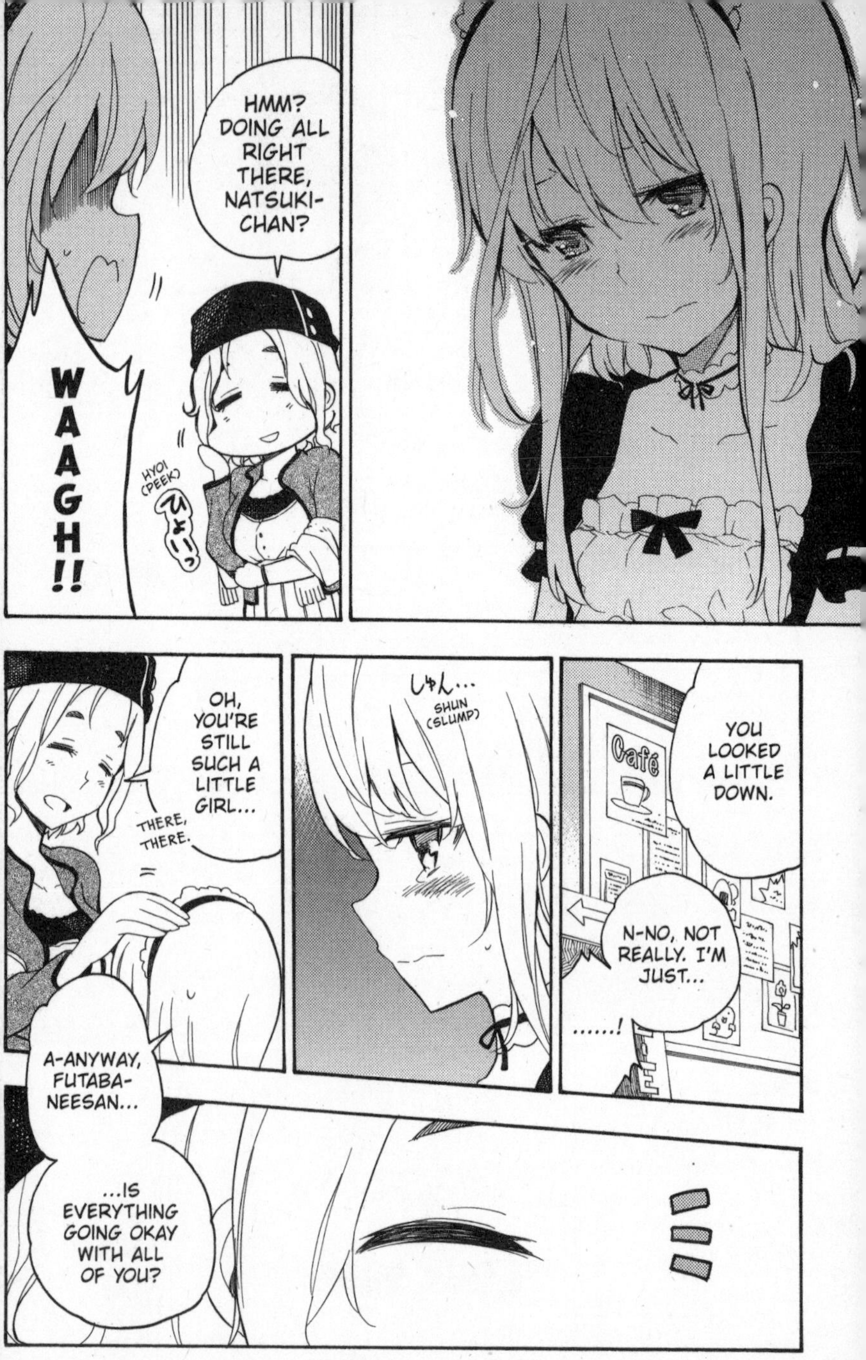
HMM? DOING ALL RIGHT THERE, NATSUKI-CHAN?
HYOI (PEEK)
ひょいっ
WAAAGH!!
YOU LOOKED A LITTLE DOWN.
N-NO, NOT REALLY. I'M JUST...
......!
しゅん...
SHUN (SLUMP)
OH, YOU'RE STILL SUCH A LITTLE GIRL...
THERE, THERE.
A-ANYWAY, FUTABA-NEESAN...
...IS EVERYTHING GOING OKAY WITH ALL OF YOU?

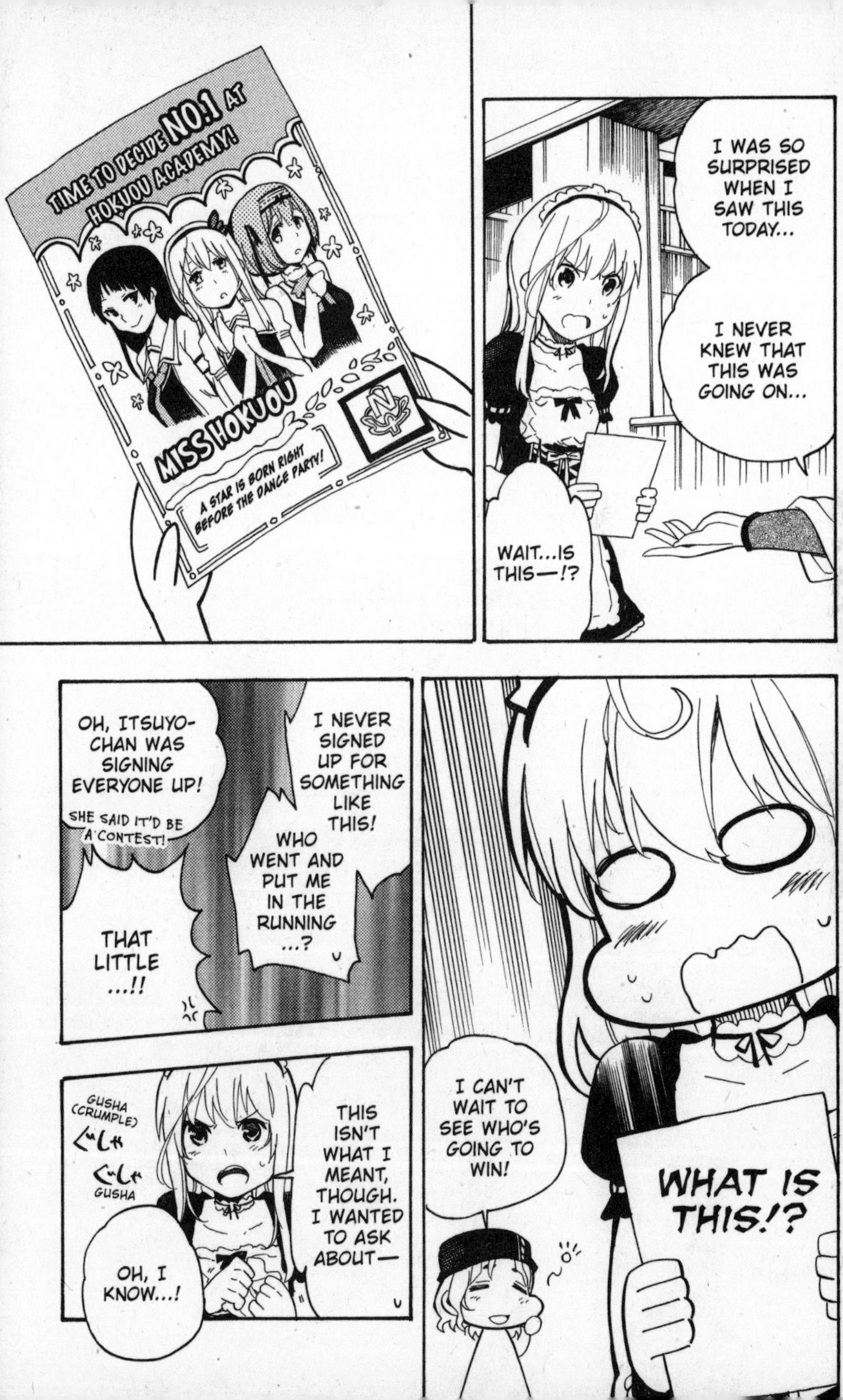
I WAS SO SURPRISED WHEN I SAW THIS TODAY...
I NEVER KNEW THAT THIS WAS GOING ON...
WAIT...IS THIS—!?
TIME TO DECIDE NO.1 AT HOKUOU ACADEMY!
MISS HOKUOU
A STAR IS BORN RIGHT BEFORE THE DANCE PARTY!
WHAT IS THIS!?
I CAN'T WAIT TO SEE WHO'S GOING TO WIN!
I NEVER SIGNED UP FOR SOMETHING LIKE THIS!
WHO WENT AND PUT ME IN THE RUNNING ...?
OH, ITSUYO-CHAN WAS SIGNING EVERYONE UP!
SHE SAID IT'D BE A CONTEST!
THAT LITTLE ...!!
THIS ISN'T WHAT I MEANT, THOUGH. I WANTED TO ASK ABOUT—
GUSHA (CRUMPLE)
ぐしゃ
ぐしゃ
GUSHA
OH, I KNOW...!

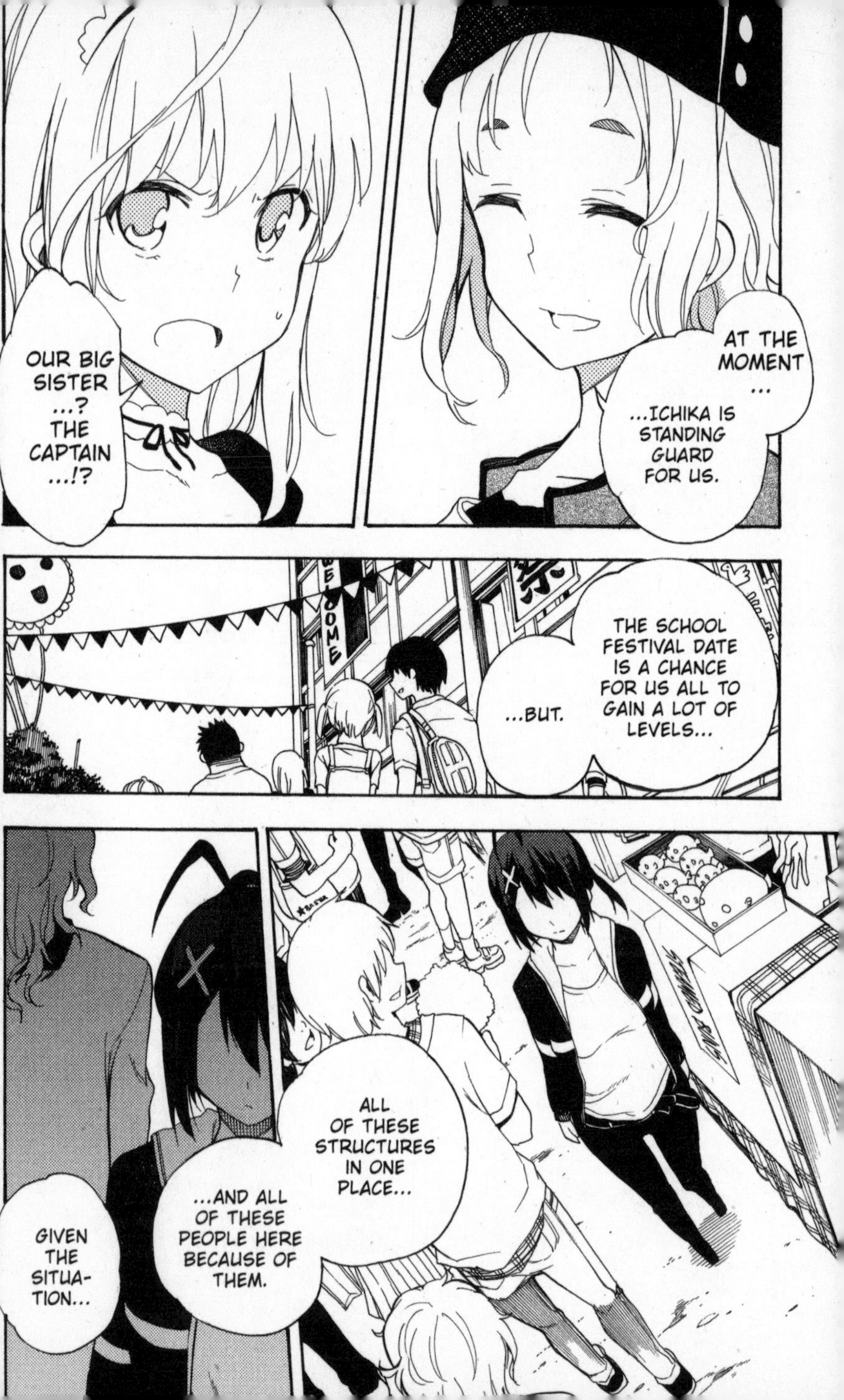
AT THE MOMENT ...
...ICHIKA IS STANDING GUARD FOR US.
OUR BIG SISTER ...? THE CAPTAIN ...!?
THE SCHOOL FESTIVAL DATE IS A CHANCE FOR US ALL TO GAIN A LOT OF LEVELS...
...BUT.
ALL OF THESE STRUCTURES IN ONE PLACE...
...AND ALL OF THESE PEOPLE HERE BECAUSE OF THEM.
GIVEN THE SITUATION...

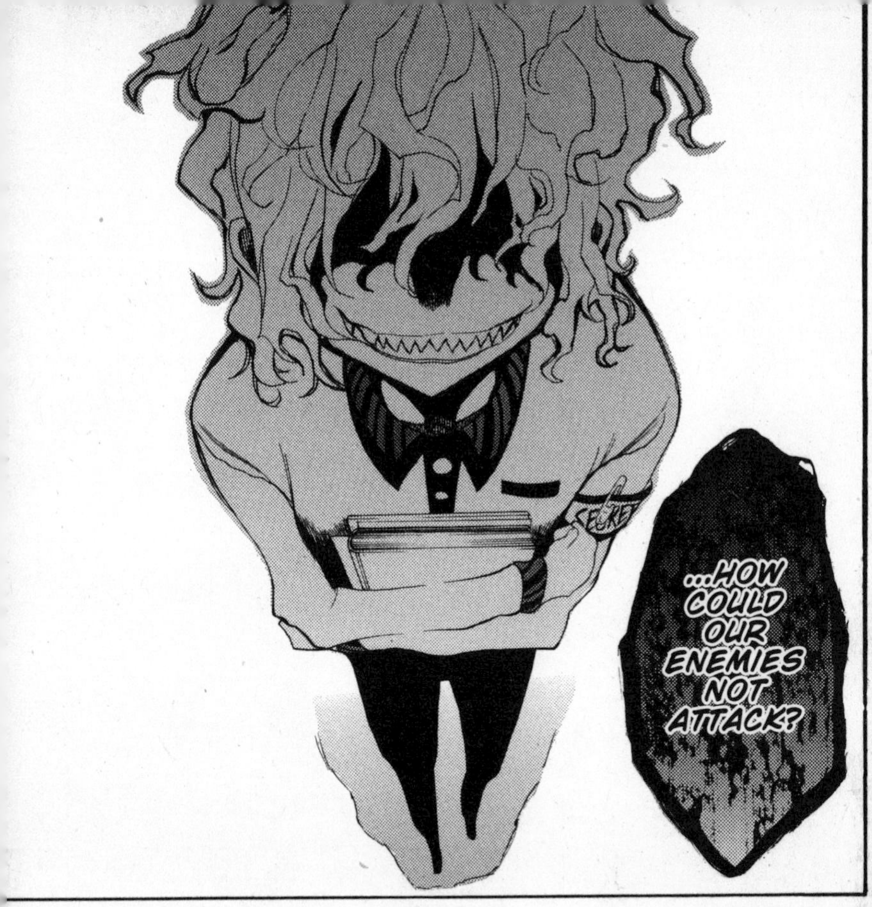
...HOW COULD OUR ENEMIES NOT ATTACK?

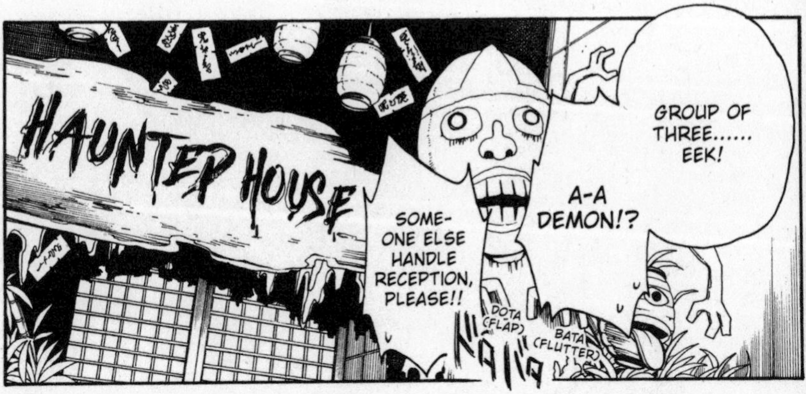
GROUP OF THREE...... EEK!
A-A DEMON!?
SOME-ONE ELSE HANDLE RECEPTION, PLEASE!!
HAUNTED HOUSE
BATA (FLUTTER)
DOTA (FLAP)

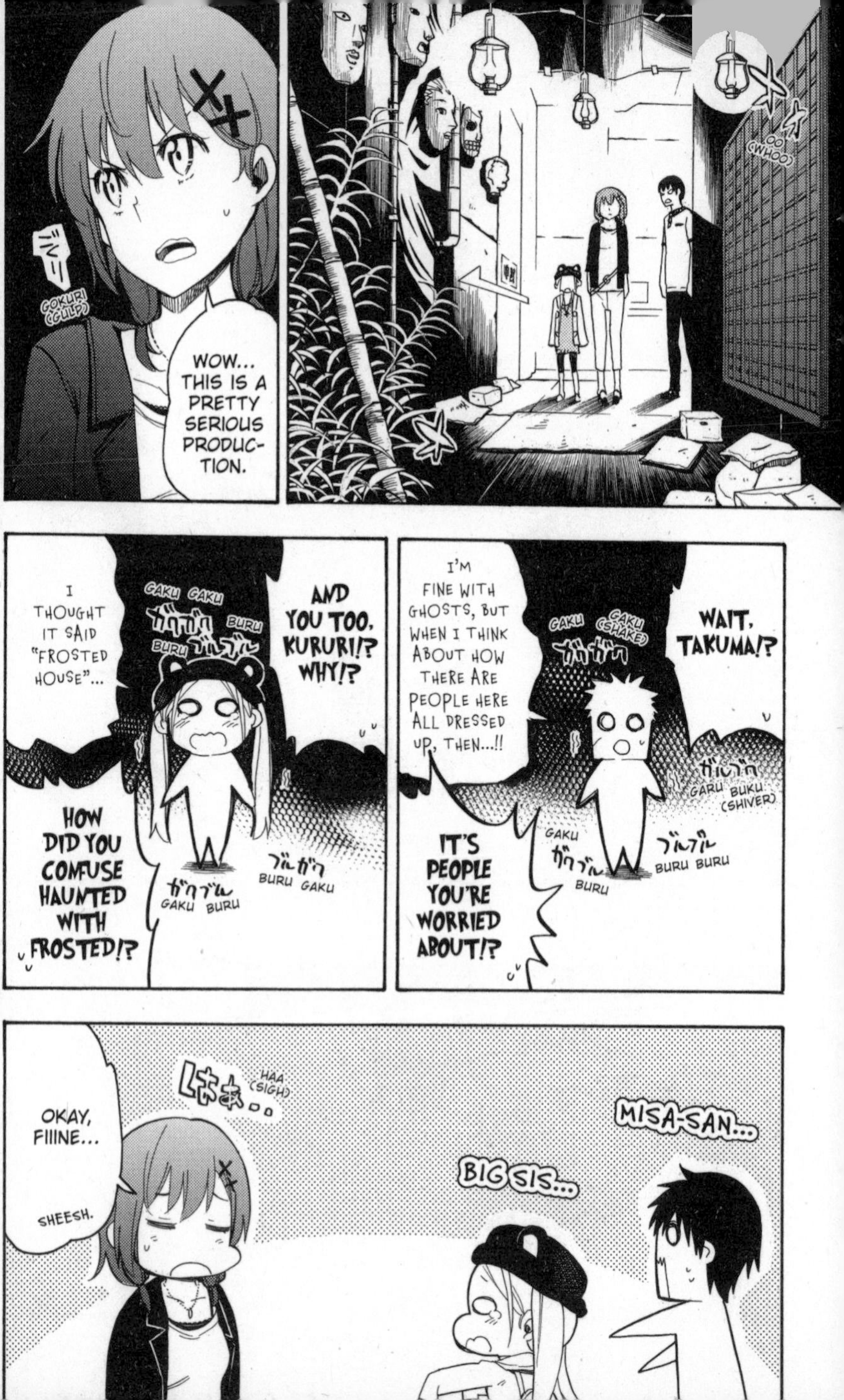
OO (WHOO)
GOKURI (GULP)
WOW... THIS IS A PRETTY SERIOUS PRODUCTION.
WAIT, TAKUMA!?
GAKU GAKU (SHAKE)
I'M FINE WITH GHOSTS, BUT WHEN I THINK ABOUT HOW THERE ARE PEOPLE HERE ALL DRESSED UP, THEN...!!
GARU BUKU (SHIVER)
BURU BURU
GAKU BURU
IT'S PEOPLE YOU'RE WORRIED ABOUT!?
AND YOU TOO, KURURI!? WHY!?
GAKU GAKU
BURU BURU
I THOUGHT IT SAID "FROSTED HOUSE"...
BURU GAKU
GAKU BURU
HOW DID YOU CONFUSE HAUNTED WITH FROSTED!?
MISA-SAN...
BIG SIS...
HAA (SIGH)
OKAY, FIIINE...
SHEESH.

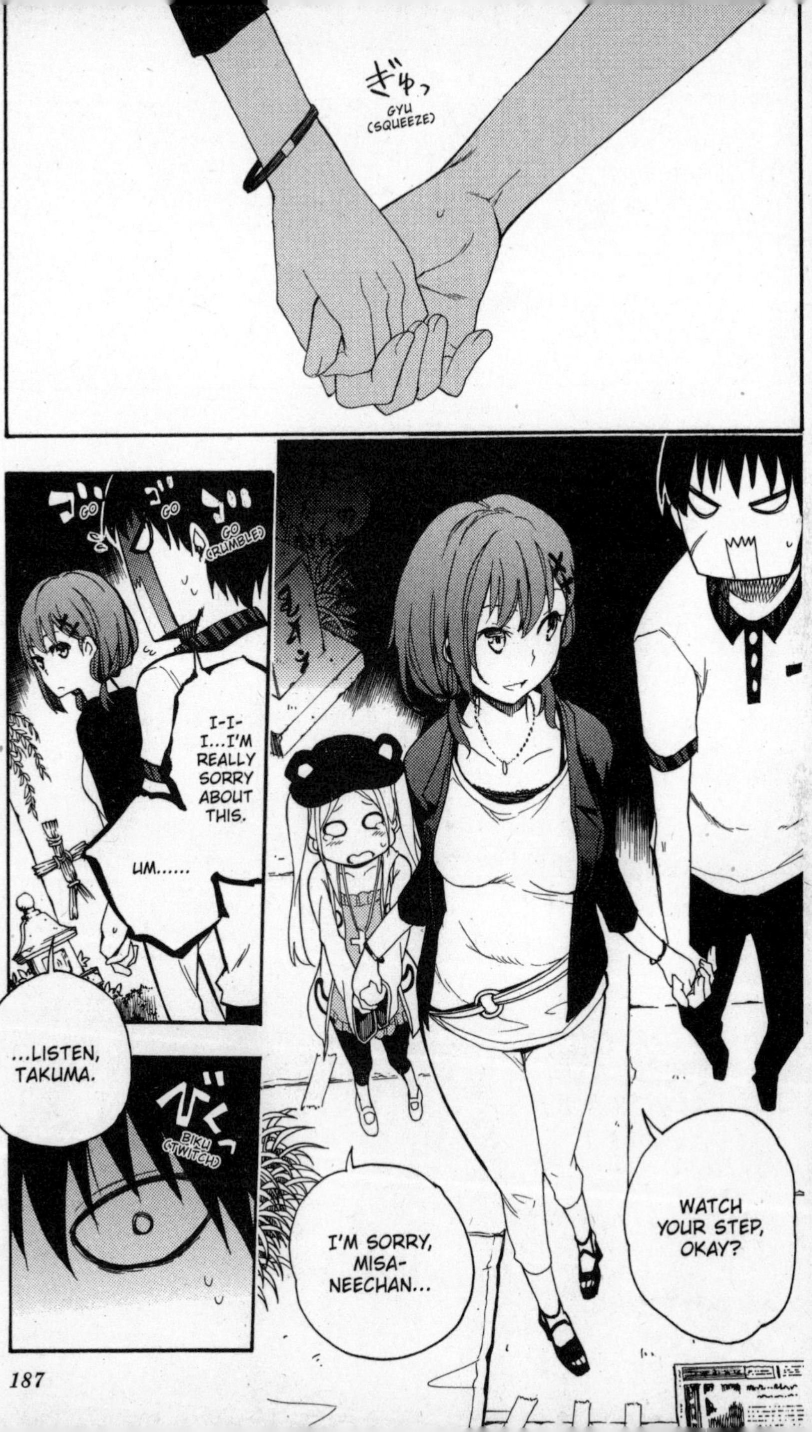
ぎゅっ
GYU (SQUEEZE)
WATCH YOUR STEP, OKAY?
I'M SORRY, MISA-NEECHAN...
ゴ GO ゴ GO ゴ GO (RUMBLE)
I-I-I...I'M REALLY SORRY ABOUT THIS.
UM......
...LISTEN, TAKUMA.
ビクっ
BIKU (TWITCH)

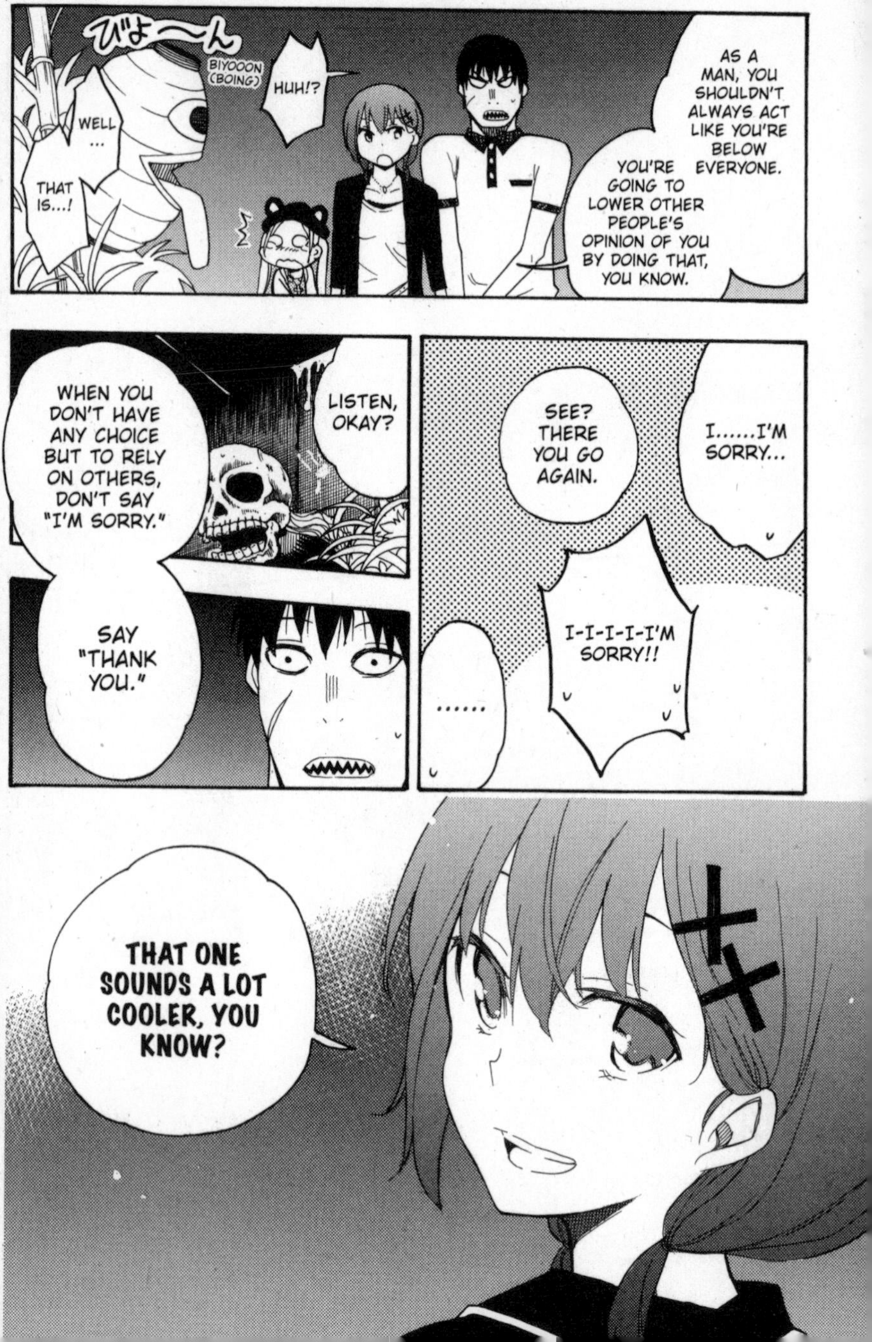
AS A MAN, YOU SHOULDN'T ALWAYS ACT LIKE YOU'RE BELOW EVERYONE.
YOU'RE GOING TO LOWER OTHER PEOPLE'S OPINION OF YOU BY DOING THAT, YOU KNOW.
HUH!?
びよ～ん
BIYOOON (BOING)
WELL...
THAT IS...!
I......I'M SORRY...
SEE? THERE YOU GO AGAIN.
I-I-I-I-I'M SORRY!!
......
LISTEN, OKAY?
WHEN YOU DON'T HAVE ANY CHOICE BUT TO RELY ON OTHERS, DON'T SAY "I'M SORRY."
SAY "THANK YOU."
THAT ONE SOUNDS A LOT COOLER, YOU KNOW?

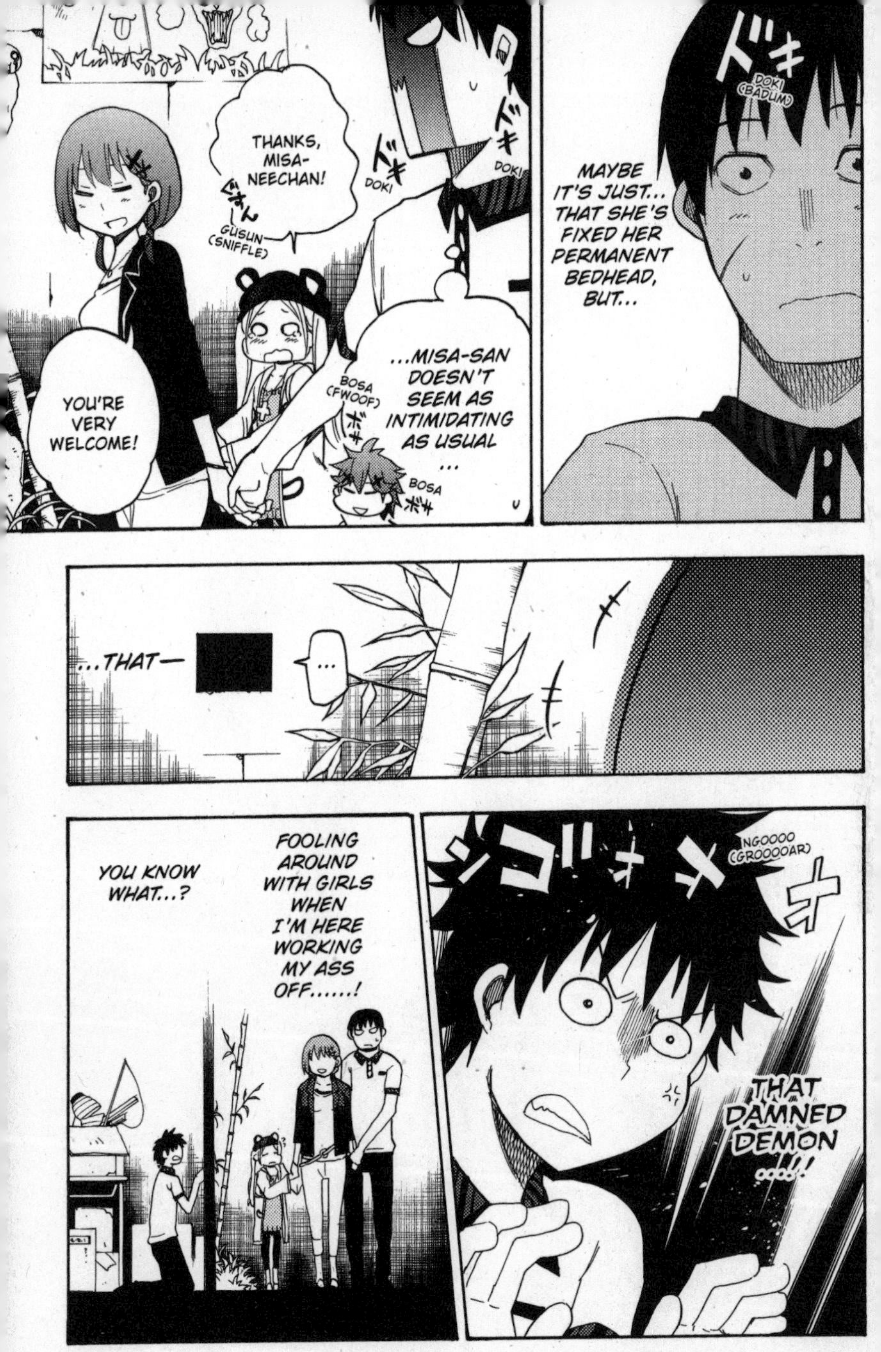

DOKI (BADUM)
MAYBE IT'S JUST... THAT SHE'S FIXED HER PERMANENT BEDHEAD, BUT...
DOKI
DOKI
THANKS, MISA-NEECHAN!
GUSUN (SNIFFLE)
...MISA-SAN DOESN'T SEEM AS INTIMIDATING AS USUAL...
BOSA (FWOOF)
BOSA
YOU'RE VERY WELCOME!
...
...THAT—
NGOOOO (GROOOOAR)
THAT DAMNED DEMON......!!
FOOLING AROUND WITH GIRLS WHEN I'M HERE WORKING MY ASS OFF......!
YOU KNOW WHAT...?

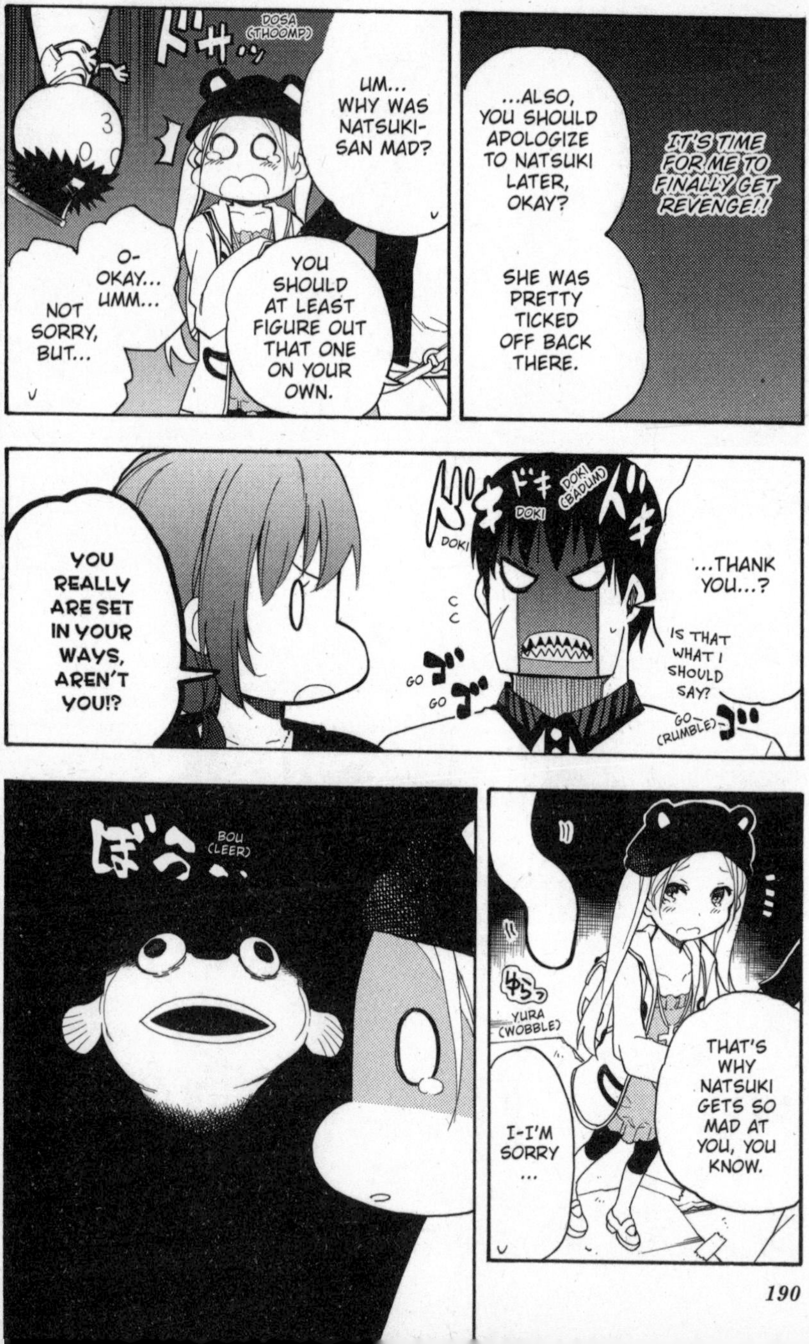
IT'S TIME FOR ME TO FINALLY GET REVENGE!!
...ALSO, YOU SHOULD APOLOGIZE TO NATSUKI LATER, OKAY?
SHE WAS PRETTY TICKED OFF BACK THERE.
DOSA (THOOMP)
UM... WHY WAS NATSUKI-SAN MAD?
YOU SHOULD AT LEAST FIGURE OUT THAT ONE ON YOUR OWN.
O-OKAY... UMM...
NOT SORRY, BUT...
...THANK YOU...?
IS THAT WHAT I SHOULD SAY?
GO (RUMBLE)
DOKI (BADUM)
DOKI
DOKI
GO
GO
YOU REALLY ARE SET IN YOUR WAYS, AREN'T YOU!?
THAT'S WHY NATSUKI GETS SO MAD AT YOU, YOU KNOW.
YURA (WOBBLE)
I-I'M SORRY ...
BOU (LEER)

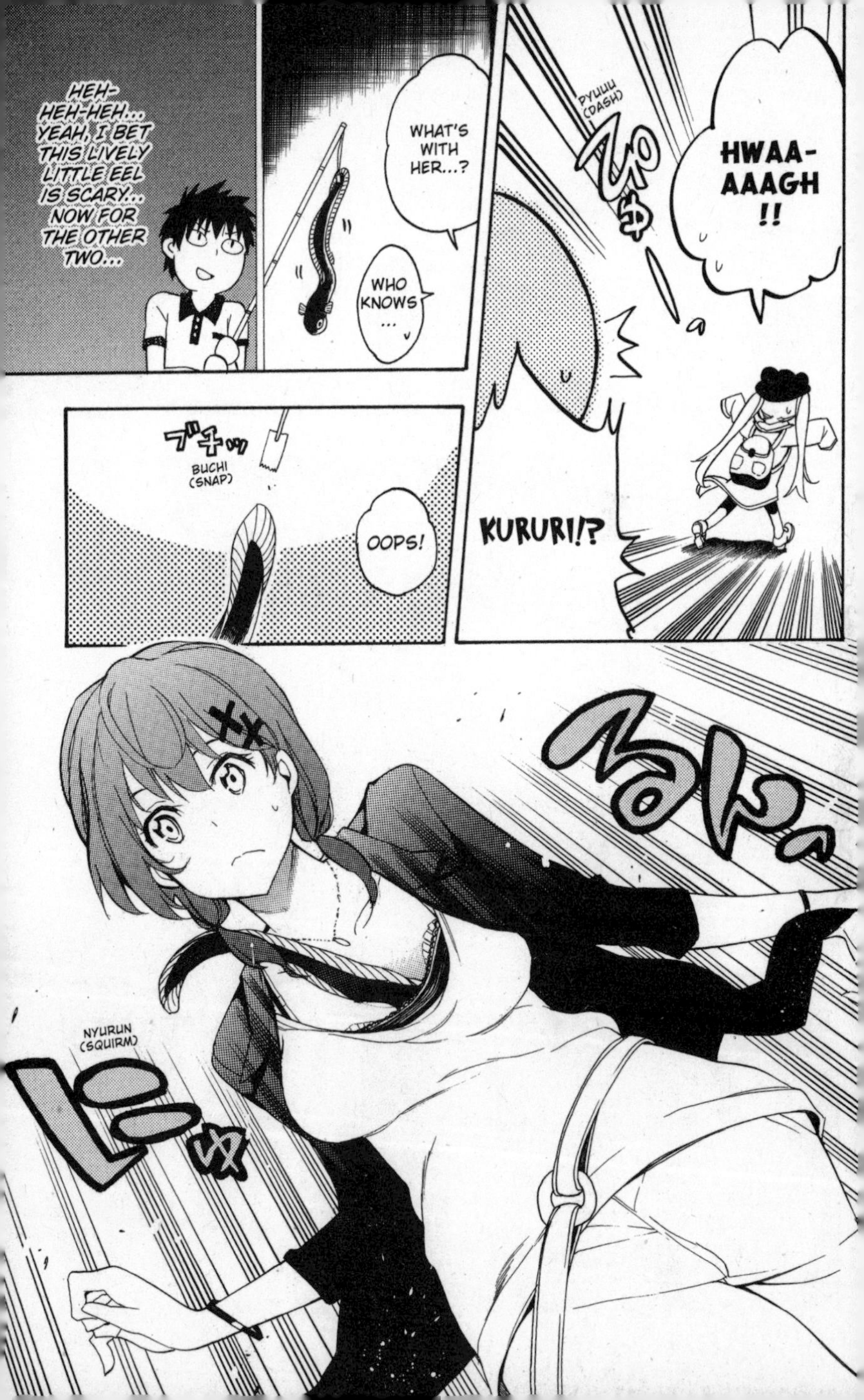
HWAAA-AAAGH!!
PYUUU (DASH)
KURURI!?
WHAT'S WITH HER...?
WHO KNOWS...
HEH-HEH-HEH... YEAH, I BET THIS LIVELY LITTLE EEL IS SCARY... NOW FOR THE OTHER TWO...
BUCHI (SNAP)
OOPS!
NYURUN (SQUIRM)

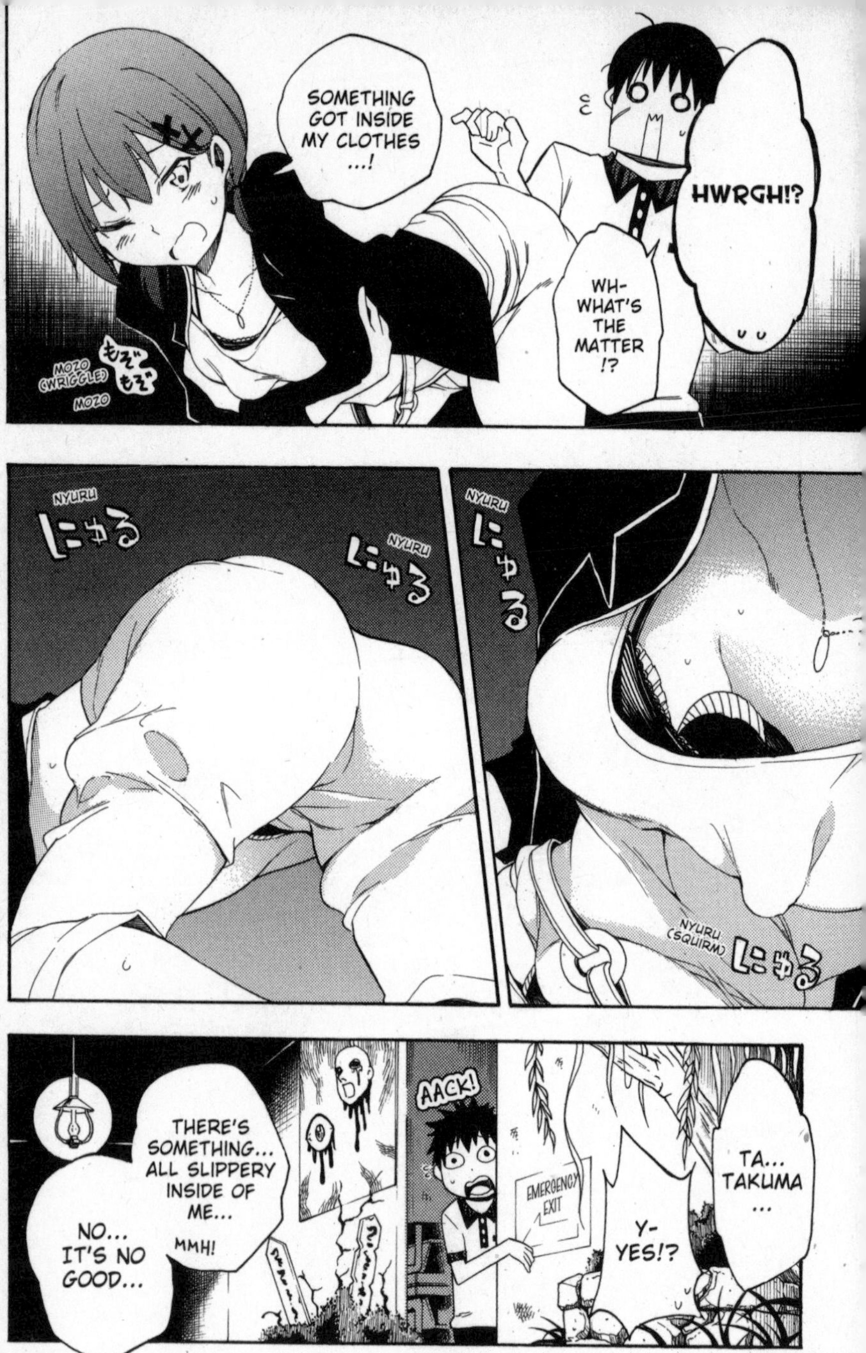
HWRGH!?
WH- WHAT'S THE MATTER !?
SOMETHING GOT INSIDE MY CLOTHES ...!
もぞもぞ
MOZO (WRIGGLE) MOZO
NYURU
にゅる
NYURU (SQUIRM)
にゅる
NYURU
にゅる
NYURU
にゅる
TA... TAKUMA ...
Y- YES!?
EMERGENCY EXIT
AACK!
THERE'S SOMETHING... ALL SLIPPERY INSIDE OF ME...
MMH!
NO... IT'S NO GOOD...

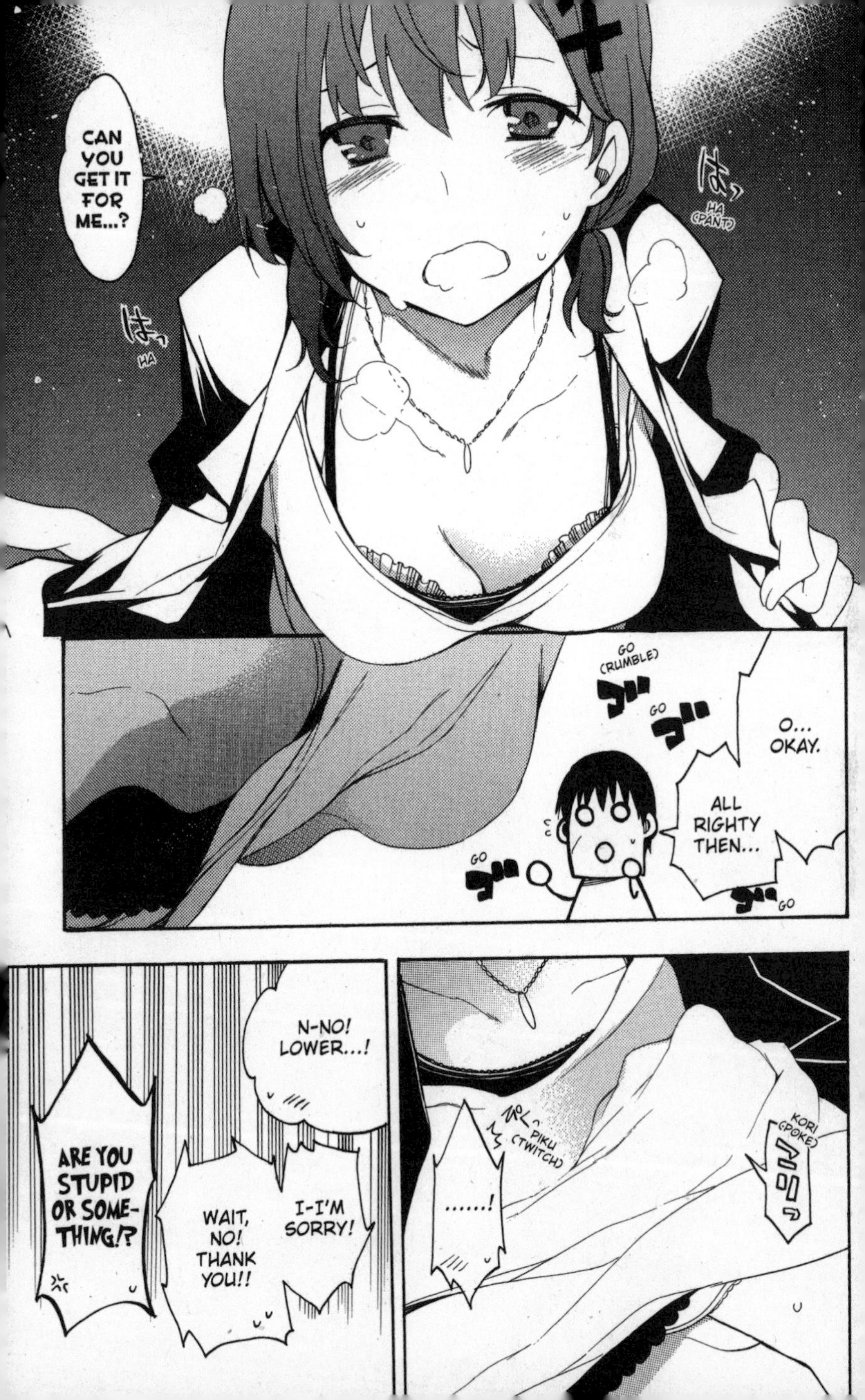
は HA (PANT)
CAN YOU GET IT FOR ME...?
は HA
GO (RUMBLE)
GO
O... OKAY.
ALL RIGHTY THEN...
GO
GO
KORI (POKE)
ぴく PIKU (TWITCH)
......!
N-NO! LOWER...!
I-I'M SORRY!
WAIT, NO! THANK YOU!!
ARE YOU STUPID OR SOME-THING!?

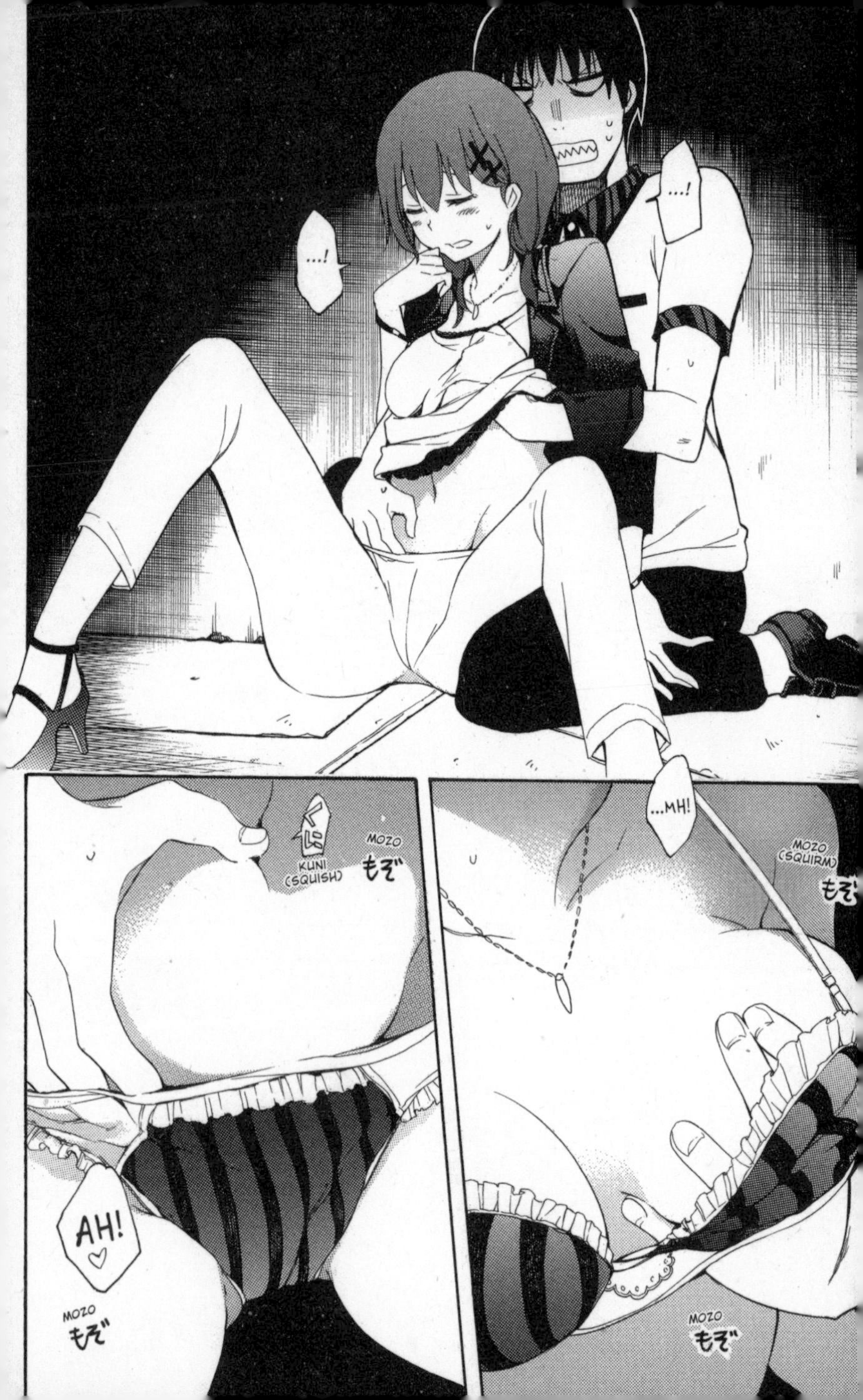
...!
...!
...MH!
MOZO (SQUIRM)
もぞ
MOZO
もぞ
くに
KUNI (SQUISH)
MOZO
もぞ
AH! ♡
MOZO
もぞ

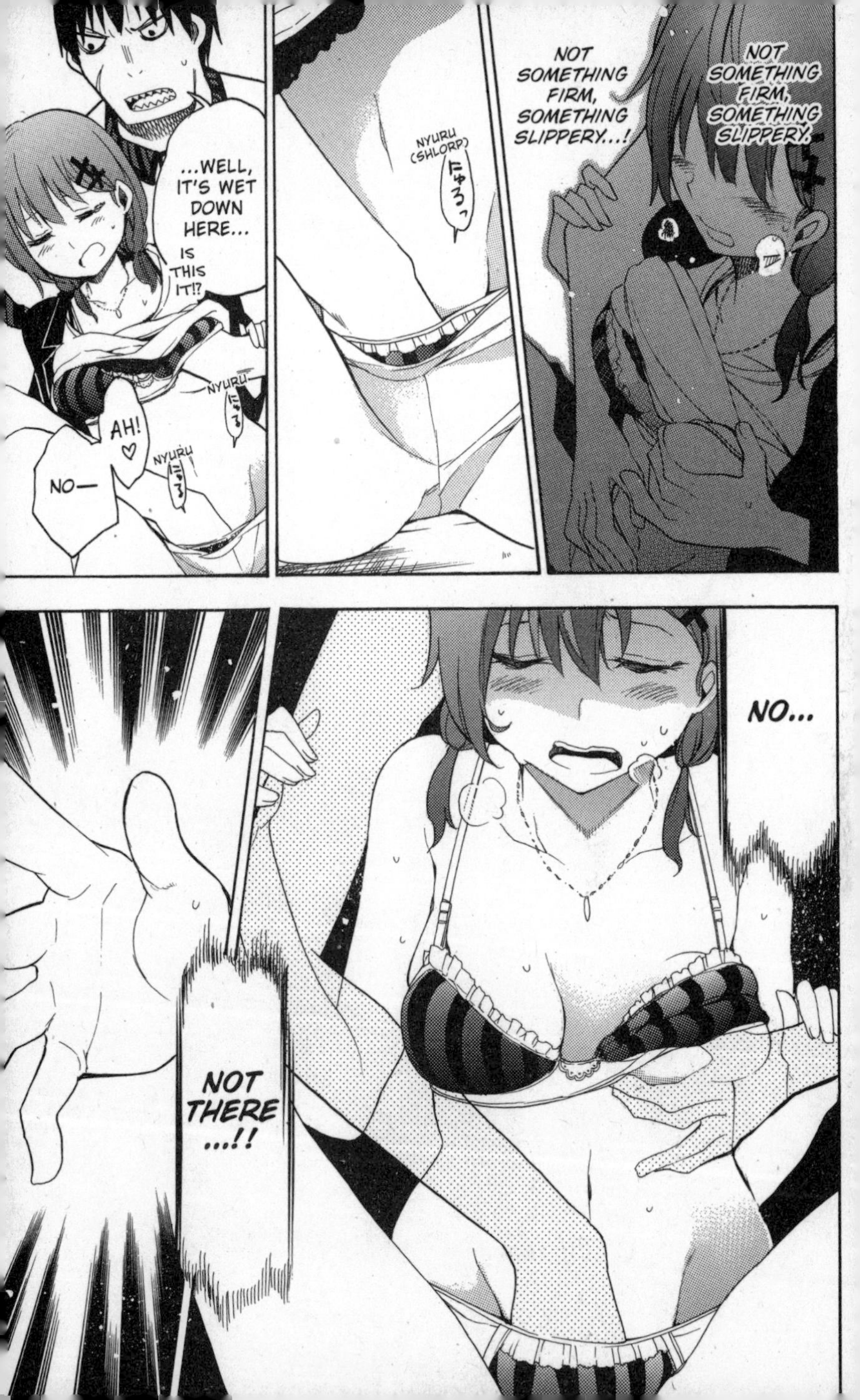
NOT SOMETHING FIRM, SOMETHING SLIPPERY.
NOT SOMETHING FIRM, SOMETHING SLIPPERY...!
NYURU (SHLORP)
にゅるっ
...WELL, IT'S WET DOWN HERE...
IS THIS IT!?
NYURU
AH! ♡
NYURU
NO—
NO...
NOT THERE ...!!

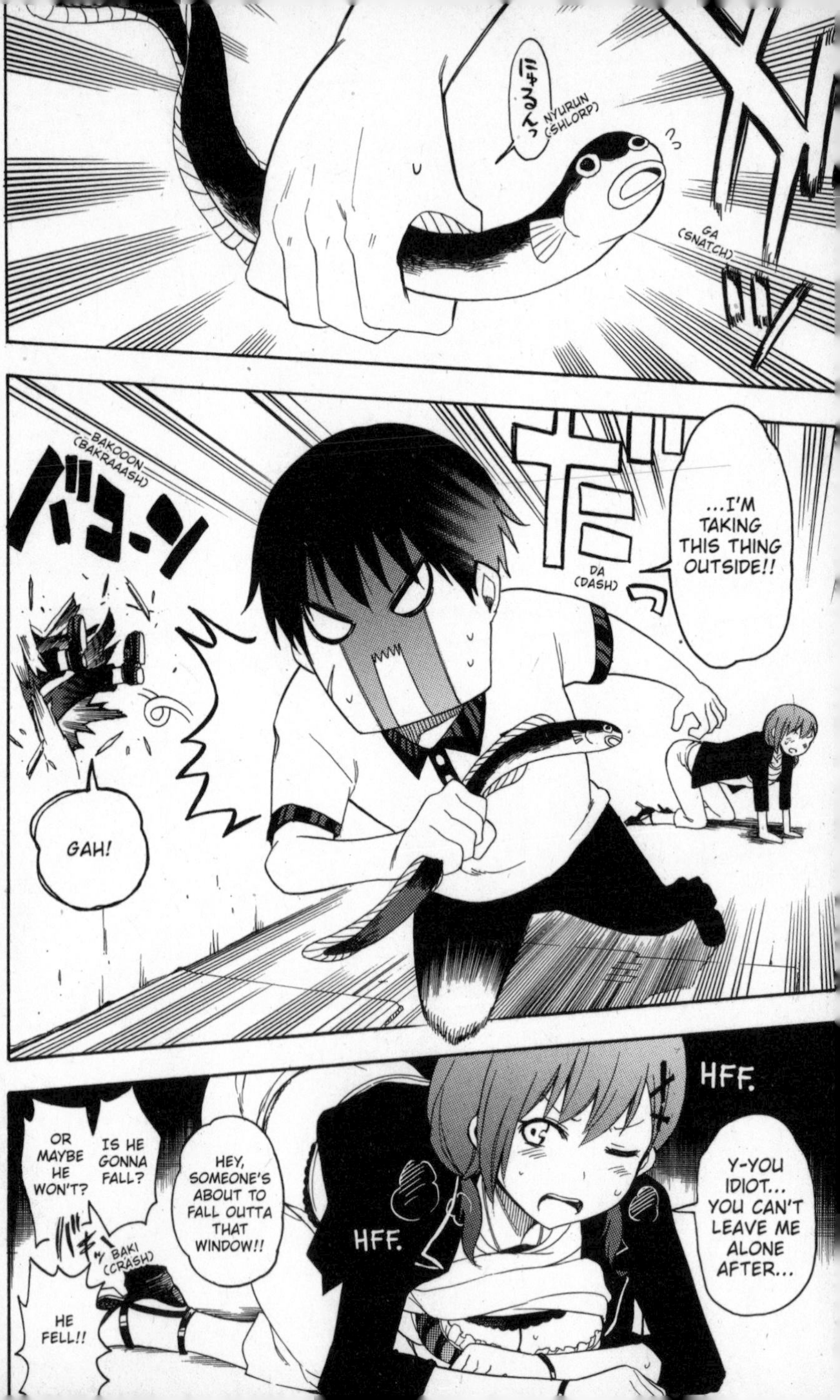
GA (SNATCH)
にゅるんっ
NYURUN (SHLORP)
...I'M TAKING THIS THING OUTSIDE!!
DA (DASH)
BAKOOON (BAKRAAASH)
GAH!
HFF.
Y-YOU IDIOT... YOU CAN'T LEAVE ME ALONE AFTER...
HFF.
HEY, SOMEONE'S ABOUT TO FALL OUTTA THAT WINDOW!!
IS HE GONNA FALL?
OR MAYBE HE WON'T?
BAKI (CRASH)
HE FELL!!

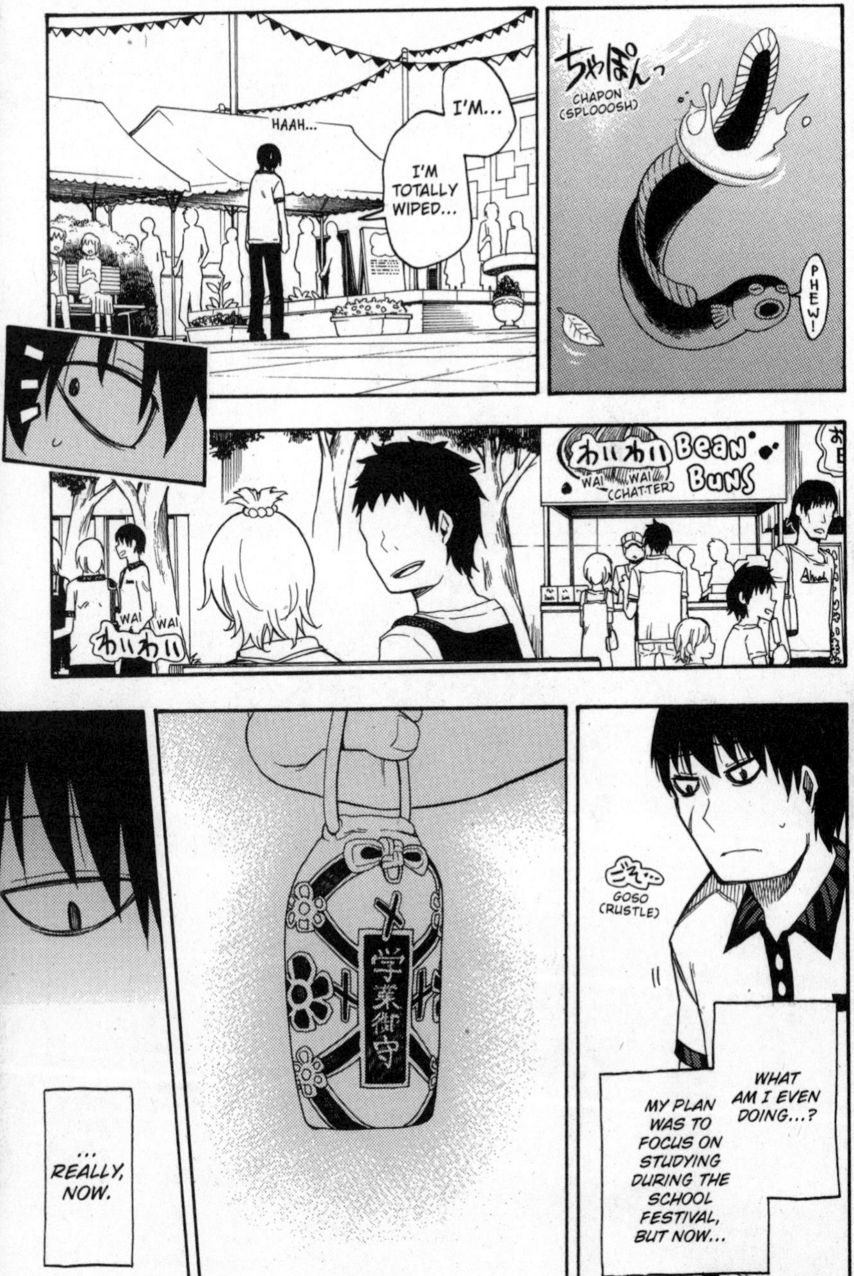
ちゃぽんっ
CHAPON (SPLOOOSH)
PHEW!
I'M...
I'M TOTALLY WIPED...
HAAH...
わいわい
WAI WAI (CHAT-TER)
BEAN BUNS
わいわい
WAI WAI
ごそ…
GOSO (RUSTLE)
WHAT AM I EVEN DOING...?
MY PLAN WAS TO FOCUS ON STUDYING DURING THE SCHOOL FESTIVAL, BUT NOW...
学業御守
... REALLY, NOW.

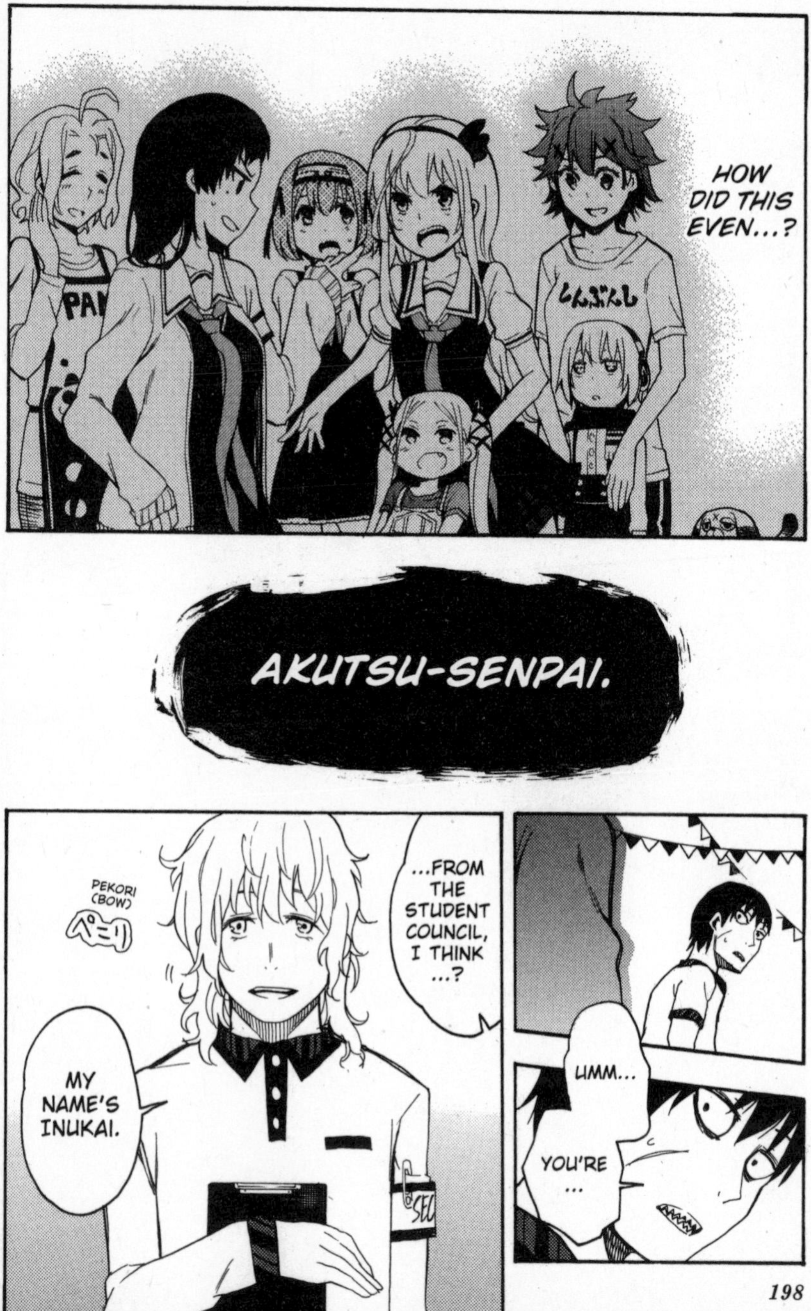
HOW DID THIS EVEN...?
AKUTSU-SENPAI.
UMM...
YOU'RE ...
...FROM THE STUDENT COUNCIL, I THINK ...?
PEKORI (BOW)
ぺこり
MY NAME'S INUKAI.

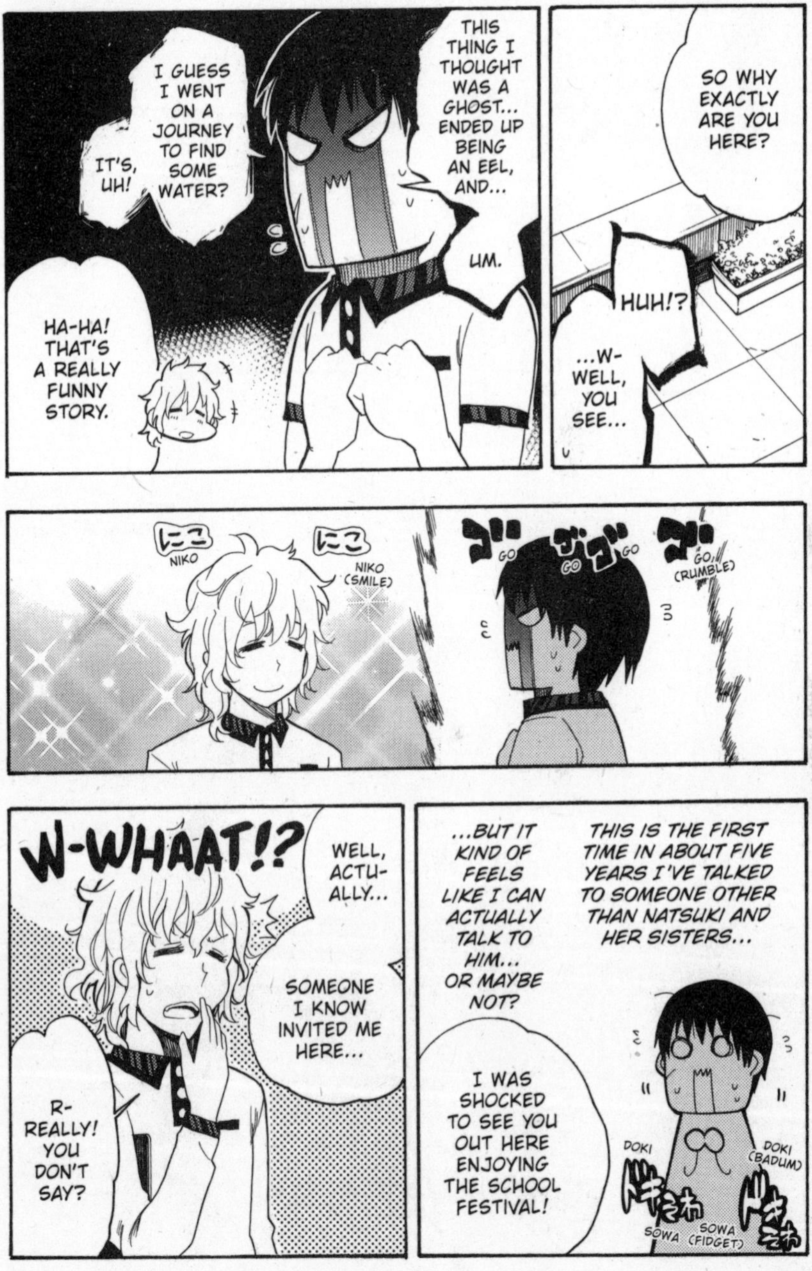
SO WHY EXACTLY ARE YOU HERE?
HUH!?
...W-WELL, YOU SEE...
THIS THING I THOUGHT WAS A GHOST... ENDED UP BEING AN EEL, AND...
UM.
I GUESS I WENT ON A JOURNEY TO FIND SOME WATER?
IT'S, UH!
HA-HA! THAT'S A REALLY FUNNY STORY.
ゴ GO
ゴ GO
ゴ GO
ゴ GO (RUMBLE)
にこ NIKO (SMILE)
にこ NIKO
THIS IS THE FIRST TIME IN ABOUT FIVE YEARS I'VE TALKED TO SOMEONE OTHER THAN NATSUKI AND HER SISTERS...
...BUT IT KIND OF FEELS LIKE I CAN ACTUALLY TALK TO HIM... OR MAYBE NOT?
I WAS SHOCKED TO SEE YOU OUT HERE ENJOYING THE SCHOOL FESTIVAL!
ドキ DOKI (BADUM)
ドキ DOKI
そわ SOWA (FIDGET)
そわ SOWA
WELL, ACTU-ALLY...
W-WHAAT!?
SOMEONE I KNOW INVITED ME HERE...
R-REALLY! YOU DON'T SAY?

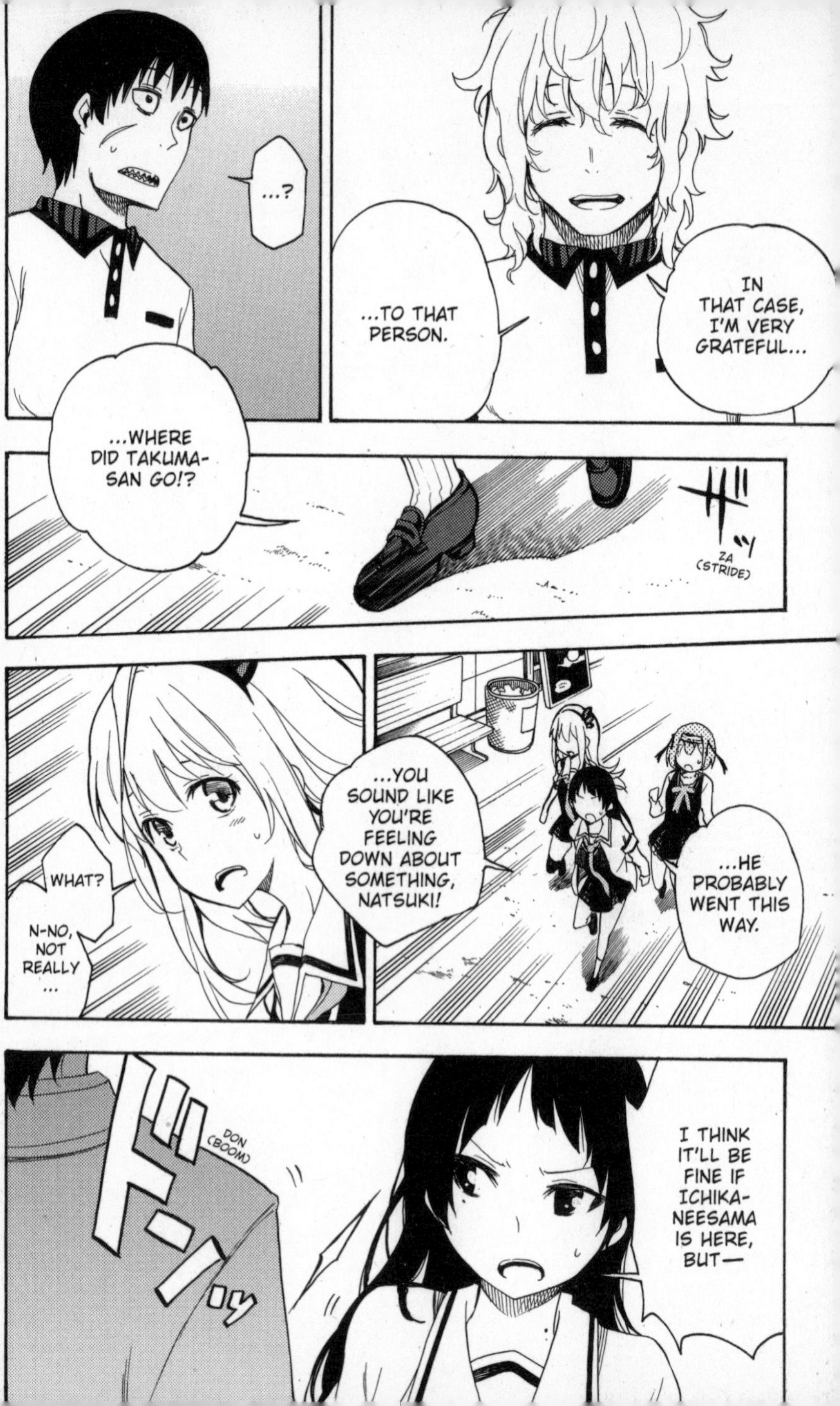
IN THAT CASE, I'M VERY GRATEFUL...
...TO THAT PERSON.
...?
...WHERE DID TAKUMA-SAN GO!?
ZA (STRIDE)
...HE PROBABLY WENT THIS WAY.
...YOU SOUND LIKE YOU'RE FEELING DOWN ABOUT SOMETHING, NATSUKI!
WHAT?
N-NO, NOT REALLY...
I THINK IT'LL BE FINE IF ICHIKA-NEESAMA IS HERE, BUT—
DON (BOOM)

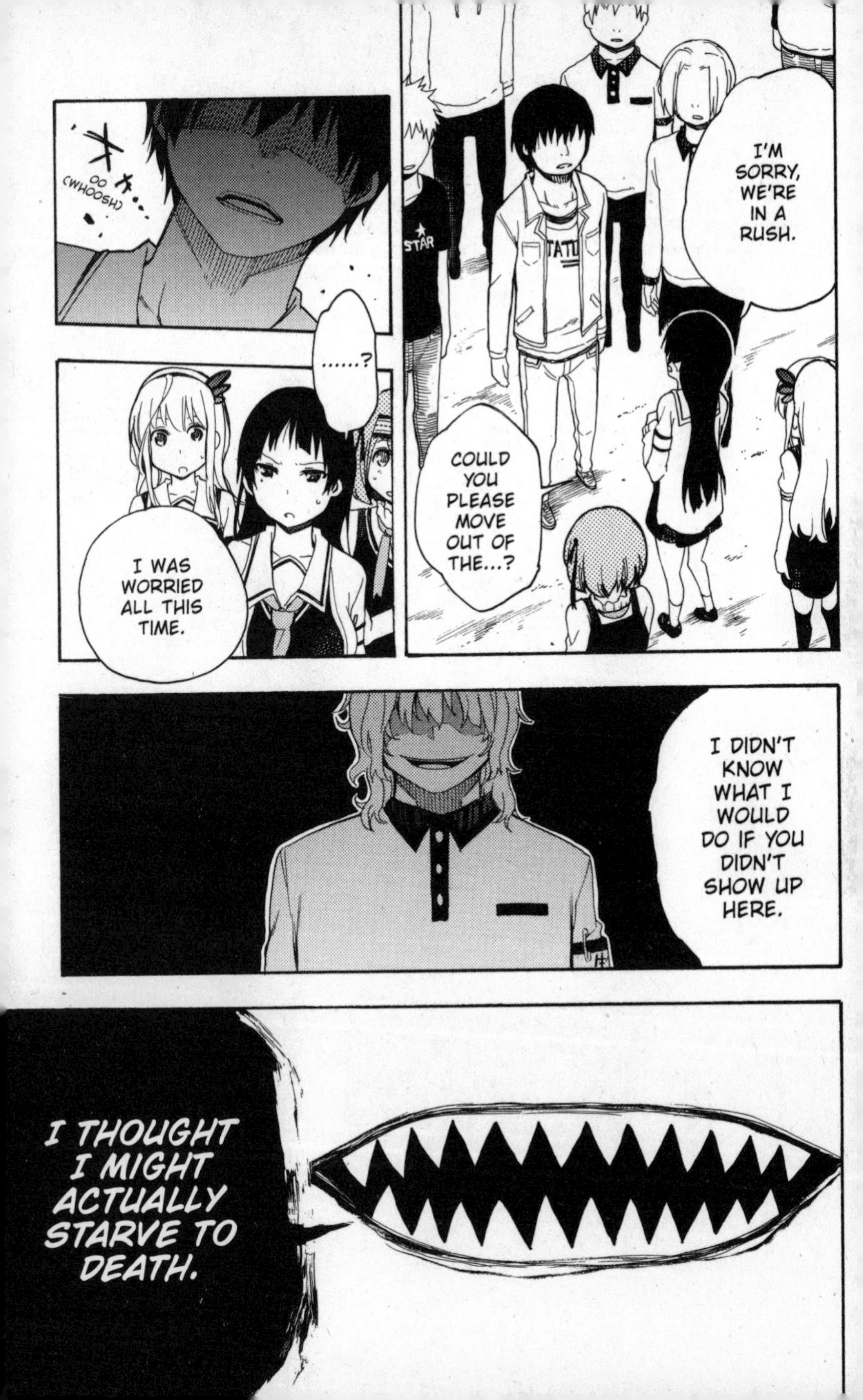
I'M SORRY, WE'RE IN A RUSH.
COULD YOU PLEASE MOVE OUT OF THE...?
OO (WHOOSH)
......?
I WAS WORRIED ALL THIS TIME.
I DIDN'T KNOW WHAT I WOULD DO IF YOU DIDN'T SHOW UP HERE.
I THOUGHT I MIGHT ACTUALLY STARVE TO DEATH.

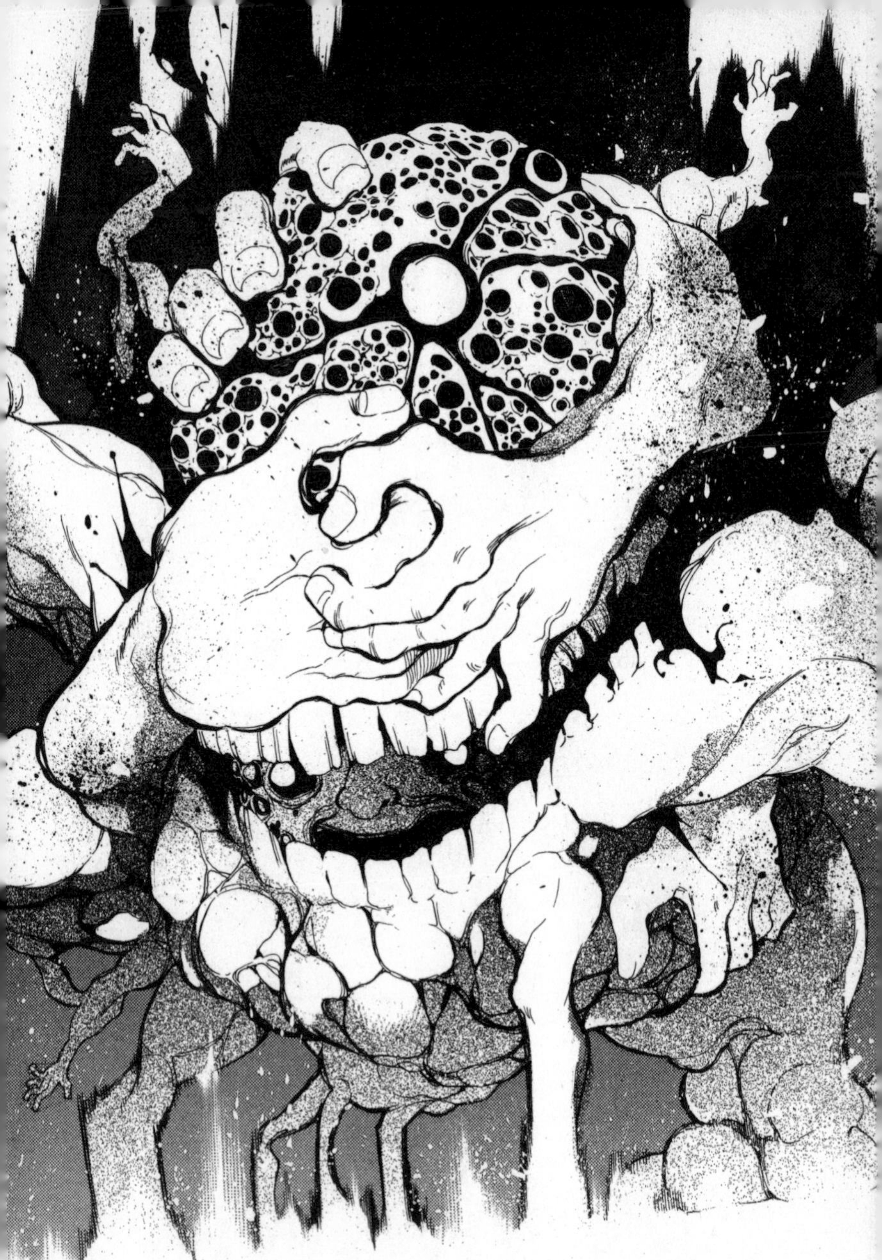

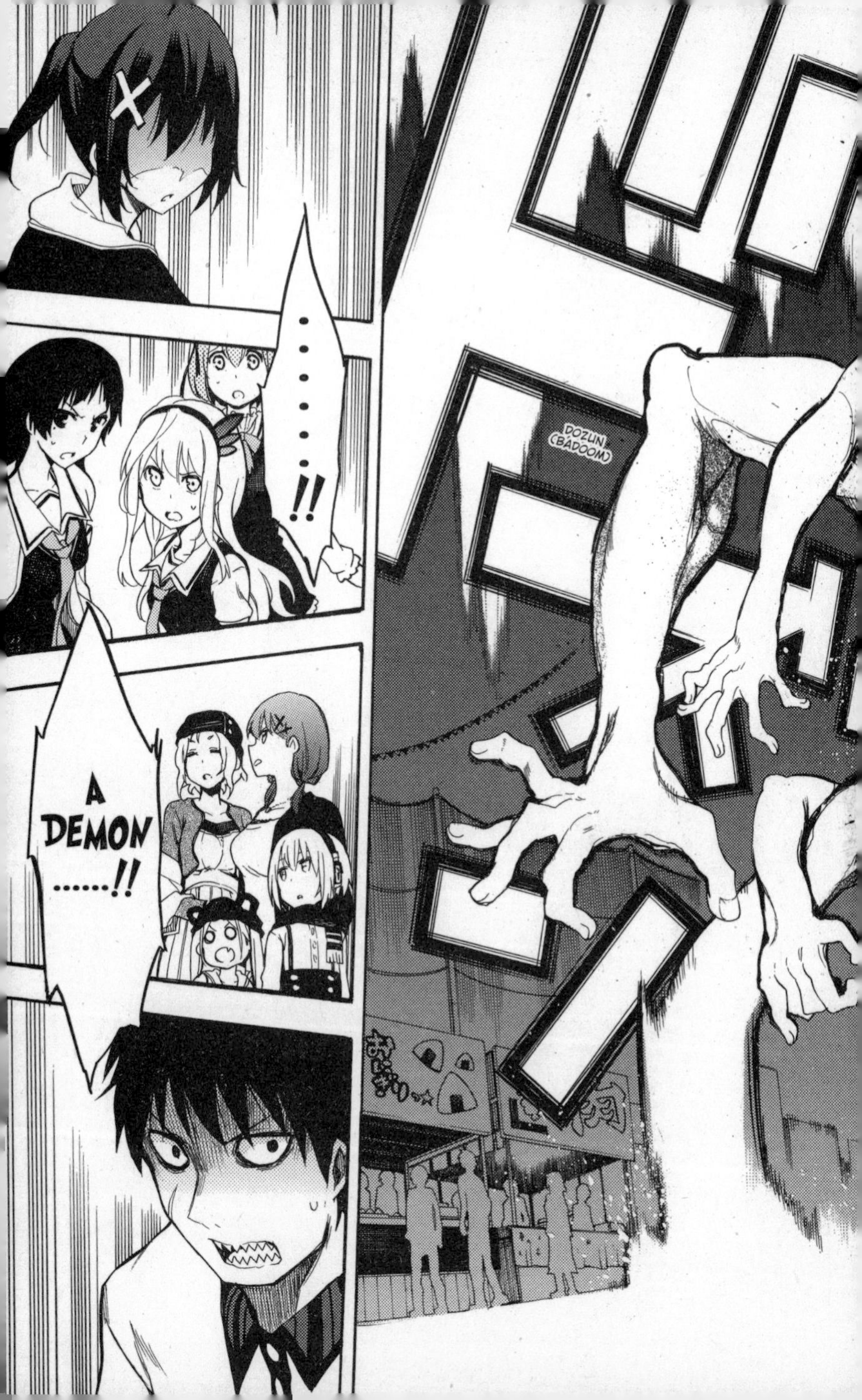
DOZUN
(BADOOM)
......!!
A DEMON ....!!

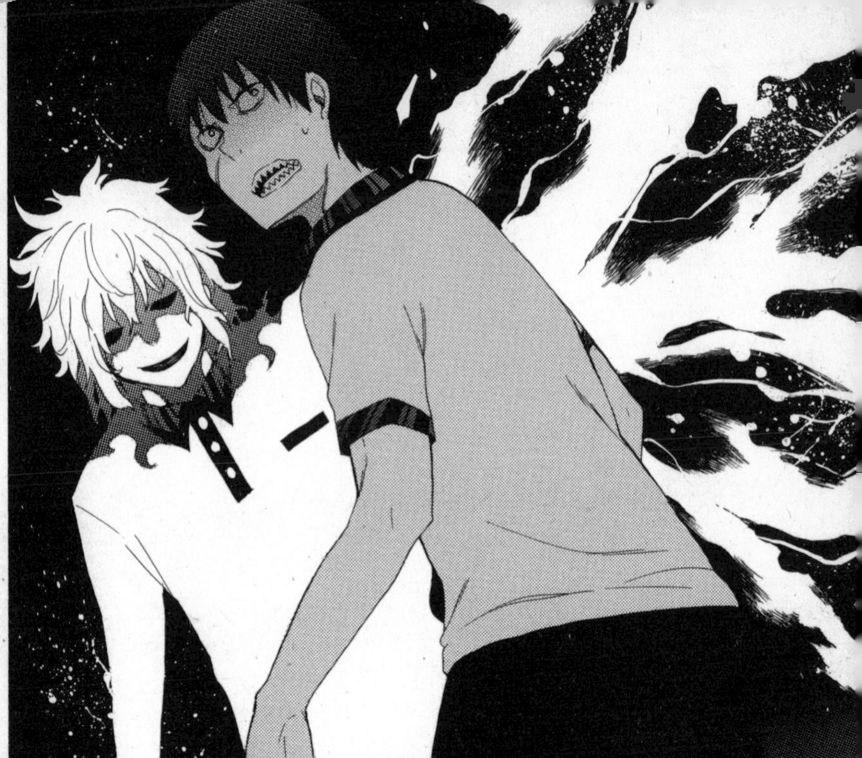

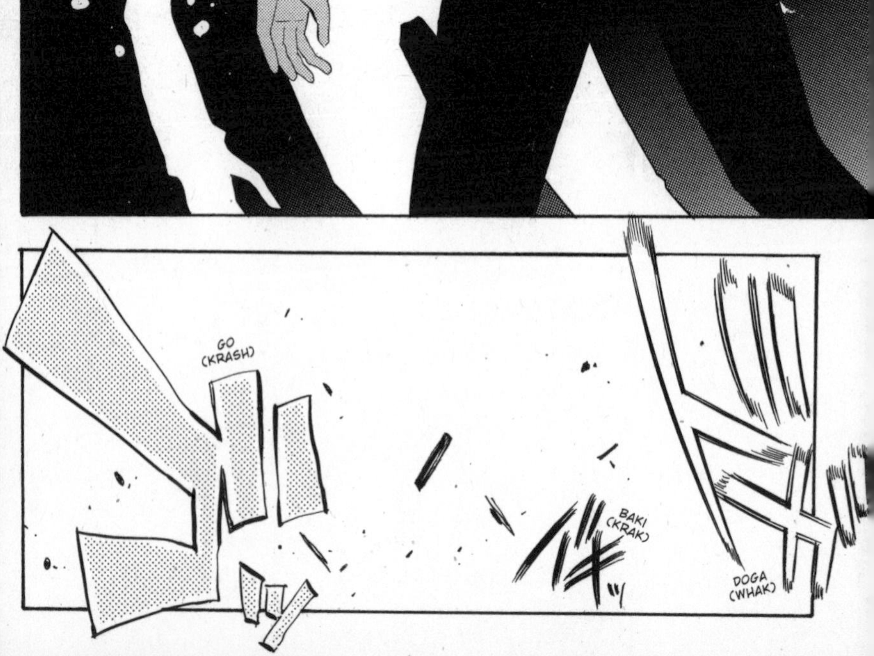
DOGA
(WHAK)
BAKI
(KRAK)
GO
(KRASH)

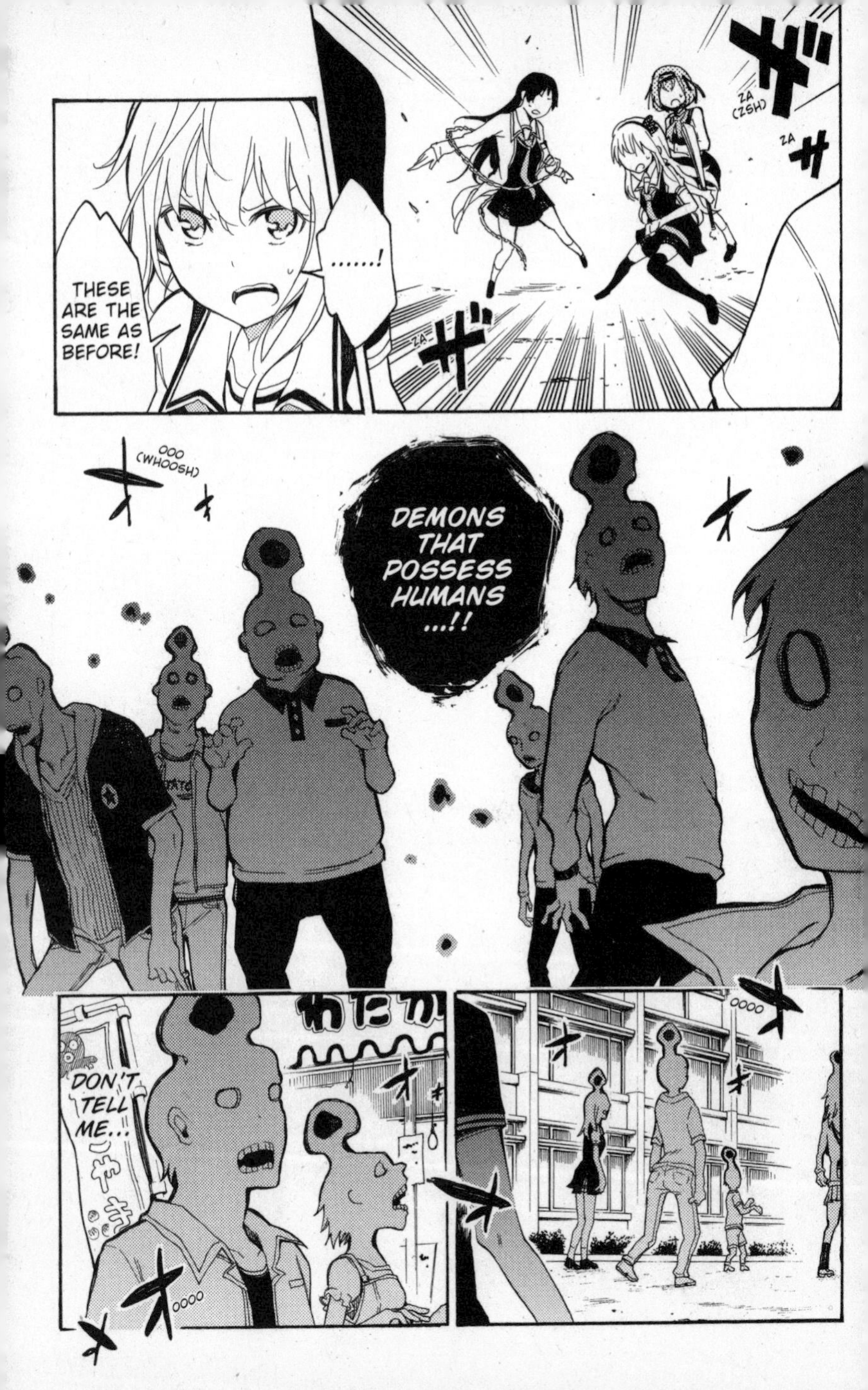
ZA (ZSH)
ZA
ZA
......!
THESE ARE THE SAME AS BEFORE!
OOO (WHOOSH)
DEMONS THAT POSSESS HUMANS ...!!
OOOO
DON'T TELL ME...
OOOO

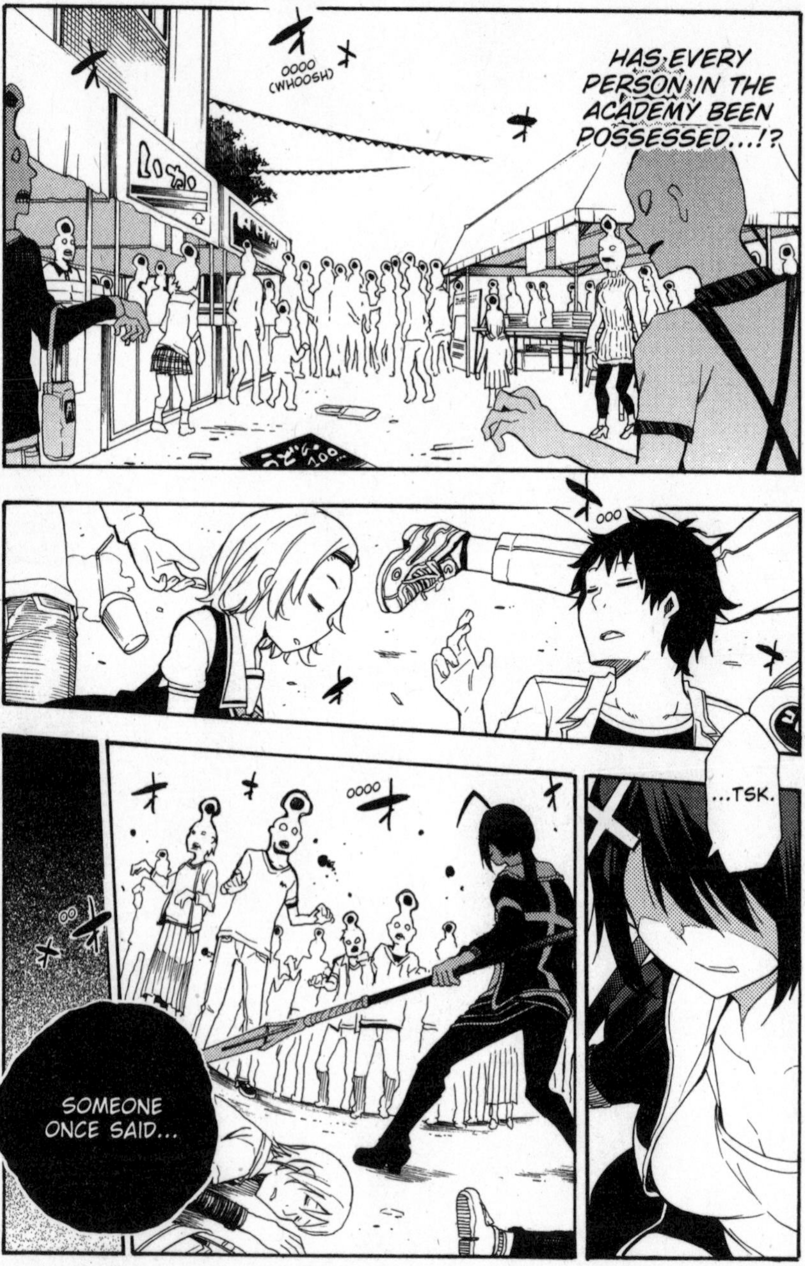
HAS EVERY PERSON IN THE ACADEMY BEEN POSSESSED...!?
OOOO (WHOOSH)
OOO
...TSK.
OOOO
OO
SOMEONE ONCE SAID...

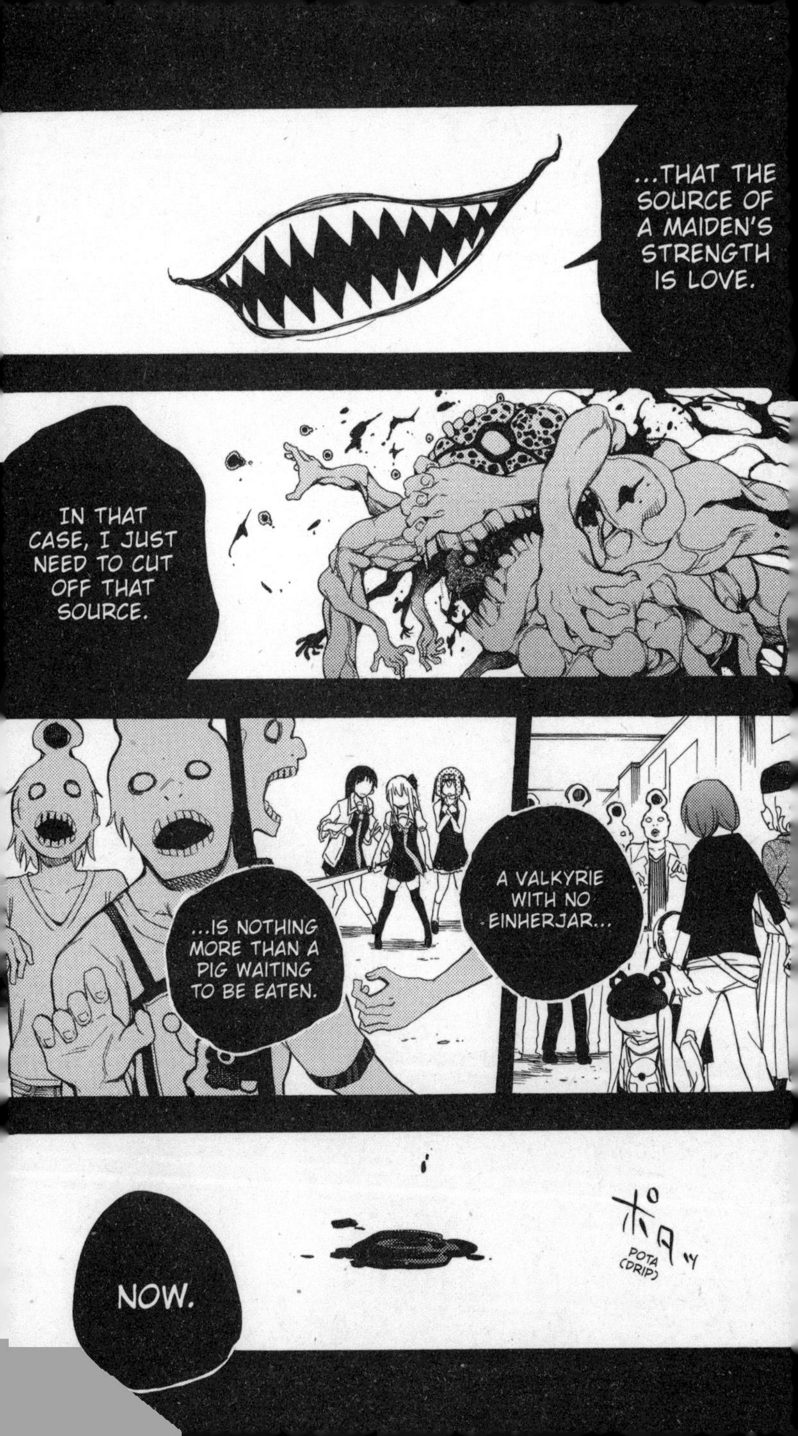
...THAT THE SOURCE OF A MAIDEN'S STRENGTH IS LOVE.
IN THAT CASE, I JUST NEED TO CUT OFF THAT SOURCE.
A VALKYRIE WITH NO EINHERJAR...
...IS NOTHING MORE THAN A PIG WAITING TO BE EATEN.
POTA (DRIP)
NOW.

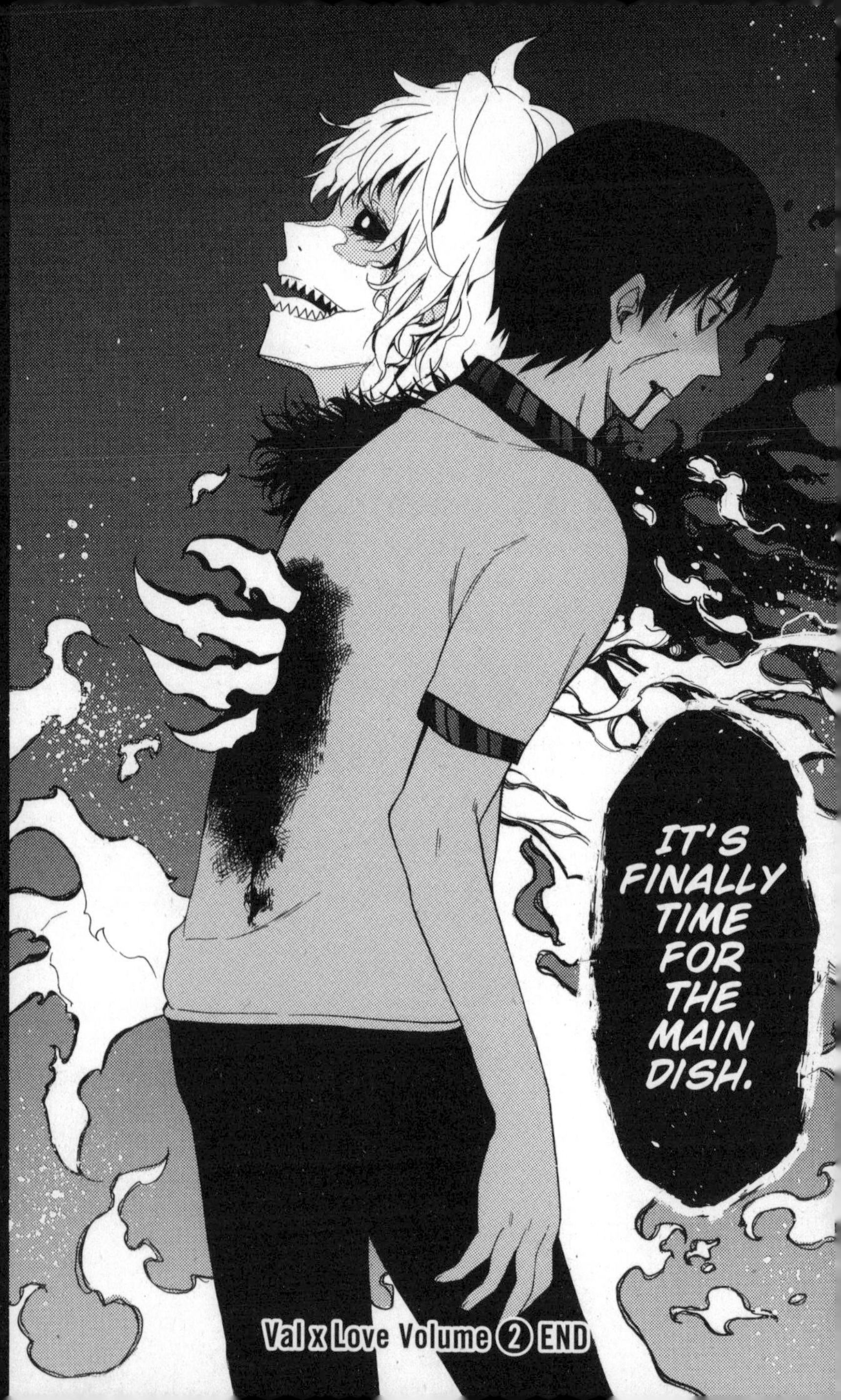
IT'S FINALLY TIME FOR THE MAIN DISH.
Val x Love Volume 2 END

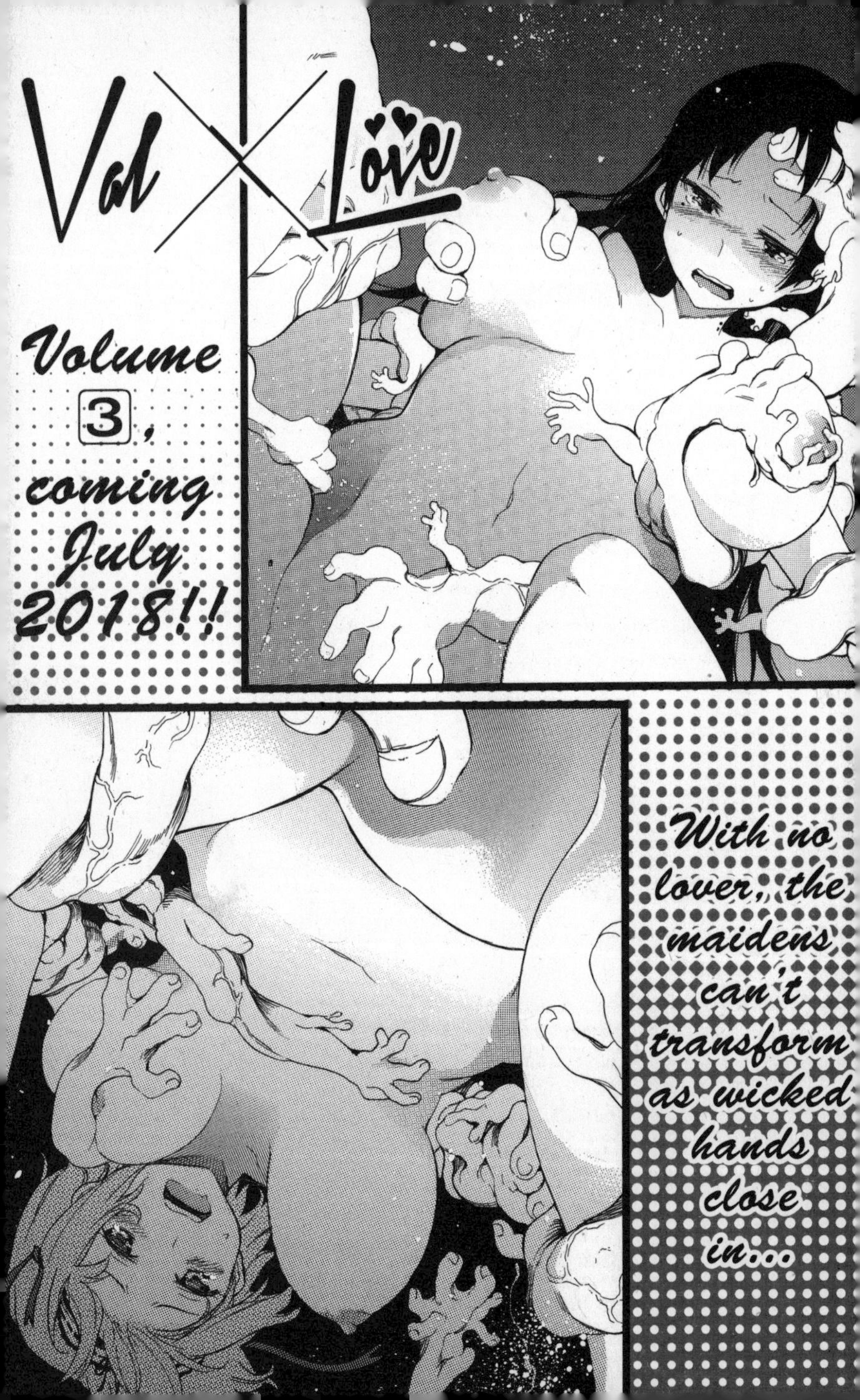
Val × Love
Volume 3, coming July 2018!!
With no lover, the maidens can't transform as wicked hands close in...

RYOSUKE ASAKURA

TRANSLATION: KO RANSOM
LETTERING: ROCHELLE GANCIO

VAL LOVE vol. 2
© 2016 Ryosuke Asakura / SQUARE ENIX CO., LTD.
First published in Japan in 2016 by SQUARE ENIX CO., LTD. English translation rights arranged with SQUARE ENIX CO., LTD. and Yen Press, LLC through Tuttle-Mori Agency, Inc.

English translation © 2018 by SQUARE ENIX CO., LTD.

Yen Press
1290 Avenue of the Americas
New York, NY 10104

Visit us at yenpress.com
facebook.com/yenpress
twitter.com/yenpress
yenpress.tumblr.com
instagram.com/yenpress

First Yen Press Edition: April 2018

Yen Press is an imprint of Yen Press, LLC.
The Yen Press name and logo are trademarks of Yen Press, LLC.

The publisher is not responsible for websites (or their content) that are not owned by the publisher.

Library of Congress Control Number: 2017954705

ISBNs: 978-0-316-44693-8 (paperback)
        978-0-316-44694-5 (ebook)

10 9 8 7 6 5 4 3 2 1

WOR

Printed in the United States of America